P9-CFC-665

Teaching as *Paul* Taught

Other Books by Roy B. Zuck

A Biblical Theology of the New Testament (editor)
A Biblical Theology of the Old Testament (editor)
Adult Education in the Church (coeditor)*
Barb, Please Wake Up!*
Basic Bible Interpretation
Biblical Archaeology Leader's Guide*
Childhood Education in the Church (coeditor)
Christian Youth: An In-Depth Study (coauthor)*
Church History Leader's Guide*
Communism and Christianity Leader's Guide*
Creation: Evidence from Scripture and Science*
Devotions for Kindred Spirits (editor)
Integrity of Heart, Skillfulness of Hands: Biblical and Leadership Studies in
    Honor of Donald K. Campbell (coeditor)
Job
Learning from the Sages: Selected Studies on the Book of Proverbs (editor)
Letter to a Jehovah's Witness
Precious in His Sight: Childhood and Children in the Bible
Reflecting with Solomon: Selected Studies on the Book of Ecclesiastes (editor)
Rightly Divided: Readings in Biblical Hermeneutics (editor)
Sitting with Job: Selected Studies on the Book of Job (editor)
Teaching as Jesus Taught
Teaching with Spiritual Power
The Bib Sac Reader (coeditor)*
The Bible Knowledge Commentary, New Testament (coeditor)
The Bible Knowledge Commentary, Old Testament (coeditor)
The Life of Christ Commentary (coeditor)*
The Speaker's Quote Book
Ventures in Family Living (coeditor)*
Vital Apologetic Issues (editor)
Vital Biblical Issues (editor)
Vital Contemporary Issues (editor)
Vital Christian Living Issues (editor)
Vital Christology Issues (editor)
Vital Ministry Issues (editor)
Vital New Testament Issues (editor)
Vital Old Testament Issues (editor)
Vital Prophetic Issues (editor)
Vital Theological Issues (editor)
Youth and the Church (coeditor)*
Youth Education in the Church (coeditor)*

* Out of print

Teaching as *Paul* Taught

Roy B. Zuck

Baker Books
A Division of Baker Book House Co
Grand Rapids, Michigan 49516

Published by Baker Books
a division of Baker Book House Company
P.O. Box 6287, Grand Rapids, MI 49516-6287

Printed in the United States of America

Library of Congress Cataloging-in-Publication Data

Zuck, Roy B.
    Teaching as Paul taught / Roy B. Zuck.
      p. cm.
    Includes bibliographical references and indexes.
    ISBN 0-8010-2159-6 (pbk.)
    1. Paul, the Apostle, Saint—Contributions in teaching. 2. Christian education—Teaching methods—History. I. Title.
BS2506.Z83   1998
268′.092—dc21   97-37902

For information about academic books, resources for Christian leaders, and all new releases available from Baker Book House, visit our web site:
http://www.bakerbooks.com/

Contents

93410

List of Tables

Introduction

Adolf Hitler.

Joseph Stalin.

Mao Zedong.

When you read these names, you no doubt think immediately of one thing that characterized all three: the brutal, barbaric slaughter of millions of people.

Take Adolf Hitler. Thinking the Aryan people were a superior race, he killed six million Jews, along with another estimated five million people in other ethnic groups including Gypsies, Poles, and Slavs. Many were imprisoned in concentration camps and then killed in gas chambers.

Joseph Stalin, U.S.S.R. dictator, exiled and executed millions who opposed his programs.

And Mao Zedong, "chairman" of China's Communist party, carried out numerous "extermination campaigns," to promote his reforms. He too was responsible for terrorizing and murdering millions of innocent people.

But suppose that somehow each of them heard the plan of salvation by faith in Christ, and accepted him as their Savior! Suppose they then turned their feverish zeal in favor of Christianity, promoting it wholeheartedly and with all their energy.

Would people believe they had a genuine change of heart? Probably most who heard of their conversions would be highly suspicious. And that's understandable, because such a revolutionary turnaround would seem unthinkable. To many, it is inconceivable that such tyrannical despots could be totally transformed. It seems impossible for anyone with such disregard for human life to become genuinely and deeply concerned for the spiritual well-being of others.

Yet that is exactly what happened in the first century A.D.! Saul ("who was also known as Paul," Acts 13:9), staunch persecutor of Christians, became a Christian, and vigorously promoted what he formerly denounced. The adversary of Christianity became its advocate; the enemy of Christians became one of them.

Years after Paul's conversion, he wrote that he "was once a blasphemer and a persecutor and a violent man" (1 Tim. 1:13). He told the believers in Philippi that before he was saved he in his zeal was "persecuting the church" (Phil. 3:6). To the Galatians he acknowledged that he "intensely[1] . . . persecuted the church of God and tried to destroy it" (Gal. 1:13). And to the Corinthians he admitted that he "persecuted the church of God" (1 Cor. 15:9). He thought that in doing so he was serving God, a fact Jesus had predicted to his disciples: "whoever kills you will think he is offering a service to God" (John 16:2). Paul was convinced that Jesus could not be the Messiah, because to die on a tree as Jesus did was to be cursed (Deut. 21:23). A crucified Messiah was a contradiction in terms! However, Paul admitted to Timothy years later that he "acted in ignorance and unbelief" (1 Tim. 1:13).

Yet this persecutor was actually persecuting Christ. The union of believers with Jesus Christ led Jesus to ask Saul on the Damascus Road, "Why do you persecute me?" (Acts 9:4; 22:7; 26:14) and to explain to Saul, "I am Jesus, whom you are persecuting" (9:5; cf. 22:8; 26:15).

Saul, the zealous Pharisee, first revealed his opposition to Christianity by guarding the clothes (probably the outer garments or cloaks) of those who were stoning Stephen, the first Christian martyr (Acts 7:58). This cloak guarding meant, as he later told a mob in Jerusalem, that as he stood there he was giving his approval (22:20).

Convinced that this new "sect" was heretical, and that Christianity, if allowed to spread, would divide and weaken Judaism, he, like modern-day vigilantes, went "from house to house," dragging off men and women who professed faith in Christ "and put them in prison" (8:3). These new Christians were no doubt afraid of Saul, for he threatened to murder them. (He was "breathing out murderous threats against the Lord's disciples," 9:1.) Obsessed with a burning passion to wipe out this

---

1. The word "intensely" is the NIV rendering of the Greek *kath hyperbolēn*, "according to excess" or "to the extreme." The RSV translates the phrase "violently" and the NEB has "savagely."

new heresy, he "went from one synagogue to another to imprison and beat" believers (22:19), something he said he did many times (26:11). He vigorously tried to force them to turn back to Judaism by blaspheming Christ (26:11). He was responsible for the deaths of many Christians, for he "persecuted the followers of this Way [as he called them] to their death" (22:4). When they were put to death, he told King Agrippa, he cast his vote in favor of their executions (26:10).

Not satisfied with his vicious attacks against the Jerusalem church, he even "went to foreign cities to persecute" Christians; he was "furiously enraged against them" (26:11).[2] One of these cities was Damascus,[3] about 150 miles from Jerusalem. He undertook this exhausting journey of seven to ten days to take believers there back as prisoners to Jerusalem (9:1–2, 14), where they would be punished (22:5). But why Damascus? Perhaps he was concerned that Christians in that great trading center would tell travelers in incoming and outgoing caravans about Jesus, thereby spreading the influence of this new belief to other lands far and wide.

These tactics of hunting, threatening, arresting, imprisoning, beating, trying to force to blaspheme, and murdering Christians were all directed toward his goal of seeking to "destroy" the church. The word "destroy" in Acts 8:3 is *lymainō*, "to injure or damage," a word used only here in the New Testament. It is used in the Septuagint in Psalm 79:13 (80:13 in English texts) of wild boars that ruin (NIV, "ravage") a vineyard. Saul's hatred against the church was like a wild animal raging against them.

In Acts 9:21 and Galatians 1:13, 23 Paul used *portheō*, a stronger word used only these three times in the New Testament, to depict his goal. (The NIV renders it "raised havoc" in Acts 9:21 and "tried to destroy" in Gal. 1:13, 23.) The verb means "to pillage, make havoc of, destroy, annihilate."[4] No wonder Ananias, a highly respected Christian Jew living in Damascus (Acts 22:12), said he had heard many reports

2. "Furiously enraged at them" translates the Greek *perissōs emmainomenōs autois*, which is softened in the NIV to "in my obsession against them."

3. Damascus, an ancient city known even to Abraham (Gen. 14:15), had a considerable Jewish population in Paul's day (S. Safrai and M. Stern, eds., *The Jewish People in the First Century* [Assen: Van Gorcum, 1974], 1:142). Josephus, first-century Jewish historian, refers in one place to 10,000 Jews being killed in Damascus by the Romans (*The Jewish Wars* 2.20.2) and in another place he refers to 18,000 (ibid., 7.8.7). For a brief history of Damascus and several photos of present-day Damascus, see F. F. Bruce, *In the Steps of the Apostle Paul* (Grand Rapids: Kregel, n.d.), 10–14.

4. Walter Bauer, William F. Arndt, and F. Wilbur Gingrich, *A Greek-English Lexicon of the New Testament and Other Early Christian Literature*, 2d ed., rev. F. Wilbur Gingrich and Frederick W. Danker (Chicago: University of Chicago Press, 1979), 693.

about all the "harm" (*kakos,* "injury, misfortune") Saul had done to saints in Jerusalem (9:13).

Knowing Paul as a great apostle, it is difficult for us to imagine him a violent man, as he called himself in 1 Timothy 1:13. He used this same word *hybistēs* in Romans 1:30 in describing depraved unbelievers (NIV, "insolent"). Paul's "before" and "after" are not unlike the imagined transformation of violent executioners like Hitler, Stalin, and Mao Zedong.

On the Damascus Road, Jesus confronted him, converted him, and commissioned him, thereby reversing his undaunting zeal against Christianity to arduous zeal for Christianity. Instead of seeking to damage and wipe out this new belief, he now sought to disseminate it.

He became the Lord's leading apostle and also one of Christianity's greatest teachers—a master teacher from whom we can learn much for our own teaching.

"J am a teacher of the true faith."

I Timothy 2:7

1

Was Paul a Teacher?

Paul, vehement opponent of Christianity, experienced the transforming grace of God and became Christianity's greatest champion and exponent. Highly educated and impassionately motivated, he ministered in multiple capacities of leadership, unmatched by few since his day. He served God as a pioneer missionary, a commissioned apostle, a zealous evangelist, an energetic church planter, a prolific writer, an insightful theologian, a vigorous apologist, a dynamic preacher, a warmhearted pastor, and a stimulating teacher.

Many writers have recognized Paul's outstanding role. He has been considered "the greatest man after Christ,"[1] "the most impressive and outstanding personage in the whole Apostolic circle [and] the most brilliant of the Apostles,"[2] "the greatest thinker of his age, if not of any age,"[3] "Christianity's foremost spokesman and by far its most exciting and vigorous theologian,"[4] "one of the finest scholars of his age [and] the greatest of all missionaries,"[5] "the greatest of Christians,"[6] "a ge-

1. Clarence Edward Macartney, *Paul the Man* (Westwood, N.J.: Revell, 1961), 9.
2. W. M. Ramsay, *Pauline and Other Studies* (New York: Armstrong & Son, 1906; reprint, Grand Rapids: Baker, 1970), 28.
3. James Stalker, *The Life of St. Paul* (New York: Revell, 1950), 91.
4. E. P. Sanders, *Paul* (New York: Oxford University Press, 1991), 18.
5. Frank E. Gaebelein, *The Pattern of God's Truth* (New York: Oxford University Press, 1954; reprint, Chicago: Moody, 1968), 105.
6. Reginald E. O. White, *Apostle Extraordinary* (Grand Rapids: Eerdmans, 1962), v.

nius,"[7] "next to Jesus . . . the most significant person in early Christianity,"[8] "one of the great characters, not only in the Bible, but in all history,"[9] "the most powerful human personality in the history of the Church,"[10] "the first great theologian of the church,"[11] "the most saintly and heroic personality who has ever born the name of Christ,"[12] "the greatest proclaimer of the cross of Christ,"[13] "one of the most significant figures in the history of civilization,"[14] "the super-missionary of the Gospel,"[15] and "the most influential Christian who ever lived."[16]

Book titles also point to Paul's uniqueness and varied functions. Some designate his primary role as apostle:

Paul the Apostle
The Apostle Paul
Apostle of the Heart Set Free
Paul: Apostle of Liberty
Apostle to the Gentiles
The Apostle: A Life of Paul
Apostle Extraordinary.?[17]

Other book titles specify other aspects of Paul's leadership:

7. Samuel Sandmel, *The Genius of Paul: A Study in History* (Philadelphia: Fortress, 1979), 35.

8. Ibid., 213.

9. Herbert Lockyer, *All the Men of the Bible* (Grand Rapids: Zondervan, 1958), 269.

10. "Paul, St.," in *The Oxford Dictionary of the Christian Church*, ed. F. L. Cross, 2d ed. (New York: Oxford University Press, 1974), 1047.

11. W. S. Reilly, "Characteristics of St. Paul," *Catholic Biblical Quarterly* 3 (1941): 218.

12. Clarence Edward Macartney, *The Greatest Men of the Bible* (New York: Abingdon-Cokesbury, 1941), 15.

13. Ibid., 21.

14. F. F. Bruce, *Paul and His Converts* (Downers Grove, Ill.: InterVarsity, 1985), 16.

15. Simon Légasse, "Paul's Pre-Christian Career according to Acts," in *The Book of Acts in Its Palestinian Setting*, ed. Richard Bauckham (Grand Rapids: Eerdmans, 1995), 383.

16. William E. Phipps, *Encountering through Questioning Paul* (Washington, D.C.: University Press of America, 1982), 84.

17. Hugh Monetfiore, *Paul the Apostle* (New York: Collins, 1981); Giuseppe Ricciotti, *Paul the Apostle*, trans. Alba I. Zizzamia (Milwaukee: Bruce, 1952); A. Sabatier, *The Apostle Paul*, trans. A. M. Hellier (London: Hodder and Stoughton, 1891); F. F. Bruce, *Apostle of the Heart Set Free* (Grand Rapids: Eerdmans, 1977); Richard N. Longenecker, *Paul: Apostle of Liberty* (New York: Harper and Row, 1964; reprint, Grand Rapids: Baker, 1976); Jürgen Becker, *Apostle to the Gentiles*, trans. O. C. Dean, Jr. (Louisville: Westminster/Knox, 1993); John Pollock, *The Apostle: A Life of Paul* (Wheaton, Ill.: Victor, 1985); Reginald E. O. White, *Apostle Extraordinary* (Grand Rapids: Eerdmans, 1962); and William Neil, *Apostle Extraordinary* (Wallington, Surrey: Religious Education, 1965).

Paul the Leader
Paul the Man
Paul the Missionary
St. Paul the Orator
Paul the Preacher
Paul: Portrait of a Revolutionary
St. Paul the Traveller and Roman Citizen
Paul the Traveller
Paul: The Man, the Missionary, and the Teacher
Saint Paul: The Man and His Mind
Paul: Follower of Jesus or Founder of Christianity?
The Genius of Paul: A Study in History
Saint Paul the Master Builder.?[18]

These are only a few of the multitudinous works on Paul. Hundreds upon hundreds of books have been written on Paul's life and ministry. Thousands of journal articles have explored various aspects of the character and works of Christianity's greatest intellect. Metzger's index of periodical literature on Paul includes 3,013 entries,[19] and Mills updated this index with an additional 2,700 entries.[20] Yet only an amazingly few books and articles address Paul's ministry as a teacher! Even the impressive *Dictionary of Paul and His Letters*,[21] with its 1,038 pages and 214 topics by 108 authors, has only one article on Paul's teaching (though admittedly a few articles refer briefly to the apostle's pedagogical methods). Petersen's extensive bibliography with its approximately

18. J. Oswald Sanders, *Paul the Leader* (Colorado Springs: NavPress, 1984); Macartney, *Paul the Man;* William M. Taylor, *Paul the Missionary* (New York: Doran, 1881); Maurice Jones, *St. Paul the Orator* (London: Hodder and Stoughton, 1910); John Eadie, *Paul the Preacher* (London: Griffin, 1859; reprint, Minneapolis: James Family, 1979); Raymond Bailey, *Paul the Preacher* (Nashville: Broadman, 1991); David Coggan, *Paul: Portrait of a Revolutionary* (London: Hodder and Stoughton, 1984); W. M. Ramsay, *St. Paul the Traveller and Roman Citizen*, 3d ed. (1895; reprint, Grand Rapids: Baker, 1949); Ernle Bradford, *Paul the Traveller* (New York: Macmillan, 1974); Orello Cone, *Paul: The Man, the Missionary, and the Teacher* (New York: Macmillan, 1898); Ernest White, *Saint Paul: The Man and His Mind* (Fort Washington, Penn.: Christian Literature Crusade, 1958); David Wenham, *Paul: Follower of Jesus or Founder of Christianity?* (Grand Rapids: Eerdmans, 1995); Sandmel, *The Genius of Paul: A Study in History*; Walter Lock, *St. Paul the Master Builder* (London: Methuen, 1899).

19. Bruce M. Metzger, *Index to Periodical Literature on the Apostle Paul*, 2d ed. (Leiden: Brill, 1970). The first edition (1966) had 2,987 entries, and the second edition (1970) added 26 more.

20. Watson E. Mills, *An Index to Periodical Literature on the Apostle Paul* (Leiden: Brill, 1993).

21. Gerald F. Hawthorne, Ralph P. Martin, and Daniel G. Reid, eds., *Dictionary of Paul and His Letters* (Downers Grove, Ill.: InterVarsity, 1993).

13,000 entries has no category on Paul's teaching.[22]

W. D. Davies's book has a chapter entitled, "The Old and New Man: Paul as Teacher of the Individual."[23] Neil's book of seven chapters on Paul includes a chapter on Paul as a missionary and a chapter on Paul as a letter writer, but no chapter on his teaching.[24] This is typical of most books on the apostle. I am aware of only two books that address Paul as a pedagogue, one of which was written more than seventy years ago.[25]

Granted, the New Testament refers to Paul's preaching more often than to his teaching (see the tables in chapter 3).[26] But just as preachers can benefit from studying how Paul preached, so can teachers gain from noting how Paul taught.

Analyzing and following Paul's educational goals and strategies can help us become better teachers of God's Word. Examining his pedagogy can acquaint us with a number of important principles and procedures in teaching. The Book of Acts and Paul's epistles show us at least thirty-two important aspects of teaching:

> how he expressed concern for his converts
> how he instructed others in doctrine and Christian living
> how he used his knowledge of contemporary cultures
> how he adapted his message and style to various audiences
> how he willingly endured hardship in order to help others
> how he showed the impact of the truth in one's life
> how he urged his learners to live for the Lord
> how he made clear his ministry aims
> how he revealed his inner motives
> how he trained others to serve the Lord
> how he shared his ministry with his companions

22. Paul D. Petersen, ed., *Paul the Apostle and Pauline Literature: A Bibliography Selected from the ATLA Religion Database*, 4th rev. ed. (Chicago: American Theological Library Association, 1984).

23. W. D. Davies, *Paul and Rabbinic Judaism* (New York: Harper and Row, 1948). In this chapter Davies writes that "Paul the κῆρυξ [herald] had to become διδάσκαλος . . ." (ibid., 112). Through his message (*kērygma*) they became converts, but in his teaching (*didachē*) the converts were nourished by "theological exposition" and "ethical instruction" (ibid.).

24. Neil, *Apostle Extraordinary*.

25. Howard Tillman Kuist, *The Pedagogy of St. Paul* (New York: Doran, 1925); and Kent L. Johnson, *Paul the Teacher* (Minneapolis: Augsburg, 1986). Some books, however, do address selected aspects of his teaching, such as his opponents, writing style, and use of illustrations and rhetoric.

26. "Paul was first and foremost a preacher" (Bailey, *Paul the Preacher*, 16). "Obviously Paul was first of all and most of all a preacher" (William Cleaver Wilkinson, *Paul and the Revolt against Him* [Philadelphia: Griffith and Rowland, 1914], 2). A comparison of New Testament references to Paul's preaching and teaching is examined in chapter 3.

how he depended on the Lord for guidance and strength
how he exemplified Christlikeness
how he exhibited qualities necessary for effective teaching
how he used letter writing as a means of communication and teaching
how he corrected his learners when they needed it
how he responded to those who opposed his teaching
how he used questions to prod his listeners' and readers' thinking
how he expressed concepts in strikingly picturesque ways
how he used contemporary illustrations to communicate his points
how he boldly gave commands for his learners to follow
how he modeled a servant attitude
how he adapted his teaching to a variety of locations and situations
how he affirmed and encouraged his learners
how he lectured with dynamic impact
how he quoted the Old Testament in his teaching
how he captured and held the attention of his listeners
how he involved learners in the teaching-learning process
how he trained and developed disciples
how he varied his teaching methods
how he shared his pastoral heart
how he relied on the Holy Spirit for spiritual power

Analyze your own teaching in the light of these thirty-two aspects of Paul's ministry and ask yourself how you can follow his example. Incorporating these principles and practices in one's ministry can certainly make any teacher more effective.

What's Your Answer?

Do you think of Paul as a great teacher? Why or why not? What aspects of his ministry contribute to his being thought of as a great instructor?

Do you think of yourself as a teacher? Why or why not?

What aspects of Paul's teaching might you emulate in order to become a more effective teacher?

"The Lord's servant must be able to teach."

2 Timothy 2:24

2

Can We Teach as Paul Taught?

Since Paul was such an outstanding theologian, thinker, scholar, and communicator, is it really possible for anyone today to teach as he did?

True, Paul was unique in a number of ways. First, he saw the resurrected Christ on the Damascus Road. This unique experience, an essential qualification for his being an apostle (1 Cor. 9:1), drastically changed his life. While many individuals' lives have been significantly altered by God's transforming grace, no one today has encountered exactly what Paul experienced. While believers know and love the same Savior Paul did, his conversion experience is unequaled in his being confronted suddenly, alarmingly, and personally by the one who identified himself as Jesus and who told Paul to go into Damascus and wait there for the Lord's instructions on what to do (Acts 9:5; 22:8–10; 26:15–16).

Second, Paul was an educated Jew, born to a Pharisee as a Roman citizen in a Greek university city, schooled in a Tarsus synagogue, and educated in Jerusalem under Gamaliel, Israel's leading rabbi. His Jewish upbringing in his home gave him a thorough acquaintance with the Old Testament, a vast knowledge that few people have today. As will be discussed in chapter 4, these and other aspects of Paul's background uniquely prepared him for his extensive ministry of about three decades. Few people today possess such a thorough preparation for teaching God's Word.

Third, Paul's ministry is inimitable because he was an apostle. The spiritual gift of apostleship was unique to the early church as a "foundational" gift, for as Paul wrote, the church, "God's household," was "built on the foundation of the apostles and prophets, with Christ Jesus himself as the chief cornerstone" (Eph. 2:20). The fact that apostles and prophets are listed first in Paul's reference to spiritual gifts in both Ephesians 4:11 and 1 Corinthians 12:28 also suggests that they are foundational gifts. Therefore, since the gift of apostleship is not functional today, Paul's role as an apostle cannot be duplicated. Another indication of this temporary nature is the fact that in listing those to whom Jesus appeared after his resurrection, Paul stated, "Last of all he appeared to me also" (1 Cor. 15:8). Paul did not say, "Then he appeared to me," but "Last of all he appeared to me," which suggests a finality to the Lord's appearances. This "serves to mark [Paul] out as the end point of such appearances and therefore the end point of apostolic appointment."[1]

A fourth aspect of his ministry that makes Paul unsurpassed is his having received revelation of truths directly from God. He referred to this fact several times. In Galatians, most likely the first epistle he wrote, he stated, "I want you to know, brothers, that the gospel I preached is not something that man made up. I did not receive it from any man, nor was I taught it; rather, I received it by revelation from Jesus Christ" (Gal. 1:11–13). He added that when God called him by his grace and revealed his Son in Paul, he "did not consult any man . . . but . . . went immediately into Arabia and later returned to Damascus" (1:16–17) and then three years later went to Jerusalem "to get acquainted with Peter" and James (1:18–19).

After his conversion, he went into Damascus (the Lord appeared to him possibly only a few miles outside the city), stayed with Judas on Straight Street,[2] and was visited by Ananias, a devout, reputable Jewish Christian. Ananias enabled him to see again after being blind for three days and then baptized him, after which Paul ate and regained his strength (Acts 9:11–19). He began preaching in the synagogues and after many days had gone by the Jews conspired to kill him, so he escaped by night by being lowered in a basket "through an opening in the [city] wall" (9:20–25; cf. 2 Cor. 11:32–33).[3] His time in Arabia (possibly

1. Paul W. Burnett, "Apostle," in *Dictionary of Paul and His Letters*, ed. Gerald F. Hawthorne, Ralph P. Martin, and Daniel G. Reid (Downers Grove, Ill.: InterVarsity, 1993), 48.

2. A street by that name still runs today from east to west in old Damascus.

3. "Saul's plans for persecuting Christians in Damascus took a strange turn; he had entered the city blind and left in a basket! Ironically he became the object of persecution" (Stanley D. Toussaint, "Acts," in *The Bible Knowledge Commentary, New Testament*, ed. John F. Walvoord and Roy B. Zuck [Wheaton, Ill.: Victor, 1983], 377–78). Pollock suggests the basket in which the new apostle was lowered from a window jutting over the city wall about eight or ten feet was "a fish basket, a large shapeless sack which folded round his body so that no casual observer would notice in the darkness that it hid a man" (John Pollock, *The Apostle: A Life of Paul* [Wheaton, Ill.: Victor, 1985], 44).

northern Arabia in Nabatean territory east of Damascus[4]) may have transpired after his beginning days in Damascus. Luke's words "after many days" in Acts 9:23 may include Paul's Arabian visit.

Probably during that secluded time in Arabia Paul meditated on the significance of his conversion, reflecting on ways Jesus was revealed in the Old Testament.[5] And this may have been when the Lord revealed to Paul many of the truths he later preached and wrote about, truths that previously had been unrevealed to humankind. He referred to one of those doctrines in his Epistle to the Ephesians. He called this "the mystery of Christ, which was not made known to men in other generations as it has now been revealed by the Spirit to God's holy apostles and prophets" (Eph. 3:4–5). Some Bible students say the word "as" means "to the same extent as," so that the verse means the mystery was partially revealed in the Old Testament but is now fully revealed in the New Testament. It is preferable, however, to understand the word "as" in a descriptive sense, with the verse meaning that the mystery was not revealed in the Old Testament at all but was revealed first in the New. In Ephesians 3:9 Paul wrote that this mystery was hidden in ages past, and in Colossians 1:26 he affirmed, "the mystery that has been kept hidden for ages and generations . . . is now disclosed to the saints."

This "mystery," a truth previously unknown but now revealed, is the truth that in the church age believing Gentiles and Jews are heirs of God's grace, "members together of one body," the church (Eph. 3:6; cf. 2:11–22). This fact, Paul wrote, "was made known to me by revelation" (3:3). The apostle wrote of the same truth in Romans 16:25–26 when he said that "the revelation of the mystery hidden for long ages past [is] now revealed and made known."

Fifth, Paul's ministry cannot be duplicated because he "was caught up to paradise" (2 Cor. 12:4), that is, he was raptured ("caught up" translates the word *harpazō*, also used in 1 Thess. 4:17 of saints at the rapture) to "the third heaven" (2 Cor. 12:2), the abode of God and the souls of believers who have died. The remarkable experience, which occurred before he began his missionary journeys ("fourteen years ago,"

4. Pliny, first-century Roman author, said Arabia was on the desert side of the three easternmost cities of the Decapolis: Damascus, Raphona, and Philadelphia (*Natural History* 5.16.74; cf. Strabo *Geography* 16.2.20).

5. Baslez and Longenecker suggest Paul's purpose in going to Arabia was for reflection and study (M.F. Baslez, *Saint Paul* [Paris: Fayard, 1991], 101; and Richard N. Longenecker, *Galatians*, Word Biblical Commentary [Dallas: Word, 1990], 34). And Jerome Murphy-O'Connor suggests the apostle's stay was brief and that he probably did not penetrate very deeply into Arabia ("Paul in Arabia," *Catholic Biblical Quarterly* 55 [1993]: 732–37).

12:2), confirmed his apostolic credentials, a subject he addressed to the Corinthians (11:16–12:10) because they questioned his authority as an apostle. If they insisted on an apostle having "visions and revelations" (12:1), he certainly qualified![6] He referred to "these surpassingly great revelations" (12:7). In fact, Paul added, the credentials of an apostle include "signs, wonders, and miracles" (12:12)—and Paul qualified in that area too (Rom. 15:19). He was used of God to perform several miracles, miracles that confirmed his apostolic authority (cf. Heb. 2:3b–4). These included his causing Elymas, a Jewish sorcerer on the island of Cyprus, to be blinded (Acts 13:6–12) and exorcising a demon from a fortune-teller slave (16:16–18). Again, since the gift of apostleship, being essential for the initial founding of the church, was temporary, the receiving of revelations and the power to perform miracles was limited to the apostles. In this way too we are unable to replicate Paul's ministry.

Sixth, Paul stands unique as a Christian leader because of his being used of God to write thirteen[7] of the New Testament's twenty-seven books. In the number of chapters, Paul's letters total exactly one-third of the New Testament (87 of 260 chapters)! Of the number of pages in

6. On four other occasions God revealed himself to Paul in a vision. The first vision of Christ was on the road to Damascus. In Acts 9:4; 22:7; and 26:14 he said he "heard" a voice, but in 9:27 Luke recorded that Barnabas told the Jerusalem disciples that Paul "had seen the Lord." And in 26:19 the apostle referred to this experience as a "vision from heaven," an indication that he saw as well as heard the Lord (cf. 1 Cor. 9:1, "Have I not seen Jesus our Lord?") Also Ananias said Paul had been chosen "to see the Righteous One" (Acts 22:14; cf. 26:16). His second vision or "revelation" was when God directed him to visit Jerusalem with Barnabas and Titus (Gal. 2:2; "I went in response to a revelation"). This visit may have been the famine visit mentioned in Acts 11:27–30. For a discussion of Paul's five Jerusalem visits, see Donald K. Campbell, "Galatians," in *The Bible Knowledge Commentary, New Testament,* 593; and for an extensive discussion of the arguments for and against identifying Galatians 2:1–10 with Acts 11:30, see David Wenham, "Acts and the Pauline Corpus: II. Pauline Parallels," in *The Book of Acts in Its Ancient Literary Setting,* ed. Bruce W. Winter and Andrew W. Clarke (Grand Rapids: Eerdmans, 1993), 226–43.

7. If Paul wrote Hebrews, the total is fourteen, slightly more than half the number of New Testament books. While a number of factors point to Pauline authorship, other points argue strongly against his having written Hebrews. For discussions of this issue, see Harold W. Attridge, *The Epistle to the Hebrews,* Hermeneia (Philadelphia: Fortress, 1989), 1–6; Donald Guthrie, *New Testament Introduction* (Downers Grove, Ill.: InterVarsity, 1990), 668–82; D. Edmond Hiebert, *An Introduction to the New Testament,* vol. 3: *The Non-Pauline Epistles and Revelation,* rev. ed. (Chicago: Moody, 1977), 71–81; Zane C. Hodges, "Hebrews," in *The Bible Knowledge Commentary, New Testament,* 777–78; Philip Edgcumbe Hughes, *A Commentary on the Epistle to the Hebrews* (Grand Rapids: Eerdmans, 1977), 19–30; William L. Lane, *Hebrews 1–8,* Word Biblical Commentary (Dallas: Word, 1991), xlvii–li; and Brooke Foss Westcott, *The Epistle to the Hebrews* (London: Macmillan, 1889), lxii–lxxix.

the Nestle-Aland Greek New Testament, one-fourth (24.6%) are Pauline.

Also three-fifths (60%) of the Book of Acts records Paul's ministry: seventeen of the twenty-eight chapters (Acts 9 and 13–28). So his life and letters (Acts 9, 13–28 and Romans through Philemon) together comprise 40 percent of the chapters of the New Testament!

These writings were given by inspiration of the Holy Spirit (2 Tim. 3:16; 2 Peter 1:21) and thus are part of the inerrant, authoritative Scriptures. And their influence is immeasurable. Writers have said Paul's epistles are "among the mightiest intellectual forces of the world,"[8] and are "one of the most influential forces in the religious and intellectual history of the world . . . whose influence through the ages cannot be estimated."[9]

These six factors about the great apostle give reason for teachers and others today to shrink back from thinking they can teach as he taught. Seeing the resurrected Christ, having a Jewish-Roman-Greek background, being an apostle, receiving revelations from God, being caught up to the third heaven, and having been used of God to write almost half of the New Testament books—these all place Paul in an incomparable position.

On the other hand, six other elements in his life enable us to affirm that we *can* teach as he taught. First, he admitted that before his salvation he, as a blasphemer and persecutor (Gal. 1:13), was "the worst of sinners" (1 Tim. 1:16). Then after serving Christ for many years he acknowledged while in prison that he had not arrived spiritually (Phil. 3:12–13). Certainly every believer can also affirm his or her need for ongoing spiritual development.

Second, we have the same message Paul had, namely, the gospel of salvation through faith in Christ (Acts 16:30–31; Rom. 3:24–25; 6:23; 10:9–10; 1 Cor. 1:23; 15:1, 3–4; 2 Cor. 8:9; Gal. 2:16; 3:26; Eph. 1:7; 2:8; 1 Tim. 1:14; Titus 2:14; 3:5). And we have the same truths to impart to believers to help them mature in Christ. The message has not changed; what Paul taught is what we are to teach.

Third, Paul was empowered in his ministry by the Holy Spirit, whose enabling is available to all believers. He wrote that his message was presented with the Holy Spirit's power (1 Cor. 2:4; 1 Thess. 1:5), and that the Spirit helped him (Phil. 1:19). The same Holy Spirit who indwelt the apostle indwells all believers (Acts 15:8; Rom. 5:5; 8:9, 11; 1 Cor. 2:12; 3:16; 2 Cor. 1:22; Gal. 3:14; Eph. 2:22; 1 Thess. 4:8; 2 Tim. 1:14; Titus 3:5–6).

8. James Stalker, *The Life of St. Paul* (New York: Revell, 1950), 91.
9. J. Oswald Sanders, *Paul the Leader* (Colorado Springs: NavPress, 1984), 57–58.

Just as Paul was filled with the Holy Spirit (Acts 9:17; 13:9), so are believers to be filled with the Spirit (Eph. 5:18), that is, controlled by him. They are to "live by dependence on him" (Gal. 5:16 NASB) and "walk in the Spirit," for he is involved in their sanctification (Rom. 15:16; 2 Thess. 2:13). Also, the Holy Spirit led Paul on several occasions. He and Barnabas undertook their first missionary journey at the prompting and leading of the Spirit (Acts 13:2, 4); he and other apostles and elders were led by the Holy Spirit in their decision in the Jerusalem Council (15:28); Paul and his companions were kept by the Spirit from going into the province of Asia (16:6–7); and he told the elders at Ephesus that he felt compelled by the Spirit "to go to Jerusalem" after his third missionary journey (20:22). The same indwelling Holy Spirit is available to guide all believers ("those who are led by the Spirit of God are sons of God," Rom. 8:14; cf. Gal. 5:18).

Fourth, the apostle's means of communication are also available to us. He taught verbally, he communicated by means of letters, and he taught by his personal example. In his verbal communication, he used methods that we too can use, including lectures, discussions, and questions, and he used a variety of figures of speech, analogies, and references to Old Testament Scripture that teachers can use today.

A fifth similarity between Paul's teaching and ours is the fact of pressure and hard work. To the Corinthians Paul wrote of his "distress and anguish of heart" (2 Cor. 2:4) and of the "pressure" he faced each day because of his "concern for all the churches" (11:28). He often addressed the problem of Judaizers and other false teachers who, disagreeing with what he taught, sought to undo what he had accomplished. He was continually burdened that his converts grow in Christ. All this demanded hard work and strenuous effort: "I have labored and toiled and have often gone without sleep" (2 Cor. 11:27). "I labor, struggling with all his [i.e., Christ's] energy" (Col. 1:29). "We labor and strive" (1 Tim. 4:10).[10] He knew what it was to be "in need" (Phil. 4:12) and to suffer emotionally and physically (2 Cor. 4:8–12; 6:4–10; 11:23–29). Many dedicated teachers can identify with Paul's efforts and his burden for those to whom he ministered.

---

10. Paul used several significant words to express his hard work on behalf of others. *Kopiaō* (in Col. 1:29 and 1 Tim. 4:10) means "to labor or work to the point of being weary or exhausted." *Mochthos* in 2 Corinthians 11:27, another word for toil, includes the idea of struggle or exertion. *Agōnizomai* in Colossians 1:29 conveys striving or putting forth effort. "The athletic picture behind the word [*agōnizomai*] emphasizes Paul's missionary work, w[ith] all its attendant toil, its tireless exertion, and its struggles against all manner of setbacks and opposition" (Fritz Rienecker, *A Linguistic Key to the Greek New Testament*, ed. Cleon L. Rogers, Jr. [Grand Rapids: Zondervan, 1980], 571).

Sixth, the apostle found it necessary to support himself financially by tentmaking (Acts 18:3).[11] To the Ephesian elders he spoke of "these hands of mine" and of his "hard work" (20:34–35). To the Thessalonian believers he said he engaged in "toil and hardship . . . night and day in order not to be a burden to anyone" (1 Thess. 2:9; 2 Thess. 3:8).[12] He wrote to the Corinthians, "we work hard with our own hands" (1 Cor. 4:12).[13] These verses no doubt refer to his physical labor in his "secular" job. His self-employment enabled him to offer the gospel "free of charge" (1 Cor. 9:18; 2 Cor. 11:7), though as an apostle he had the right to be supported financially by those to whom he ministered (1 Cor. 9:12–18). By his tentmaking he met his own material needs and even the needs of others, as he told the Ephesian elders: "These hands of mine have supplied my own needs and the needs of my companions" (Acts 20:34).

Similarly, many today who teach or disciple others find it necessary to be engaged in employment in order to meet their financial needs. In doing so, they are not unlike the great apostle.

So while it is impossible for us to imitate Paul in his teaching ministry in a number of ways, it is possible for us to teach as he did because of several factors we have in common with him. With the church's

11. Many have assumed that the tents Paul made were from a cloth made of black goats' hair known as *cilicium*, named after the province of Cilicia, where Tarsus, Paul's hometown, was located. (Those holding this view include, among others, E. Plumptre, "St. Paul as a Man of Business," *Expositor* [1985]: 259–66; and Gustav A. Deismann, *Paul: A Study in Social and Religious History* [New York: Hodder and Stoughton, 1926], 48–50.) It seems preferable, however, to understand "tentmaking" (*skēnopoios*) as referring to leathermaking (Livy *History of Rome* 5.2.7; 37. 39.2; J. Curle, *A Roman Frontier Post and Its People* [Glasgow: Maclehose & Sons, 1911], 66) for leather goods were associated with Cilicia (T. R. S. Broughton, "Roman Asia," in *An Economic Survey of Ancient Rome*, ed. T. Frank [Baltimore: John Hopkins University Press, 1938], 5:823–24). Perhaps Paul worked in both leather and goats' hair cloth (Pollock, *The Apostle: A Life of Paul*, 16).

Engaged primarily in making tents out of leather, Paul may have made and repaired other products from leather and woven goods, such as booths, canopies, and awnings for soldiers, sailors, and travelers (Paul W. Barnett, "Tentmaking," in *Dictionary of Paul and His Letters*, 926; Ronalds F. Hock, *The Social Context of Paul's Ministry: Tentmaking and Apostleship* [Philadelpia: Fortress, 1980], 20–25; W. Michaelis "οκυροττοιος," in *Theological Dictionary of the New Testament*, 7 [1971], 393–94). "Tentmaker," then, may have been a broad term, just as a saddler does not make only saddles (Martin Hengel, *The Pre-Christian Paul*, trans. John Bowden [Philadelphia: Trinity, 1991], 17). In his travels Paul could have easily carried with him cutting tools, awls, a sharpening stone, and such (Brian Rapske, "Acts, Travel and Shipwreck," in *The Book of Acts in Its Graeco-Roman Setting*, ed. David W. J. Gill and Conrad Gempf [Grand Rapids: Eerdmans, 1994], 7).

12. "Toil" translates *kopos*, from *kopiaō*, "to work to exhaustion"; and "hardship" translates *mochthos*, "work involving exertion."

13. Literally, "We labor [from *kopiaō*; see note 10], doing manual labor [from *ergazomai*] with our own hands."

greatest apostle we can share his desire to advance spiritually; his commitment to communicating the gospel and essential doctrines; his empowering and leading by the Holy Spirit; his effective avenues of communication; his sense of pressure, concern, and struggle for others; and his involvement in self-supporting means. With these common elements we can thrill at the thought of teaching as Paul taught.

Mulling It Over . . .

Have you ever thought of yourself as a teacher similar to Paul? If not, are there reasons why you could and should?

Think of ways God has uniquely equipped you to teach.

Consider each of the six factors in Paul's teaching that we can share with him. Ask the Lord to enable you to use each of them more effectively as you teach.

*"J was appointed a herald and
an apostle and a teacher."*

2 Timothy 1:11

3

What Place Did Teaching
Have in Paul's Ministry?

You no doubt have a number of "titles," terms that represent your relationships and responsibilities. Your "relationship" titles, for example,
may include your being a son or daughter, a grandson or granddaughter,
brother or sister, nephew or niece, husband or wife, father or mother,
father-in-law or mother-in-law, uncle or aunt, grandfather or grandmother. Others include friend, fiancé, neighbor, customer, or client.

Your "responsibility" titles may include student, teacher, parent,
homemaker, worker, employee, employer, supervisor, manager, director, agent, committee member, board member, chairperson, administrator, officer, or president.

Like most people, Paul too had numerous titles. In his human relationships he was "the son of a Pharisee" (Acts 23:6) and an uncle and
brother (23:16 refers to "the son of Paul's sister"). Also he referred to his
being "a child" (26:4; 1 Cor. 13:11). Religiously he was a leader among
the Pharisees (Acts 23:6; 26:5; Phil. 3:5). As a believer in Christ, he was
spiritually related to the Lord as his son (e.g., Rom. 8:14, 19, 23; Gal.
3:26; 4:6; Eph. 1:5) and heir (Rom. 8:17; Gal. 3:29; 4:7; Eph. 3:6; Titus

3:7). In addition, with all believers he was a member of the universal church, the body of Christ (Rom. 12:4–5; 1 Cor. 10:17; 12:12–13, 27; Eph. 1:23; 3:6; 4:25; 5:30; Col. 1:18, 24; 3:15).

Though imprisoned by Roman authorities, Paul viewed himself as the Lord's prisoner because Paul was there as a result of his serving Christ: "the prisoner of Christ Jesus" (Eph. 3:1), "a prisoner for the Lord" (4:1), "his prisoner" (2 Tim. 1:8), and "a prisoner of Christ Jesus" (Philem. 1).

The apostle also had eight responsibility titles: instrument, teacher, witness, servant, slave, herald, minister, and apostle.

Instrument

When God told Ananias in Damascus to go restore Saul's sight, the Lord gave the reason: "This man is my chosen instrument" (Acts 9:15). That is, Paul was to be like a tool or implement in God's hand. Ananias also said, as Paul reported later, "The God of our fathers has chosen you" (22:14).

Teacher

Twice he reminded Timothy that he, Paul, was a teacher: "I was appointed . . . a teacher" (1 Tim. 2:7; 2 Tim. 1:11).

Witness

In keeping with the Lord's instruction to the Eleven ("You will be my witnesses," Acts 1:8), Jesus told Paul he would be his "witness" (*martys*, 22:15; 26:16; cf. testifying [*martyromai*, "witnessing"] in 26:22).

Servant

Twice the apostle is said to be Christ's servant (*hypēretēs*, "a helper, one who assists or serves others"; Acts 26:16; 1 Cor. 4:1).[1] Paul also called

---

1. This word is used of John Mark who went with Barnabas and Paul to be their "helper" (Acts 13:5). Originally, it referred to oarsmen on a warship to distinguish them from soldiers on the ship. Then it came to mean anyone who was an underling, such as a physician's assistant or a military adjutant (Jerome Murphy-O'Connor, *Paul on Preaching* [New York: Sheed and Ward, 1963], 60–64). Also see Karl H. Ringstorf, "ὑπερέτης, ὑπερετέω," in *Theological Dictionary of the New Testament*, 8 (1972), 530–44.

himself a servant *(diakonos)* of Christ (1 Cor. 3:5; 2 Cor. 11:23), a servant of God (6:4), a servant of the new covenant (3:6), a servant of the gospel (Eph. 3:7; Col. 1:23), and a servant of the church (Col. 1:25).

Slave

Five times Paul referred to himself as a slave *(doulos,* one who is owned by another) of the Lord. He was "a servant [*doulos*] of Christ Jesus" (Rom. 1:1; Phil. 1:1), "a servant [*doulos*] of Christ" (Gal. 1:10), "a servant [*doulos*] of God" (Titus 1:1), and Paul and Timothy were "servants [*douloi*] for Jesus' sake" (2 Cor. 4:5). Just as some Old Testament slaves bound themselves in appreciation to their masters (Exod. 21:2–6), so Paul willingly bound himself over to serve the Lord all his life. He was proud, not ashamed, of being that kind of slave.

Only one person called Paul a slave, and that was a demon-possessed girl, who herself was a slave, making a lot of money for her owners by her fortune-telling (Acts 16:16–17).

Herald

Twice Paul wrote, "I was appointed a herald" *(kēryx;* 1 Tim. 2:7; 2 Tim. 1:11). The *kēryx* was a person who announced public events or proclaimed good news. "The herald's most important qualification was that he faithfully represent or report the word of the one by whom he had been sent. He was not to be 'original'—it was imperative that the message he brought *not* be his own, but that it be the message of another."[2]

Minister

A title Paul used of himself only once is *leitourgos* ("minister") of Christ Jesus (Rom. 15:16). This relates to *leitourgia,* a word often used of the religious duties of priests and others. Thus in proclaiming the gospel, as Paul wrote in this same verse, he was performing a priestly duty. Like a priest, he presented the believing Gentiles as an offering to the Lord.

2. Victor Paul Furnish, "Prophets, Apostles, and Preachers: A Study of the Biblical Concept of Preaching," *Interpretation* 17 (January 1963): 55 (italics his). For a summary of the use of *kēryx* in classical Greek before Christ and in Greek papyri after Christ, see Murphy-O'Connor, *Paul on Preaching,* 48–51.

Apostle

The most common title of Paul is "apostle" *(apostolos)*, which means one sent with the authority and as a representative of the one sending him.[3] Thus Paul and the other apostles were commissioned by God by divine authority and as his representatives or spokesmen. Paul used this term of himself in the salutations of nine of his epistles.

"Paul, a slave of Christ Jesus, a called apostle" (Rom. 1:1, author's trans.)

"Paul, a called apostle of Christ Jesus through the will of God" (1 Cor. 1:1, author's trans.)

"Paul, an apostle of Christ Jesus by the will of God" (2 Cor. 1:1).

"Paul, an apostle, not from men nor through man, but through Jesus Christ and God the Father" (Gal. 1:1, author's trans.)

"Paul, an apostle of Christ Jesus by the will of God" (Eph. 1:1)

"Paul, an apostle of Christ Jesus by the will of God" (Col. 1:1)

"Paul, an apostle of Christ Jesus by the command of God our Savior and of Christ Jesus our hope" (1 Tim. 1:1)

"Paul, an apostle of Christ Jesus by the will of God" (2 Tim. 1:1)

"Paul, a slave of God and an apostle of Jesus Christ" (Titus 1:1, author's trans.)

Twice Luke referred to Paul and Barnabas as apostles: in Iconium (Acts 14:4) and in Lystra (14:14). Eleven other times Paul wrote about his role as Jesus' apostle, as seen in the following verses.

"We received grace and apostleship to call people from among all the Gentiles" (Rom. 1:5).

"I am the apostle to the Gentiles" (Rom. 11:13).

---

3. Jesus was called an "apostle" (Heb. 3:1) because he was sent by God. Forty-two times the Gospel of John mentions that Jesus was "sent" by the Father. In turn Jesus, having chosen twelve apostles, sent them out to preach (Mark 3:14). Paul acknowledged that he was sent by God (1 Cor. 1:17; 2 Cor. 2:17; Gal. 1:1) for God had said to him, "I am sending you" to open the eyes of the Gentiles (Acts 26:17). The concept of an apostle being sent as an authoritative representative is seen in late rabbinic literature, in which the *šālîaḥ* was one who was sent by another as an agent to act on his behalf and with his authority. "The-one-whom-a-person-sends *(šālîaḥ)* is like the sender" (Mishnah, *Berakot* 5.5). Cf. Paul W. Barnett, "Apostle," in *Dictionary of Paul and His Letters,* ed. Gerald F. Hawthorne, Ralph P. Martin, and Daniel G. Reid (Downers Grove, Ill.: InterVarsity, 1993), 45–46; J. B. Lightfoot, "The Name and Office of Apostle," in *The Epistle of St. Paul to the Galatians,* 10th ed. [reprint, London: Macmillan, 1986], 92–101; and R. K. Rengstorf, "ἀπόστολος," in *Theological Dictionary of the New Testament,* 1 (1964), 407–47.

"God has put us apostles on display" (1 Cor. 4:9).

"Even though I may not be an apostle to others, surely I am to you!" (1 Cor. 9:2a).

"For you are the seal of my apostleship in the Lord" (1 Cor. 9:2b).

"For I am the least of the apostles and do not even deserve to be called an apostle" (1 Cor. 15:9).

"God . . . was also at work in my ministry as an apostle" (Gal. 2:8).

"As apostles of Christ, we could have been a burden to you, but we were gentle among you" (1 Thess. 2:6–7).

"I was appointed a herald and an apostle . . . and a teacher" (1 Tim. 2:7).

"I was appointed a herald and an apostle and a teacher" (2 Tim. 1:11).

His apostleship was unique in that the Lord appointed him to that responsibility the moment he was saved (Acts 9:15). In fact, God had set him apart for this ministry "from birth" (Gal. 1:15). Another aspect of his apostolic uniqueness is that God designated him as the Lord's emissary to the Gentiles, a point that the New Testament notes repeatedly (Acts 9:15; 13:46–47; 14:27; 15:12; 18:6; 21:19; 22:21; 26:17, 20; 28:28; Rom. 1:5, 13; 11:13; 15:16; Gal. 1:16; 2:2, 7–9; Eph. 3:8; Col. 1:27; 1 Tim. 2:7; cf. Eph. 3:6; 1 Thess. 2:16; 2 Tim. 4:17).

Other Indications of Paul's Emphasis on Teaching

Of these eight titles—instrument, teacher, witness, servant, slave, herald, minister, and apostle—it may seem surprising that "teacher" occurs only twice (and both times in Paul's letters to Timothy). However, a number of verbs and other nouns are used to call attention to Paul's important role as a teacher. Table 1 demonstrates the prominence of teaching in the apostle's service for the Lord.

Table 1
References to Paul's Teaching

Verses Using the Verb *Didaskō*[4]

"Barnabas and Paul met with the church [at Antioch] and taught great numbers of people" (Acts 11:26).

---

4. The word *didaskō*, the normal word for teach or instruct (K. H. Rengstorf, "διδάσκω *ktl.,*" in *Theological Dictionary of New Testament Theology,* 2 [1964],135), is used ninety-five times in the New Testament, with forty-seven of them referring to Jesus' teaching (Roy B. Zuck, *Teaching as Jesus Taught* [Grand Rapids: Baker, 1995], 29).

"Paul and Barnabas remained in Antioch, where they and many others taught and preached the word of the Lord" (Acts 15:35).

"So Paul stayed for a year and a half [in Corinth], teaching them the word of God" (Acts 18:11).

"You know that I have . . . taught you publicly and from house to house" (Acts 20:20).

"They have been informed that you teach all the Jews . . . to turn away from Moses" (Acts 21:21).

"This is the man who teaches all men everywhere" (Acts 21:28).

"Boldly and without hindrance he preached the kingdom of God and taught about the Lord Jesus Christ" (Acts 28:31).

"Timothy . . . will remind you of my way of life in Christ Jesus, which agrees with what I teach everywhere in every church" (1 Cor. 4:17).

"You . . . were taught in him" (Eph. 4:21).

"We proclaim him, admonishing and teaching everyone with all wisdom" (Col. 1:28).

"Hold to the traditions which we taught whether by our word or by letter" (2 Thess. 2:15, author's trans.).

Verses Using the Noun *Didachē*

"The proconsul . . . was amazed at the teaching about the Lord" by Barnabas and Paul (Acts 13:12).

"May we know what this new teaching is that you are presenting?" (Acts 17:19).

"You wholeheartedly obeyed the form of teaching to which you were entrusted" (Rom. 6:17).

"Watch out for those who cause divisions and put obstacles in your way that are contrary to the teaching you have learned" (Rom. 16:17).

"Holding firmly to the trustworthy message according to the teaching" (Titus 1:9, author's trans.).

Verses Using the Noun *Didaskalia*

"The sound doctrine . . . which he entrusted to me" (1 Tim. 1:10–11).

"You will be a good minister of Christ Jesus, brought up in the truths of the faith and of the good teaching that you have followed" (1 Tim. 4:6).

"All who are under the yoke of slavery should consider their masters worthy of full respect, so that God's name and our teaching may not be slandered" (1 Tim. 6:1).

"You . . . know all about my teaching" (2 Tim. 3:10).

"In every way they will make the teaching about God our Savior attractive" (Titus 2:10).

In both classical Greek and the New Testament *didaskō* is often used with the accusative of the person(s) taught and/or the accusative of the subject(s) taught. The eleven occurrences of *didaskō* in Table 1 show that Paul taught "great numbers" (Acts 11:26), "them" (i.e., believers in Corinth; Acts 18:11), "you" (i.e., believers in Ephesus; Acts

20:20; Eph. 4:21), Jews (Acts 21:21), "all men" (21:28), and "everyone" (Col. 1:28). The content of his teaching was the word of the Lord (Acts 15:35; 18:11), the Lord Jesus Christ (28:31), and traditions[5] (2 Thess. 2:15; cf. 3:6). Places where he taught included churches everywhere (1 Cor. 4:17).

Didachē denotes the context of teaching, "what is taught," and *didaskalia* suggests either the act of teaching or the content of one's teaching. "Perhaps some distinction between the two can be noted if *didachē* is translated 'doctrine' (suggesting *what* is taught) and if *didaskalia* is translated 'instruction' or 'instructing' (suggesting the act of teaching)."[6] Interestingly, *didaskalia* often relates to false teaching (Eph. 4:14; Col. 2:22; 1 Tim. 4:1; 6:3; 2 Tim. 4:3; Titus 1:11).

Teaching *(didaskalia)* is to be "sound" (from *hygiainō*, "to be healthy"), as Paul stated in 1 Timothy 1:10; 2 Timothy 4:3; Titus 1:9; and 2:1. He also wrote in 1 Timothy 6:3 of "sound instruction" and in 2 Timothy 1:13 of "sound teaching" (both are literally "healthy words"). And older men, he told Titus, are to be "sound in faith, in love, and in endurance" (Titus 2:2).

Paul also used a few other words related to teaching. In the synagogue in Thessalonica (Acts 17:3) he was "explaining" *(dianoigō,* "to open up"; used elsewhere in the New Testament only of Christ who opened up the Old Testament Scriptures to the Emmaus disciples, Luke 24:31–32, 45) and "proving" or setting forth *(paratithēmi)* from the Old Testament that the Messiah "had to suffer and rise from the dead."[7] *Paratithēmi* means "to place beside"; thus Paul was placing the facts of Christ's life alongside the Old Testament, showing how he fulfills those scriptural predictions.

Paratithēmi conveys also the idea of entrusting, committing, or depositing something with someone.[8] In several cities Paul committed elders to the Lord (Acts 14:23; 20:32), and he told Timothy to entrust to others what Paul had taught him (2 Tim. 2:2). And he also wrote to Timothy, "I give *[paratithēmai]* you this instruction *[parangelia,* 'a com-

5. The traditions *(paradosis)* Paul referred to are literally "what is passed on." He commended the Corinthians for holding to the traditions (NIV, "teachings") he had passed on (lit., "delivered over") to them (1 Cor. 11:2; cf. 2 Thess. 2:15; 3:6). In other contexts *paradosis* refers to the oral traditions of the Pharisees (Matt. 15:2–3, 6; Mark 2:5–9; Gal. 1:14).

6. Roy B. Zuck, "Greek Words for 'Teach,' " *Bibliotheca Sacra* 122 (April–June 1965): 161 (italics mine).

7. As stated in the Introduction, in his preconversion days Paul challenged the idea that the Messiah had to be crucified. But here, as an apostle, he argued in defense of that truth.

8. A. T. Robertson suggests this term was used of banking—entrusting money to another *(Word Pictures in the New Testament,* [New York: Harper and Row, 1930–1933], 4:614).

mand from a superior'], 1 Tim. 1:18). To the Thessalonians he said, "You know what instructions [*parangelias,* 'commands'] we give you by the authority of the Lord Jesus" (1 Thess. 4:2).

Another teaching-related word is *ektithēmi,* "to set forth the meaning of, or to explain." When in Rome, Paul explained the kingdom of God (Acts 28:23).[9]

Katēcheō, still another word for teaching, was used by Paul of Jews who were "instructed" by the law (Rom. 2:18), of himself in preferring to "speak five intelligible words to instruct [*katēcheō*] others than ten thousand words in a tongue" (1 Cor. 14:19), and of the instructor who should be supported financially by those he instructs (Gal. 6:6).[10] The word seems to suggest informing or passing on information orally.[11]

Teaching sometimes calls for telling others of the dangers of straying from obeying the Lord, warning *(noutheteō)* them of the hazards of their wrong ways and admonishing or urging them to return. Several times Paul referred to his having done this with his learners. He warned the Ephesian elders of the potential danger of false teachers (Acts 20:31), whom he called savage wolves (20:29). Paul was confident the Roman believers were capable of warning (NIV, "instruct") each other (Rom. 15:14). He said he wrote to the Corinthians to warn them (1 Cor. 4:14) possibly of the problem of complacency or arrogance. Proclaiming Christ involved his warning (NIV, "admonishing") and "teaching" [*didaskō*] everyone (Col. 1:28), and similarly he urged the Colossians to "teach [*didaskō*] and warn [*noutheteō*] one another with all wisdom" (3:16). Spiritual leaders who warn believers are to be respected, he told the Thessalonians (1 Thess. 5:12); and believers in turn are to warn the idle (5:14). Any disobedient believer is to be warned "as a brother" (2 Thess. 3:15) for the purpose of restoring him to an obedient walk with the Lord.

Occasionally Paul found it necessary to warn others of the risks involved in going their self-focused ways and to admonish them to return to God's way. Teaching occasionally involves this negative aspect.

These several words for teaching reveal the vital place of pedagogy in the apostle Paul's ministry. This is not surprising since teaching was also a significant part of the work of the early church. In assuming a leadership role in the church, Paul taught, just as those before him had

9. All three New Testament occurrences of this word are in Acts. Peter explained his Joppa experience to the Jerusalem leaders (11:4), and Aquila and Priscilla "explained to [Apollos] the way of God more adequately" (18:26).

10. Luke also used *katēcheō* when he stated that his purpose in writing the Gospel of Luke for Theophilus was "so that you may know the certainty of the things concerning which you have been instructed" (Luke 1:4, author's trans.).

11. David W. Bennett, *Metaphors of Ministry* (Grand Rapids: Baker, 1993), 153; and Zuck, "Greek Words for 'Teach,'" 162.

done and as the Lord himself had done.[12] In addition, the Lord taught his disciples to teach (Mark 6:30).

The three thousand who were saved on the day of Pentecost "devoted themselves to the apostles' teaching" (*didachē*, Acts 2:42). Peter and John were "teaching [*didaskō*] the people" in Jerusalem (4:2) the way of salvation. And he and other apostles did the same (5:21, 28), filling Jerusalem with their "teaching" (*didachē*, 5:28), though it resulted in their being flogged (5:40). Even though they were ordered not to "speak in the name of Jesus" (5:40), the apostles daily "in the temple courts and from house to house . . . never stopped teaching [*didaskō*] and proclaiming the good news [*euangelizomai*] that Jesus is the Christ" (5:42). Their dedication to the Lord resulted in their boldly instructing people about Christ and sharing the gospel both publicly (in the temple courts where many Jews gathered) and privately (going "from house to house" to be sure no one failed to hear of Christ).

Apollos, too, was a fervent evangelist and teacher. A Jewish native of Alexandria, Egypt, he knew the Old Testament well, having been "instructed [*katēchēmenos*, from *katēcheō*, 'to teach or inform'] in the way of the Lord," and so "he taught [*didaskō*] accurately the things concerning Jesus" (18:25, author's trans.).

Besides teaching large numbers of people, Paul also taught individuals. Two such young men were Timothy and Titus. Having been instructed by Paul, they were to teach others. In fact, in his Pastoral Epistles Paul repeatedly encouraged them to be teaching others.

Table 2
Paul's Instructions to Timothy and Titus to Teach

"Command and teach [*didaskō*] these things" (1 Tim. 4:11).
"Until I come, devote yourself to the public reading of Scripture, to preaching [*logos*, 'the word'] and to teaching [*didaskalia*]" (1 Tim. 4:13).

---

12. On Jesus' extensive teaching ministry, see my *Teaching as Jesus Taught*. Similarities and differences between Jesus' teaching and Paul's teaching are evident. For example, both were called "teacher" by themselves and others, their ministry goals were similar, they both faced opponents, they both taught with a sense of urgency and compassion, they both taught with a variety of picturesque expressions and illustrations, they both used many questions in their teaching, they both developed disciples, they both stood before a high priest and were smitten and insulted, they both suffered death at the hands of their enemies. Both were Jews, both were raised and educated in Jewish homes, both learned a trade, both knew and quoted the Old Testament, both debated with religious leaders.

In their differences Jesus often taught outdoors, and Paul often taught in synagogues. Jesus did not travel outside Palestine, whereas Paul traveled extensively. Jesus did not write any letters, whereas Paul wrote many. Jesus had a limited formal education, but Paul was schooled under Gamaliel. Paul lived almost twice as long as Jesus.

"Watch your life and doctrine [*didaskalia*] closely" (1 Tim. 4:16).

"These are the things you are to teach [*didaskō*] and urge on them" (1 Tim. 6:2).

"And the things you have heard me say in the presence of many witnesses entrust [*paratithēmi*] to reliable men who will also be qualified to teach [*didaskō*] others" (2 Tim. 2:2).

"Correct, rebuke and encourage—with great patience and careful instruction [*didachē*]" (2 Tim. 4:2).

"You must teach [lit. 'speak'] what is in accord with sound doctrine [*didaskalia*]" (Titus 2:1).

"Teach the older men to be temperate" (Titus 2:2).

"Teach the older women to be reverent in the way they live" (Titus 2:3).[13]

"In your teaching [*didaskalia*] show integrity" (Titus 2:7).

"These, then, are the things you should teach [lit., speak]" (Titus 2:15).

These verses in this table show that what Paul valued for his own ministry was then to be replicated by others. And what they taught was to be matched by consistent living (1 Tim. 4:16; Titus 2:7), thus showing that one's life is as important as one's teaching. In fact, without Christlike living, doctrine becomes hypocritical.

Paul's list of qualifications for elders includes the ability to teach (*didaktikos*, 1 Tim. 3:2)—another indication of the importance of teaching. Paul noted that elders are responsible primarily for preaching (*logos*, "the word") and teaching (*didaskalia*, 1 Tim. 5:17) because of the prominence of these two functions in church ministry. Elders, Paul told Titus, are to "hold firmly to the trustworthy message as it has been taught" (Titus 1:9). The words "as it has been taught" literally read, "according to the teaching" (*didachē*). An elder must be concerned for conserving the truth, encouraging others by it, and defending it against those who oppose it. So significant is the teaching of God's Word that Paul affirmed that any servant of the Lord, not just elders, must be "able to teach" (*didaktikos*, 2 Tim. 2:24).

The spiritual gift of teaching also points up the value Paul placed on teaching. Of special note is the fact that teachers stand near the beginning (in third place) of Paul's lists of spiritual gifts in Romans 12:6–8 and 1 Corinthians 12:28–30. And in Ephesians 4:11 teachers are linked with pastors as a single gifted office.[14] Teachers are to lead and care for those they instruct much as a shepherd (*poimēn*, rendered "pastor," means shepherd) cares for his flock. And local-church pas-

---

13. "Teach" is not in the Greek in Titus 2:2 and 3, but is included in English translations to carry through the command to teach from verse 1.

14. Pastors and teachers are considered as one gift (we may think of the two words as hyphenated: "pastor-teachers") because the one article "the" introduces "pastors" but does not precede "teachers," and because the word "and" (*kai*), which connects them, differs from the other "and's" (*de*) in the verse.

tors, in shepherding their people are to "feed" them by teaching God's Word. Thus the "shepherds" and "teachers" constitute one group thought of as "teaching shepherds."[15] Teaching requires a heart of concern, comforting and guiding those taught, which in turn calls for careful instruction in biblical truths, the "food" needed for spiritual growth.

Paul explained that some believers have certain spiritual gifts, while other Christians have others: "We have different gifts" (Rom. 12:6). "There are different kinds of gifts . . . different kinds of service . . . different kinds of working" (1 Cor. 12:4–6). "He gives them to each one" (12:11). Apparently God provides one or more divine enablings at the moment of salvation by his Holy Spirit: "Now to each one the manifestation of the Spirit is given for the common good" (12:7). Paul's frequent mention of the Holy Spirit—nine times in eight verses (12:3–10)—emphasizes that these abilities do not stem from one's own desires. This is God's working.

Yet each believer is responsible to cultivate ("fan into flame the gift of God, which is in you," 2 Tim. 1:6) and utilize his spiritual gift or gifts. If a believer has the gift of teaching Paul wrote, "let him teach" (Rom. 12:7). While the Holy Spirit has endowed some Christians with the God-given ability to teach—to explain and apply the Scriptures[16]—all believers are responsible to teach. "The Lord's servant must [be] able to teach" (2 Tim. 2:24), and believers are to "teach and admonish one another" (Col. 3:16). This fact seems to be true of other spiritual gifts as well. For example, while some have a special capacity for serving, encouraging, giving, leadership, or showing mercy (Rom. 12:7–8), all followers of Christ are to engage in these functions as they have opportunity.

Most of the spiritual gifts Paul listed are mentioned only once; but the fact that he referred to teaching in all three listings underscores the significance God places on this activity.[17]

15. Markus Barth, *Ephesians 4–6,* Anchor Bible (Garden City, N.Y.: Doubleday, 1974), 482.

16. For more on the meaning of this spiritual empowerment to teach, see Roy B. Zuck, *Teaching with Spiritual Power* (1963; reprint, Grand Rapids: Kregel, 1993), 80–97.

17. God designed certain spiritual gifts to serve as a foundation for the church, including apostles, prophets (Eph. 2:20; 3:5; 4:11), tongues (the ability to speak a foreign language without having learned it), interpretation of tongues, and healing. On this foundation the church is now being built by the use of other gifts. For discussion of the temporary, founding nature of some gifts and the permanent, ongoing nature of others, see William J. McRae, *The Dynamics of Spiritual Gifts* (Grand Rapids: Zondervan, 1976), 90–99; Zuck, *Teaching with Spiritual Power,* 83; and John F. Walvoord, *The Holy Spirit* (Grand Rapids: Zondervan, 1958), 173–88.

How Did Paul's Teaching Differ from His Preaching?

As discussed earlier in this chapter, Paul was more than a teacher. He was also a preacher (*kēryx*, "herald"). This Greek word derives from the verb *kēryssō*, "to announce or proclaim as a herald,[18] to make public announcements or verbally publicize good news." That he engaged in both is not surprising, since Jesus had commissioned his disciples to do both: to preach (*kēryssō*) the kingdom (Matt. 10:7; Mark 3:14; Luke 9:2) and to teach (*didaskō*, Matt. 28:20). Jesus himself engaged in both.[19]

References to Paul's preaching ministry abound in both the Book of Acts and his epistles, as noted in tables 3 and 4.

Table 3
References in Acts to Paul's Preaching

Verses Using the Verb *Kēryssō* ("to Preach")

"At once he began to preach in the synagogues that Jesus is the Son of God" (Acts 9:20).

"But Paul and Barnabas remained in Antioch, where they and many others taught and preached the word of the Lord" (15:35).

"In the name of Jesus whom Paul preaches, I command you to come out" (19:13).

"Now I know that none of you among whom I have gone about preaching the kingdom will ever see me again" (20:25).

"Boldly and without hindrance he preached the kingdom of God and taught about the Lord Jesus Christ" (28:31).

Verses Using the Verb *Euangelizomai* ("to Announce Good News")

In "Lystra and Derbe . . . they continued to preach the good news" (14:7).

"They preached the good news in that city [Derbe] and won a large number of disciples" (14:21).

"After Paul had seen the vision, we got ready at once to leave for Macedonia, concluding that God had called us to preach the gospel to them" (16:10).

"Paul was preaching the good news about Jesus and the resurrection" (17:18).

Verses Using Other Verbs

Laleō ("to Speak")

"We had to speak the word of God to you first" (13:46).

---

18. Walter Bauer, William F. Arndt, and F. Wilbur Gingrich, *A Greek-English Lexicon of the New Testament and Other Early Christian Literature*, 2d ed., rev. F. Wilbur Gingrich and Frederick W. Danker (Chicago: University of Chicago Press, 1979), 431.

19. Forty-seven times the Gospels refer to Jesus' teaching (*didaskō*) and eighteen times to his preaching (*kēryssō*). See Zuck, *Teaching as Jesus Taught*, 93–96.

"And when they had preached the word in Perga, they went down to Attalia" (14:25).

"Paul and his companions [were] kept by the Holy Spirit from preaching the word in the province of Asia" (16:6).

"Then they spoke the word of the Lord to him and to all the others in his house" (16:32).

Anangellō ("to Proclaim")

"You know that I have not hesitated to preach anything that would be helpful to you" (20:20).

"For I have not hesitated to proclaim to you the whole will of God" (20:27).

"I preached that they should repent and turn to God" (26:20).

Katangellō ("to Proclaim Solemnly")

"They proclaimed the word of God in the Jewish synagogues" (13:5).

"Through Jesus the forgiveness of sins is proclaimed to you" (13:38).

"Let us go back and visit the brothers in all the towns where we preached the word of the Lord and see how they are doing" (15:36).

"These men are servants of the Most High God, who are telling you the way to be saved" (16:17).

"This Jesus I am proclaiming to you is the Christ" (17:3).

"When the Jews in Thessalonica learned that Paul was preaching the word of God at Berea, they went there too, agitating the crowds and stirring them up" (17:13).

Parrēsiazomai ("to Speak Openly or Boldly")

"Barnabas . . . told them . . . how in Damascus [Paul] had preached fearlessly in the name of Jesus" (9:27).

"So Saul stayed with them and moved about freely in Jerusalem, speaking boldly in the name of the Lord" (9:28).

"Then Paul and Barnabas answered them boldly: 'We had to speak the word of God to you first'" (13:46).

"So Paul and Barnabas spent considerable time [in Iconium], speaking boldly for the Lord" (14:3).

"Paul entered the synagogue and spoke boldly there for three months" (19:8).

Diamartyromai ("to Declare Thoroughly or Solemnly")

"Paul devoted himself exclusively to preaching [*logos*, 'the word'], testifying to the Jews that Jesus was the Christ" (18:5).

"I have declared to both Jews and Greeks that they must turn to God in repentance and have faith in our Lord Jesus" (20:21).

"If only I may finish the race and complete the task . . . of testifying to the gospel of God's grace" (20:24).

"From morning till evening he explained and declared to them the kingdom of God" (28:23).

These thirty-one verses with seven different verbs demonstrate Paul's deep commitment to and unrelenting involvement in sharing Christ with others. The content of this Good News (the gospel) included Jesus (Acts 19:13), that Jesus is the Son of God (9:20) and the Messiah (17:3; 18:5), the word of God (13:5, 46; 14:25; 15:35–36; 16:6, 32; 17:13),[20] the forgiveness of sins (13:38), the way to be saved (16:17), repentance (26:20), repentance and faith (20:21), God's grace (20:24), the kingdom of God (20:25; 28:23, 31),[21] anything that would be helpful (20:20), and the whole will of God (20:27). The apostle's communicating the gospel was done for the Lord (14:3) and in his name (9:28), that is, as his representative.

Table 4
References in Paul's Epistles to His Preaching[22]

Verses Using the Verb *Kēryssō*

"We preach Christ crucified" (1 Cor. 1:23).

"No, I beat my body and make it my slave so that after I have preached to others, I myself will not be disqualified for the prize" (1 Cor. 9:27).

"Whether, then, it was I or they, this is what we preach, and this is what you believed" (1 Cor. 15:11).

"But if it is preached that Christ has been raised from the dead, how can some of you say that there is no resurrection of the dead?" (1 Cor. 15:12).

"Jesus Christ . . . was preached among you" (2 Cor. 1:19).

"For we do not preach ourselves, but Jesus Christ as Lord, and ourselves as your servants for Jesus' sake" (2 Cor. 4:5).

"For if someone comes to you and preaches a Jesus other than the Jesus we preached . . . you put up with it easily enough" (2 Cor. 11:4).

"I . . . set before them the gospel that I preach among the Gentiles" (Gal. 2:2).

"Brothers, if I am still preaching circumcision, why am I still being persecuted?" (Gal. 5:11).

"This is the gospel that you heard and that has been proclaimed to every creature under heaven, and of which I, Paul, have become a servant" (Col. 1:23).

"We worked night and day in order not to be a burden to anyone while we preached the gospel of God to you" (1 Thess. 2:9).

---

20. The apostle's emphasis on the Word of God, the content of his preaching, is also noted in Acts 13:7, 44, 48–49; 15:27; 18:11; and 19:10, 20.

21. Toussaint rightly sees Luke's references in Acts to the kingdom of God (1:3–6; 8:12; 14:22; 19:8; 20:25; 28:23, 31) as referring to the eschatological forthcoming millennial kingdom (Stanley D. Toussaint, "Acts," in *The Bible Knowledge Commentary, New Testament,* ed. John F. Walvoord and Roy B. Zuck (Wheaton, Ill.: Victor, 1983), 430.

22. This table excludes references Paul made to the preaching of others.

Verses Using the Verb *Euangelizomai*

"That is why I am so eager to preach the gospel also to you who are at Rome"
(Rom. 1:5).

"It has always been my ambition to preach the gospel where Christ was not
known" (Rom. 15:20).

"For Christ did not send me to baptize, but to preach the gospel" (1 Cor. 1:17).

"Yet when I preach the gospel, I cannot boast, for I am compelled to preach"
(1 Cor. 9:16a).

"Woe to me if I do not preach the gospel!" (1 Cor. 9:16b).

"What then is my reward? Just this: that in preaching the gospel I may offer it
free of charge" (1 Cor. 9:18).

"Now, brothers, I want to remind you of the gospel I preached to you" (1 Cor.
15:1).

"By this gospel you are saved, if you hold firmly to the word I preached to you"
(1 Cor. 15:2).

"So that we can preach the gospel in the regions beyond you" (2 Cor. 10:16).

"Was it a sin for me to lower myself in order to elevate you by preaching the
gospel of God to you free of charge?" (2 Cor. 11:7).

"But even if we or an angel from heaven should preach a gospel other than the
one we preached to you, let him be eternally condemned!" (Gal. 1:8).

"If anybody is preaching to you a gospel other than what you accepted, let him
be eternally condemned!" (Gal. 1:9).

God revealed "his son in me so that I might preach him among the Gentiles"
(Gal. 1:16).

"They only heard the report, 'The man who formerly persecuted us is now
preaching the faith he once tried to destroy'" (Gal. 1:23).

"As you know, it was because of an illness that I first preached the gospel to
you" (Gal. 4:13).

"Although I am less than the least of all God's people, this grace was given me:
to preach to the Gentiles the unsearchable riches of Christ" (Eph. 3:8).

Verses Using Other Verbs

Katangello ("to Proclaim Solemnly")

"The Lord has commanded that those who preach the gospel should receive
their living from the gospel" (1 Cor. 9:14).

"We proclaim him, admonishing and teaching everyone with all wisdom" (Col.
1:28).

Parrēsiazomai ("to Speak Openly or Boldly")

"Pray that I may declare it [the gospel] fearlessly, as I should" (Eph. 6:20).

"We dared to tell you his gospel in spite of strong opposition" (1 Thess. 2:2).

Diamartyromai ("to Declare Thoroughly or Solemnly")

"The Lord will punish men for all such sins, as we have already told you and
warned you" (1 Thess. 4:6).

As in Acts, these five verbs in thirty-one verses in the Pauline letters underscore the apostle's concern for spreading the gospel.[23] He was indeed a herald of good news! He put into action his desire that many others hear the wonderful verses of salvation and place their faith in Jesus Christ. The content of Paul's preaching included Christ, his resurrection, the gospel, the faith (i.e., the doctrine of salvation by faith; Gal. 1:23), and the unsearchable riches of Christ.[24]

Paul, then, clearly engaged in both preaching and teaching. And others, including Timothy (see table 2) and church elders (1 Tim. 5:17),[25] were to do the same.

Is there a difference between preaching and teaching? When we read in the New Testament about Jesus, Paul, and others preaching, we should not think of them standing behind pulpits, preaching sermons. The words for preaching, seen in tables 3 and 4, refer instead to telling, declaring, announcing, sharing, or communicating the good news of salvation in Christ to the unsaved, whether crowds or individuals. In the New Testament, "preaching" is better thought of as "conveying." And of course the goal was to persuade others, by the Holy Spirit's enabling, to receive Christ as their personal Savior from sin. This is the responsibility of all believers, not just a few so-called gifted evangelists. Besides being a teacher, Timothy, Paul told him, was to "do the work of an evangelist" (2 Tim. 4:5), that is to share the Good News, winning the unsaved to Christ.

Preaching is for evangelization, to bring sinners to the Savior. Teaching, however, is for edification, to instruct and thereby spiritually nurture believers in Christ. One calls for repentance; the other for discipleship. One is to bring spiritual birth; the other is for spiritual growth.

---

23. In addition to these verbs, Paul used the noun "gospel" (*euangelion*, "good news") fifty-one times! He called it "the gospel of God," "the gospel of Christ," "the gospel of his Son," "the gospel of the glory of Christ," "my gospel," "our gospel," "the gospel of peace," and "the gospel of your salvation." In Romans 15:19 the NIV has "I have fully proclaimed the gospel of Christ." A more literal rendering is, "I have filled up [from *pleroo*] the gospel of Christ." This may mean he filled up the "space" where the gospel had not been conveyed, namely, from Jerusalem to Illyicum, also known as Dalmatia, on the eastern coast of the Adriatic Sea and roughly equivalent to present-day Albania and former Yugoslavia (John Knox, "Romans 15:14–33 and Paul's Conception of His Apostolic Mission," *Journal of Biblical Literature* 83 [March 1964]:11). Or Paul's statement may mean he had discharged his commission, preaching the gospel and founding churches, and leaving to others the task of building on his foundation (John Murray, *The Epistle to the Romans* [Grand Rapids: Eerdmans, 1965], 2:214).

24. *Kērygma*, his message, or what he heralded, is mentioned in 1 Corinthians 1:21; 2:4; 15:12; 2 Timothy 4:17; and Titus 1:3.

25. In 1 Timothy 5:17 "preaching" translates *logos*, "word." Elders were to give attention to the word (i.e., to proclaim it) and to teaching (*didaskalia*).

Evangelizing is bringing lost sheep into the fold; teaching is feeding and guiding those sheep.

However, was not teaching involved in evangelizing? This seems to be the case in Cyprus, when Sergius Paulus, the proconsul of the town of Paphos, was "amazed at the teaching [*didachē*] about the Lord" (Acts 13:12). Teaching was also involved in Paul's evangelizing in Athens. As a result of his "preaching the good news about Jesus and the resurrection" (17:18), some Athenians said they wanted to know more about his "new teaching" (*didachē*, 17:19). Peter's evangelistic efforts also involved teaching (Acts 4:2; 5:21, 28, 42).

This shows that teaching and preaching, while different, overlap in some ways. Evangelizing involves telling certain truths, instructing people about their lost condition and the Lord's provision of salvation (and in Paul's case, explaining how Jesus fulfills Old Testament prophecies, Acts 17:3). More often, however, teaching is directed toward those who have become Jesus' followers.

As an energetic missionary Paul took the gospel to many places in Syria, Asia Minor, Greece, and Italy. Of note is the fact that in many of those same places he followed up his evangelizing/preaching with a teaching ministry. These included Antioch of Syria (Acts 11:26; 15:35), Thessalonica (17:1–4; 2 Thess. 2:15; 3:6), Corinth (Acts 18:11), Ephesus (20:20; Eph. 4:21), and Rome (Acts 28:23, 31).

In light of the frequent mention of teaching in the apostle's ministry, as recorded in Acts and in his epistles—he referred to teaching in twelve of his thirteen letters (all except Philemon)—we can readily agree with Horne that Paul was "a master teacher second in greatness only to the Master himself."[26]

Check Yourself . . .

Do you, like Paul, see yourself as God's instrument, teacher, witness, servant, slave, herald, and minister? What can you do to enhance your role in each of these areas?

---

26. Herman Harrell Horne, "Foreword," in Howard Tillman Kuist, *The Pedagogy of St. Paul* (New York: Doran, 1925), viii.

Do you sense the high significance of teaching? Are you encouraging some of your students to become teachers? What can you do to develop the teaching skills of others?

If you believe you have the gift of teaching, what can you do to cultivate that gift?

"Under Gamaliel I was thoroughly trained in the law."

Acts 22:3

4

How Did Paul's Background Prepare Him as a Teacher?

In September 1996 the National Commission on Teaching and America's Future issued a report on the nation's teachers. The report, "What Matters Most: Teaching for America's Future," said that more than one-fourth of newly hired teachers enter public school classrooms with inadequate skills or training in their subjects. And twelve percent of new teachers begin with no training at all in teaching skills and subjects, having entered on emergency or substandard certification. In addition, only five hundred of the nation's twelve hundred education schools meet professional standards of accreditation.

Could a similar indictment be leveled against many volunteer teachers in church educational programs? How many Sunday school teachers have been adequately trained for their tasks? How many are sufficiently prepared in Bible content, teaching methods, and student characteristics? How many lay teachers are recruited to teach Sunday school, children's church, or Bible studies, or to lead youth groups or even to teach adult Bible classes with adequate preparation? How many are enlisted on an emergency, fill-in basis, with the attitude, "You can do it. It doesn't take much time or preparation"?

Regrettably, this approach in many churches may mirror a lack of dedication to giving God the highest level of competency possible.

This problem of training deficiency in public and church education was not the case, however, with the apostle Paul! He entered his "career" as an evangelist, missionary, church planter, theologian, teacher, and discipler with the highest qualifications possible. He was eminently prepared!

God orchestrated several factors in the apostle's background that enabled him to become one of the most significant leaders and teachers in the history of the church. These elements included his family background, birthplace, citizenship, education, and upbringing as a Pharisee. All contributed to his becoming a herald and teacher of the gospel, whose Jewish-Roman background and cosmopolitan outlook fitted him for a unique ministry as the apostle to the Gentiles.

Family Background

Paul was born to Jewish parents living in Tarsus of Cilicia (Acts 9:11; 21:39; 22:3; cf. 23:34) in present-day southeastern Turkey. He stated, as recorded in Acts 21:39 and 22:3, "I am a Jew." He also wrote of his Jewish lineage that he was a descendant of Abraham (Rom. 11:1; 2 Cor. 11:22), an Israelite (Rom. 11:1; 2 Cor. 11:22; Phil. 3:5). Like all Jewish males, he was circumcised on the eighth day (Phil. 3:5). He also wrote that he was "a Hebrew of Hebrews" (Phil. 3:5). This phrase may mean he was genuinely Jewish with no Gentile blood in his genealogy,[1] but this seems superfluous since he had already referred to his Israelite/Benjamite lineage. Another view is that "a Hebrew of Hebrews" indicates he was born in Palestine; but this runs counter to his claim to have been born in Tarsus. A preferable view is that he had a Hebraic religious background, speaking Aramaic (Acts 21:40; 22:2) in his childhood,[2] rather than being brought up as a Hellenistic Jew. In other words, he was "a Hebraicist as against a Hellenist."[3] In the first century A.D. many Jews living outside Palestine were Greek-speaking Hellenists. But this

---

1. The Living Bible paraphrases these words with the sentence, "So I was a real Jew if there ever was one!"

2. F. F. Bruce, "Is the Paul of Acts the Real Paul?" *Bulletin of the John Rylands University Library* 59 (1976): 285.

3. Richard N. Longenecker, *Paul: Apostle of Liberty* (New York: Harper and Row, 1964; reprint, Grand Rapids: Baker, 1976), 22.

need not mean all Jews of the Diaspora were Greek in outlook.[4] And this may be the point of Paul's statement: he was not like many Hellenistic Jews of the Diaspora; he was a true Hebrew.[5] His use of Aramaic suggests "a deeper bond with the land" of Palestine[6] than was true of Jews who had assimilated Greek thought and ways.

Paul's statement, however, does not exclude his knowledge of Greek life, philosophy, and language. In his epistles he quoted or alluded to several Greek writers (Acts 17:28; 1 Cor. 15:33; Titus 1:12), his letters were composed in Greek, and he evidences awareness of Greek culture and rhetoric. Also, the fact that he often quoted from the Septuagint, the Greek translation of the Old Testament, points to his knowledge of Greek. From childhood he could speak Greek, the lingua franca of that part of the Roman Empire, and he no doubt knew Latin, but at home his family spoke Aramaic (similar to Hebrew), the language of their homeland[7] and the language of the Jewish people in Syria and eastern Asia Minor. Paul's mastery of the Greek language means he "is hardly likely to have learned it as a second language."[8] He handled everyday Greek with ease, showing he had spoken it since childhood. He was "at home" in the Septuagint,[9] as well as the Hebrew Scriptures. With bilingual ability he switched readily from Greek (Acts 21:37) to Aramaic (21:40).[10] This ability in Greek from childhood had a great effect on the

4. Ibid., 25–32. Longenecker cites several authors who feel that Paul's birthplace inevitably made him a liberal Hellenist (e.g., T. R. Glover, *Paul of Tarsus* [London: SCM, 1925], 5–23; and Martin Dibelius, *Paul*, ed. Werner Georg Kümmel, trans. Frank Clark [Philadelphia: Westminster, 1953]; see Longenecker, *Paul: Apostle of Liberty*, 25, n. 9).

5. This meant that the Jewish side of his nature, as Ramsay suggested, was more significant than his Roman side (W. M. Ramsay, *St. Paul the Traveller and the Roman Citizen*, 3d ed. [1895; reprint, Grand Rapids: Baker, 1949], 32).

6. Jerome Murphy-O'Connor, *Paul: A Critical Life* (Oxford: Clarendon, 1996), 36.

7. John Pollock, *The Apostle: A Life of Paul* (Wheaton, Ill.: Victor, 1985), 16. Martin Hengel states that because Paul traveled to Rome, possibly to Spain (Rom. 15:24), and to major capital cities of Roman colonies, the apostle probably spoke Latin (*The Pre-Christian Paul*, trans. John Bowden [Philadelphia: Trinity, 1991], 10–11; cf. Gerd. Lüdemann, *Earliest Christianity according to the Traditions in Acts: A Commentary* [Minneapolis: Fortress, 1989], 241, n. 6). E. G. Sihler advanced the opinion that Paul "picked up Greek as easily as an American child of Scandanavian or German descent would gain English in Fort Wayne, St. Louis, or St. Paul" ("Review of *Licht von Osten*, by Adolf Deissmann," *Biblical Review* 3 [October 1923]: 625).

8. Hengel, *The Pre-Christian Paul*, 35; cf. 3.

9. Simon Légasse, "Paul's Pre-Christian Career according to Acts," in *The Book of Acts in Its Palestinian Setting*, ed. Richard Bauckham (Grand Rapids: Eerdmans, 1995), 374.

10. Years ago Albert Schweitzer drew a sharp distinction between Palestinian Judaism and Hellenistic or Diaspora Judaism. He said Paul was a Palestinian Jew and therefore not of Tarsus (*Paul and His Interpreters: A Critical History*, trans. W. Montgomery [London: Adam and Black, 1912]). Conversely, Claude Goldsmid Montefiere, holding the

apostle as he "spent so large a portion of his active public life in the very centers of Greek philosophy, learning, and power."[11]

Jerome wrote that Paul's parents were from Gischala in Galilee and were taken to Tarsus as prisoners-of-war by Mark Antony.[12] However, this theory seems questionable.[13] Ramsay suggested the plausible view that Paul's family may have been settled in Tarsus in approximately 170 B.C. "by one of the Seleucid kings in order to strengthen their hold on the city" who "seem to have had a preference for Jewish colonies in their foundations in Asia Minor."[14] Had Paul's parents settled in Tarsus

---

same Judaistic dichotomy, believed Paul was familiar with only Diaspora Judaism (*Judaism and St. Paul* [London: Goschen, 1914]). Others who agree with Montefiere include James William Parkes (*A History of the Jewish People* [London: Weidenfeld and Nicholson, 1962]); Joseph Klausner (*From Jesus to Paul*, trans. William F. Stinespring [New York: Macmillan, 1943]); and Samuel Sandmel (*A Jewish Understanding of the New Testament* [Cincinnati: Hebrew Union College Press, 1956], 37–51).

Emil Schürer writes against this false demarcation (*The Jewish People in the Age of Jesus Christ (175 B.C.–A.D. 135)*, ed. Geza Vermes, Fergus Millar, and Martin Goodman [Edinburgh: Clark, 1986], 1 [div. 2]: 29–50), as does I. Howard Marshall ("Palestinian and Hellenistic Christianity: Some Critical Comments," *New Testament Studies* 19 [1972–1973]: 271–87). W. D. Davies rightly affirms that Paul was both Hellenistic and Judaistic: "The Judaism within which [Paul] grew up, even in Jerusalem, was largely Hellenized, and the Hellenism he encountered in his travels [was] largely Judaized" (*Paul and Rabbinic Judaism* [New York: Harper and Row, 1948], x–xi). Cf. Martin Hengel, *The "Hellenization" of Judaea in the First Century after Christ*, trans. John Bowden [Philadelphia: Trinity, 1989).

Palestine was influenced by Hellenistic thinking, since the land had been dominated by Greeks from 333 B.C. and by Romans from 63 B.C. The Seleucids, who ruled Palestine from 198 to 168 B.C., introduced strong Greek influence. Along with the Greek language, "Hellenistic names, customs, and amusements were inevitably assimilated" (ibid., 5), and rabbinic sources often reflect Greek influence in their vocabulary (ibid., viii). Yet, even though Paul was from a Hellenic city and spoke Greek, "he belonged to the main stream [*sic*] of first-century Judaism" (ibid., 1).

11. Albert Barnes, *Scenes and Incidents in the Life of the Apostle Paul* (reprint, Grand Rapids: Baker, 1950), 20.

12. Jerome *Lives of Illustrious Men* 5.

13. Brian Rapske, *The Book of Acts and Paul in Roman Custody* (Grand Rapids: Eerdmans, 1994), 87; A. N. Sherwin-White, *Roman Society and Roman Law in the New Testament* (Oxford: Clarendon, 1963), 152; Murphy-O'Connor, *Paul: A Critical Life*, 37–39; and William Barclay, *The Mind of St. Paul* (New York: Harper and Brothers, 1958), 29. Cf. Kirsopp Lane and Henry J. Cadbury, *The Acts of the Apostles: English Translation and Commentary* (reprint, Grand Rapids: Baker, 1979), 284–85.

14. Ramsay, *St. Paul the Traveller and the Roman Citizen*, 32. The number of Jews who lived in the Roman Empire in the time of Caesar Augustus (63 B.C.–A.D. 14) may have been four and a half million, with a half to three-fourths of a million in Palestine. "In the time of Jesus and the first Christians, far more Jews lived in the Diaspora than in the land of Israel" (Eduard Lohse, *The New Testament Environment*, trans. John E. Steely [Nashville: Abingdon, 1976], 120). Robert A. Kraft suggests that two-thirds of the Jews in Paul's day lived outside of Palestine ("Judaism on the World Scene," in *The Catacombs and the*

only shortly before his birth, they would have been merely Tarsian "residents," not Tarsian citizens.[15]

Birthplace

Born in Tarsus,[16] Paul held citizenship in a Greek-Roman city that he called "no ordinary city" (Acts 21:39). Why would he say Tarsus was an extraordinary city? Several factors suggest its exceptional nature. First, it was a large city. Ruins beneath the present city, with its population of about fifty thousand, suggest a population of half a million in Paul's day.

Second, it was an ancient city. It is mentioned in Hittite records in the second millennium B.C. The Assyrian king Shalmaneser III conquered Tarsus in 883 B.C., a feat he mentioned in his Black Obelisk. Then the Assyrian King Sennacherib conquered it again in 698 B.C. Persians, Greeks, and Romans all ruled the city. Antiochus settled a colony of Jews in Tarsus around 170 B.C. Philo, a contemporary of Paul, listed Cilicia among the countries inhabited by Jews.[17]

Third, Tarsus was ideally situated. Because of the fertile soil around Tarsus, grapes, wheat, and flax were grown in abundance. It had its own seaport, though the city was a few miles inland. The Cydnus River flowed through the heart of the city to the harbor. The location of Tarsus on a great trade route contributed to the city's commerce and wealth, so Xenophon called it "a great and prosperous city."[18] As a boy, Paul would no doubt have watched merchant ships anchor at the harbor, seen travelers enter the city from east and west, and heard merchants busily and noisily hawking their wares. The city's cosmopolitan nature may well have contributed to Paul's desire to travel to other major cities with the gospel. Brought up in a metropolitan environment, in a city that linked East with West and the Greek with the Oriental, Paul was ideally suited to become a world missionary.

Fourth, Tarsus had favorable political ties with Rome. The city enthusiastically supported Julius Caesar, who visited the city in 47 B.C.[19]

Colosseum, ed. Stephen Benko and John J. O'Rourke [Valley Forge, Penn.: Judson, 1971], 83–84; cf. V. Tcherikover, *Hellenistic Civilization and the Jews* [Philadelphia: Jewish Publication Society, 1959], 284–95).

15. Lohse, *The New Testament Environment,* 31–32.

16. For a listing of numerous ancient and secondary sources on Tarsus, see Hengel, *The Pre-Christian Paul,* 90–92, n. 11.

17. Philo *Legation against Gaius* 281. "During the early period of Roman rule we find large numbers of Jews in the various towns of Asia Minor" (S. Safrai and M. Stern, eds., *The Jewish People in the First Century* [Assen: Van Gorcum, 1974], 143).

18. Xenophon *Anabasis* 1.2.23.

19. Dio Chrysostom *Discourses* 34.21–23.

Five years later Mark Antony granted Tarsus the status of *libera civitas* ("free city"), which meant it was self-governing and exempt from paying taxes to Rome, a rare privilege for a city that was not a Roman colony. One of Tarsus's famous citizens was Athenodorus, a Stoic who taught philosophy to the emperor Augustus and was the emperor's adviser. Roman citizenship was granted to a large number of Tarsus residents, and other Tarsians could purchase their Roman citizenship for five hundred drachmae.[20]

Fifth, Tarsus was a great educational center. The city was so dedicated to education that Strabo, Greek geographer and contemporary of Paul, wrote, "The people at Tarsus have devoted themselves so eagerly, not only to philosophy, but also [to] the whole round of education in general, that they have surpassed Athens [and] Alexandria. . . . Further the city of Tarsus has all kinds of schools of rhetoric."[21]

Many philosophers lived and taught in Tarsus, including Antipater, Archedemus, Athenodorus, and Nestor; and "in the nearby town of Soloi, Chrysippus and Aratus, two of the greatest of all the Stoics, were born."[22] Athenodorus died in A.D. 7 when Paul was a boy. No doubt young Saul heard of him and other Stoic philosophers. In fact, in Athens Paul quoted from Aratus (Acts 17:28).

The bustling metropolis of Tarsus had "such a desire for knowledge, such a respect for scholarship, and such an intellectual format of thought that no thinking young man would entirely escape the contagion of the thronging ideas which crowded the air."[23]

How significant that Paul should be born in Tarsus, a large, Roman university city, a Hellenic-Oriental metropolis of wealth and culture. Unlike the twelve apostles, he was "city born and city bred."[24] Coming from such a city, it is no surprise his missionary work took him to numerous other strategic cities of the empire.

Citizenship

Of greater importance than Paul's being a citizen of Tarsus was his Roman citizenship, a fact mentioned several times in Acts. The Roman officers in Philippi, embarrassed to learn they had beaten and impris-

---

20. Colin J. Hemer, "Tarsus," in *International Standard Bible Encyclopedia,* 4 (1988), 735.

21. Strabo *Geography* 14.5.13.

22. Barclay, *The Mind of St. Paul,* 25.

23. Ibid.

24. Roland Q. Leavell, *The Apostle Paul: Christ's Supreme Trophy* (Grand Rapids: Baker, 1963), 13.

oned two Roman citizens, Paul and Silas, escorted them from prison (Acts 16:36–39). About to have Paul flogged in Jerusalem, a Roman commander was alarmed to learn he had chained a Roman citizen (22:23–28). When the commander told Paul he "had to pay a big price" for his citizenship, the apostle replied, "But I was born a citizen" (22:28). This commander, Claudius Lysias, sent Paul to Governor Felix in Caesarea, with a letter in which he affirmed Paul's Roman citizenship (23:26–27). Two years later (24:27), Felix's successor Festus offered to put Paul on trial in Jerusalem, but Paul refused and appealed to be tried before Caesar (25:8–12; cf. vv. 20–21), a right belonging to Roman citizens. King Agrippa, to whom Paul witnessed, referred to Paul's appeal to Caesar (26:32).

Not everyone of the fifty million inhabitants (including slaves) of the Roman Empire possessed Roman citizenship. Only about one of ten enjoyed that honor.[25] Being a Roman citizen provided special privileges, including exemption from being flogged[26] or executed[27] by crucifixion and the right to appeal to Rome for a trial against capital sentences.[28]

Why then did Paul and Silas not say anything about their Roman citizenship when they were stripped, flogged, and imprisoned in Philippi (16:22–24)?[29] Presumably their silence was deliberate because of their desire to follow Christ in his sufferings (2 Cor. 4:10–11; Phil. 3:10–11; Col. 1:24).

Paul's having been born a Roman citizen meant his parents were citizens. But how did they attain it? No one knows for sure, but several writers say Paul's ancestors had been slaves of the Romans and were granted freedom and citizenship by a Roman citizen.[30] Others suggest Paul's forebears received citizenship in return for some service rendered

---

25. Augustus *Res Gestae* 8.

26. "Also liable under the *lex Julia* on *vis publicia* is anyone who, while holding *imperium* or office, puts to death or flogs a Roman citizen contrary to his right of appeal, or orders any of the above mentioned things to be done, or puts [a yoke] on his neck so that he may be tortured" (Justinian *Digest* 48.6.7).

27. Peter Garnsey and Richard Saller, *The Roman Empire: Economy, Society and Culture* (Berkeley, Calif.: University of California Press, 1987), 117.

28. Schürer, *The History of the Jewish People in the Age of Jesus Christ (175 B.C.–A.D. 135)*, 3:135, n. 34.

29. This was one of three times he was flogged (2 Cor. 11:25) by Roman authorities, not to be confused with the five times he was beaten by Jews with thirty-nine lashes (11:24). Several other times he referred to being beaten (6:5, 9; 11:23; cf. Gal. 6:17).

30. Hengel, *The Pre-Christian Paul*, 14; John Clayton Lentz, *Luke's Portrait of Paul* (Cambridge: Cambridge University Press, 1993), 47–48; Murphy-O'Connor, *Paul: A Critical Life*, 41. See P. R. C. Weaver, "Social Mobility in the Early Roman Empire: The Evidence of the Imperial Freedmen and Slaves," *Past and Present* 37 (1967): 3–20.

to the Roman cause.[31] Some obtained citizenship in return for military service, but this would hardly have been the case with Paul's family who were Pharisees. More likely is the conjecture that Tarsus residents were granted full citizenship in the empire en masse. Josephus wrote that Nicator, a Seleucid king, gave citizenship to Jews in certain cities.[32] On several occasions a number of Tarsian Jews became Roman citizens: when Antiochus Epiphanes reorganized the city around 175 B.C.; when the Roman general Pompey made Cilicia a Roman province in 65–64 B.C.;[33] when Julius Caesar was welcomed into Tarsus in 47 B.C.; when General Mark Antony headquartered in Tarsus in 42 B.C.; and when Augustus conferred benefits on Tarsus in 31 B.C. On any one of these occasions Paul's precursors may have first received citizenship.[34] Roman citizenship bestowed by such grants, however, was uncommon[35] and was a "mark of distinction"[36] as was a Greek-city citizenship.[37] In fact, holding dual citizenship meant Paul was among the elite of Tarsus.[38]

However, was it incompatible for a Jew to be a Roman citizen? Rapske cites evidence showing that this did not pose a problem for Jews.[39] Paul's citizenship saved him from a Roman flogging on at least two occasions, and resulted in his voyage to Rome. His Roman ties led him to write of the believers' even greater citizenship in heaven (Phil. 3:20; cf. Eph. 2:19). As a Jewish citizen of the Roman Empire, he was uniquely "the man of two worlds"[40]—Israel and the Greco-Roman Empire. His vision for oth-

31. Strabo *Geography* 5.1.6. F. F. Bruce says that an archaeologist, William Calder, suggested in 1953 that a guild of tentmakers would have been useful to the Roman army (*Paul: Apostle of the Heart Set Free* [Grand Rapids: Eerdmans, 1977], 37; idem, *In the Steps of the Apostle Paul* [Grand Rapids: Kregel, n.d.], 8; and idem, "Paul the Apostle," in *International Standard Bible Encyclopedia*, 3 [1986], 709).

32. Josephus *The Antiquities of the Jews* 12.3.1.119.

33. Henry J. Cadbury, *The Book of Acts in History* (New York: Harper and Brothers, 1955), 73–74.

34. E. M. Blaicklock favors the time of Pompey's settlement ("Tarsus," in *The Illustrated Bible Dictionary* [Downers Grove, Ill.: InterVarsity, 1980], 3:1519. Cf. Suetonius *Julius* 28; and E. Brewer, "Roman Citizenship and Its Bearing on the Book of Acts," *Restoration Quarterly* 4 [1960]: 207–8).

35. A. N. Sherwin-White, *The Roman Citizenship*, 2d ed. (Oxford: Clarendon, 1973), 273. John J. O'Rourke says no Jewish community was given Roman citizenship as part of a general grant ("Roman Law and the Early Church," in *The Catacombs and the Colosseum*, 184, n. 164; cf. M. Adinolfi, "Stato Civile dei Christiani 'Forestieri e Pellegrini," *Antonianum* 42 [1967]: 420–34.

36. Lentz, *Luke's Portrait of Paul*, 25.

37. Ibid., 43.

38. F. F. Bruce, *The Acts of the Apostles; The Greek Text with Introduction and Commentary*, 2d ed. (Grand Rapids: Eerdmans, 1952), 399.

39. Rapske, *The Book of Acts and Paul in Roman Custody*, 89.

40. Barclay, *The Mind of St. Paul*, 31.

ers was universal, not provincial; and his outlook was broad, not paro-
chial. As a world citizen, he was at ease in all surroundings—with his
own people in synagogues, with pagan Gentiles in Phyrgia, with refined
philosophers of Athens, or with governors and kings.[41]

Paul's citizenship in Tarsus meant he came from a family of moder-
ate wealth. Athenodorus, the Stoic philosopher and one-time leader of
Tarsus, required the payment of five hundred drachmae for full citizenship in Tarsus, which may have been paid by Paul's father.[42] Other indications of Paul's wealth are his paying for the purifying rite of four
Nazarites (Acts 21:23–24), which would involve considerable expense;
Felix's expecting a bribe from Paul (24:26); Paul's ability to keep himself
for two years in Caesarea; his having to pay for his travel to Rome; and
his renting a house in Rome for two years (28:30).[43] Being a citizen of
a Greek city and a citizen of the Roman Empire would both indicate
high social status and some wealth.[44]

Education

Paul's schooling also equipped him to become an outstanding theologian and teacher. His educational training included instruction at home,
attendance at a synagogue school, and enrollment in advanced training
under Gamaliel in Jerusalem to become a rabbi. Paul's upbringing in a
Jewish home meant he was "brought up to consider the study and observance of the Laws of Jehovah as the supreme aim in life."[45] And having a father who was a Pharisee ("I am a Pharisee, the son of a Pharisee,"
Acts 23:6) meant his learning at home was especially profound.

Like all Jewish children, Paul would have been taught the Law at an
early age, both formally and informally. "As soon as a child can speak
(that is, after his third year) he is to be instructed in the Law by his father."[46] Consistent with Moses' instructions in Deuteronomy, Paul's

41. Maurice Jones, *St. Paul the Orator* (London: Hodder and Stoughton, 1910), 279.

42. A. H. M. Jones, *The Greek City from Alexander to Justinian* (Oxford: Clarendon,
1940), 174.

43. Colin J. Hemer, *The Book of Acts in the Setting of Hellenistic History* (Tübingen:
Mohr, 1989), 192.

44. Longenecker, *Paul: Apostle of Liberty*, 31.

45. Howard Tillman Kuist, *The Pedagogy of Paul* (New York: Doran, 1925), 22.

46. William Barclay, *Educational Ideals in the Ancient World* (1959; reprint, Grand
Rapids: Baker, 1974), 17 (based on *Mishnah Sukkah* 42a). According to Josephus, every
Jewish boy was taught the Scriptures and oral traditions "from our first consciousness"
(*Against Apion* 2.18). Philo referred to this instruction being given "from earliest youth"
(*Legation against Gaius*, 210).

home schooling was given formally ("impress them"—these command-ments—"on your children," Deut. 6:7a) and informally ("Talk about them when you sit at home and when you walk along the road, when you lie down and when you get up,"[47] 6:7b; cf. 4:9; 11:19). Jewish customs observed by parents profoundly influenced their children. As families kept the Sabbath[48] and participated in certain annual Jewish feasts,[49] and as children were taken by their parents to the synagogue each week to hear the Old Testament read and explained, Jewish pre-schoolers, including the young boy Paul, could not help but be vividly impressed. As the Passover was observed annually in the homes of Jews, children, naturally curious, would ask about its significance, and parents were ready to explain the ceremony (Exod. 12:26–27). In the weekly synagogue meeting on the Sabbath, boys and girls learned the Old Testament—learning that supplemented what they received at home. Synagogue services included reading portions of the Scriptures, usually from the Pentateuch first and then from the Prophets, followed by explanations and applications of the Scriptures, and congregational reciting of psalms and prayers.[50] By repeatedly hearing, memorizing, and reciting the Old Testament, young Saul, like all Jewish children in his day, would have become well acquainted with the nation's patriarchs, leaders, kings, prophets, and priests. Not surprisingly, the Jews viewed their synagogues as places of religious instruction. "The main object of the synagogue was the teaching of the people."[51]

47. "When you lie down and when you get up" is probably intended as a merism, a figure of speech that states two opposites with the intention of referring to everything in between. Thus Deuteronomy 6:7 emphasizes informal teaching of God's ways anytime "teachable moments" arise, whether in the evening, morning, or during the day.

48. Children were to be encouraged to observe the Sabbath laws (*Shabbath*, 166).

49. These feasts included the Passover, Unleavened Bread, Firstfruits, and Weeks (Pentecost) in the spring, and the Trumpets, Day of Atonement, and the Tabernacles in the fall (Lev. 23). It is unknown, however, how many of the feasts could be celebrated by Jews in the Diaspora, though undoubtedly at least the Passover was observed in each Jewish home. That Jews from the Diaspora did travel to Jerusalem to attend the three feasts of Unleavened Bread, Weeks, and Tabernacles (Deut. 16:16) is evident from Acts 2, which records that the Jews from remote parts of the Roman Empire attended the Feast of Weeks (Pentecost) in Jerusalem (Acts 2:9–11). Shammai, a Jewish leader, said children should attend these festivals when they were old enough to ride on their father's shoulders, and Hillel, another Jewish leader, said the children must attend when they could see their father's hand and walk (*Hagigah* 1.1).

50. On the proceedings in synagogue services in first-century Jewry, see S. Safrai and M. Stern, eds., *The Jewish People in the First Century* (Assen: Van Gorcum, 1976), 1:918–33.

51. Alfred Edersheim, *Sketches of Jewish Social Life in the Days of Christ* (1876; reprint, Grand Rapids: Eerdmans, 1967), 267. Appropriately, then, Philo called the synagogues "houses of instruction" (*Life of Moses* 3.27).

Later in his writings, Paul referred to Abraham twenty-one times and to Isaac three times. In his speeches in Acts and in his epistles, Paul referred by name to Israel's great Lawgiver, Moses, thirteen times; to David, Israel's greatest king, eight times; and to Isaiah six times. Adam is mentioned seven times. He revealed his familiarity with the Old Testament by quoting from it approximately one hundred times, with a possible additional one hundred more allusions to Old Testament passages.[52] The personal piety, authoritative preaching, illustrative teaching, and dynamic writing of the Old Testament writers unquestionably impacted and shaped Paul in significant ways.[53]

In addition to the learning received from an early age at home and weekly in the synagogues, children were taught in elementary schools. Picture young Saul starting school at age six or seven[54] along with other Jewish boys of Tarsus. Unlike their Gentile neighbors who attended pagan schools, they went to the synagogue where a school building had been built as an annex.[55] The school was called Beth Ha-Sepher ("House of the Book") because its primary purpose was to teach young boys the Torah (the first five books of the Old Testament). These schoolboys would learn to read and write Hebrew; they would learn to read the Greek Septuagint, the Jews' Bible of the first century and a few centuries before and after;[56] they would memorize significant portions of the Old Testament. These boys learned by constant repetition. Their teacher had them repeat their lessons after him until they were "able to recite it with great fluency."[57] "Who learns the Torah without repetition is like one who sows but does not reap."[58] Repetition enabled the boys to memorize the passages. Acrostics, catchwords, and rhythm in certain Old Testament passages also helped the students learn them by heart.

Is it any wonder that Paul in his thirteen epistles quoted or alluded to the Old Testament scores of times? As a typical Jewish student, he was saturated with the Old Testament. He knew it thoroughly; he could

52. These are discussed in chapter 14.

53. For more on the impact of these Old Testament leaders on Paul's training, see Kuist, *The Pedagogy of St. Paul*, 24–31.

54. Jerusalem Talmud, *Ketuboth* 32c.4. "Do not receive a boy into school before his sixth year" (ibid., 50a).

55. Barclay, *Educational Ideals in the Ancient World*, 37.

56. The Septuagint was the Old Testament translated into Greek from Hebrew by Jewish scholars in Alexandria, Egypt, about 200 B.C. to enable Hellenistic Jews of the Greco-Roman world who grew up speaking only Greek to know the Old Testament.

57. Rabbi Akiba, *Erubin* 54a (cited in ibid., 41).

58. *Essays on Jewish Life and Thought, The Letters of Benammi*, Second Series, 54, cited in Barclay, *The Mind of St. Paul*, 41, n. 135.

cite it readily; he could repeat it accurately. After having studied the Old Testament for about four years, Saul and his schoolmates at the age of ten[59] began studying the Mishnah, the oral interpretation of the Law, in a secondary school known as the Beth Ha-Midrash ("House of the Traditions").[60]

Paul received advanced schooling in Jerusalem under the respected rabbi Gamaliel, whom the apostle mentioned in Acts 22:3 and whom Luke called "a teacher of the law, who was honored by all the people" (5:34). Paul's father, a Pharisee, sent him, an adolescent about fifteen years old,[61] to study for five or six years under "the most significant and influential Pharisaic educator in the early 1st century A.D."[62] Some say Gamaliel was the son of Rabbi Hillel, founder in 10 B.C. of the more broadminded of the two main Jewish sects (Shammai founded the more literal and strict Jewish party). However, the Talmud speaks of Gamaliel as Hillel's grandson, a more likely tradition.[63] Gamaliel's tolerance showed itself when he urged the Sanhedrin, the temple council,

59. Mishnah, *'Aboth* 5.21.

60. John T. Townsend, "Ancient Education in the Time of the Early Roman Empire," in *The Catacombs and the Colosseum*, 156. E. G. Sihler is probably incorrect in suggesting that after Jewish secondary school Paul would have attended a Hellenistic secondary school known as a *grammatikos* in Tarsus ("Review of *Licht vom Osten*, by Adolf Deissmann," *Biblical Review* 3 [October 1923]: 625). In the *grammatikos* Greek and Roman boys studied Greek literature (mainly Homer's writings), grammar, writing, mathematics, science, geography, physical training, and music (Mark Golden, *Children and Childhood in Classical Athens* [Baltimore: Johns Hopkins University Press, 1990], 62). This is not to suggest, however, that Paul was unfamiliar with some Greek writings. Being brought up in Tarsus, he probably became familiar with some Greek literature through informal contact with non-Jews in the Hellenistic society around him.

61. Writers differ in their opinions on Paul's age when he moved to Jerusalem. Edwin M. Yamauchi says "about the age of twelve" ("Hellenism," in *Dictionary of Paul and His Letters*, ed. Gerald F. Hawthorne, Ralph P. Martin, and Daniel G. Reid [Downers Grove, Ill.: InterVarsity, 1993], 386); several suggest "about the age of thirteen" (James Stalker, *The Life of St. Paul* [New York: Revell, 1950], 26; Robert E. Speer, *Studies of the Man Paul* [New York: Revell, 1900], 20; and F. W. Farrar, *The Life and Work of St. Paul* [New York: Dutton, 1902; reprint, Minneapolis: Klock & Klock, 1981], 1:25); and Francis Lyall says Paul's age "might have been anywhere from the age of eight until the age of approximately fifteen" (*Slaves, Citizens, Sons: Legal Metaphors in the Epistles* [Grand Rapids: Zondervan, 1984], 240). But W. M. Ramsay says Paul's reference in Acts 26:4 to his "youth" (*neotēs*, the same word Paul used of Timothy in 1 Tim. 4:12; cf. Matt. 19:20) means that the future apostle was several years older. A young boy of thirteen, he believes, would not have said, "from my youth up" but "from my childhood up" (*The Teaching of Paul in Terms of the Present Day* [London: Hodder and Stoughton, 1913], 41).

62. Rapske, *The Book of Acts and Paul in Roman Custody*, 94. Joachim Jeremias notes that Gamaliel was, like Paul, a Benjamite (*Jerusalem in the Time of Jesus*, trans. F. H. Cave and C. H. Cave [London: SCM, 1969], 278, 287).

63. W. Bacher, "Gamaliel I," in *Jewish Encyclopedia*, 5:558–59.

not to execute Peter and other apostles who were arrested for preaching Jesus (5:33–40). That they followed his advice shows his influence among the Jewish aristocracy. The people so respected him that they called him Rabban ("Our master"), a title even more honorable than Rabbi ("My master"), and which was later ascribed to seven other teachers of the school of Hillel. The Mishnah records that "when Rabban Gamaliel the Elder died, the glory of the Torah ceased and purity and abstinence died."[64]

Paul's statement to a crowd in Jerusalem that he "was brought up in this city" (Acts 22:3) has led some scholars to insist that he moved to the Palestinian capital in his early childhood, not his youth. Van Unnik argues that as a boy Paul was "brought up" by his parents in Jerusalem and that he then studied in Jerusalem under Gamaliel.[65] The New American Standard Bible supports this view ("I am a Jew, born in Tarsus, but brought up in this city, educated under Gamaliel, strictly according to the law of our fathers, being zealous for God, just as you are today"), as does the New English Bible ("I am a true-born Jew, a native of Tarsus in Cilicia. I was brought up in this city, and as a pupil of Gamaliel I was thoroughly trained in every point of our Jewish law").

A preferred view omits the comma after "city" and understands the verse this way: "I am a Jew, born in Tarsus of Cilicia, brought up (*anatrephō* [66]) in this city at the feet of Gamaliel, trained (*paideuō*) according to the exactness (*akribeia*) of the law of our fathers, being zealous for God as all of you are today" (author's trans.). This rendering keeps all four Greek participles parallel: "born," "brought up," "trained," and "being" (zealous).[67]

---

64. Mishnah, *Sotie* 9.15. "Abstinence" may be translated "separateness," implying some loss of attention to his Pharasaic teachings. See Jacob Neusner, *The Rabbinic Traditions about the Pharisees before 70* (Leiden: Brill, 1971), 351–52; and idem, *The Pharisees: Rabbinic Perspectives* (Hoboken, N.J.: KTAV, 1985), 23–56.

65. W. C. van Unnik, *Tarsus or Jerusalem: City of Paul's Youth*, trans. George Ogg (London: Epworth, 1962). Cf. George Ogg, "Review of *Tarsus of* [*sic*] *Jerusalem*, by W. C. van Unnik," *Scottish Journal of Theology* 8 (1955): 94–97; and Everett F. Harrison, "Acts 22:3—A Test Case for Luke's Reliability," in *New Dimensions in New Testament Study*, ed. Richard N. Longenecker and Merrill C. Tenney (Grand Rapids: Zondervan, 1974), 251–53.

66. *Anatrephō*, "to be brought up," may also mean "to educate" (Stanley D. Toussaint, "Acts," in *The Bible Knowledge Commentary, New Testament*, ed. John F. Walvoord and Roy B. Zuck [Wheaton, Ill.: Victor, 1983], 418; and R. C. H. Lenski, *The Interpretation of the Acts of the Apostles* [Minneapolis: Augsburg, 1961], 901–2).

67. Longenecker, *Paul: Apostle of Liberty*, 23–26; and Nigel Turner, *Grammatical Insights into the New Testament* (Edinburgh: Clark, 1965), 83–84. This view is also suggested in a footnote on Acts 22:3 in *The NIV Study Bible*, 1689. Van Unnik's view wrongly requires that *paideuō* ("trained") be related to *two* phrases, "at the feet of Gamaliel" and "according to the exactness of the law of our fathers."

Studying under Gamaliel, Paul learned the techniques of debating, of posing questions raised by an imaginary opponent and answering those questions, of discussion and argumentation, of satirical criticism.[68] The apostle often used these techniques in his ministry and writings, as discussed later in chapters 11–14. Paul also learned under this great rabbi-teacher how to expound the Old Testament. "Paul's clear and logical manner of explaining the great doctrines of the Christian faith was no doubt the result, at least in part, of his schooling 'at the feet of Gamaliel.'"[69]

Pharisaic Background

Three times Paul stated he was a Pharisee. On trial before the Sanhedrin, he exclaimed, "I am a Pharisee, the son of a Pharisee" (Acts 23:6). The second occurrence of the word "Pharisee" in this statement is plural, so that the plural should read "a son of Pharisees." That is, he was raised in a family of Pharisees, with his father and grandfather (and/or uncles?) belonging to this religious group. To Agrippa he said he lived according to the "strictest sect" of Judaism "as a Pharisee" (26:5). And to the Philippians he proudly claimed that "in regard to the law," he was "a Pharisee" (Phil. 3:5).

The phrase "a son of Pharisees" means, according to some, that Paul was referring to his membership in a Pharisaic association or that he was a pupil of Pharisaic teachers.[70] However, while "the son of" can mean "one who belongs to" or "one who has the characteristics of," the specific term "a son of Pharisees" is used nowhere else in the New Testament or rabbinic writings.[71] Also, when Josephus used the phrase "sons of the high priest," he was referring to the physical lineage of three sons of Ishmael the high priest,[72] not to their being students of Ishmael. Thus Paul was not merely saying he had Pharisaic connections; he was asserting his familial upbringing in a genuine Pharisaic family.[73]

When he spoke to Agrippa about his living "according to the strictest sect of our religion" (Acts 26:5), he was affirming his meticulous adher-

68. Kuist, *The Pedagogy of St. Paul*, 39–41, 48.

69. James I. Packer, Merrill C. Tenney, and William White, Jr., eds., *The Bible Almanac* (Nashville: Nelson, 1980), 557.

70. Jeremias, *Jerusalem in the Time of Jesus*, 252, n. 26; Rapske, *The Book of Acts and Paul in Roman Custody*, 96; and A. F. Weiss, "Φαρισαῖος," in *Theological Dictionary of the New Testament*, 9 (1974), 46 and n. 215.

71. Lentz, *Luke's Portrait of Paul*, 52.

72. Josephus *The Jewish Wars* 6.114.

73. Lenski, *The Interpretation of the Acts of the Apostles*, 934.

ence to Pharisaic standards. Like all Pharisees, he took holiness and purity seriously, gave avid attention to religious obligations, was concerned about the welfare of his people, and sought to relate God's Word to everyday life.[74]

Several other times Paul expressed his serious commitment to Pharisees. To a crowd in Jerusalem he said he "was just as zealous for God as any of you are today" (Acts 22:3). Before he was saved, he lived out his zeal for God by persecuting the church (Phil. 3:6; cf. Gal. 1:13), and he was "faultless" regarding legalistic righteousness (Phil. 3:6). In Rome he told the Jewish leaders that he had done nothing amiss regarding "the customs [*ethos*] of our ancestors" (Acts 28:17). In fact, he even exceeded other Jews in their devotion, as he told the Galatians: "I was advancing in Judaism beyond many Jews of my own age and was extremely zealous for the traditions of my fathers" (Gal. 1:14). The Greek word for "traditions" is *paradosis,* a technical term that in this context designates the oral law (cf. Matt. 15:2–3, 6; Mark 7:5, 8–9, 13)[75] which the Pharisees were careful to keep along with obedience to the commands of the Torah, the written law.

While some Jews possessed citizenship in a Greek city, is it likely that Pharisees would reside in the Diaspora and hold citizenship in a city of Gentiles? Lentz says that they may or may not have resided outside Palestine[76] and that their being Greek citizens was "highly improbable."[77] This, however, runs counter to Paul's statement that he, a Pharisee, was a citizen of Tarsus. Also, as Lentz admits, "there is some evidence that suggests the presence of Pharisees outside of Palestine before the destruction of the Temple."[78] Though a citizen of a Greek city, a Pharisee,

---

74. The Pharisee party originated in Jewry in the second century B.C. possibly from the Hasidim (loyal ones) who continued Ezra's work of studying and meticulously obeying the law (R. Travers Herford, *Pharisaism: Its Aim and Method* [London: Williams and Norgate, 1912], 19). The word "Pharisee" derives from the Hebrew $p^erush\hat{i}m,$ the "separated ones," which may mean they (most of whom were laymen and some of whom were scholars) sought to separate themselves from the common people in order to be ceremonially clean (Eduard Lohse, *The New Testament Environment,* trans. John E. Steely [Nashville: Abingdon, 1976], 77; R. J. Wyatt, "Pharisees," in *International Standard Bible Encyclopedia,* 2 [1986], 822). For more on the Pharisees in Jesus' day—their numbers, practices, beliefs, shortcomings, and responses to Jesus—see Roy B. Zuck, *Teaching as Jesus Taught* (Grand Rapids: Baker, 1995), 130–50.

75. William R. Stegner, "Jew, Paul the," in *Dictionary of Paul and His Letters,* 504. These were the traditions of the rabbis, which were accepted by the Pharisees but rejected by the Sadducees (Walter Bauer, William F. Arndt, and F. Wilbur Gingrich, *A Greek-English Lexicon of the New Testament and Other Early Christian Literature,* 2d ed., rev. F. Wilbur Gingrich and Frederick W. Danker [Chicago: University of Chicago Press, 1979], 616).

76. Lentz, *Luke's Portrait of Paul,* 54–55.

77. Ibid., 56.

78. Ibid., 54.

holding to ritual purity, would certainly not be involved in worship of local Greek gods or participate in pagan, Hellenistic practices.

Of interest is the fact that the apostle said, "I am a Pharisee," not "I was a Pharisee." Even some Christians in Jerusalem "belonged to the party of the Pharisees" (Acts 15:5). But how could believers remain as Pharisees, especially in light of Jesus' strong denunciations of them as ostentatiously displaying their devotion (Matt. 6:2, 5; 23:5, 28), seeking the attention of others (6:3, 5; 23:5–7, 28; Luke 16:15), following oral traditions some of which violated the Scriptures (Matt. 15:3, 6–7; Mark 7:3–4, 8–9, 13), considering themselves superior to others (Luke 18:9), neglecting moral issues (Matt. 23:23; Luke 11:42), greedily loving money (Matt. 23:25; Luke 11:39; 16:14), adding burdensome regulations on the populace (Matt. 23:4; Luke 11:46), and being hypocritical (Matt. 6:2; 22:18; 23:3, 13, 15, 23, 25, 27, 29; Mark 12:15)?[79] How could Paul the apostle affirm his being a Pharisee when Jesus said the Pharisees were spiritually blind (Matt. 15:14; 23:16–17, 19, 24, 26) and like vipers (12:34; 23:33)? How is it that Paul never said he became an ex-Pharisee?[80] How is it that he "remained a Pharisee to his dying day"?[81]

Perhaps the answer lies in the teachings that Pharisaism and Christianity have in common, and in Paul's having rejected those teachings, practices, and attitudes of the Pharisees that Jesus vehemently criticized. Those truths held in common include God's sovereignty, self-revelation, and creative work; man's sin and death; the hope of the resurrection (Acts 23:6; 24:15, 21);[82] the existence of angels (23:8); the future reign of Messiah, the "hope" of Israel (24:15; 26:6–7; 28:20); and God's mercy.[83] Yet Paul, in his conversion, became a transformed, regenerated Pharisee. As Sanders put it, he became "a Christianized Pharisee,"[84] which means he renounced all in Pharisaism that would have contradicted the gospel and he embraced Jesus Christ as the Savior and pronounced belief in him as the only way of salvation. He now saw Christ as the fulfillment of Old Testament prophecies about the Messiah.

As a Pharisee, with a significant education in his adolescent years under the leading rabbi, Gamaliel, and having excelled "beyond many

79. Zuck, *Teaching as Jesus Taught*, 134–38.
80. Jacob Jervell, *The Unknown Paul* (Minneapolis: Augsburg, 1984), 71.
81. Frederick C. Grant, *Roman Hellenism and the New Testament* (New York: Scribner's Sons, 1962), 136.
82. The Sadducees, however, denied a future resurrection (Matt. 22:23; Mark 12:18; Luke 20:27; Acts 23:8).
83. Grant, *Roman Hellenism and the New Testament*, 136–37.
84. J. T. Sanders, "The Pharisee in Luke-Acts," in *The Living Text: Essays in Honor of Ernest W. Saunders*, ed. D. E. Groh and R. Jewett (New York: University Press of America, 1985), 166.

Jews" (Gal. 1:14), the apostle would have been highly respected by fellow Jews. In fact, when he gave his defense speech before the Sanhedrin, the Pharisees asserted, "We find nothing wrong with this man" (Acts 23:9).

Conclusion

In the first of Paul's thirteen epistles, he told the Galatians that God had set him apart from birth (Gal. 1:15). The verb "set apart" *(aphorizō)* means "to mark off by a boundary line or set aside for a purpose,"[85] and "from birth" is literally "from my mother's womb." From the very time he was born—and even long before!—circumstances converged to shape him to become the church's greatest apostle, emissary, and teacher.

From eternity God had determined where Paul would be born, when he would be born, and to whom he would be born. He also foreordained Paul's educational training: in the home of a Pharisee, in a synagogue school, and in a rabbinical "college" of the Jews' most honored rabbi-teacher of that day. Paul was Hebraic by parentage, Hellenic by birthplace, Roman by citizenship, and Jewish by upbringing and schooling.

Knowing Aramaic and Greek; being raised in a metropolitan center of education and commerce; being surrounded by debased, corrupt, pagan culture and conduct; possessing full citizenry rights as a Roman; being devoutly religious; being educated for rabbinical service; knowing the Old Testament and Jewish traditions thoroughly, Paul qualified remarkably well for the multicultural, multinational ministry to which God had set him apart.

How about You?

What factors in your background has God used to help prepare you to teach his Word?

If you do not have some of the advantages Paul had in his background, how might you overcome some deficiencies?

---

85. Paul used the same word in Romans 1:1 ("set apart for the gospel of God"), and Luke wrote that the Holy Spirit directed the Antiochian church to set apart Barnabas and Saul for the work to which God had called them (Acts 13:2).

What specific steps can you take to become more knowledgeable of the Scriptures, and thus be a better Bible teacher?

How does your background "fit" with the ministry you sense God has given you?

"You . . . know all about my . . . way of life."

2 Timothy 3:10

5

What Qualities Made Paul a Great Teacher?

Your telephone rings. You pick up the receiver. A voice at the other end says a national organization is taking a survey and the person asks if you have a minute to answer one question. Assuming this won't take much time, you agree to hear the question. He asks, "What do you think are the most important qualities a teacher should have?"

What answer would you give to that question? How do you think others would respond? Would you say, "A pleasant personality"? "Knowledge of his or her subject"? "Intelligence"? "Creativity"? "A stern disciplinarian, one who makes students behave"? "One who is admired by his students"? "Interest in his students"? "Open-minded and fun-loving"? "Control of the class"?

Responses to such an alleged survey may differ depending on the respondents' background and outlook. One actual survey, taken several years ago among student teacher candidates at Concordia College in River Forest, Illinois, included 257 responses.[1] The admirable qualities

1. Carl J. Moser, "The Most Important Characteristic of an Effective Teacher," *Journal of Christian Education* 2 (1981): 51–55.

of effective teachers cited by these students indicate that a teacher's personality is much more important than his or her knowledge, classroom ability, or teaching methods.[2] While teaching skills, knowledge of one's subject, and classroom creativity are important, these were not ranked high in the survey. In the opinions of these college students, who were training to teach in Christian elementary schools, love for and patience with pupils are the two most significant factors in effective teaching. "What a teacher *is* is the most important characteristic . . . followed closely by what a teacher does."[3] These exceed the concern for what the teacher knows. Most likely if students of any age were asked to evaluate their own teachers, similar results may be uncovered.

How would Paul rate as a teacher? The Book of Acts and the Pauline Epistles reveal a number of the apostle's qualities. Unquestionably he knew his subject matter, and certainly he possessed excellent teaching skills. But were these the features that radiate in the written records of his ministry? Occurring far more frequently are his personality traits— traits that reveal his deep love and genuine concern for those to whom he ministered. The New Testament information on the church's outstanding apostle repeatedly manifests his godly devotion; his God-given authority and confidence; his personal integrity, honesty, and consistency; genuine humility; thoughtful courtesy; compassionate sensitivity to God and others; bold severity against his and God's opponents; unquenching fervency; dauntless tenacity when beset with numerous adversities and difficulties; deep-seated serenity; heartfelt felicity, and comprehensive mastery of doctrinal and ethical subjects. Of these qualities (discussed in this chapter and the next), all except the last one focus on Paul's character. And the last one, pertaining to knowledge and teaching skill, is true of Paul because of who he was—a man deeply committed to God and genuinely interested in others.[4]

As we examine these features in Paul's personality and experience, ask yourself how well you parallel these in your life and teaching. Are you deeply devoted to God—or are you "faking" it? Do you teach with his authority—or do you teach as if your authority is self-induced? Are you genuinely humble—or has pride crept in? Are you courteous to your students—or do you easily become rude toward them? Are you sensitive to God's leading and the feelings of your students—or are you unconcerned

2. Ibid., 52.
3. Ibid., 55 (italics his).
4. In my *Teaching as Jesus Taught*, I discuss fourteen qualities that marked Jesus as the world's most outstanding teacher: maturity, mastery, certainty, humility, consistency, spontaneity, clarity, urgency, variety, quality, empathy, intimacy, sensitivity, and relevancy (*Teaching as Jesus Taught* [Grand Rapids: Baker, 1995], 61–90).

and calloused? Are you stern as necessary with those who contradict the Scriptures—or do you disregard false teaching with indifference? Are you energetic and enthusiastic about your teaching—or do you merely endure the process? When distress intrudes into your life, do you persevere—or are you easily disheartened? Do you enjoy God's peace and joy—or are you easily perturbed and despondent? Do you give your mind to the study of the Scriptures—or are you lackadaisical in preparation? Do you spend adequate time in seeking to know the subject(s) you teach—or do you spend as little time as possible, simply to "get by"?

If you tend to slip into the second option in any of these categories, then let Paul's high standards of teaching challenge you afresh to excel in your teaching responsibilities.

Piety

Foundational to effective Christian teaching is the teacher's relationship to God. How can you possibly introduce others to Christ and challenge them to walk with him if you yourself are not dedicated to the Lord? If Paul was not godly, he certainly could not have challenged others toward godly living. Yet he was so devoted to God that his piety is evidenced by seven factors. First, his focus on Christ stands as his unsurpassing quality, his "supreme characteristic."[5] "For Paul, life began in the apprehension of Christ, aims at the imitation of Christ, is directed by identification with Christ, is sustained by union with Christ, rejoices in the expectation of Christ."[6]

To the Philippians, Paul wrote, "For to me, to live is Christ" (Phil. 1:21), and "I can do everything through him who gives me strength" (4:13). So central was Christ to Paul's life that he told the Galatians, "Christ lives in me" (Gal. 2:20). He expressed his wholehearted devotion for Christ by saying that he served him "with my whole heart" (Rom. 1:9) for he was compelled by the love of Christ (2 Cor. 5:14). This phrase may be understood as Paul's love for Christ, but more likely it means Christ's love for Paul. The Greek word for "compels" is *synechei*, "to hold or press together, or to constrain," implying a pressure that confines and restricts as well as controls.[7] So driven was Paul by Christ's

---

5. James Stalker, *The Life of St. Paul* (New York: Revell, 1950), 102.

6. Reginald E. O. White, *Apostle Extraordinary* (Grand Rapids: Eerdmans, 1962), 99.

7. Fritz Rienecker, *A Linguistic Key to the Greek New Testament*, ed. Cleon L. Rogers, Jr. (Grand Rapids: Zondervan, 1980), 469; and Alfred Plummer, *A Critical and Exegetical Commentary on the Second Epistle of St Paul to the Corinthians*, International Critical Commentary (Edinburgh: Clark, 1915), 173.

controlling love that his overriding goal was "that he might serve Christ, know Christ, and become like Christ."[8] Everything was secondary compared to "the surpassing greatness of knowing Christ Jesus" (Phil. 3:8). As Christ's servant, Paul's ambition was to please him, not others (Gal. 1:10; 1 Thess. 2:4).

Second, Paul's piety is evidenced by his prayer life. The Book of Acts records numerous occasions when he prayed—occasions so varied that his praying, one senses, was natural, spontaneous, and frequent: in the house of Judas in Damascus immediately after his conversion (Acts 9:11); with other prophets and teachers as he and Barnabas were commissioned for their first missionary journey (13:1–4); in Lystra, Iconium, and Antioch as he and Barnabas appointed elders (14:23); during his incarceration in the Philippian jail (16:25); in Miletus with elders from Ephesus (20:36); with disciples in Tyre on the beach (21:5); in the temple in Jerusalem (22:17); and on the island of Malta praying for the healing of Publius's father (28:7–8). Only the last of these eight references is the request of his praying specified: for healing. Of interest are the petitions in Paul's prayers, listed in table 5.

Table 5
Petitions in Paul's Prayers

That "the way may be opened for me to come to you . . . so that I may impart to you some spiritual gift to make you strong [that we] may be mutually encouraged by each other's faith" (Rom. 1:10–12)

That "the Israelites . . . may be saved" (Rom. 10:1).

"That you will not do anything wrong . . . and that you will do what is right" (2 Cor. 13:7).

"Our prayer is for your perfection"[9] (2 Cor. 13:9).

"That the eyes of your heart may be enlightened in order that you may know the hope to which he has called you, the riches of his glorious inheritance in the saints, and his incomparably great power for us who believe" (Eph. 1:18–19).

"That out of his glorious riches he may strengthen you with power through his Spirit in your inner being, so that Christ may dwell in your hearts through faith" (Eph. 3:16–17a).

---

8. William M. Taylor, *Paul the Missionary* (New York: Doran, 1881), 547. For more on the centrality of Christ in Paul's life and teachings, see Robert E. Speer, *The Man Paul* (New York: Revell, 1900), 115–67.

9. *Katartisis*, a noun used only here in the New Testament, stems from the common verb *katartizō*, "to make complete, put in order," as in Galatians 6:1 ("restore"), 2 Corinthians 13:11 (be "made complete," author's trans.), and 1 Thessalonians 3:10 ("supply"). *Katartisis* conveys the thought of completion, so that Paul's prayer in 2 Corinthians 13:9 was for the Corinthians' spiritual growth or advancement. Paul used a related noun, *katartismos*, in Ephesians 4:12 in the sense of being "equipped for service."

"That you . . . may have power . . . to grasp how wide and long and high and deep is the love of Christ and to know this love that surpasses knowledge—that you may be filled to the measure of all the fullness of God" (Eph. 3:17b–19).

"That your love may abound more and more in knowledge and depth of insight, so that you may be able to discern what is best and may be pure and blameless . . . [and] filled with the fruit of righteousness" (Phil. 1:9–11).

"That you may live a life worthy of the Lord and may please him in every way" (Col. 1:10).

"That we may see you again and supply what is lacking in your faith" (1 Thess. 3:10).

"That our God may count you worthy of his calling, and that by his power he may fulfill every good purpose of yours and every act prompted by your faith . . . so that the name of our Lord Jesus Christ may be glorified in you, and you in him" (2 Thess. 1:11–12).

"That you may be active in sharing your faith, so that you will have a full understanding of every good thing we have in Christ" (Philem. 6).

All these petitions, remarkably, pertain not to physical needs but to spiritual issues. He prayed for the Romans' spiritual blessings;[10] the Israelites' salvation; the Corinthians' right conduct and spiritual growth; the Ephesians' spiritual insight and power; the Philippians' growth in love, spiritual discernment, and purity; the Colossians' conduct as worthy of the Lord; the Thessalonians' spiritual advancement and worthy conduct; and Philemon's active witnessing for Christ. How many Christians today voice these kinds of requests to the Lord on behalf of others?

At least six times the apostle wrote that he was praying for his readers (including believers in four cities, and two individuals), without mentioning a specific request: "I remember you in my prayers" (Rom. 1:9–10); "Remembering you in my prayers" (Eph. 1:16); "In all my prayers for all of you, I always pray with joy" (Phil. 1:4–5); "We pray for you" (Col. 1:3); "I constantly remember you in my prayers" (2 Tim. 1:3); "I remember you in my prayers" (Philem. 4).

Also, his frequent encouragement to his readers to pray speaks of his own unswerving commitment to prayer: "Be . . . faithful in prayer" (Rom. 12:12); "Pray in the Spirit on all occasions with all kinds of prayers and requests . . . and always keep on praying for all the saints" (Eph. 6:18); "In everything, by prayer and petition, with thanksgiving,

10. The term "spiritual gift" *(charisma . . . pneumatikon)* in Romans 1:11 probably refers to Paul's imparting spiritual favors or blessings to the Romans by his ministry to them (John A. Witmer, "Romans," in *The Bible Knowledge Commentary, New Testament,* ed. John F. Walvoord and Roy B. Zuck [Wheaton, Ill.: Victor, 1983], 440); cf. God's "gifts" [*charisma*] i.e., "blessings," on Israel in Rom. 11:29. This does not imply that Paul could bestow spiritual gifts on others, since those are given sovereignly by the Holy Spirit (1 Cor. 12:7–11).

present your requests to God" (Phil. 4:6); "Devote[11] yourselves to prayer" (Col. 4:2); "Pray continually" (1 Thess. 5:17); "I urge, then, first of all, that requests, prayers, intercession and thanksgiving be made for everyone" (1 Tim. 2:1); "I want men everywhere to lift up holy hands in prayer" (1 Tim. 2:8).

In return Paul did not hesitate to ask believers to pray for him, and most of those requests were for his spiritual effectiveness in ministry (Rom. 15:30–31; Eph. 6:19–20; Col. 4:3–4; 1 Thess 5:25; 2 Thess. 3:1–2; 2 Tim. 1:16). And those who he said were praying on his behalf included the Corinthians (2 Cor. 1:11), the Philippians (Phil. 1:19), and Philemon (Philem. 22).

Another feature of Paul's supplications on behalf of others included his many benedictions (Rom. 15:5, 13; 16:20; 1 Cor. 16:23; 2 Cor. 13:14; Gal. 6:18; Eph. 6:23–24; Phil. 4:23; Col. 4:18; 1 Thess 5:23; 2 Thess 3:18; 1 Tim. 6:21; 2 Tim. 4:22; Titus 3:15; Philem. 25).

Prayer is more than presenting requests to God; it also includes giving thanks to the Lord, which Paul often did (Acts 28:15; Rom. 7:25; 1 Cor. 10:30; 15:57; 2 Cor. 2:14; 8:16; 9:15; Eph. 1:16; 1 Tim. 1:12; 2 Tim. 1:3). He voiced his thanks to the Lord for those to whom he wrote (Rom. 1:8; 1 Cor. 1:4; Eph. 1:16; Phil. 1:3; Col. 1:13; 1 Thess. 1:2; 2:13; 3:9; 2 Thess. 1:3; 2:13; Philem. 4), and he frequently encouraged others to be grateful to the Lord (Eph. 5:4, 20; Phil. 4:6; Col. 1:12; 2:7; 3:15–17; 4:2; 1 Thess. 5:18; 1 Tim. 4:4). Unquestionably, prayer constituted a vital part of this master teacher's strategy in fostering his students' spiritual growth.

A third indication of Paul's allegiance to God is his acts of worship. He fasted (Acts 13:2–3; 14:23), kept a vow he made (18:18),[12] participated in worship with others (13:2; 16:13, 16, 25; 20:7; 24:11, 17–18; 28:8–9), and attended Israel's annual feasts in Jerusalem including the Feast of Unleavened Bread (20:6) and the day of Pentecost (20:16).

Fourth, the strength of Paul's spiritual life stemmed from his dependence on the indwelling Holy Spirit. Luke recorded that the Spirit filled Paul (Acts 9:17; 13:9), called and sent him on his missionary work (13:2, 4), guarded him from entering the provinces of Asia and

---

11. The Greek word rendered "be faithful" in Romans 12:12 and "devote" in Colossians 4:2 is *proskartereō*, "to persist in, be busily engaged in, spend much time in" (Walter Bauer, William F. Arndt, and F. Wilbur Gingrich, *A Greek-English Lexicon of the New Testament and Other Early Christian Literature*, 2d ed., rev. F. Wilbur Gingrich and Frederick W. Danker [Chicago: University of Chicago Press, 1979], 715; and Walter Grundmann "προσκαρτερέω," in *Theological Dictionary of the New Testament*, 3 [1969], 618).

12. The time and nature of this vow are not stated, but during the vow he let his hair grow and when the time of the Nazirite vow was over he got a haircut at Cenchrea, Corinth's seaport.

Bithynia (16:6–7) and to Jerusalem (20:22), and informed[13] him of dangers he would face in Jerusalem (20:23). In addition, Luke wrote that the Holy Spirit gives encouragement (9:31) and guides in decision-making (15:28). The apostle wrote repeatedly about the Holy Spirit, urging believers to live by means of the Spirit (Gal. 5:16), and to be filled (i.e., controlled) by the Spirit (Eph. 5:18). The Holy Spirit's central role in the lives of believers is seen in his many ministries as listed in table 6.

Table 6
Paul's Affirmations about the Ministry
of the Holy Spirit in Believers

Regenerates	Titus 3:5
Justifies	1 Corinthians 6:11
Baptizes	1 Corinthians 12:13
Seals	Ephesians 1:13; 4:30
Indwells	Romans 5:5; 8:9, 11
	1 Corinthians 2:12; 3:16; 6:19
	2 Corinthians 1:22; 5:5
	Galatians 3:2, 5; 4:6
	Ephesians 2:22
	1 Thessalonians 4:8
	2 Timothy 1:14
Adopts	Romans 8:15[14]
Sanctifies	Romans 1:4;[15] 15:16
	2 Thessalonians 2:13
Leads	Romans 8:14
	Galatians 5:18
Controls	Romans 8:6, 9
Teaches	1 Corinthians 2:14
Reveals	1 Corinthians 2:10–11
	Ephesians 3:5
Liberates	2 Corinthians 3:17
Empowers	Romans 15:13, 19
	1 Corinthians 2:4

13. The word *diamartyromai*, sometimes translated "warns" (Acts 2:40; 1 Thess 4:6; 2 Tim. 2:14), or "give a charge" (1 Tim. 5:21; 2 Tim. 4:1), more probably here in Acts 20:23 conveys the idea of declaring or testifying solemnly as in verses 21 and 24 (and 8:25; 10:42; 18:5; 28:23). See table 3 in chapter 3.

14. His title, "the Spirit of sonship" (or adoption), refers to his ministry of placing an individual at the moment of salvation into the position of being God's adopted sons (Gal. 4:5; Eph. 1:5).

15. His title, "the Spirit of holiness," suggests either that he possesses holiness or that he gives holiness in his sanctifying ministry.

	2 Corinthians 6:6[16]
	Ephesians 3:16
	1 Thessalonians 1:5
Loves	Romans 15:30
	Colossians 1:8
Intercedes	Romans 8:26–27
Helps	Romans 8:26
	Philippians 1:19
Verifies	Romans 8:16; 9:1
Resurrects	Romans 8:11
Gives believers joy	Romans 14:17[17]
Gives spiritual gifts	1 Corinthians 12:4–11
Produces spiritual "fruit"	
or inner qualities	Galatians 5:22–23
Unites	Ephesians 4:3
Brings fellowship	2 Corinthians 13:14
	Philippians 2:1
Enables believers to pray	Romans 8:15
	Galatians 4:6
	Ephesians 2:18; 6:18
Enhances worship	Philippians 3:3
Hopes	Galatians 5:5

The prominence given to the Spirit's ministry in Paul's theology demonstrates that living "in accord with the Spirit" (Rom. 8:5) and "by the Spirit" (Gal. 5:16) is essential to spiritual progress and maturity. Godliness is impossible without the Holy Spirit. Because the apostle enjoyed the benefits of the Spirit working in his own life, he, as a caring teacher, wanted others to have the same.

Fifth, the apostle's piety is seen in his unflinching trust in the Lord. Besides Paul's many statements about salvation being attained by faith (trust) in Christ (e.g., Acts 24:24; Rom. 3:22; 4:5; 5:1; Gal. 2:16, 20; 3:24–25; Eph. 2:8; Phil. 3:9), the apostle attested to his ongoing confidence in the Lord. He assured the Corinthians that God gives us victory (1 Cor. 15:57) for "we live by faith, not by sight" (2 Cor. 5:7). To the believers of Philippi he affirmed that "he who began a good work in you will carry it on to completion until the day of Christ Jesus" (Phil. 1:6). About to be

16. In 2 Corinthians 6:6–7a, Paul listed eight qualities that authenticated his apostolic authority (David K. Lowery, "2 Corinthians," in *The Bible Knowledge Commentary, New Testament*, 569). One such credential, he wrote, was "in the Holy Spirit," which may suggest that he ministered in the power of the Holy Spirit.

17. "Joy in the Holy Spirit" may mean joy supplied by the Spirit or joy experienced in the sphere of the Spirit; that is, in the spiritual realm "in union with or in connection with" the Holy Spirit (R. C. H. Lenski, *The Interpretation of St. Paul's Epistle to the Romans* [Minneapolis: Augsburg, 1961], 841).

shipwrecked on the island of Malta on the way to Rome, Paul assured the crew that their lives would be spared. He said, "I have faith in God" (Acts 27:25) because an angel had appeared to him and told him that none of them would lose their lives. From a Roman prison he told Timothy he was not ashamed of the gospel or of his confined condition "because I know whom I have believed, and am convinced that he is able to guard what I have entrusted to him for that day" (2 Tim. 1:12).

Sixth, another factor demonstrating the apostle's godly character is his hope, that is, his confidence in what God will do in his future program. This included his assurance of the "resurrection of the dead" (Acts 23:6; 24:15), the fulfillment of Old Testament promises to Israel (26:6–7; 28:20), sharing Christ's glory (Rom. 5:2; 2 Cor. 3:11–12; Col. 1:27), the liberation of creation from its present bondage (Rom. 8:21), the redemption (*apolytrōsis*, "release or deliverance") of our bodies (8:23–24), deliverance from afflictions (2 Cor. 1:10), bestowal of full righteousness when Christ returns (Gal. 5:5; cf. 2 Tim 4:8), inheritance of God's riches (Eph. 1:18; cf. v. 14), eternal life (Titus 1:2; 3:7), and the Lord's return (the "blessed hope," 2:13). Because of his confidence in God's actions in the future, Paul wanted his readers to have that same sense of certainty. He encouraged the Christians in Rome to "be joyful in hope" (Rom. 12:12) and "to overflow [or 'be abounding'] with hope."

The seventh indicator of the apostle's godly living is his clear conscience. When on trial he spoke to the Sanhedrin of his "good" conscience (Acts 23:1), and to Felix he referred to his "clear"[18] conscience (24:16). His conscience confirmed his honesty (Rom. 9:1; 2 Cor. 1:12), and he affirmed to Timothy that he, the apostle, had a "clear [lit., 'clean'] conscience" (2 Tim. 1:3).

Paul encouraged Timothy to maintain a "good conscience" (1 Tim. 1:19) and stated that deacons are to have a "clear [lit., 'clean'] conscience" (3:9).

An eighth factor pointing up Paul's piety is his sensitivity to the Lord's leading in his life. His desire to visit believers in Rome was tempered by his submission to God's will (Rom. 1:10; 15:32). The same was true of his plans to return to Corinth ("if the Lord is willing," 1 Cor. 4:19; "if the Lord permits," 16:7).

These eight elements in Paul's life cogently demonstrate his allegiance to and intimacy with God. His Spirit-filled devotion to the Savior served as the underlying basis of a highly effective preaching and teach-

---

18. *Aproskopon,* used only three times in the New Testament and each time by Paul (Acts 24:16; 1 Cor. 10:32; Phil. 1:10), means "not giving offense, not causing others to stumble." In the papyri it is used in the sense of "free from hurting others" and "not causing injury to others" (Rienecker, *A Linguistic Key to the Greek New Testament,* 422).

ing ministry. Without this essential quality, his work would have been impotent and ineffectual.

Authority

As a teacher of God's Word, you can and should teach with authority. But this does not mean you should "lord it over" your students in a domineering way. Nor does it mean you should seek to show off your knowledge or think of yourself as superior to others. Teaching with spiritual authority is not to be equated with teaching authoritatively.

Teaching with God's authority means two things: recognizing your message comes from him, and recognizing your ability comes from him. Having these two factors can enable you, like Paul, to speak and teach boldly.

Paul spoke with authority because he was an apostle (1 Cor. 9:1; 15:9). Twice he referred to "that authority the Lord gave" him (2 Cor. 10:8; 13:10). This meant he was chosen not by men but by God (Gal. 1:1) and that his message was not something he made up but was received "by revelation from Jesus Christ" (1:11–12).

We cannot replicate his experience as an apostle because the era of apostleship ended with Paul (see chapter 2). However, the message he communicated is our message as well. And the Holy Spirit, who empowered him in his teaching, is available to assist us in ours as well. Table 7 lists the many references to Paul's speaking God's words, not his own.

Table 7
References to Paul's Content Being Authoritative

References to the Word[19] of God

Barnabas and Paul "proclaimed the word of God" (Acts 13:5).
Sergius Paulus "wanted to hear the word of God" (13:7).
"Almost the whole city [of Pisidian Antioch] gathered to hear the word of the Lord" (13:44).
"We had to speak the word of God to you" (13:46).
"The word of the Lord spread though the whole region" (13:49).
Paul and Barnabas "preached the word in Perga" (14:25).

19. In each of the following twenty-three verses "word" translates *logos*, the subject matter revealed by God.

"Paul and Barnabas remained in Antioch, where they and many others taught and preached the word of the Lord" (15:35).

"Let us go back and visit the brothers in all the towns where we preached the word of the Lord" (15:36).

The Holy Spirit kept Paul and Silas "from preaching the word in the province of Asia" (16:6).

"Then they spoke the word of the Lord to him [the Philippian jailer] and to all the others in his house" (16:32).

"Paul was preaching the word of God at Berea" (17:13).

"So Paul stayed for a year and a half [in Corinth], teaching them the word of God" (18:11).

"All the Jews and Greeks who lived in the province of Asia heard the word of the Lord" (19:10).

"The word of the Lord spread widely" (19:20).

"Now I commit you to God and to the word of his grace" (20:32).

"Hold firmly to the word I preached to you" (1 Cor. 15:2).

"You have . . . heard . . . the word of truth, the gospel" (Col. 1:5).

"God gave me to present to you the word of God in its fullness" (Col. 1:25).

"When you received the word of God, which you heard from us, you accepted it not as the word of men, but as it actually is, the word of God" (1 Thess. 2:13).

"According to the Lord's own word, we tell you. . . ." (1 Thess 4:15).

"God's word is not chained" (2 Tim. 2:9).

"Preach the Word" (2 Tim. 4:2).

"He brought his word to light through the preaching entrusted to me" (Titus 1:3).

References to the Message[20] of God

"It is to us that this message of salvation has been sent" (Acts 13:26).

"The Lord opened her [Lydia's] heart to respond to Paul's message" (Acts 16:14).

The Bereans "received the message with great eagerness" (Acts 17:11).

"Faith comes from hearing, and hearing comes through the word of Christ" (Rom. 10:17, author's trans.).

"For the message of the cross is foolishness to those who are perishing" (1 Cor. 1:18).

"My message and my preaching were not with wise and persuasive words" (1 Cor. 2:4).

"Our message to you is not 'Yes' and 'No'" (2 Cor. 1:18).

God "has committed to us the message of reconciliation" (2 Cor. 5:19).

"Pray for us, too, that God may open a door for our message" (Col. 4:3).

"You welcomed the message" (1 Thess. 1:6).

20. In eleven of the following fifteen verses "message" is the NIV translation of *logos*—all except Acts 16:14 (*tois laloumenois*, "the things spoken"); Romans 10:17 (*rhēmatos*, "saying, or spoken word"); 2 Timothy 4:15 (*logoi*, the plural of *logos*); and 2 Timothy 4:17 (*kērygma*, "preached message"). These are essentially synonyms of *logos*.

"The Lord's message rang out from you" (1 Thess. 1:8).

"Pray for us that the message of the Lord may spread rapidly and be honored" (2 Thess. 3:1).

Alexander "strongly opposed our message" (2 Tim. 4:15).

The Lord "gave me strength, so that through me the message might be fully proclaimed" (2 Tim. 4:17).

An elder "must hold firmly to the trustworthy message as it has been taught" (Titus 1:9).

These many verses emphasize the point that Paul could speak with authority and confidence to others because he shared God's message. And the same stands true for believers today. We can teach with authority because we are communicating divine truth—truth that can change lives. Having God's powerful Word means we, like the apostle, "do not preach ourselves, but Jesus Christ" (2 Cor. 4:5).

As stated earlier, teaching with authority means not only having a divinely authoritative message; it also means having God's enabling by the Holy Spirit. The power of the Holy Spirit (or the power of God) is mentioned several times in the Pauline Epistles in relation to Paul's ministry. He said God enabled him to win Gentiles to Christ "through the power of the Spirit" (Rom. 15:19). His message was given in "demonstration of the Spirit's power" (1 Cor. 2:4),[21] so that the fruit of those to whom he preached and whom he taught would focus not on having wisdom "but on God's power" (2:5). Because Paul was God's servant (2 Cor. 4:1, 5; Gal. 1:10; Eph. 3:7; Col. 1:23, 25),[22] his empowerment or capability (*hikanotēs*, 2 Cor. 3:5) came not from himself but from God (cf. 13:4). One of the eight inner qualities Paul enumerated in 2 Corinthians 6:6–7a is "the power of God." Thus as Paul preached and taught, he was not just talking; he was communicating with spiritual power: "our gospel came to you not simply with words, but also with power, with the Holy Spirit" (1 Thess. 1:5).[23] His spiritual potency was evident even in Damascus right after his conversion: he was "powerful" (*endynamai*, "to be filled with power") and he "baffled" (*synchynnō*, "to confuse or confound") the Jews (Acts 9:22).[24]

---

21. This Greek phrase is literally "demonstration of the Spirit and power," a figure of speech known as a hendiadys in which two parallel nouns are to be understood as one subordinate to the other: "the power of the Spirit."

22. "His authority was grounded in his commission as a servant. . . . His authority was derived from the Lord of heaven and earth" (Kent L. Johnson, *Paul the Teacher* [Minneapolis: Augsburg, 1986], 20).

23. The Greek reads, "and in power and in the Holy Spirit," which may be another hendiadys like that in 1 Corinthians 2:4 (see note 21).

24. For more on teaching with the power of the Holy Spirit, see my *Teaching with Spiritual Power* (1963; reprint, Grand Rapids: Kregel, 1993).

The apostle carefully explained to the Corinthians that he never abused his authority. He said he was not "harsh in [his] use of authority" (2 Cor. 13:10) because it was "authority the Lord gave" him (10:8; 13:10). Having God's authoritative message and spiritual enabling means we can share the truth with boldness, not shyness; with certainty, not timidity; with conviction, not cowardice.

This was clearly true of Paul. Soon after his conversion he spoke boldly to Jews in Damascus (Acts 9:27) in their synagogues, the very place where he had gone to arrest Christian Jews! Later he and Barnabas spoke boldly in Pisidian Antioch to Jews who opposed what they were teaching (13:46) and to Jews in the Iconium synagogue (14:3). Then in Ephesus, Paul spoke boldly in the synagogue there for three months (19:8). In each of these verses Luke used the same verb, "to speak freely, openly, fearlessly, boldly," in referring to Paul's authoritative ministry. Also Apollos, a Christian Jew, spoke boldly to the Jews in the Corinthian synagogue (18:26). When the apostle was giving his defense before King Agrippa[25] and Governor Festus, the latter interrupted Paul, accusing him of being insane (26:24). In response, Paul said, "I can speak freely [*parrēsiazomai*] to Agrippa" (26:26). Years before, Paul used the same verb when he told the Thessalonians that he "dared" to tell them the gospel "in spite of strong opposition" (1 Thess. 2:2), that is, he spoke boldly or courageously. Potential conflict did not deter him from speaking of the Good News. When in prison in Rome, he asked the Ephesians to pray that he would "declare it fearlessly" (*parrēsiazomai*, Eph. 6:20).

This verb, a composite word meaning "having all speech," was used in classical Greek to designate possessing freedom of speech, often with a political connotation.[26] The noun *parrēsia*, derived from this verb, means boldness or confidence, also suggestive of freedom of expression before others (as in Acts 2:29; 4:13, 30–31; 28:20 [Paul preached and taught "boldly" while under house arrest in Rome]; 2 Cor. 7:4; Eph. 6:19) or before God in faith and prayer. (The NIV translates this noun

25. This Agrippa was Agrippa II, son of Herod Agrippa I (Acts 12:1) and a great-grandson of Herod the Great (Matt 2:1). "At this time he was a young man of about 30 years of age and the ruler of territories northeast of Palestine with the title of King. Because he was a friend of the Roman imperial family he was awarded the privilege of appointing the Jewish high priest and also had been made the custodian of the temple treasury. His background made him eminently qualified to hear Paul; he was well acquainted with the Jews' religion" (Stanley D. Toussaint, "Acts," in *The Bible Knowledge Commentary, New Testament*, 423).

26. A. L. Moore, *The First and Second Thessalonians*, New Century Bible (London: Nelson and Sons, 1969), 33; and Heinrich Schlier, "παρρησία, παρρησιάζομαι," in *Theological Dictionary of the New Testament*, 5 (1967), 871–73.

"freedom" in Eph. 3:12; "assurance" in 1 Tim. 3:13; "courage" in Phil. 1:20 and Heb. 3:6; and "confidence" in Heb. 4:16; 10:19; 1 John 2:28; 3:21; and 4:17.) With a divine, Christ-centered message and a divine, Spirit-given enabling, we, like Paul, can feel free and open in conveying divine truth. Even in the face of opposition believers can impart God's Word dauntlessly and without shame (Rom. 1:16; Phil. 1:20; 2 Tim. 1:8, 12; 2:15).

Even in his epistles Paul presented God's Word staunchly and without flinching. When he told the Romans, "I have written you quite boldly on some points" (Rom. 15:15), he used the adverb *tolmēroterōs*, which occurs only here in the New Testament and which stems from *tolmaō*, "to dare, to be brave or courageous."

Paul's boldness in preaching and teaching also is seen in his courageous leadership before others. "Wherever he went, Paul stood out as a man of unusual authority and force of personality—a man who was every inch a leader."[27] Several times we read of his looking straight at others: at Elymas the sorcerer in Paphos (Acts 13:9), at a crippled man in Lystra (14:9), and at the Sanhedrin in Jerusalem (23:1).[28] The apostle was courageous in disputing with Jewish Christians who insisted that salvation required circumcision (15:2); in confronting the demon-possessed slave girl in Philippi (16:16–18); in informing the prison officers that they should escort them out of prison (16:37); in wanting to speak to the riotous crowd in Ephesus (19:28–31); in addressing the wild Jerusalem crowd who had him arrested (21:27–36, 40–22:1); in challenging the centurion who was about to flog him (22:25); in speaking to the Sanhedrin and even causing them to argue among themselves (23:1–11); in ordering a centurion, while he, Paul, was in jail, to take a young man (his own nephew) to the commander (*chiliarchon*, a leader of about six hundred soldiers; 23:17); in defending himself in Caesarea before Governor Felix and his Jewish accusers (24:10–21); before Governor Festus (25:7–11)[29] two years later (24:27) and before King Agrippa, his sister Bernice, and Festus (26:1–29); in warning the crewmen on the ship to Rome that they would face difficulties on the voyage (27:10); in urging them to take courage in the storm (27:21–26) and encouraging the crew and passengers to eat (27:31–35);[30] in confronting Peter in his hypocritical actions (Gal. 2:11–13); and in speak-

27. J. Oswald Sanders, *Paul the Leader* (Colorado Springs: NavPress, 1984), 39.

28. The word *atenizō*, "to look intently or to gaze," is also used of Peter and John (Acts 3:4), who looked straight at a crippled man in Jerusalem.

29. Porcius Festus was Roman procurator of Judea from A.D. 58 to 62.

30. Amazingly, "the apostolic prisoner commanded the captain!" (Sanders, *Paul the Leader*, 40).

ing forthrightly to the Galatians ("You foolish Galatians!" 3:1; "Mark
my words!" 5:2). He also spoke to the Corinthians about being bold
(*tharreō*, "to be courageous or confident") with them (2 Cor. 10:1–2).

Another evidence of the apostle's implacable valor is seen in the
many commands he issued to his readers. (See appendix B for a listing
of these commands.)

Such intrepid staunchness on the part of this courageous prisoner
emanated from his confidence in the Lord, who lived in him (Gal. 2:20)
and for whom he, Paul, lived (2:19; cf. 2 Cor. 5:15).

Integrity

In the last several years a number of prominent Christian leaders have
been found guilty of immorality or other heinous sins. How dishearten-
ing to learn that some who teach others God's ways fail to follow his
ways themselves! To teach one way but live another discredits the gospel, resulting in unbelievers making a mockery of Christianity.

Was this kind of deleterious hypocrisy ever true of Paul? Indeed not!
He was through and through a man of integrity, one whose life matched
his words, a person of honesty, a man who not only spoke the truth but
also lived it with unsullied, unabated consistency. His life was never
marred by pretense, pretending to be one thing but actually being another. Paul set a high example of integrity, honesty, and consistency,
showing that such a life is indeed possible.

Teachers today do well to note what this authentic apostle said about
his life—and then with the help of God's Spirit to emulate that pattern
of genuine, consistent living. This is so important that failure to do so
may well cause students to reject the truth teachers seek to teach.

Negatively, Paul wrote that he harbored no impure motives: "For the
appeal we make does not spring from error or impure motives, nor are
we trying to trick you" (1 Thess. 2:3). Nor did he use deception (2 Cor.
4:2) or flattery (1 Thess 2:5), or seek to please people (Gal. 1:10; 1 Thess
2:4), or engage in the ministry out of greed or for personal gain (2 Cor.
2:17).[31] Neither was he guilty of lying: "God . . . knows that I am not lying" (2 Cor. 11:31); "I am telling the truth, I am not lying" (1 Tim. 2:7);
or exploiting others for his own aggrandizement (2 Cor. 7:2). Luke re-

---

31. "He refused amenities to which he believed he was rightfully entitled because he
did not want to be accused of preaching for the money. Wandering sophists, willing to
speak on any subject or represent any cause for money, had been a part of Greco-Roman
culture" (Raymond Bailey, *Paul the Preacher* [Nashville: Broadman, 1991], 77).

ported that Paul told the Ephesian elders he had never coveted others' possessions (Acts 20:33).

Positively, he affirmed the sincerity of his speech: "In Christ we speak before God with sincerity [*eilikrineia*],[32] like men sent from God" (2 Cor. 2:17). What he said was always truthful. "I speak the truth in Christ—I am not lying" (Rom. 9:1; cf. Gal. 4:16); "Everything we said to you was true," he affirmed to the believers in Corinth (2 Cor. 7:14). "The truth of Christ is in me" (11:10). "Truthful speech" was one of the qualities that enabled Paul to endure hardships for Christ (6:7).

He also vouched for the sincerity of his conduct: We have contented ourselves . . . "in the holiness and sincerity [*eilikrineia*] that are from God" (2 Cor. 1:12). "We have wronged no one, we have corrupted no one, we have exploited no one" (7:2). "For we are taking pains to do what is right, not only in the eyes of the Lord but also in the eyes of men" (8:21). And he reminded the Thessalonians that they knew of his "holy, righteous, and blameless" life (1 Thess. 2:10). So open and consistent was Paul that he told the elders of Ephesus, "You know how I lived the whole time I was with you" (Acts 20:18; cf. vv. 33–34), and he wrote to Timothy, "You, however, know all about my . . . way of life" (2 Tim. 3:10). His conduct always aligned perfectly with what he taught, as Timothy, his co-worker, well knew: "He will remind you of my way of life in Christ Jesus, which agrees with what I teach everywhere in every church" (1 Cor. 4:17).

The apostle's genuineness meant he could even call on God to attest to his upright conduct. Five times he affirmed that God was his witness and knew of his life (Rom. 1:9; 2 Cor. 1:23; 5:11; 1 Thess. 2:5, 10; cf. Phil. 1:8).

As a person of flawless honesty, Paul never pretended to be something he was not. He admitted his inadequacies, including his conflict with sin (Rom. 7:15–20); his weakness, fear, and trembling before the Corinthians (1 Cor. 2:3); his dependence on Christ's power (2 Cor. 12:9; cf. 11:30) because of his weakness (13:4); and the fact that he still needed to progress spiritually (Phil. 3:12–13).

As I wrote elsewhere,

> One of the quickest ways to discourage learners from living out the Word of God is inconsistency. Instructing students in the way to live, but not living that way ourselves, bottlenecks learning. When students see that we are not "practicing what we teach" (as Jesus accused the Pharisees, Matt. 23:3), they lose

32. In its etymology *eilikrineia* means "judged by the sun." Paul's speech was so honest it was like being exposed to the penetrating rays of the sun. This word is also used in 2 Corinthians 1:12.

confidence in us, in the Bible, and in the Lord. When we lead lives of integrity in modeling the truths we teach, our students are encouraged to develop similar qualities in themselves. Exemplifying the truth reinforces what we teach, added to the impact of our words. [33]

Paul, like Jesus, demonstrated full harmony between his life and his teachings. For example, he urged his readers to be humble (Rom. 12:3, 16; Eph. 4:2; Phil. 2:3–4)—and he was (Eph. 3:8; 1 Tim. 1:15). He challenged others to be filled with the Holy Spirit (Eph. 5:18)—and he was (Acts 9:17; 13:9). He advised Timothy not to be ashamed of the gospel (2 Tim. 1:8)—and he wasn't (Rom. 1:16; 2 Tim. 1:12). He prompted Philemon to share his faith (Philem. 6)—and Paul did (1 Thess. 1:5; 2:2). He instructed believers to "serve [*douleuō*, 'to serve as a slave'] one another" (Gal. 5:13)—and he did (2 Cor. 4:5).

What he asked others to do, he himself carried out. "With all his high demands Paul asked no more commitment than he himself gave. . . ."[34] His many appeals "would have been instantly self-defeating had his own character belied them."[35] The same is true of teachers today.

Humility

If anyone had reason to be proud or to boast, Paul certainly did. His educational background exceeded that of most of those to whom he ministered.[36] He had seen the resurrected Lord. He was commissioned by God as a specially called apostolic delegate. He was used by God to lead many people to Christ, to plant numerous churches, and to disciple hundreds of believers in Christian doctrine and living. He was unflagging in his zeal for the Lord and unfaltering in spite of severe opposition and personal hardships.

Yet he was one of God's most humble servants. In following the example of Christ (1 Cor. 11:1), he demonstrated the same humility Christ had (Phil. 2:5–8). When people in Lystra began worshiping Barnabas and Paul, calling him Hermes, the Greek messenger god, he urged them

---

33. Roy B. Zuck, *Teaching as Jesus Taught* (Grand Rapids: Baker, 1995), 67–68.
34. Reginald White, *Meet St. Paul* (Wilton, Conn.: Morehouse, 1989), 34.
35. Ibid.
36. "Highly educated, he did his work among people who never went to school. His converts were with few exceptions from the uncultivated classes, peasants, small shopkeepers, slaves. Even in Corinth, the Church was made up for the most part of humble folk" (Charles Edward Jefferson, *The Character of Paul* [New York: Macmillan, 1927], 143–44).

to spurn such actions, shouting, "We too are only men, human like you" (Acts 14:15).

That was on his first missionary journey. Then on his third journey, as he was saying farewell to the Ephesian elders, he avowed that he "served the Lord with great humility and tears" (20:19). To the Corinthians he made it plain that he was not promoting himself ("Was Paul crucified for you?" 1 Cor. 1:13), because though like a farmer he planted seed, it was God who made the seed grow (3:6). As he explained, "neither he who plants nor he who waters is anything" (3:7). Nor did he "preach" himself (2 Cor. 4:5) because he was like a valueless clay jar in which God had "placed" the priceless gospel of salvation through Christ (4:7).[37]

Boasting, then, was totally out of place in Paul's life. He insisted, "I cannot boast," and "I will not boast about myself" (1 Cor. 9:16; 2 Cor. 12:5; cf. 2 Cor. 10:13, 15). In fact, a "thorn in the flesh," he explained, kept him "from being conceited" (*hyperairomai*, "to exalt oneself," a word used only three times—twice in 2 Cor. 12:7 and once in 2 Thess. 2:4). In referring often to his inner feelings as he wrote 2 Corinthians, Paul also referred to his being humble (*tapeinos*, 2 Cor. 10:1 NIV, "timid") and making himself low or humble (11:7).

The least of the apostles (1 Cor. 15:9) and the worst of sinners (1 Tim. 1:15) are two ways the apostle described his humble position. When he wrote that he was "less than the least of all God's people" (Eph. 3:8), he used a strange word, *elachistoteros*, a comparative piled on top of a superlative,[38] thereby suggesting deep self-abasement.

Paul also signaled his humility by referring to himself as a slave (*doulos*) of Christ (Rom. 1:1; Gal. 1:10; Phil. 1:1), of God (Titus 1:1), and of the saints (2 Cor. 4:5)—one who served (*douleō*) the Lord humbly like his slave (Acts 20:19). Just as Jesus said he was "among you as one who serves" (Luke 22:27), so Paul spoke of his serving the saints (Rom. 15:25). "To serve" in these two verses translates *diakoneō*, which refers to carrying out "undone activities, such as waiting on tables or caring for household needs—activities without apparent dignity."[39] To the Greeks, such lowly, undignified work was disdained. With their love for wisdom and freedom they had little appreciation for servants.[40] Yet ser-

---

37. In the ancient world, treasures were stored in earthen jars (Plummer, *A Critical and Exegetical Commentary on the Second Epistle of St Paul to the Corinthians*, 126).

38. Ronald Coggan, *Paul: Portrait of a Revolutionary* (London: Hodder and Stoughton, 1984), 235, n. 39. In 1 Corinthians 15:9 the word "least" is the superlative *elachistos*.

39. J. Gary Inrig, "Called to Serve: Toward a Philosophy of Ministry," *Bibliotheca Sacra* 140 (October–December 1983): 336.

40. K. Hess, "Serve, Deacon, Worship," in *New International Dictionary of New Testament Theology*, 3:545; and H. W. Beyer, "διακονέω, διακονία, διάκονος," in *Theological Dictionary of the New Testament*, 2 (1964), 82–83.

vanthood is to be a salient mark of Jesus' followers. Paul spoke of his service *(diakonia)* for Christ (1 Tim. 1:12) and for Christians (2 Cor. 9:1; 11:8), and he denoted himself as a servant *(diakonos,* 1 Cor. 3:5) of Christ (2 Cor. 11:23), of God (6:4), of the new covenant (3:5), of the gospel (Eph. 3:7; Col. 1:23), and of the church (Col. 1:25).

As discussed in chapter 3, the apostle twice called himself a *hypēretēs,* "a helper" (Acts 26:16; 1 Cor. 4:1). He also spoke of his serving God in the sense of carrying out his religious duty *(latreuō,* Acts 27:23; Rom. 1:9; 2 Tim. 1:3).

Not surprisingly, this humble, self-abased, spiritual slave/servant/ helper urged others to be humble (Eph. 4:2; Phil. 2:3–4; Col. 3:12). Boasting and pride are to have no place in a believer's life (Rom. 12:3, 16; 1 Cor. 3:21; 4:7; 13:4) because "boasting is not good" (5:6). Any boasting is to be in the Lord, not oneself (1:29, 31; 2 Cor. 10:17).

Teaching is serving, humbly pointing others not to oneself but to the Lord. Students do not respect teachers who exalt themselves, boast of their accomplishments, or proudly display their knowledge. Pride, in fact, obstructs learning; refusing to assume the role of a servant before one's students aborts the learning process. So as Paul admonished, we are to "clothe" *(endyō)* ourselves with humility (Col. 3:12), that is, to be so endowed with absence of pride that others readily see our humility as if it were our clothing.

Courtesy

Another striking feature of Paul's character is his gracious, courteous attitude toward others. In his speeches in Acts he showed himself a true gentleman, as seen in the way he addressed his audiences. In Pisidian Antioch he referred to the Jews as "brothers," that is, he was related to them racially (Acts 13:26). On Mars' Hill he began his message to the philosophically minded Athenians by the commendatory words, "Men of Athens! I see that in every way you are very religious" (17:22).[41] Arrested by a Jewish mob in Jerusalem he calmly and kindly asked the commander, "Please let me speak to the people" (21:39). Then, beginning his defense to the Jews, he courteously addressed them as "brothers and fathers" (22:1). About to be flogged, he did not yell at or revile the centurion; he simply asked a penetrating question that jolted the centurion (22:25–26). He called the Sanhedrin his "brothers" (23:1, 5–6), twice he addressed Agrippa courteously by his

41. "His address in Athens is a model of courteous speech" (Jefferson, *The Character of Paul,* 190).

title "King Agrippa" (26:2, 27), and he called Festus "most excellent Festus" (26:25). Christians are "brothers" in the sense that they are children born of God and, being spiritually related, they are equal in God's sight. Luke often used this word when referring to Christians, including those in Asia Minor (Acts 15:36, 40), Lystra and Iconium (16:2), Philippi (16:40), Thessalonica (17:10), Berea (17:14), Corinth (18:10, 27), Ptolemais, south of Tyre (21:7), Jerusalem (21:17), Damascus (22:5), and Puteoli, Italy (28:14).

In addition, Paul referred to each of seven individuals as his brother: Quartus (Rom. 16:23), Sosthenes (1 Cor. 1:1), Timothy (2 Cor. 1:1, Col. 1:1; 1 Thess. 3:2; Philem. 1), Titus (2 Cor. 2:13; 8:22), Tychicus (Eph. 6:21; Col. 4:7), Epaphroditus (Phil. 2:25), and Onesimus (Col. 4:9; Philem. 16). Scores of times, in seven of his epistles, he addressed his Christian readers as brothers: in Romans, 1 and 2 Corinthians, Galatians, Philippians, and 1 and 2 Thessalonians.

How thoughtful of the apostle to commend believers for their spiritual progress. He applauded the Corinthians' enrichment by God's grace (1 Cor. 1:4–5); their excelling in several spiritual virtues (2 Cor. 8:7); their eagerness to help other believers materially (9:2); the Ephesians' and the Colossians' faith in the Lord and love for other saints (Eph. 1:15–16; Col. 1:4–5); the Philippians' partnership with Paul in the gospel (Phil. 1:5); the Colossians' orderliness and firm faith (Col. 2:5); and the Thessalonians' work, faith, love, endurance, hope, and witnessing (1 Thess. 1:3, 8; 4:10).

Again Paul modeled for all teachers one of the most essential qualities for effective communication. Competent teachers, being concerned for their students, are kind, gracious, and considerate, never discourteous, blunt, or tactless. They listen carefully to students' needs, questions, and concerns, giving thoughtful consideration to ways they can help them. Capable teachers view their Christian students as their equals, as their brothers and sisters in Christ.

Sensitivity

You can hardly read Paul's letters without noting his constant emphasis on love and his repeated expressions of affectionate concern for others. This recurring theme of the great apostle stands in astounding contrast to his preconversion days. The man who once condemned men to death without wincing[42] was now the one who expressed his deep love and warm affection for believers and unbelievers alike. The one who

42. Ibid., 224.

once murdered Christians was now the one who loved them and encouraged them to love each other. The one whose heart was hard set against people who professed faith in Christ was now the one whose heart was soft, tender, sensitive, and loving. The one who hated Christians was now the one who wrote some of the world's best statements about love in 1 Corinthians 13:1–7, 13.

If Paul were not a man of heartfelt sensitivity, genuine compassion, and tender love, his teaching would have fallen on deaf ears. Instructors who love their students, and whose students know it, communicate with far greater impact than those whose love is lacking or is not readily detected.

Several features display Paul's sensitive, tenderhearted affection for others. One is his shedding of tears. He told the elders of Ephesus, "I served the Lord with great humility and with tears" (Acts 20:19). He reminded the Corinthians that he had written them "out of great distress and anguish of heart and with many tears" (2 Cor. 2:4). And as he wrote to the Philippians, he voiced with tears his concern that many people opposed the message of Christ's death as its "enemies" (Phil. 3:18). Many people today feel it is inappropriate for a man to shed tears, but for Paul there was no conflict between his being a courageous, strong leader and a sensitive, warm friend.

A second way in which Paul's compassion shows itself is his forthright statements about his love, seen in these verses:

> I am writing "to warn you, as my dear children" (1 Cor. 4:14).
> "You know the depth of my love for you" (2 Cor. 2:4).
> "We have . . . opened wide our hearts to you" (2 Cor. 6:11).
> "We are not withholding our affection[43] from you" (2 Cor. 6:12).
> "I speak as to my children" (2 Cor. 6:13).
> "You have such a place in our hearts that we would live or die with you" (2 Cor. 7:3).
> "I have you in my heart" (Phil. 1:7).
> "God can testify how I long for all of you with the affection of Christ Jesus" (Phil. 1:8).
> "You had become so dear to us" (1 Thess. 2:8).

43. "Affection" in 2 Corinthians 6:12 and Philippians 1:8 renders *splanchnois*, literally, inner body parts, which were believed to be the seat of feeling or "deep compassion" (Helmut Koster, "σπλάγχνον *ktl.*," in *Theological Dictionary of the New Testament,* 7 [1971], 548–59). Elsewhere the NIV translates it "affection" (2 Cor. 7:15), "compassion" (Phil. 2:1), "hearts" (Philem. 7), and "heart" (Philem. 12, 20). The Gospels often use the related verb *splanchnizomai* in reference to Jesus (Matt. 9:36; 14:14; 20:34; Mark 1:41; 6:34; 8:2; Luke 7:13). This verb occurs only in the Gospels and the noun occurs most often, though not exclusively, in Paul's epistles.

"We loved[44] you so much" (1 Thess. 2:8).

"When we were torn away[45] from you for a short time . . . out of our intense longing we made every effort to see you" (1 Thess. 2:17).

Onesimus "is my very heart" (Philem. 12).

The great pedagogue also wrote of his "sincere love" (2 Cor. 6:6) and his overflowing love for the Thessalonians (1 Thess. 3:12). So strong was his love for the believers of Thessalonica that he said he was "like a mother caring for her little children" and like a father who "deals with his own children, encouraging, comforting, and urging" them (2:7, 11–12). The word "mother" translates not the normal word for mother, but *trophos,* a nursing mother, or wet nurse (used only here in the New Testament), who warms and cherishes *(thalpō)* her children. "The gentleness and unselfishness of Paul as a spiritual parent shines through in this illustration."[46] He also said his leading others to Christ was like becoming their father ("I became your father through the gospel," 1 Cor. 4:15). And like a father caring for his spiritual children he did not want to be a burden to them (2 Cor. 12:14–15). He told the Philippians they were his brothers whom he loved and longed for (Phil. 4:1).

Third, Paul's sensitivity is apparent from his expressions of joy over his convert-students. "I am full of joy over you," he exclaimed to the Romans (Rom. 16:19). While absent from those in Corinth and Colossae he wrote, "I am with you in spirit" (1 Cor. 5:3–4; Col. 2:5). He informed the Corinthians he knew they "would all share my joy" (2 Cor. 2:3), and "my joy knows no bounds" (7:4).

A fourth sign of Paul's sensitive soul was his grieving over believers who had sinned ("stop sinning," he exhorted; 1 Cor. 15:34). He was troubled that Hymenaeus and Alexander, blasphemers, had "shipwrecked their faith" (1 Tim. 1:19–20) and that Phygelus, Hermogenes, and Demas had deserted him (2 Tim. 1:15; 4:10). He showed his heart concern in writing to the Corinthians, "Who is led into sin, and I do not inwardly burn?" (2 Cor. 11:29). To burn inwardly probably does not mean burn with anger, but rather with shame, distress, and remorse. By adding the emphatic Greek word for "I," Paul stressed his

---

44. The unusual rare Greek verb here for love, used only here in the New Testament, is *homeiromenoi,* "to feel kindly toward or to long for someone." A grave inscription in Lycaonia (in south-central Asia Minor) includes the adjective *homeiromenoi* in the parents' sorrowing for and longing for their son (W. M. Ramsay, "The Utilisation of Old Epigraphic Copies," *Journal of Hellenistic Studies* 38 [1918]: 157).

45. "Torn away" translates a strong verb *aporphanizō,* "to be orphaned."

46. Thomas L. Constable, "1 Thessalonians," in *The Bible Knowledge Commentary, New Testament,* 694.

own grief: "Who is entrapped into sin and my heart is not ablaze with pain?"[47]

Fifth, the endearing terms by which Paul addressed a number of his coworkers also speaks of his love, friendship, and concern. These terms are shown in table 8.

Table 8
Paul's Terms of Endearment for His Coworkers

My son: Timothy, Onesimus
My dear (lit., "true") son: Timothy, Titus
My/our brother: Timothy, Titus, Epaphroditus, Quartus, Onesimus
Beloved *(agapētos)*:[48] Timothy, Luke, Philemon, Epenetus, Ampliatus, Stachys,
    Persis
Beloved brother *(agapētos adelphos)*: Timothy, Philemon, Tychicus, Onesimus
Beloved son *(agapētos teknon)*: Timothy
Fellow worker: Timothy, Titus, Aquila, Priscilla, Mark, Aristarchus, Demas,
    Luke, Epaphroditus, Philemon
Fellow soldier: Epaphroditus, Aristarchus, Archippus
Fellow prisoner: Aristarchus, Epaphroditus, Epaphras
Fellow servant: Epaphras, Tychicus
Faithful servant: Tychicus
My partner: Titus
Servant: Timothy, Epaphras

Obviously, these eighteen individuals meant much to Paul. It is interesting to note in the chart that several were referred to by a number of different terms. For example, Paul called Timothy "my son" (1 Tim. 1:18; 2 Tim. 2:1), "my dear son" (2 Tim. 1:2), "our brother" (2 Cor. 1:1; Col. 1:1; 1 Thess 3:2; Philem. 1), "beloved son" (1 Cor. 4:17; 2 Tim. 2:1), "fellow worker" (1 Thess. 3:2), and "servant" (Phil. 1:1). Titus is called "my true son" (Titus 1:4), "my brother" (2 Cor. 2:13), "fellow worker" (2 Cor. 8:23), and "my partner" (2 Cor. 8:23). To identify the verses where others are called by various terms, look up these references: Romans 16:5, 8, 9, 12; Ephesians 6:21; Philippians 2:25; Colossians 1:7; 4:7, 9, 10, 14; Philemon 1, 2, 10, 16, 23.

Other times Paul called entire church assemblies "friends," "dear friends" *(agapētoi)*, "brothers" *(adelphoi)*, or "dear brothers" (*adelphoi agapētoi;* Rom. 12:19; 1 Cor. 10:14; 15:58; 2 Cor. 7:1; 8:1; 12:19; Phil. 2:12; 4:1; cf. 1 Thess. 2:8, "you had become so dear [*agapētoi*] to us"), or

---

47. Plummer, *A Critical and Exegetical Commentary on the Second Epistle of St. Paul to the Corinthians,* 331.
48. The NIV usually renders *agapētos* "dear friend," and *agapēos adelphos* "dear brother."

"dear children" (*tekna agapēta;* 1 Cor. 4:14; Eph. 5:1), or "my dear children" (*tekna mou,* Gal. 4:19).

The apostle's fondness for Timothy may stem from his having been led to the Lord by Paul, since he called Timothy "my true son in the faith" (1 Tim. 1:2). On the other hand, perhaps the young man's mother Eunice and grandmother Lois led him to the Lord (2 Tim. 1:5). In the Lord's work Paul viewed Timothy as a son serving with his father (Phil. 2:22).

A sixth mark of Paul's sensitivity and kind heart is his longing to see his friends and coworkers when they were away from him. He was waiting for Timothy to come to him in Macedonia from Corinth (1 Cor. 16:11), and Titus's coming to him was a comfort (2 Cor. 7:6). When he was alone in Athens (1 Thess. 3:1), he wanted Silas and Timothy to join him from Berea "as soon as possible" (Acts 17:15). When Paul was in Nicopolis in Greece he asked Titus to join him there (Titus 3:12), and later when the apostle was imprisoned in Rome, he asked Timothy to come see him quickly (2 Tim. 4:9) because he said, "I long to see you" (1:4). Earlier in his ministry Paul longed to go see several congregations to whom he had earlier ministered, including the Thessalonians (1 Thess. 2:17–18), and the Philippians (Phil. 1:8). When he wrote to the Christians in Rome, he expressed his desire to travel there to see them (Rom. 1:10–11; 15:31–32)—people whom he had not yet met. And even when he was imprisoned, he anticipated being released so he could visit the Philippian believers (Phil. 2:24).

To receive good news from the churches about their spiritual progress always heartened Paul. Timothy brought him encouraging news from Thessalonica (1 Thess. 3:6–10), and he hoped to send Timothy to Philippi (Phil. 2:19, 23).

Paul also wanted to be encouraged by having Philemon receive back his slave Onesimus, whom the apostle had led to the Lord in Rome (Philem. 10–15). Onesimus had become "a dear brother" (*adelphon agapēton*) to Paul (Philem. 16). By receiving the born-again slave as a spiritual brother, Philemon would "refresh [Paul's] heart in Christ" (Philem. 20).

A seventh token of the apostle's tender heart is his concern for his coworkers in their illnesses. These include Epaphroditus, who almost died from his sickness (Phil. 2:26–30), Timothy (1 Tim. 5:23), and Trophimus (an Ephesian, Acts 21:29), whom Paul had to leave sick in Miletus (2 Tim. 4:20).

An eighth clue to the apostle's compassionate soul is his longing for the unsaved to come to Christ. These included not only Gentiles but also his own people, the Jews, whose spiritual lostness gave him "great sorrow and unceasing anguish" of heart (Rom. 9:2; 10:1). He felt inwardly compelled to continue sharing the good news of salvation in Christ (1 Cor. 9:16; 2 Cor. 5:11).

Ninth, Paul showed concern for the churches he had planted and the congregations he established. After his and Barnabas's first missionary journey into Asia Minor, they retraced their steps to Lystra, Iconium, and Antioch and encouraged and strengthened the churches (Acts 14:21–22). This no doubt meant that the two leaders engaged in a teaching ministry. When Paul and Barnabas had a sharp disagreement over Mark, Paul took Silas with him and they went through Syria and Cilicia, the region where Tarsus (Paul's birthplace) is located, to strengthen the churches there (15:39–41). Along with the varied kinds of persecution and hardship he experienced, he also carried the burden of his "concern for all the churches" (2 Cor. 11:28). This undaunting dedication to his work reveals Paul's heart of compassion toward his disciples. His heart for them is also seen in his mention of love in at least two of his benedictions: "My love to all of you" (1 Cor. 16:24), and "Peace to the brothers, and love with faith from God the Father and the Lord Jesus Christ" (Eph. 6:23).

A tenth indication of his warm relationship with his disciple-learners is that he felt free to ask them to pray for him. This request is mentioned in at least five of his epistles (Rom. 15:30–31; Eph. 6:19–20; Col. 4:3–4; 1 Thess. 5:25; 2 Thess 3:1–2).

An eleventh point to note is that Paul's church congregations expressed their love to him. Being fully aware of his love for them, they willingly reciprocated by extending their compassion to him. For example, in their letter stating the decision of the Jerusalem Council regarding circumcision, the church leaders referred to "our dear friends Barnabas and Paul" (Acts 15:25). At Miletus, after Paul gave his farewell speech to the elders of the Ephesian church, they prayed together and in a show of affection "they all wept as they embraced him and kissed him" (20:36). That must have been a moving moment as they realized they would never see their beloved friend-pastor-teacher again.

The Galatian believers welcomed Paul as if he were an angel or even Christ himself, and, if possible, they would have even torn out their eyes and given them to Paul because of his illness (Gal. 4:14–15). Some scholars feel this statement about their eyes suggests that Paul's ailment was failing eyesight.

Aquila and Priscilla's love for their friend Paul was so deep and genuine that Paul wrote that this husband-wife team risked their lives for him (Rom. 16:4). Though the circumstances of this sacrificial act are not known, obviously they loved their fellow tentmaker.

Paul expressed delight that the Corinthians had an "ardent concern" for him (2 Cor. 7:7) and excelled in their love for him (8:7).

On his way to Jerusalem, at the conclusion of his third missionary journey, Paul stayed for a week with believers in Tyre. When he left, they all accompanied him to the beach where he was to board a ship, and they prayed with him there and bade him farewell (Acts 21:3–6). Arriving in Jerusalem, he was "cordially" welcomed by Christians there (21:17).

Wherever he went, Paul had friends who loved him and were concerned about him. When Felix held Paul over in Caesarea, the governor allowed friends to visit him and provide for his needs (24:23). The same occurred when Paul landed at Sidon (27:3).

Paul also had friends on the island of Crete because when he wrote to Titus on that island (Titus 1:5), he instructed Titus to "greet those who love us" (3:15).

Because of his strong commitment to the supremacy of love (1 Cor. 13:13), the apostle often urged Christians to love each other—and he recorded these commands in every one of his epistles![49]

Teachers do well to follow Paul's grand model of intense sensitivity to the needs of others, heartfelt burden for the unsaved, warm concern for his learners, and open expressions of love and compassion for believers in various locations.

To Think About . . .

Do you constantly give attention to your spiritual life, seeking to be a model of Christ-centeredness, prayer, heartfelt worship, dependence on the Holy Spirit, confidence in the Lord, and a clear conscience?

Do you teach with a sense of authority and boldness, not from yourself but from the Bible content you seek to convey?

Do you endeavor with the Holy Spirit's help to lead a life of consistency, sincerity, and integrity?

---

49. Romans 12:9–10; 13:8–10; 1 Corinthians 8:1; 13:1–4, 6, 8, 13; 16:14; 2 Corinthians 6:13; 8:24; Galatians 5:13–14, 22; Ephesians 4:2, 15; 5:2; Philippians 1:9; 2:2; Colossians 2:2; 3:14; 1 Thessalonians 3:12; 4:10; 5:18; 2 Thessalonians 3:5; 1 Timothy 4:12; 6:11; 2 Timothy 2:22; Titus 2:2; Philemon 9.

Are you careful to avoid pride, recognizing your humble position before the Lord?

Are you courteous, considerate, and tactful with your students?

In which ways do you seek to communicate compassion toward your students and sensitivity to their needs?

*"We are hard pressed on every side,
but not crushed."*

2 Corinthians 4:8

6

What Other Qualities Marked Paul as an Outstanding Teacher?

In the previous chapter we considered six qualities that marked Paul's teaching. Now we will examine six additional features that show us Paul was a remarkable teacher.

Fervency

Few servants of Christ have exhibited the driving zeal and limitless energy seen in the apostle Paul. Just as he excelled in fervor before his conversion in doggedly tracking down and imprisoning Christians, so he was unstoppable in his relentless passion for Christ. As he told the Romans, he served God with his "whole heart" (lit., "in my spirit," Rom. 1:9). An inner driving force—the person of the indwelling Holy Spirit—made him "eager"[1] to share the good news of Christ (1:15). In writing

---

1. The adjective *prothymos*, "eager, willing," occurs only in Romans 1:15 in the New Testament, though the related noun *prothymia*, "eagerness," occurs five times (Acts 17:11; 2 Cor. 8:11–12, 19; 9:2). Both words are emotion-laden.

of his undaunted "ambition" to preach Christ (15:20) and to please Christ (2 Cor. 5:9), Paul used a word that means to devote oneself zealously to a cause, to consider one's commitment to the cause an honor. In fact, he felt "compelled" to share the Good News (1 Cor. 9:16), knowing that if he neglected this responsibility he would be under distress ("woe to me"). He likened his determination to that of a debtor: he "owed" others the truth (Rom. 1:14), including "Greeks and non-Greeks" (*barbaros*, "one who does not speak Greek properly, an uncultured person") and the wise and unwise (*anoētos*, "ignorant").

The apostle's dynamic intensity led to his working hard, as he wrote several times. "I worked harder than all of them" (1 Cor. 15:10), that is, harder than the other apostles. This was not a proud boast; it was simply reporting a fact. "He traveled more, suffered more opposition, wrote more New Testament epistles, and founded more churches"[2] than the others, but yet he did so not in his own strength or for his own acclaim, but by the grace of God (15:10). He affirmed the same fact in 2 Corinthians 11:23 ("I have worked much harder"), and to achieve his goal of bringing others to maturity in Christ he said "I labor" (*kopiaō*, "to work hard, to toil to the point of exhaustion," Col. 1:29). His devotion to Christ and to his convert-learners led him to tell the Corinthians that he would gladly "spend for you everything I have" and to be completely spent for them (2 Cor. 12:15), like parents spending money on their children (v. 14).[3] Similarly, he told the Thessalonian believers he delighted in sharing with them not only biblical content but also "our lives as well" (1 Thess. 2:8). Desiring the Galatians to become like Christ, this apostolic leader suffered pain like that of a mother's pains in childbirth (Gal. 4:19). Zealous for their spiritual development and concerned that they not be influenced by false teachers, Paul experienced intense inner agony on their behalf. What resolute and impressive commitment to others!

Paul's ministry was no nine-to-five job. He worked "night and day," as he said four times (Acts 20:31; 26:7; 1 Thess. 2:9; 2 Thess. 3:8). In his untiring dedication he was even willing to risk his life for Christ as those at the Jerusalem Council knew (Acts 15:26) and as he told the Ephesians ("I consider my life worth nothing to me," 20:24). When his friends urged him not to go to Jerusalem, he rejected their advice and said he was "ready not only to be bound, but also to die" (21:13). He wanted Christ to be glorified through him, whether he lived or died (Phil. 1:23).

---

2. David K. Lowery, "1 Corinthians," in *The Bible Knowledge Commentary, New Testament*, ed. John F. Walvoord and Roy B. Zuck (Wheaton, Ill.: Victor, 1983), 543.

3. In 2 Corinthians 12:14–15 Paul used a related pair of words: *dapanaō*, "to spend," and *ekdapanaō*, "to be spent out."

He pictured his intrepid service for Christ as being like a race (Acts 20:24; 1 Cor. 9:24–26; 2 Tim. 4:7) and a fight (2 Tim. 4:7; cf. 1 Tim. 1:18; 6:12). A runner must keep going, whether tired or not; a boxer must "hang in there" with gusto even when he may feel like quitting.

This pioneer's vitality is also seen in the extent of his travels. Traveling overland and by sea, he may have covered about 6,200 miles in his three missionary trips and his journey to Rome and other minor excursions, thus becoming "perhaps the most traveled person within the NT world."[4]

He had no concern for fringe benefits. No health insurance or life insurance. No vacation time. No thought of "striking" for higher wages. No retirement to a rocking chair. Paul's energy and abandonment to Christ propelled him on with no consideration of the cost. In his burning zest for the Savior he possessed "a mind aflame with the truth of God, and a will fired with a passion for the glory of God."[5] "So swiftly did he move that his accomplishments leave us breathless."[6]

Yet all this immense energy and unusual stamina is remarkable when we consider his physical condition. He acknowledged that his opponents said that "his personal appearance is unimpressive" (2 Cor. 10:10 NASB). Some writers say this Greek phrase (lit., "the appearance of his body") refers to his character or attitude,[7] whereas others say it refers to his physical appearance,[8] which seems more likely. The second-century apocryphal Acts of Paul and Thecla includes the following description of the apostle: "a man of small stature, with a bald head and crooked legs, in a good state of body, with eyebrows meeting and nose somewhat crooked, full of friendliness."[9] In this legend, Onesiphorus, a

---

4. Larry J. Kreitzer, "Travel in the Roman World," in *Dictionary of Paul and His Letters*, ed. Gerald F. Hawthorne, Ralph P. Martin, and Daniel G. Reid (Downers Grove, Ill.: InterVarsity, 1993), 945. Ronald F. Hock suggests Paul may have traveled as much as 10,000 miles (*The Social Context of Paul's Ministry: Tentmaking and Apostleship* [Philadelphia: Fortress, 1980], 27).

5. J. Oswald Sanders, *Paul the Leader* (Colorado Springs: NavPress, 1981), 66.

6. James Stalker, *The Life of St. Paul* (New York: Revell, 1950), 5.

7. Giuseppe Ricciotti, *Paul the Apostle*, trans. Alba I. Zizzamia (Milwaukee: Bruce, 1952), 151–52; and Alfred Plummer, *A Critical and Exegetical Commentary on the Second Epistle of St. Paul to the Corinthians*, International Critical Commentary (Edinburgh: Clark, 1915), 282.

8. For example, Fritz Rienecker, *A Linguistic Key to the Greek New Testament*, ed. Cleon L. Rogers, Jr. (Grand Rapids: Zondervan, 1980), 487; Richard N. Longenecker, *The Ministry and Message of Paul* (Grand Rapids: Zondervan, 1971), 23; T. R. Glover, *Paul of Tarsus* (London: Student Christian Movement, 1925), 172–73; and Abraham J. Malherbe, "A Physical Description of Paul," *Harvard Theological Review* 79 (1986): 171.

9. Wilhelm Schneemelcher, ed., *New Testament Apocrypha*, trans. R. McL. Wilson (Louisville: Westminster/Knox, 1992), 2:239. This description was known to Tertullian (*On Baptism* 17) of the second century and to Jerome (*Lives of Illustrious Men* 7) of the fourth century.

resident of Iconium, waited with his wife and two children outside his city for Paul to arrive, and seeing the apostle coming, he described him in this way. Some say this description is unreliable,[10] whereas others assert that the description may rest on genuine recollections from an earlier day.[11] These features of a bald head, bowed legs, hooked nose, and meeting eyebrows were not regarded unfavorably in the ancient world.[12] And yet if Paul were short in height, he may have seemed unimpressive to the Corinthians.

In his rigorous schedule Paul carried some physical ailment, which he called "a thorn in my flesh" (2 Cor. 12:7). Writers have suggested a variety of views on the identity of this malady.[13] They include epilepsy,[14] ophthalmia,[15] stuttering or other speech impediment,[16] or malarial fever.[17] Other suggestions include hysteria, migraine headaches, severe sciatica, rheumatism, poor hearing, and leprosy.[18] One view that seems more favorable than the others is ophthalmia, some form of eye disease. This seems possible because he said the Galatians would have torn out their eyes for him (Gal. 4:15), a statement he made right after he referred twice to his "illness" (4:13–14). And in the same letter he referred to the "large letters" in which he wrote that epistle (6:11), possi-

---

10. Robert M. Grant, "The Description of Paul in the Acts of Paul and Thecla," *Vigilae Christianae* 36 (1982): 1–4; and John Bradner, "Paul's Physical Appearance according to Early Christian Literature and Iconography," *Hartford Quarterly* 7 (1967): 73.

11. Longenecker, *The Ministry and Message of Paul*, 23; Ricciotti, *Paul the Apostle*, 152–53; F. W. Farrar, *The Life and Work of St. Paul* (New York: Dutton, 1902; reprint, Klock & Klock, 1981), 2:628–29; and Richard J. Bauckham, "Apocryphal Pauline Literature," in *Dictionary of Paul and His Letters*, 36. Ricciotti cites descriptions of the apostle from the sixth, tenth, and fourteenth centuries, which also refer to Paul's short stature, baldness, and touching eyebrows (*Paul the Apostle*, 153).

12. Bauckham, "Apocryphal Pauline Literature," 36.

13. The view that Paul's thorn in the flesh was a physical problem stems from as early as Tertullian. Others, however, view the "thorn" as a personal enemy (e.g., Terrence Y. Mullins, "Paul's Thorn in the Flesh," *Journal of Biblical Literature* 76 [1976]: 299–303). This "persecution-by-opponents view was common in the early church, being proposed by Chrysostom, Eusebius, Hilary of Ambrose, Augustine, Theodore of Mopsustia, Theodoret, and Theophylact" (J. B. Lightfoot, *The Epistle of St. Paul to the Galatians* [1865; reprint, Grand Rapids: Zondervan, n.d.], 187).

14. Holsten, *Zum Evangelium des Paulus* (1980); Lightfoot, *The Epistle of St. Paul to the Galatians*, 186–91; and Dorothy E. Donley, "The Epilepsy of St. Paul," *Catholic Biblical Quarterly* 6 (1944): 358–59.

15. Farrar, *The Life and Work of St. Paul*, 1:652–61.

16. Edward A. Mangan, "Was Saint Paul an Invalid?" *Catholic Biblical Quarterly* 5 (1943): 68–72.

17. W. M. Ramsay, *St. Paul the Traveller and Roman Citizen* (London: Hodder and Stoughton, 1908), 94–97; and idem, *The Church in the Roman Empire before A.D. 70* (New York: Putnam's Sons, 1893), 63–64.

18. Graham H. Twelftree, "Healing, Illness," in *Dictionary of Paul and His Letters*, 379.

bly pointing to his poor eyesight, though this is not certain.[19] Some say the large letters were only for emphasis.

In spite of this handicap, whatever it was, he kept going, with remarkable drive, spirited and energetic in his dedicated zeal for Christ.

Tenacity

To be fervent and zealous is one thing. But to endure in that zeal in the face of difficult odds is another. Have you ever started out enthusiastically on some project and then got discouraged and quit because of problems along the way?

Perhaps many Christians face that weakness. But not Paul. He never let his trials lead him to consider throwing in the towel. He refused to resign simply because of problems. He persisted in his task of preaching and teaching even though he constantly confronted obstacles and hardships.

Like a long-distance runner—exhausted, thirsty, breathing hard, and muscles aching—Paul steadfastly endured in his work. Tenacity marked his life; endurance was his motto. Suffering, persecution, physical danger, criticism, illness, insults, open opposition to his teaching, mental anguish, even incarceration—Paul knew them all, and yet he never gave up or bailed out.

So extensive and frequent were Paul's sufferings in his three decades of ministry that he wrote, perhaps in hyperbole, that his life was endangered "every hour" (1 Cor. 15:30). In his epistles he spoke of affliction and suffering over sixty times, using words for "suffering" (*pathēma, paschō*[20]), "affliction" (*thlipsis, thlibō*), and "weakness" (*astheneia, astheneō*).[21] He suffered at the hands of Gentiles and false teachers (2 Cor. 11:26) and especially unbelieving Jews (Rom. 15:31; 2 Cor. 11:24, 26; Gal. 5:11; 1 Thess. 2:14–16).

A stunning prediction that suffering would suffuse Paul's entire ministry was given to Ananias in Damascus: "I will show him how much he must suffer for my name" (Acts 9:16). And that adversity began almost immediately. As soon as he began preaching in the synagogues, his Jew-

19. Donald K. Campbell, "Galatians," in *The Bible Knowledge Commentary, New Testament*, 610.

20. *Pathēma* ("suffering") occurs in Romans 8:18; 2 Corinthians 1:5–7; Galatians 5:24; Philippians 3:10; Colossians 1:24; and 2 Timothy 3:11; and *paschō* ("to suffer") is in 1 Corinthians 12:26; 2 Corinthians 1:6; Galatians 3:4; Philippians 1:29; 1 Thessalonians 2:14; 2 Thessalonians 1:5; and 2 Timothy 1:12.

21. S. J. Hafemann, "Suffering," in *Dictionary of Paul and His Letters*, 919.

ish hearers suspected him of being a spy (9:20–21). Then "after many days"[22] Jews in Damascus planned to kill him (9:23), so he escaped by being lowered over the city wall in a basket (9:25). This was the first of many such efforts to eliminate the new apostle, attempts that resulted in his often being "on the run."

When Hellenistic Jews with whom he debated in Jerusalem tried to kill him, his friends sent him to Tarsus, his hometown (9:30). On the apostle's first missionary journey, Elymas, the sorcerer on the island of Cyprus, opposed Paul's work (13:8). In Antioch of Pisidia Jews spoke against Paul (13:45) and chased him out of town (13:50). Jews in Iconium spoke to the Gentiles against Paul (14:2) and when they planned to stone him, he fled to Lystra and Derbe (14:5–6). Then in Derbe Jews "won the crowd over [and] stoned Paul and dragged him outside the city" (14:19).

On his second missionary journey, when he first entered Europe, Paul was falsely accused, flogged, and imprisoned in Philippi (16:19–24). After his miraculous release, he went to Thessalonica and even there Jews started a riot, based on false accusations, in an effort to capture Paul (17:5–9). Paul escaped to Berea and again Thessalonian Jews agitated the crowds (17:13). In Athens some listeners sneered at him (17:32). Paul went from Athens to Corinth, where again Jews abused the apostle (18:6) and attacked him and took him to court, again with false accusations (18:12–13).

From Corinth Paul went to Ephesus and even there Jews "publicly maligned the Way" (19:9).[23] Opposition also came from silversmith Demetrius, who led his coworkers to start a citywide riot against Paul (19:23–41). Once again the Jews plotted against him when he returned to Greece (20:3).

When Paul arrived in Jerusalem, Jews from the province of Asia (present-day western Turkey) saw him there and, like other Jews on previous occasions, stirred up the city and tried to kill the apostle (21:27–31). After he gave his daring defense speech to the mob, they still wanted him dead (22:22–23). Cleverly playing on the differences of belief in the Sanhedrin led to such violent dispute "that the commander was afraid Paul would be torn to pieces by them" (23:10).

Still the Jews did not give up. In a conspiracy, forty men pledged their determination to kill him (23:12–15). Arrested, he was taken to Caesarea and there a lawyer brought charges against him before Gov-

22. This probably includes time in Arabia, which he referred to briefly in Galatians 1:17.
23. "The Way" is a term used only in the Book of Acts (9:2; 19:9, 23; 22:4; 24:14, 22), highlighting the uniqueness of Christianity.

ernor Felix (24:1–8) and, charging him with being a troublemaker and ringleader, "the Jews joined in the accusation" (24:9). Then in Jerusalem the apostle was accused by the Jewish religious leaders before Festus (25:2, 7; cf. v. 15). In testifying before King Agrippa, Paul explained "why the Jews seized" him and tried to kill him (26:21).

Almost everywhere he went—Damascus, Jerusalem, Antioch of Pisidia, Iconium, Lystra, Philippi, Thessalonica, Berea, Corinth, Ephesus, Caesarea—people were anxious to get rid of him because they did not like his message. And in most cities Jews were his opponents. Near the end of his life, looking back on some of his persecutions, he wrote, "the Lord rescued me from all of them" (2 Tim. 3:11; cf. 4:18).

In eleven of his thirteen epistles (all except 1 Timothy and Titus) Paul mentioned suffering, persecution, hardship, and opposition, as seen in the following list of 101 verses.

"We also rejoice in our sufferings" (Rom. 5:3).

"Now if we are children, then we are heirs—heirs of God and co-heirs with Christ, if indeed we share in his sufferings in order that we may also share in his glory" (Rom. 8:17).

"I consider that our present sufferings are not worth comparing with the glory that will be revealed in us" (Rom. 8:18).

"Not only so, but we ourselves, who have the firstfruits of the Spirit, groan inwardly as we wait eagerly for our adoption as sons, the redemption of our bodies" (Rom. 8:23).

"Who shall separate us from the love of Christ? Shall trouble or hardship or persecution or famine or nakedness or danger or sword?" (Rom. 8:35).

"For I am convinced that neither death nor life, neither angels nor demons, neither the present nor the future, nor any powers, neither height nor depth, nor anything else in all creation, will be able to separate us from the love of God that is in Christ Jesus our Lord" (Rom. 8:38–39).

"For it seems to me that God has put us apostles on display at the end of the procession, like men condemned to die in the arena. We have been made a spectacle to the whole universe, to angels as well as to men. We are fools for Christ, but you are so wise in Christ! We are weak, but you are strong! You are honored, we are dishonored! To this very hour we go hungry and thirsty, we are in rags, we are brutally treated, we are homeless. We work hard with our own hands. When we are cursed, we bless; when we are persecuted, we endure it; when we are slandered, we answer kindly. Up to this moment we have become the scum of the earth, the refuse of the world" (1 Cor. 4:9–13).

"There are many who oppose me" (1 Cor. 6:9).

"We put up with anything rather than hinder the gospel of Christ" (1 Cor. 9:12).

"And as for us, why do we endanger ourselves every hour? I die every day—I mean that, brothers—just as surely as I glory over you in Christ Jesus our Lord. If I fought wild beasts in Ephesus for merely human reasons, what have I gained?" (1 Cor. 15:30–32).

"Praise be to the God and Father of our Lord Jesus Christ, the Father of compassion and the God of all comfort, who comforts us in all our troubles, so that we can comfort those in any trouble with the comfort we ourselves have received from God. For just as the sufferings of Christ flow over into our lives, so also through Christ our comfort overflows. If we are distressed, it is for your comfort and salvation; if we are comforted, it is for your comfort, which produces in you patient endurance of the same sufferings we suffer. And our hope for you is firm, because we know that just as you share in our sufferings, so also you share in our comfort. We do not want you to be uninformed, brothers, about the hardships we suffered in the province of Asia. We were under great pressure, far beyond our ability to endure, so that we despaired even of life. Indeed, in our hearts we felt the sentence of death. But this happened that we might not rely on ourselves but on God, who raises the dead. He has delivered us from such a deadly peril, and he will deliver us. On him we have set our hope that he will continue to deliver us" (2 Cor. 1:3–10).

"I wrote you out of great distress and anguish of heart and with many tears" (2 Cor. 2:4).

"But we have this treasure in jars of clay to show that this all-surpassing power is from God and not from us. We are hard pressed on every side, but not crushed; perplexed, but not in despair; persecuted, but not abandoned; struck down, but not destroyed. We always carry around in our body the death of Jesus, so that the life of Jesus may also be revealed in our body. For we who are alive are always being given over to death for Jesus' sake, so that his life may be revealed in our mortal body. So then, death is at work in us, but life is at work in you" (2 Cor. 4:7–12).

"Therefore we do not lose heart. Though outwardly we are wasting away, yet inwardly we are being renewed day by day. For our light and momentary troubles are achieving for us an eternal glory that far outweighs them all" (2 Cor. 4:16–17).

"For while we are in this tent, we groan and are burdened" (2 Cor. 5:4).

"Rather, as servants of God we commend ourselves in every way: in great endurance; in troubles, hardships and distresses; in beatings, imprisonments and riots; in hard work, sleepless nights and hunger" (2 Cor. 6:4–5).

"Through glory and dishonor, bad report and good report; genuine, yet regarded as impostors; known, yet regarded as unknown; dying, and yet we live on; beaten, and yet not killed; sorrowful, yet always rejoicing; poor, yet making many rich; having nothing, and yet possessing everything" (2 Cor. 6:8–10).

"In all our troubles my joy knows no bounds" (2 Cor. 7:4).

"For when we came into Macedonia, this body of ours had no rest, but we were harassed at every turn—conflicts on the outside, fears within" (2 Cor. 7:5).

"Are they servants of Christ? (I am out of my mind to talk like this.) I am more. I have worked much harder, been in prison more frequently, been flogged more severely, and been exposed to death again and again. Five times I received from the Jews the forty lashes minus one. Three times I was beaten with rods, once I was stoned, three times I was shipwrecked, I spent a night and a day in the open sea, I have been constantly on the move. I have been in danger from rivers, in danger from bandits, in danger from my own countrymen, in danger from Gentiles; in danger in the city, in danger in the country, in danger at sea; and in danger from false brothers. I have labored and toiled and have often gone without sleep; I have known hunger and thirst and have often gone without food; I have been cold and naked. Besides everything else, I face daily the pressure of my concern for all the churches. Who is weak, and I do not feel weak? Who is led into sin, and I do not inwardly burn?" (2 Cor. 11:23–29).

"To keep me from becoming conceited because of these surpassingly great revelations, there was given me a thorn in my flesh, a messenger of Satan, to torment me" (2 Cor. 12:7).

"But he said to me, 'My grace is sufficient for you, for my power is made perfect in weakness.' Therefore I will boast all the more gladly about my weaknesses, so that Christ's power may rest on me. That is why, for Christ's sake, I delight in weaknesses, in insults, in hardships, in persecutions, in difficulties. For when I am weak, then I am strong" (2 Cor. 12:9–10).

"As you know, it was because of an illness that I first preached the gospel to you" (Gal. 4:13).

"My dear children, for whom I am again in the pains of childbirth until Christ is formed in you, how I wish I could be with you now and change my tone, because I am perplexed about you!" (Gal. 4:19–20).

"Brothers, if I am still preaching circumcision, why am I still being persecuted?" (Gal. 5:11).

"Finally, let no one cause me trouble, for I bear on my body the marks of Jesus" (Gal. 6:17).

"I ask you, therefore, not to be discouraged because of my sufferings for you, which are your glory" (Eph. 3:13).

"I am an ambassador in chains" (Eph. 6:20).

"It is right for me to feel this way about all of you, since I have you in my heart; for whether I am in chains or defending and confirming the gospel, all of you share in God's grace with me" (Phil. 1:7).

"Now I want you to know, brothers, that what has happened to me has really served to advance the gospel. As a result, it has become clear throughout the whole palace guard and to everyone else that I am in chains for Christ. Because of my chains, most of the brothers in the Lord have been encouraged to speak the word of God more courageously and fearlessly" (Phil. 1:12–14).

"The former preach Christ out of selfish ambition, not sincerely, supposing that they can stir up trouble for me while I am in chains" (Phil. 1:17).

"For it has been granted to you on behalf of Christ not only to believe on him, but also to suffer for him, since you are going through the same struggle you saw I had, and now hear that I still have" (Phil. 1:29–30).

"But even if I am being poured out like a drink offering on the sacrifice and service coming from your faith, I am glad and rejoice with all of you" (Phil. 2:17).

"What is more, I consider everything a loss compared to the surpassing greatness of knowing Christ Jesus my Lord, for whose sake I have lost all things. I consider them rubbish, that I may gain Christ" (Phil. 3:8).

"I want to know Christ and the power of his resurrection and the fellowship of sharing in his sufferings, becoming like him in his death" (Phil. 3:10).

"I am not saying this because I am in need, for I have learned to be content whatever the circumstances. I know what it is to be in need, and I know what it is to have plenty. I have learned the secret of being content in any and every situation, whether well fed or hungry, whether living in plenty or in want" (Phil. 4:11–12).

"Yet it was good of you to share in my troubles" (Phil. 4:14).

"Now I rejoice in what was suffered for you, and I fill up in my flesh what is still lacking in regard to Christ's afflictions, for the sake of his body, which is the church" (Col. 1:24).

"And pray for us, too, that God may open a door for our message, so that we may proclaim the mystery of Christ, for which I am in chains" (Col. 4:3).

"Remember my chains" (Col. 4:18).

"In spite of severe suffering, you welcomed the message with the joy given by the Holy Spirit" (1 Thess. 1:6).

"We had previously suffered and been insulted in Philippi, as you know, but with the help of our God we dared to tell you his gospel in spite of strong opposition" (1 Thess. 2:2).

"You remember, brothers, our toil and hardship" (1 Thess. 2:9).

"You suffered from your own countrymen the same things those churches suffered from the Jews, who killed the Lord Jesus and drove us out . . . in their effort to keep us from speaking to the Gentiles so that they may be saved" (1 Thess. 2:14–16).

"For we wanted to come to you—certainly I, Paul, did, again and again—but Satan stopped us" (1 Thess. 2:18).

"We sent Timothy . . . to strengthen and encourage you in your faith, so that no one would be unsettled by these trials. You know quite well that we were destined for them. In fact, when we were with you, we kept telling you that we would be persecuted. And it turned out that way, as you well know" (1 Thess. 3:2–4).

"Therefore, brothers, in all our distress and persecution we were encouraged about you because of your faith" (1 Thess. 3:7).

"Therefore, among God's churches we boast about your perseverance and faith in all the persecutions and trials you are enduring" (2 Thess. 1:4).

"Join with me in suffering for the gospel, by the power of God" (2 Tim. 1:8).

"I am suffering" (2 Tim. 1:12).

"You know that everyone in the province of Asia has deserted me, including Phygelus and Hermogenes" (2 Tim. 1:15).

"Endure hardship with us like a good soldier of Christ Jesus" (2 Tim. 2:3).

"This is my gospel, for which I am suffering even to the point of being chained like a criminal" (2 Tim. 2:8–9).

"Therefore I endure everything for the sake of the elect" (2 Tim. 2:10).

"You, however, know all about my . . . persecutions, sufferings— what kinds of things happened to me in Antioch, Iconium, and Lystra, the persecutions I endured. Yet the Lord rescued me from all of them" (2 Tim. 3:10–11).

"In fact, everyone who wants to live a godly life in Christ Jesus will be persecuted" (2 Tim. 3:12).

"I am already being poured out like a drink offering" (2 Tim. 4:6).

"Demas, because he loved this world, has deserted me" (2 Tim. 4:10).

"Alexander the metalworker did me a great deal of harm" (2 Tim. 4:14).

"At my first defense, no one came to my support, but everyone deserted me. May it not be held against them" (2 Tim. 4:16).

"The Lord will rescue me from every evil attack and will bring me safely to his heavenly kingdom. To him be glory for ever and ever" (2 Tim. 4:18).

"I appeal to you for my son Onesimus, who became my son while I was in chains" (Philem. 10).

"I would have liked to keep him with me so that he could take your place in helping me while I am in chains for the gospel" (Philem. 13).

These verses mention almost every kind of hardship imaginable. Terms Paul used in these verses to describe his sufferings may be grouped as follows:

Bodily abuse: beaten, imprisoned, in the midst of riots, persecuted, brutally treated, endangered every day, struck down, flogged, lashed, beaten with rods,[24] stoned, shipwrecked,[25] and in chains.[26]

---

24. Five times Paul said he received thirty-nine lashes from Jews (2 Cor. 11:24)—a total of 195! Christ had warned his disciples they would be scourged by Jews in the synagogues (Matt. 10:17; Mark 13:9). Before his conversion Paul, the unbelieving Jew, had been the persecutor of Christians (putting them to death, Acts 22:4). Now Paul, the Christian, was persecuted by unbelieving Jews! Only one of the three beatings with rods, which was by Romans, is recorded in Acts. This was at Philippi (Acts 16:23), and was what was used on Jesus (Matt. 27:26).

25. Only one of Paul's three shipwrecks (2 Cor. 11:25) is mentioned in Acts—the one on the island of Malta, on his way to Rome, three years after he wrote 2 Corinthians. Hughes lists nine of Paul's voyages where shipwrecks may have occurred (Philip Edgcumbe Hughes, *Paul's Second Epistle to the Corinthians*, New International Commentary on the New Testament [Grand Rapids: Eerdmans, 1962], 411): the journeys from Caesarea to Tarsus (Acts 9:30), from Tarsus to Antioch (11:25–26), from Seleucia to Salamis (13:4), from Paphos to Perga (13:13), from Attalia to Antioch (14:25–26), from Troas to Neapolis (16:11), from Berea to Athens (17:14–15), from Corinth to Ephesus (18:18–19), and from Ephesus to Caesarea (18:21–22).

26. Paul was chained in a Philippian jail (Acts 16:24, 26), in Jerusalem (21:33; 22:29; 26:29), and in Rome (28:20; Eph. 6:20; Phil. 1:7, 13–14, 17; Col. 4:3, 18; 2 Tim. 1:16; Philem. 10, 13).

Physical difficulties: toil, hard work, insomnia, hunger, thirst, weakness, wasting away, cold, nakedness, illness, exposure to death, and dying.[27]

Emotional burdens: falsely criticized, dishonored, slandered, treated as scum and refuse, insulted,[28] treated as a criminal, sorrowful, distressed, pressured, in anguish of heart, shedding tears, perplexed, burdened, in despair, and distressed over the lost and over fellow believers' problems.

Financial lack: poor, having nothing, homeless, in rags, and in need.

Spiritual opposition: hindered and harassed by opponents and false brethren, deserted by friends,[29] facing evil attacks.

Is it any wonder Paul spoke of suffering "everything" (2 Tim. 2:10)?

In several of his epistles Paul included lists or catalogs of his afflictions, including Romans 8:35; 1 Corinthians 4:9–13; 2 Corinthians 4:8–9; 6:4–5, 8–10; 11:23–29; and Philippians 4:12. Some Greek writers, especially Stoics, included "peristasis ['circumstances'] catalogs" of hardships, including Plutarch, Epictetus, Seneca, and Dio Chrysostom, and some Jewish writers did the same.[30] Paul's lists, while similar in some

---

27. Paul often spoke of his being subject to death, a fact he described in various ways: "like men condemned to die" (1 Cor. 4:9), "we despaired even of life" (2 Cor. 1:8), "we felt the sentence of death" (1:9), "deadly peril" (1:10), "we carry about in our body the death of Jesus" (4:10), "given over to death" (4:11), "death is at work in us" (4:12), and "exposed to death again and again" (11:24). When he wrote about carrying in his body "the death of Jesus" (4:10), he used *nekrōsis*, "the process of dying," not *thanatos*, the final condition of death (Timothy B. Savage, *Power through Weakness: Paul's Understanding of the Christian Ministry in 2 Corinthians* [Cambridge: Cambridge University Press, 1996], 172).

28. "Insulted" in the NIV is better translated "mistreated," as in the NASB, or "shamefully treated." The word *hybrizō* means "to undergo ignominious punishment" (Georg Bertram, "ὕβρις *ktl.*," in *Theological Dictionary of the New Testament*, 8 [1972], 305). The missionaries' treatment at Philippi included being dragged before the magistrates (Acts 16:19–20), on a false accusation (16:20–21), being stripped of their clothes (16:22) and publicly beaten without a trial (16:22–23), and being thrown into an inner prison with their feet fastened in the stocks (16:24) as though they were dangerous criminals (Warren E. Becker, "Paul, the Suffering Apostle: The Place of Suffering in His Life and Theology" [Ph.D. diss., Fuller Theological Seminary, 1982], 25, n. 15).

29. Mark had deserted Paul and Barnabas when they were in Pamphylia on their first missionary journey (Acts 15:38). Others who left him were Phygelus and Hermogenes (2 Tim. 1:15) and Demas (4:10); and at his first defense in Rome everyone had abandoned him (4:16).

30. Colin G. Kruse, "Afflictions, Trials, Hardships," in *Dictionary of Paul and His Letters*, 19; Robert Hodgson, "Paul the Apostle and First Century Tribulation Lists," *Zeitschrift für die neutestamentiche Wissenschaft* 74 (January–February 1983): 59–80; Susan R. Garrett, "The God of This World and the Affliction of Paul," in *Greeks, Romans, and Christians*, ed. David L. Balch, Everet Ferguson, and Wayne A. Meeks (Minneapolis: Fortress, 1990), 99–117; Nills Willert, "The Catalogues of Hardships in the Pauline Correspondence:

ways to this literary convention, differed from secular catalogs in that he saw in them not a demonstration of his own power, but of God's power.[31]

Paul mentioned several triads in 1 Corinthians 4:10–13: three ironic antitheses in verse 10 (fools, but wise; weak, but strong; honored but dishonored); two triads in verses 11–12a on physical hardships (hungry, thirsty, in rags; and brutally treated, homeless, and hardworking); and three kinds of oppression with accompanying responses in verses 12b–13 (cursed, persecuted, and slandered).[32] Second Corinthians cites four antitheses; the nine hardships in 2 Corinthians 6:4b–5 are listed in three triads;[33] 2 Corinthians 6:8–10 includes nine pairs of antithetical, even paradoxical items; and Philippians 4:12 lists three pairs of opposites.

Between the nine hardships in 2 Corinthians 6:4b–5 and the nine pairs of opposites in verses 8–10, the apostle listed nine virtues. His life of purity, knowledge, patience, kindness, filling by the Holy Spirit,[34] sincere love, honest speech, empowerment by God, and use of spiritual weapons all enabled him to endure his toils and afflictions.

Paul often wrote that all believers can expect to experience suffering and persecution, and that many of his readers had in fact already suffered for Christ (Rom. 8:17–18; 2 Cor. 1:6–7; Phil. 1:29; 1 Thess. 1:6; 2:14; 3:3–4; 2 Thess. 1:5; 2 Tim. 3:12). One means by which he and Barnabas encouraged new believers in Lystra, Iconium, and Antioch was informing them that hardships, rather than being abnormal, are normal

---

Background and Function," in *The New Testament and Hellenistic Judaism,* ed. Peter Borgen and Søren Giversen (Oakville, Conn.: Aarhus University Press, 1995), 217–43; Savage, *Power through Weakness,* 169–70; and Abraham J. Malherbe, "The Beasts at Ephesus," *Journal of Biblical Literature* 87 (1968): 72, n. 11.

31. Kruse, "Afflictions, Trials, Hardships," 19.

32. John T. Fitzgerald, *Cracks in an Earthen Vessel: An Examination of the Catalogues of Hardship in the Corinthian Correspondence* (Atlanta: Scholars, 1988), 132.

33. In 2 Corinthians 6:4b–5 the first three—troubles (*thlipsis*), hardships, and distresses—are general; the next three—beatings, imprisonments, and riots—are specific; and the last three—hard work, sleepness nights, and hunger—are difficulties related to his occupation of tentmaking (ibid., 192–94).

34. Plummer suggests that Paul probably did not place the Holy Spirit in a list of human virtues, and that the words *en pneumati hagiō* should be rendered "in a spirit that is holy," that is, "in the spirit of holiness which distinguishes true ministers from false" (Plummer, *A Critical and Exegetical Commentary on the Second Epistle of St Paul to the Corinthians,* 196). However, it may not be unfitting for the apostle to have referred to the Holy Spirit as the fifth and thus central element in these nine factors. Another, divine element, "the power of God" is also included in the list. If he had meant "a spirit of holiness," he would have written *en pneumati hagiosynēs* (Hughes, *Paul's Second Epistle to the Corinthians,* 228).

for Christians (Acts 14:22). Yet there is value in suffering; benefits come from buffeting. Paul said, "Suffering produces perseverance" (Rom. 5:3), that is, it gives believers opportunity to demonstrate steadfastness while undergoing hardship. Also, suffering is a sharing in or identity with Christ's sufferings (8:17; Phil. 3:10), and results in the enjoyment of God's glory (Rom. 8:18). Eternal perspective enables Christ's spiritual children to be encouraged even when facing troubles (2 Cor. 4:17–18), for present hardships are "light and momentary," compared with heaven's delight (cf. Rom. 8:18).

Paul's suffering, though difficult, resulted in others hearing the gospel and being saved. Had he refrained from preaching and teaching Christ, Paul would have had a much easier life, but others would not have learned of the Good News. "If we are distressed," he told the Corinthians, "it is for your comfort and salvation" (2 Cor. 1:6). He told the Ephesians that his sufferings were "your glory" (Eph. 3:13), that is, they led to their spiritual advancement; and he told the Colossians his troubles were "for you" (Col. 1:24). He endured everything that "the elect . . . may obtain the salvation that is in Christ Jesus" (2 Tim. 2:10). He "put up with anything" necessary "rather than hinder the gospel of Christ" (1 Cor. 9:12). Even his imprisonment in Rome, rather than hindering the gospel, advanced it because his guards heard the gospel and others were encouraged by his boldness to speak out for Christ (Phil. 1:12–14). That is why he said his suffering was "for the gospel" (2 Tim. 1.8) and "for Christ's sake" (2 Cor. 12:10). When he stated that what he suffered filled up what was lacking in Christ's afflictions (Col. 1:24), he did not mean Christ's atoning sacrifice on the cross was inadequate. Instead he was saying that his sufferings added to those of Christ in order to spread the gospel. The apostle's ministry did not supplement Christ's suffering; it extended the truth of the cross to others,[35] thus in a sense helping to complete the "quota" of sufferings that remained to be filled before Christ's return.[36]

What a marvelous example of a person so committed to Christ and others that he willingly suffered! But that wasn't all. Most people would complain bitterly about their hardships, anxious to gain relief. But not Paul.

Encouraged by the positive benefits stemming from his afflictions, he was glad for them! How many suffering Christians could honestly

35. James D. E. Dunn, *The Epistles to the Colossians and to Philemon,* New International Greek Testament Commentary (Grand Rapids: Eerdmans, 1996), 113–17.

36. C. F. D. Moule, *The Epistles of Paul the Apostle to the Colossians and to Philemon*, Cambridge Greek Testament Commentary (Cambridge: Cambridge University Press, 1957), 78.

say, "we rejoice in the hope of the glory of God" and "we rejoice in our sufferings"? (Rom. 5:2–3; cf. v. 11). How many could join with the apostle in being glad because his life would soon end like a poured-out drink offering (Phil. 2:17; 2 Tim. 4:6)? How many could rejoice, as Paul did, knowing their hardships were "for the sake of [Christ's] body, which is the church" (Col. 1:24)? This attitude of his explains why he could "boast of the things that show [his] weakness" (2 Cor. 11:30) and "boast all the more gladly about [his] weaknesses" (12:9), and why he would sing in jail (Acts 16:25). He delighted in weakness "for Christ's sake" (2 Cor. 12:10), for as he wrote, "in all our troubles my joy knows no bounds" (7:4). In fact, affliction in Christian service was a high privilege. When Paul wrote, "It has been granted to you . . . to suffer for him" (Phil. 1:29), he used the word *charizō*, translated "granted," which means "to give graciously, to bestow favor." To suffer for Christ is a sign of his favor.

Yet this remarkable statesman stood confident that God would give him strength to endure his troubles (2 Tim. 4:17) and would deliver him from them (2 Cor. 1:10–11; 2 Tim. 3:11; 4:17–18). Though his unending persecutions were like being confronted with "beasts" in Ephesus (1 Cor. 15:32, probably a figure of speech referring to his fierce, beastly opponents), he "was delivered from the lion's mouth" (2 Tim. 4:17).[37] Since the Christian life is like a battle (Eph. 6:10–18), believers are to "be strong" in the Lord and to "endure hardship" like soldiers of Christ (2 Tim. 2:1, 3). Paul even encouraged Timothy to "join" with him in suffering (1:8).

Though he had every reason to be discouraged and give up, Paul kept going. He persisted in the ministry in spite of persecutions from the ministry. He made this abundantly clear in 2 Corinthians 4:8–9. He was

> hard pressed (*thlibō*, "to be under pressure or afflicted")
> but not crushed (*stenochōreō*, "to be pressured in a narrow space")
> perplexed (*aporeō*, "to be at a loss, at wits end")
> but not in despair (*exaporeomai*, "to be completely baffled")
> persecuted (*diōkō*, "to be hunted like an animal")
> but not forsaken (*enkataleipō*, "to be deserted or abandoned")
> struck down (*kataballō*, "to be knocked down as in wrestling")
> but not destroyed (*apollymi*, "to destroy or perish").[38]

37. "Since, as a Roman citizen, Paul could not be thrown to the lions in the amphitheater, this must be a figurative way of saying that his first hearing [in Rome] did not result in an immediate guilty verdict" (*The NIV Study Bible*, ed. Kenneth Barker [Grand Rapids: Zondervan, 1985], 1847).

38. Cf. Savage, *Power through Weakness*, 169–72; and Fitzgerald, *Cracks in an Earthen Vessel*, 180–84.

As stated earlier, Paul's hardships gave opportunity for God's power, not Paul's, to be demonstrated. He referred to "the Spirit's power" and "God's power" in 1 Corinthians 2:4–5. He said his suffering enabled him to rely on God (2 Cor. 1:9) and "to show that this all-surpassing power is from God and not from us" (4:7). Boasting and delighting in his weaknesses enabled Christ's power to rest on him (12:9) so that he became strong (12:10). In contrast to the secular attitude in Corinth that valued self-exalting behavior, contempt for humility, projection of vigor and force, and even abusive and arrogant speech, Paul "boasted" because of his weakness.[39] The Corinthians denigrated his failure to boast, his timid personal appearance, his amateurish speech, and his refusal of support. They saw these as signs of weakness. "Paul accepts this caricature but adds the stunning qualification that it is precisely in such 'weakness'—in his mind, such humble faith—that true power, the power of God, becomes effective in his ministry."[40] Wrongly evaluating the apostle according to the standards of their secular environment, the believers in Corinth questioned whether he was a true minister of Christ. Paul turned their logic on its head by affirming that it was precisely his "weakness" that demonstrated his apostolic authority and ensured that his ministry was by means of God's power.[41]

Can there be any doubt that Paul was a man of incredible courage, one whose tenacity is unequaled? Unshakable and unmovable, he determined to communicate the truth regardless of the cost. Individuals of lesser character would have jumped ship when the waves got turbulent. But not Paul!

He evidenced remarkable bravery and stick-to-itiveness right from the start. Jews opposed him in Damascus, the very first place he ministered after his conversion. Gentiles stoned him and left him for dead on his very first missionary journey. He even went back to Lystra (Acts 14:21–22), the very place where he had been stoned (14:8, 19). Imagine such courage! Later he traveled on to Jerusalem against the unanimous advice of friends, knowing that perils awaited him there (20:22–23). Imagine such determination! He faced an infuriated Jewish mob that was anxious to kill him and he addressed them in the outer court of the temple (21:37–40). Imagine such daring!

Determined to carry on for Christ, this warrior never wavered or waffled; he never vacillated or veered from his commitment. As he told the Ephesians, "none of these things move me" (Acts 20:24 NKJV). Because he steadfastly gave himself to the Lord's work, he could encour-

---

39. Savage, *Power through Weakness*, 54–99.
40. Ibid., 185.
41. Ibid., 187–88.

age others to do the same. He urged the Corinthian Christians to stand firm, to let nothing move them, and to give themselves "fully to the work of the Lord" (1 Cor. 15:58). Since he had endured hardship, he encouraged Timothy to do the same (2 Tim. 2:1, 3). He did not become disheartened (2 Cor. 4:1, 16) for the Lord stood with him and gave him strength (2 Tim. 4:17).

Are you facing some hardships? Is your heart heavy? Do some people oppose your work? Are you undergoing difficulties in your teaching ministry? Then be encouraged by this great teacher whose tenacity in adversity gives us a great example to follow. Criticism, abuse, opposition, and discouragement need not hinder if we focus on doing God's will in God's strength.

Severity

As discussed earlier, Paul was certainly a compassionate, loving teacher, deeply affectionate toward his students. Yet there were times when he was stern with some of them. These stern rebukes or severe warnings, however, were not inconsistent with his love. They stemmed from his love. Because of his compassion for his students he was concerned that they not be led astray into false teaching and that their conduct be consistent with the truths they knew.

Sensing problems in some of his converts' thinking and living, Paul did not hesitate to confront those believers. He did not skirt issues or sidestep problems. His rebukes were like warning signals, alerting them to dangers ahead. His stern confrontations were like flashing red lights, pointing to serious consequences if they continued on their wayward path.

One of the first instances of Paul's forthrightness was his sharp dispute with some Jews who were teaching Christians in Antioch that without circumcision a person could not be saved (Acts 15:1–2).[42] Also in his Epistle to the Galatians Paul expressed concern several times about false teaching, what he called "a different gospel" (Gal. 1:6) and a perversion of the true gospel (1:7). This statesman-teacher was so disturbed that he wished that anyone who taught falsehood would be

---

42. Other individuals Paul confronted include Elymas (Acts 13:9–11) because of his sorcery (Paul called him "a child of the devil" and "full of all kinds of deceit and treachery," perverting "the right ways of the Lord"), and Ananias the high priest because of the priest's inconsistency in judging Paul and yet violating the law by having Paul struck on the mouth (23:3). Paul also sternly warned sailors in Crete against continuing their voyage to Rome because of potentially inclement weather (27:9–10)—and later, after they ignored his advice and then were shipwrecked, he said in essence, "I told you so" (27:21).

"eternally condemned" (1:8–9).[13] Strong language indeed! In Galatians 2:4 he said the "false brothers," those who claimed to be believers but weren't, were seeking to enslave the Galatian Christians, apparently by urging them to be circumcised (cf. 2:3). He accused the heretical teachers of cutting in on the believers, like people disrupting a race by stepping in front of runners (5:7). This resulted, he said, in the Galatians being kept from obeying the truth. He even called his opponents "agitators" (5:12), people who were disturbing the believers and bringing confusion to the congregations. Since these heretics wanted others to be circumcised, Paul in sarcastic irony wrote that he wished they themselves would not only be circumcised but would even be emasculated.[44] Certainly in this epistle he was deeply disturbed by erroneous teaching.[45] "The whole letter [of Galatians] is like a thunderstorm. He scolds, he pleads, he denounces, he exhorts, he argues, he asserts dogmatically, all in a whirlwind of emotion."[46]

In 1 Corinthians Paul denounced the Corinthian believers' quarreling and divisive spirit (1:11–12), their spiritual immaturity (3:1–4), their failure to deal with a man guilty of incest (5:1–5), their boasting (5:6), their taking disputes among themselves to unsaved judges (6:1–8), their disorderly conduct in observing the Lord's Supper (11:17–22). He even wished that those who were going their own way and not loving the Lord would be cursed (16:22: the Greek word is *anathema*). He was even ready himself to punish those who deliberately disobeyed the Lord (2 Cor. 10:6), though he did not say how he would do so. He did add that he would not "spare" them (13:2) from public censure or even excommunication.[47]

Paul daringly confronted Peter who was hypocritical in his conduct and who even influenced Barnabas to be hypocritical (Gal. 2:11–14). Since salvation is available only by faith in Christ, it was unquestionably wrong for the Galatians to think they could be saved by observing the Mosaic law. To attempt to add to salvation by law observance meant

43. "Eternally condemned" translates the Greek *anathema*, which refers to some one or thing that is devoted to destruction, like the Hebrew *ḥerem*, or is accursed. The same word is used in Romans 9:3; 1 Corinthians 12:3; and 16:22, and each time it is translated "cursed."

44. F. F. Bruce translates the verse, "I wish that those who are upsetting you would complete their cutting operation—on themselves!" (*The Epistle to the Galatians*, New International Greek Testament Commentary [Grand Rapids: Eerdmans, 1982], 238). Some writers suggest this may have referred subtly to the practices of the cult of Cybele, which was led by emasculated priests, but other commentators, including Bruce, question this.

45. He also warned the Ephesian elders about the danger of false teachers (Acts 20:31), who would distort the truth and whom he likened to wolves (20:29–30).

46. Jefferson, *The Character of Paul*, 210.

47. Alfred Plummer, *A Critical and Exegetical Commentary on the Second Epistle of St Paul to the Corinthians*, International Critical Commentary (Edinburgh: Clark, 1915), 374.

they were "foolish" (3:1, 3), and observing special days meant they were going backwards to the world's "principles" (4:9), that is, elementary aspects of Jewish or pagan religion (cf. 4:3),[48] and living like slaves. This concern about the Galatians' interest in law-keeping called forth an alarming denunciation by the apostle, beginning with the exclamation "Mark my words!" (5:2) and concluding with the observation that they were "alienated from Christ" and had "fallen away from grace" (5:4).[49] And he warned the Philippians to beware of "men who do evil," calling them dogs (Phil. 3:2).[50]

Confrontation is never easy, but it sometimes becomes necessary when our students tend to veer from the truth or become involved in sin.

Serenity

Along with fervency, tenacity, and severity, Paul's gamut of emotions also included serenity. Though suffering many hardships and though agitated by false teachers, this early-church leader also knew inner peace and contentment. In each of his letters he greeted his readers by wishing them God's peace and he often concluded in a similar way. This theme could hardly have been on his mind so often if he himself did not enjoy God's inner peace. Knowing contentment in spite of his difficulties (Phil. 4:10–11), he urged others to experience the same serenity (1 Tim. 6:6–8), which is evidence of the filling of the Holy Spirit (Gal. 5:22).

Felicity

As already discussed, the apostle knew the Lord's joy in all his adversities. He never moaned or complained; he never groaned or grumbled. Instead, joy accompanied his tribulations. But he wrote of his joy in the

48. For a discussion on the meaning of "basic principles" (*stoicheia*, 4:3), which are "weak and miserable" (4:9), see Bruce, *The Epistle to the Galatians*, 193–94, 202–5. Clinton E. Arnold presents strong arguments for viewing the *stoicheia* as evil spiritual powers (*The Colossian Syncretism: The Interface between Christianity and Folk Belief at Colossae* [Grand Rapids: Baker, 1996], 158–94); also see my chapter 10, n. 64.

49. These statements do not mean they lost their salvation. Instead Paul meant they were not able to enjoy full fellowship with Christ because they were moving from trusting in God's grace and relying on their works.

50. Jews despised dogs because those animals, unlike house pets today, roamed about, feeding on garbage and attacking people. Thus Paul's description of those false teachers who advocated circumcision as necessary for salvation ("mutilators of the flesh," Phil. 3:2) was fitting for the Gentiles.

Lord on other occasions as well. Several things made him glad: the Romans' obedience to Christ (Rom. 16:19), the Philippians' and Thessalonians' conversion (Phil. 4:1; 1 Thess. 2:19–20; 3:9), the arrival of his friend (1 Cor. 16:17), the Corinthians' strength (2 Cor. 13:9), the fact that Christ was preached even though some were doing so out of impure motives (Phil. 1:18–19), the Philippians' concern for him (4:18), and Philemon's love for him (Philem. 7). In turn, Paul often urged his readers to be joyful (Rom. 12:15; Phil. 1:25–26; 2:18, 29; 3:1; 4:4), since this too is a fruit of the Spirit (Gal. 5:22). Do these things make you glad? The sharing of Christ, the salvation of others, the obedience and spiritual strength of believers, the concern of others for your own spiritual welfare, the fellowship of Christians—all these should bring joy to the heart of any teacher! Surely the kingdom of God consists of "righteousness, peace, and joy in the Holy Spirit" (Rom. 14:17).

Mastery

Teaching requires mastering certain things, and in this respect Paul was an impressively ideal teacher. For one thing, he was a master of people. He knew human nature—people's needs and emotions, their differences in background, upbringing, and customs. With this knowledge he could readily adapt his approach to various audiences. For example, he taught and ministered to Jews, to Gentiles, a ruler (Acts 13:7), women (e.g., women of high social standing [13:50; 17:12] and Lydia [16:13–15]), a "blue-collar" jailer (16:27–33), philosophically oriented Athenians (17:16–34), governors (23:33; 24:10), a king and a queen (25:13), sailors (27:10, 21–26, 33–34), and a slave (Philem. 10).

Even the places he taught varied: in synagogues, by a riverside (Acts 16:13), in a prison (16:23–28), in the marketplace of Athens (17:5), on a hilltop (Mars' Hill, 17:22), in a lecture hall in Ephesus (19:9), in an upstairs room in Troas (20:8), from the temple steps in Jerusalem (21:40), in the Sanhedrin's assembly room (22:30–23:10), in a courtroom in Caesarea (25:6, 25), on a ship (27:10, 21–26, 33–34), and in a private house in Rome (28:30–31).[51]

He often taught Jews on the Sabbath (13:14, 42, 44; 15:21; 16:13; 17:2; 18:4), and he taught on the first day of the week (20:7). "His life was one teaching experience after another. He taught whenever an occasion presented itself,"[52] thus demonstrating knowledge of people and his adaptability to various audiences and situations.

---

51. Howard Tillman Kuist, *The Pedagogy of St. Paul* (New York: Doran, 1925), 49–50.
52. Ibid., 50.

Paul also used his ability in languages, speaking sometimes in Greek (21:37) and other times in Aramaic (21:40; 22:2), depending on his listeners. Aware of customs and religious beliefs, he could tell Gentile peasants in Lystra about God's creation (14:8–18), confront Athenians about their idolatry (17:22–23), and divide the Sanhedrin by referring to Jesus' resurrection (23:6–9). He revealed his knowledge of Greek literature by his quotations from Hellenistic poets: Epimenides in his *Cretica*, and Aratus in his *Phaenomena* and Cleanthes in his *Hymn to Zeus* (17:28); Menander in his Greek comedy *Thais* (1 Cor. 15:33); and Epimenides again in Titus 1:12. As Johnson explains, "He recognized that it wasn't helpful to approach every person and situation in the same way, and therefore he accommodated himself to fit the contexts in which he taught."[53] Unquestionably, his ability to "become all things to all men" (1 Cor. 9:22) speaks of his keen mind and adaptable spirit.

Paul also knew the content of his teaching—not only whom he taught, but what he taught. His mastery of the Scriptures is seen in his many quotations and allusions from the Old Testament.[54] He revealed his knowledge of history (e.g., Acts 13:16–22), including many references to Israel's great leaders such as Abraham (13:26; Rom. 4:1–3, 9, 12–13, 16, 18; 9:7; 11:1; 2 Cor. 11:22; Gal. 3:6–9, 14, 16, 18, 29; 4:22), Moses (Acts 13:39; 26:22; 28:23; Rom. 5:14; 9:15; 10:5, 19; 1 Cor. 9:9; 10:2; 2 Cor. 3:7, 13, 15; 2 Tim. 3:8), David (Acts 13:22 [twice], 34, 36; Rom. 1:3; 4:6; 11:9; 2 Tim. 2:8), Isaiah (Acts 28:25; Rom. 9:27, 29; 10:16, 20; 15:12), and the prophets (Acts 13:20, 27, 40; 24:14; 26:22, 27; 28:23, 25; Rom. 1:2; 3:21; 11:3). Also, he frequently pointed out how Jesus fulfilled Old Testament prophecies (Acts 13:27, 32–33; 17:2; 18:28).

His intellectual mastery is also seen in the breadth of his theological topics, listed in table 14 in chapter 9. He was a great thinker, a theologian of the highest order with unusual mental acuity.

Clearly, these twelve characteristics—piety, authority, humility, integrity, courtesy, sensitivity, fervency, tenacity, severity, serenity, felicity, mastery—marked the apostle Paul as a truly outstanding teacher, one who stands as a supreme model for all teachers today.

To Reflect On . . .

As a teacher are you energetic and fervent in both your preparation and your actual teaching?

53. Kent L. Johnson, *Paul the Teacher* (Minneapolis: Augsburg, 1986), 14.
54. See chapter 14 for a discussion of these many references.

Do you have some physical handicap or drawback? If so, how do you react to that difficulty? Do you refuse to let it keep you from being faithful in serving the Lord?

Are you, like Paul, burdened for those you teach?

Have some people opposed what you teach by presenting false doctrine or falsely criticizing you? Do you keep your eyes on the Lord, confident that he can give you the strength to overcome those hardships?

Do you sense that someone in your class is adamantly going his own way, disobeying the Lord? How and when can you confront that person regarding his sin?

Do you sense the Lord's peace and joy in spite of your difficulties?

Do you seek to know your students well, adapting your lessons to their needs?

Do you seek to master the content of your lessons, so that you can present Christ most effectively?

"Teaching . . . so that we may present everyone perfect [mature] in Christ."

Colossians 1:28

7

What Were Paul's Goals and Motives in His Teaching?

Why did Paul give himself so unselfishly and unreservedly to his ministry? Why did he put his life on the line, not just once but repeatedly? Why did he travel hundreds, even thousands, of miles across much of the Roman Empire, facing one hazard and heartache after another?

What was he trying to accomplish? What were his goals? And why was he working toward these goals? What motivated him? What compelling forces kept him going?

We can learn much from this exemplary teacher on what our own goals should be in teaching, and what should propel us toward those goals.

Paul's Goal of Winning People to Christ

Having himself experienced the joy of receiving forgiveness of his sins and the gift of eternal life through Christ, Paul wanted everyone else to have that same joy. Knowing that without Christ people are lost eternally, he felt under compulsion to communicate the Good News wherever he went.

Immediately after his own conversion, he began seeking to win his fellow Jews in Damascus to Christ, proclaiming that Jesus is the Son of God (Acts 9:20) and proving (*symbibazō*, "to bring together, prove, conclude, give conclusive proof";[1] cf. 16:10; 19:33; Eph. 4:16) that Jesus is the Messiah (Acts 9:22). Also he explained to Jews and Greeks in Thessalonica (Acts 17:3) and Corinth (18:4–5) that Jesus is the Messiah. The Good News (13:22; 14:7, 21; 17:18) was that forgiveness of sins is available to those who believe in Jesus Christ (13:39; 20:21; cf. 26:27–29). To people in Lystra he and Barnabas explained, "We are bringing you good news, telling you to turn . . . to the living God" (14:15). And to the Thessalonians Paul wrote that they, on hearing the gospel from him, should turn to God (1 Thess. 1:9). Also, he told King Agrippa that he had preached to Jews and Gentiles that they needed to "turn to God" (Acts 26:20).

Having seen Jesus Christ in his resurrected state, it was natural for Paul to speak of Jesus' resurrection as he shared the gospel (13:30, 34, 37; 17:18, 32; 24:21). In nine of his epistles the apostle mentioned Jesus' resurrection thirty-four times (Rom. 1:4; 4:24–25; 6:4–5, 9; 7:4; 8:11 [twice], 34; 10:9; 14:9; 1 Cor. 6:14; 15:4, 12–14, 15 [twice], 16–17, 20; 2 Cor. 4:14; 5:15; Gal. 1:1; Eph. 1:20; 2:6; Phil. 3:10; Col. 2:12; 3:1; 1 Thess. 1:10; 4:14; 1 Tim. 3:16; 2 Tim. 2:8).[2]

When Paul called his message of salvation "the word of the Lord" (Acts 13:44; 16:32; 19:10, 20) and "the word of God" (13:5, 7, 46; 17:13; 18:11), he meant that what the apostle taught was not something he or someone else made up (Gal. 1:11–12a). It is God's message in that it came from him (1:12b), and it is "the word of life" (Phil. 2:16) because it brings eternal life to those who accept it. Paul equated coming to Christ for salvation with hearing, coming to, believing, or knowing the truth (Gal. 2:5; Eph. 1:13; Col. 1:5–6; 2 Thess. 2:13; 1 Tim. 2:4; 4:3; 2 Tim. 2:25; Titus 1:1; cf. Titus 1:14).

Paul spoke of the people's openness and receptivity to the gospel. First, since people must hear the gospel before they can believe it (Rom. 10:14, 17), Paul referred several times to their hearing the gospel or the

---

1. According to Gerhard Delling, this word in this context means "to prove conclusively or to give a compelling demonstration" ("συμβιβάζω," in *Theological Dictionary of the New Testament*, 7 [1971], 764. Also see my chapter 9, n. 10.

2. For a discussion of the several Greek words used for Jesus' resurrection, see Larry J. Kreitzer, "Resurrection," in *Dictionary of Paul and His Letters*, ed. Gerald F. Hawthorne, Ralph P. Martin, and Daniel G. Reid (Downers Grove, Ill.: InterVarsity, 1993), 807.

Word of God or their hearing of Christ (Acts 13:7, 44, 48; 15:7; 17:32; 19:10; 28:22; Eph. 1:13; 4:21; Col. 1:6, 23; 1 Thess. 2:13; 2 Tim. 4:17). Second, he said they received or welcomed *(dechomai)* the message (Acts 17:11; 2 Cor. 6:1; 1 Thess. 2:6, 13), a word also used of welcoming an individual (2 Cor. 7:15; Gal. 4:14; Col. 4:10). A third way the apostle spoke of people's receptivity to salvation was by the word *paralambanō*, "to receive or accept" (1 Cor. 15:1; Col. 2:6; 1 Thess. 2:13).[3] A fourth way he addressed this subject was that by faith in Christ they came to know *(ginōskō)* God (Gal. 4:9) and his grace (2 Cor. 8:9).

Think of the joy Paul felt in seeing people respond to his presentation of the gospel. Though many who heard him rejected him and his message, many were saved, including people in Antioch of Pisidia (Acts 13:48), Iconium (14:4), Derbe (14:21), Philippi (16:32–34), Thessalonica (17:4), Berea (17:12), Athens (17:34), Corinth (18:8), Ephesus (19:10), and Rome (28:23–24). Both Jews and Greeks in these ten major cities of the empire came to Christ. Their spiritual eyes were opened and they turned from the darkness of their lost, unsaved condition to the light of the gospel, from being under the power of Satan to being under God (26:18; cf. v. 23).

Before Paul could serve as a teacher of believers, he needed to win converts to Christ. Burdened for the lost, he was a fiery evangelist, eager and willing to tell others about Christ (Rom. 1:14–15; 1 Cor. 9:16; 2 Cor. 5:14). Because God called him as an apostle, he felt obligated to share salvation's Good News to both the Gentiles (Rom. 1:5; Col. 1:27) and Jews (Rom. 9:3; 10:1; 11:14), in fact, to everyone (Acts 26:20, 22; 1 Cor. 9:22; 10:33). Teachers today who neglect to present the plan of salvation or who do not present it clearly fail to follow this master teacher's initial strategy.

Paul's Teaching-Related Goals

Having won people to Christ and established them in local churches, Paul and his associates gave much of their time to strengthening and encouraging these new believers. Without apostolic encouragement, they might have become lax in their Christian living when non-Christians made fun of them or they faced other hardships (Acts 14:22–23). *Episterizō*, "to strengthen," combines *sterizō*, "to fix firmly" with the prefix *epi*, which seems to augment or strengthen the verb's meaning. Luke used

---

3. *Paralambanō* is also used of believers "receiving" teaching (Phil. 4:9; 1 Thess. 4:1, "you received from us how you ought to walk and to please God" [NKJV]; 2 Thess. 3:6, "the teaching you received from us").

this verb of Paul's ministry in Acts 14:22 and 15:41, and he used *sterizo* in 18:23. To strengthen believers means Paul helped them become more deeply committed spiritually. Paul also "encouraged" converts (14:22; 16:40; 20:1–2).

The Goal of Communicating Knowledge

One goal Paul set before his convert-learners was that they come to know or recall certain truths. He expressed this in a number of ways. For example, he wrote, "I want you to know or realize" (1 Cor. 11:3; 2 Cor. 8:1; Gal. 1:11; Phil. 1:12; Col. 2:1); "I don't want you to be ignorant or unaware" (Rom. 1:13; 11:25; 1 Cor. 10:1; 12:1; 2 Cor. 1:8; 1 Thess. 4:13); "Don't you know?" (Rom. 6:3, 16; 7:1; 11:2; 1 Cor. 3:16; 5:6; 6:2–3, 9, 15–16, 19; 9:13, 24); "We know" (e.g., Rom. 3:19; 5:3; 6:6, 9; 7:14; 8:22, 28; 1 Cor. 8:1, 4; 13:9; 2 Cor. 1:7; 4:14; 5:1, 6, 11; Gal. 2:16; 1 Thess 1:4; 1 Tim. 1:8–9); and "You know" (1 Cor. 12:2; 15:58; 16:15; 2 Cor. 8:9; Gal. 4:13; Eph. 6:8–9; Phil. 2:22; 4:15; Col. 3:24; 4:1; 1 Thess. 1:5; 2:1–2, 5, 11; 3:3–4; 4:2; 5:2; 2 Thess. 2:6; 3:7; 2 Tim. 1:15, 18; 2:23; 3:10, 14). He also challenged them to remember certain facts: "I want to remind you" (1 Cor. 15:1; 2 Tim. 1:6); "Don't you remember?" (2 Thess. 2:5); "You remember" (1 Thess 2:9); and "Remember" (2 Cor. 9:6; Gal. 2:10; Eph. 2:11–12; Col. 4:18; 2 Tim. 2:8).[4] For an interesting study, look up these verses to see what Paul wanted his readers to know and to remember.

The apostle also wrote of "the knowledge of the Son of God" (Eph. 4:13), "the [intimate] knowledge of him," that is, Christ (2 Cor. 2:14), "the knowledge of the glory of God" (4:6), the fact that the Corinthians excelled in knowledge (8:7), intimate knowledge of Christ (Eph. 1:7), knowledge of "the hope to which he has called"[5] believers (1:18), knowing the love of Christ (3:19), reaching unity "in the [intimate] knowledge of his will" (Col. 1:9), "the growing in [intimate] knowledge of God" (1:10), "being renewed in [intimate] knowledge" (3:10), and "[intimate] knowledge of the truth" (2 Tim. 2:25; Titus 1:1).

---

4. Paul's literary style in 1 Thessalonians is typical of the paraenetic devices employed by Hellenistic philosophers, who sought to confirm their audiences in what they already knew (cf. 1 Thess. 1:5; 2:1–2, 5, 11; 3:3–4; 4:2; 5:2) by reminding them of it (2:9; 3:6), complimenting them on what they had already accomplished, and encouraging them to continue in their practice (4:1, 10; 5:11). See George R. Beasley-Murray, "Pastor, Paul as," in *Dictionary of Paul and His Letters*, 655.

5. The Greek phrase, "the hope of his calling," suggests that at salvation, when God calls us to be his own (Rom. 1:6; 8:30; Eph. 4:1, 4; 2 Tim. 1:9), he places within believers' hearts the sense of certainty ("hope") about the future glorious inheritance (Eph. 1:14, 18) they will experience in heaven.

In 2 Corinthians 2:14; 4:6; 8:7; and Ephesians 3:19 the Greek word for knowledge is *gnōsis;* in Ephesians 1:17; 4:13; Colossians 1:9–10; 3:10; 2 Timothy 2:25; and Titus 1:1 the word is *epignōsis;* and the word in Ephesians 1:18 is *oida. Epignōsis,* used fifteen times by Paul, connotes a full or intimate inner experience, so that in the seven occurrences listed above it conveys an "active conscious recognition" or "taking knowledge of" God.[6] *Oida* in Ephesians 1:18 means "to grasp intuitively or directly," and *ginōskō* (used 45 times by Paul) in 3:19 means "to come to know, to know by experience, to ascertain." While 90 of the 103 occurrences of *oida* in Paul's epistles maintain this distinction, a few, including possibly Ephesians 1:18, may convey basically the same idea as *ginōskō.*[7]

The Goal of Spiritual Growth

Many teachers seemingly teach as if helping students acquire facts is all they need to do. However, though Paul's teaching goals included gaining knowledge, they went far beyond that. Even the words for knowledge, as we have seen, convey more than a mere intellectual comprehension of information. Many of Paul's goal-oriented statements and exhortations show his deep concern not only about what his readers knew, but also about what they were to be and to do. These aims may be summarized in one phrase: to foster spiritual growth and maturity. This is essentially the same goal Jesus had in his ministry.[8]

Paul addressed the concept of spiritual growth several times. As already noted, in Colossians 1:10 he spoke of believers "growing in the [intimate] knowledge [*epignōsis*] of God." Ephesians 4:13 presents the same thought: maturity comes "in [by means of] the [intimate] knowledge [*epignōsis*] of the Son of God." Spiritual growth occurs as Christians know the Lord more fully and intimately; their growth is by means

6. Fritz Rienecker, *A Linguistic Key to the Greek New Testament*, ed. Cleon L. Rogers, Jr. (Grand Rapids: Zondervan, 1980), 565.

7. Donald W. Burdick, "Οἶδα and Γινώσκω in the Pauline Epistles," in *New Dimensions in New Testament Study*, ed. Richard N. Longenecker and Merrill C. Tenney (Grand Rapids: Zondervan, 1974), 344–56. On these and similar verbs, see Moisés Silva, "The Pauline Style as Lexical Choice: GINOSKEIN and Related Verbs," in *Pauline Studies*, ed. Donald A. Hagner and Murray J. Harris (Grand Rapids: Eerdmans, 1980), 184–207.

8. See Roy B. Zuck, *Teaching as Jesus Taught* (Grand Rapids: Baker, 1995), 98–101. This is strong verification that Paul's teachings confirm and harmonize with Jesus' teachings, rather than contradict them. For a full discussion of this issue, see J. M. G. Barclay, "Jesus and Paul," in *Dictionary of Paul and His Letters*, 442–503.

of that intimacy.[9] In Colossians 1:6 the apostle used the related verb *epiginōskō,* which denotes the experience as well as the mental apprehension of God's grace.[10] Christian growth also includes increasing in righteousness (2 Cor. 9:10), faith (10:15), love (Phil. 1:9), and in fact, "in all things" (Eph. 4:15), that is, in every area of life. This growth is to be "into him," or perhaps better, "unto him," in the sense that Christ-likeness is the goal of our growth. As Paul put it in Ephesians 4:13, we are to attain "to the whole measure of the fullness of Christ," that is, to become fully like Christ, who is our measure or standard of moral character (cf. 3:19).

The ultimate goal for which God has predestined believers is that they "be conformed to the likeness of his Son" (Rom. 8:29). "Conformed" renders the Greek adjective *symmorphos,* "having the same form or likeness," a word used elsewhere only in Philippians 3:21, where it is translated "like." Since believers will be like Christ ("we shall be like him," 1 John 3:2) when they are with him in heaven, they are challenged to become more like him now. Paul stated that he agonized over the Galatians like a woman in child labor pains, so that Christ would be "formed" *(morphoō)* in them (Gal. 4:19), a picturesque way of expressing his desire that they become Christ-like.

That is the goal every teacher should have for each of his or her pupils: that each student become like Christ by coming "to know him better" (Eph. 1:17, "in [intimate] knowledge [*epignōsis*] of him"). Even Paul, who knew Christ so well, longed to know him better (Phil. 3:10).

Babies are enjoyable, but no parent wants his or her offspring to remain an infant. Just as stunted growth gravely concerns parents, so lack of spiritual development should be of concern to teachers. Paul addressed the problem of lack of maturity several times (1 Cor. 3:1–4; 4:21; 6:5–6; 14:20; Eph. 4:14). As believers are united, Christ's body, the church, grows like a building under construction (Eph. 2:21), like a human body (Col. 2:19), and like a plant (1 Cor. 3:6–7). This growth "presumably includes both growth in size (numbers becoming Christians) and character."[11] As the gospel is shared with others and thus spreads, it is like a tree "bearing fruit and growing" (Col. 1:6). As believ-

9. The phrase *tē epignōsei tou theou* is probably to be understood as instrumental ("by means of") rather than referential ("in"). If it were the latter (acquiring more knowledge of God), one would expect the preposition *en* ("in") to be included in the phrase (James D. G. Dunn, *The Epistles to the Colossians and to Philemon,* New International Greek Testament Commentary [Grand Rapids: Eerdmans, 1996], 72, n. 16). See John Eadie, *Commentary on the Epistle of Paul to the Colossians* (1856; reprint, Minneapolis: Klock and Klock, 1977), 27.

10. Dunn, *The Epistles to the Colossians and to Philemon,* 62–63.

11. Ibid., 186.

ers are "united in love," they come to know Christ more intimately (Col. 2:2, *eis epignōsin . . . Christou*).

Spiritual maturity of Paul's converts unquestionably stood as the paramount target of his ministry. He prayed for the Corinthians' maturity[12] (2 Cor. 13:9), and urged them to aim for it (13:11). He admonished and taught others so that he could guide them to maturity in Christ (Col. 1:23).

Paul also spoke of spiritual growth as overflowing or excelling (*perisseuō,* "to abound"). Believers are to excel in hope or confidence in the Lord (Rom. 15:13), in the exercise of spiritual gifts that will edify other believers (1 Cor. 14:12), in working for the Lord (1 Cor. 15:58; 2 Cor. 9:8), in joy (2 Cor. 8:2; Phil. 1:26), gratitude (2 Cor. 9:12; Col. 2:7), love (Phil. 1:9; 1 Thess. 3:12; 4:10), and, in fact, in everything, as Paul stated in 2 Corinthians 8:7, including faith, speech,[13] knowledge, earnestness,[14] love, and giving.

Being strengthened or built up is another way Paul described spiritual maturation. He used at least seven words to depict this concept. Paul desired that believers be made strong (*stērizō,* "to fix firmly"; Rom. 1:11; 1 Thess. 3:2), a task which only God can do (Rom. 16:25; 1 Thess. 3:13; 2 Thess. 2:17; 3:3); that they be firmly established (*bebaioō,*[15] 1 Cor. 1:8; 2 Cor. 1:21; Col. 2:7) in Christ and in the faith; that they be strong (*krataioomai,*[16] 1 Cor. 16:13; Eph. 3:16); that they stand firm (*stēkō,* 1 Cor. 16:13; Gal. 5:1; Phil. 1:27; 4:1; 2 Thess. 2:15); that they be empowered (*dynamoō,* Col. 1:11; *endynamoō,* Eph. 6:10; 2 Tim. 2:1; cf. Phil. 4:13; 2 Tim. 1:12; 4:17); that they be built up (*oikodomeō,* "to build or edify";[17] 1 Cor. 8:1; 14:4, 17; 1 Thess. 5:11).

A Christian who is mature in Christ is one whose conduct ("walk") accords with his position in Christ. Four times Paul challenged believers to walk worthily of the Lord (Eph. 4:1; Phil. 1:27; Col. 1:10; 1 Thess. 2:12). The word "worthy" *(axiōs)* means "of equal weight," or "with

---

12. *Teleios*, used by Paul in 2 Corinthians 13:9, 11; Ephesians 4:13; and Colossians 1:28; 4:12, means "fully developed, complete, or mature." When used of believers, it does not convey the idea of reaching sinless perfection in this life.

13. In this verse the word *logos* may mean "the ability to instruct others" (Albert Barnes, *Barnes' Notes on the New Testament* [reprint, Grand Rapids: Baker, 1962], 875).

14. Earnestness here refers to readiness to discharge one's duty (ibid.).

15. This verb is used in the papyri in the sense of a legally guaranteed (confirmed) security (Adolf Deissmann, *Bible Studies*, trans. Alexander Grieve, 2d ed. [Edinburgh: Clark, 1903], 104–9).

16. Simpson suggests this word means "to be fortified, braced, invigorated" (E. K. Simpson and F. F. Bruce, *Commentary on Ephesians and Colossians*, New International Commentary on the New Testament [Grand Rapids: Eerdmans, 1975], 78, n. 25.

17. Paul used the related noun *oikodomē* ("building up, edification") more often than the verb (Rom. 14:19; 15:2; 1 Cor. 14:3, 5, 12, 26; 2 Cor. 10:8; 12:19; 13:10; Eph. 4:12, 16, 29).

scales in balance," in the sense of our lives being in full accord with the standards of the gospel and of the Lord himself. Paul was concerned that his converts' deeds match their words (Col. 3:17; 2 Thess. 2:16–17). The apostle also challenged believers to live a new life (Rom. 6:4), to live according to and by the enabling of the Holy Spirit (8:4; Gal. 5:16), to live decently (Rom. 13:13) and by faith (2 Cor. 5:7). Spiritually mature Christians live for Christ, not themselves (5:15). They are filled with or controlled by the Holy Spirit (Eph. 5:18), manifesting spiritual "fruit" or virtues (Gal. 5:22–23; cf. Phil. 1:11).

Paul also wrote of spiritual development as "learning," related to both content and experience. *Manthanō*, "to learn," carries the concept of learning subject matter through instruction, as in 2 Timothy 3:14 ("continue in what you have learned"), or appropriating something to oneself through experience or practice,[18] as in Romans 6:17 ("the teaching [*didachē*] you have learned"); Ephesians 4:20 ("You however, did not come to know ['learn,' *manthanō*] Christ that way"); Philippians 4:9 ("Whatever you have learned . . . from me"); and 2 Timothy 3:14 ("continue in what you have learned").[19]

When we and our students are appropriating the truth, growing in Christ, becoming more like him by evidencing his character, we please God (Rom. 14:18; 2 Cor. 5:9; Gal. 1:10; Eph. 5:10; Col. 1:10; 1 Thess. 4:1) and bring glory to him (Rom. 15:6; 2 Cor. 4:15; Eph. 1:12, 14; 2 Thess. 1:12).

Can spiritual maturity be measured? How do we know if our students are maturing in Christ? Paul's writings include sixty-four references to numerous traits of spiritual quality—attributes that should characterize a growing Christian. They may be grouped according to their relationship to God, to others, and to circumstances. Paul longed for his learners to become more Christlike (Gal. 4:19) and thus more mature by evidencing these qualities in their lives. For a helpful devotional study, look up these verses, perhaps taking a few each day, and ask the Lord to help you increase in each of these areas and to help your students do the same.

Qualities in Relationship to God

Blamelessness: Philippians 2:14–15; 1 Timothy 3:2; 6:14; Titus 1:7
Clear conscience: 1 Timothy 1:5, 19; 3:9

---

18. Walter Bauer, William F. Arndt, and F. Wilbur Gingrich, *A Greek-English Lexicon of the New Testament and Other Early Christian Literature*, 2d ed., rev. F. Wilbur Gingrich and Frederick W. Danker (Chicago: University of Chicago Press, 1979), 491.
19. Compare 1 Corinthians 4:6; Colossians 1:7; and Titus 3:14.

Decency: Romans 13:13
Dedication: Romans 12:1
Faithfulness: 1 Corinthians 4:2; Galatians 5:22
Godliness: 1 Timothy 2:2; 4:7–8; 6:6, 11; Titus 1:1
Holiness: 2 Corinthians 7:1; 1 Thessalonians 4:3–4, 7; Titus 1:8
Hope: Romans 15:13; 1 Corinthians 13:13; 1 Timothy 4:10
Insight: Ephesians 1:17
Love: Ephesians 3:17–19
Obedience: Romans 16:19; 2 Corinthians 2:9
Power: Ephesians 1:19; 3:16, 20; 2 Timothy 1:7
Praise: Romans 15:7; Ephesians 5:19
Prayerfulness: Romans 12:12; 15:30–31; Philippians 4:6; Colossians
    4:2; 1 Thessalonians 5:17; 1 Timothy 2:1, 8
Purity: Romans 13:14; 2 Corinthians 6:14; Philippians 1:10; 1 Timo-
    thy 1:5; 5:22; Titus 2:5
Service: Romans 12:11; 1 Corinthians 15:58; Ephesians 6:7
Sincerity: 1 Timothy 3:8
Singing: Ephesians 5:19; Colossians 3:16
Thankfulness: Ephesians 5:20; Colossians 3:16–17: 1 Thessalonians
    5:18
Trust: Romans 15:13; 1 Corinthians 13:13; Ephesians 6:16; Philippi-
    ans 1:6; 4:13
Zeal: Romans 12:11; Titus 2:14

Qualities in Relationship to Others

Acceptance: Romans 15:7
Blessing: Romans 13:14
Concern: Philippians 2:3
Edification: Romans 14:19; 15:2; 1 Corinthians 14:4–5, 17; 1 Thessa-
    lonians 5:11
Encouragement: 1 Thessalonians 4:18; 5:11, 14; 2 Timothy 4:2
Forbearance: Ephesians 4:2
Forgiveness: Ephesians 4:32; Colossians 3:13
Generosity: 1 Timothy 6:18
Gentleness: Galatians 5:23; Philippians 4:5; Colossians 3:13; 1 Timo-
    thy 6:11
Goodness: Romans 12:11, 21; Ephesians 5:9; 1 Thessalonians 5:21,
    1 Timothy 6:18; Titus 3:1, 14
Graciousness: Colossians 4:5–6
Harmony, unity: Romans 12:16, 18; 1 Corinthians 1:10; 7:15; 14:19,
    33; 2 Corinthians 13:11; Philippians 2:15; 4:2; 1 Thessalonians
    5:13

Helpfulness: Romans 12:13; 1 Thessalonians 5:14
Honor, respect: Romans 12:10; 13:7; Ephesians 6:5; 1 Thessalonians
    5:13; 1 Timothy 6:1–2
Hospitality: Romans 12:13; 1 Timothy 3:2; Titus 1:8
Humility: Philippians 2:3; Colossians 3:12; Titus 3:2
Impartiality: 1 Timothy 5:21
Integrity: 2 Corinthians 4:2–3; Titus 2:7
Kindness: Galatians 5:22; Ephesians 4:32; Colossians 3:12
Love: Romans 12:9–10; 13:9–10; 1 Corinthians 13:13; Galatians 5:14;
    Ephesians 5:1–2; Colossians 3:14; 1 Thessalonians 3:12; 4:9;
    1 Timothy 1:5; 2 Timothy 1:7
Mercy: Romans 12:8
Moderation: 1 Timothy 3:2, 11; Titus 2:2
Nonjudgmental spirit: Romans 14:1, 13
Obedience: Ephesians 6:1, 5; Colossians 3:20, 22; Titus 3:1
Rebuking: 1 Timothy 5:20; 2 Timothy 4:2; Titus 2:15
Sharing: Ephesians 4:28
Sincerity: 2 Corinthians 2:17; 1 Timothy 3:8
Submission: Romans 13:5; Ephesians 5:21–22; Titus 2:9; 3:1
Sympathy: Romans 12:15
Trustworthiness: 1 Timothy 3:11; Titus 2:10
Truthfulness: 2 Corinthians 4:2; Ephesians 4:15, 25

Qualities in Relationship to Circumstances

Contentment: Philippians 4:6, 11–12; 1 Thessalonians 5:6; 1 Timothy
    6:6
Courage: 1 Corinthians 16:13
Diligence: Colossians 3:23; 1 Timothy 4:15
Discernment: Ephesians 1:18; 5:15, 17; Philippians 1:10; Colossians
    2:2; Philemon 6
Moderation: 1 Timothy 3:2, 11; Titus 2:2
Patience: Romans 12:12; Colossians 3:12; 1 Thessalonians 5:14
Peace: Romans 15:13; Philippians 4:6–7; Colossians 3:15
Perseverance: 2 Corinthians 4:1, 16; Colossians 1:11; 1 Timothy 4:16;
    6:11
Quietness: 1 Thessalonians 4:11; 1 Timothy 2:2
Self-control: Galatians 5:23; 2 Timothy 1:7; Titus 1:8; 2:5–6
Vigilance: 1 Corinthians 15:58; 1 Thessalonians 5:6
Work: 1 Thessalonians 4:11; 2 Thessalonians 3:9–10

Christian maturity has a negative side too. The Pauline Epistles mention many sins believers should avoid. These include anger, arguing,

complaining, conformity to the world, criticism, deceit, discord, discouragement, disobedience, divisiveness, disputing, drunkenness, envy, favoritism, fellowship with unbelievers, folly, godless chatter, gossip, greed, hatred, idleness, idolatry, immorality, impurity, ingratitude, loving money, lust, lying, malice, meaningless talk, overbearing, pride, quarreling, quick temper, rebellion, resentfulness, revenge, slander, self-centeredness, slander, theft, violence, worry, and yielding to the devil.

The Goal of Imitating Paul

In five epistles Paul set before his readers another goal: to imitate him.

"Therefore I urge you to imitate me [lit., 'become imitators, *mimētai*, of me']" (1 Cor. 4:16).

"Follow my example [lit., 'become imitators, *mimētai*, of me'], as I follow the example of Christ" (1 Cor. 11:1).

"I plead with you, brothers, become like me" (Gal. 4:12).

"Join with others in following my example [lit., 'become fellow imitators, *symmimētai*, of me'], brothers, and take note of those who live according to the pattern [*typos*] we gave you" (Phil. 3:17).

"Whatever you have learned or received or heard from me, or seen in me—put it into practice" (Phil. 4:9).

"You became imitators [*mimētai*] of us and of the Lord" (1 Thess. 1:6).

"For you, brothers, become imitators [*mimētai*] of God's churches in Judea" (1 Thess. 2:14).

"For you yourselves know how you ought to follow our example [lit., 'to imitate, *mimeomai*, us']" (2 Thess. 3:7).

"We did this . . . in order to make ourselves a model for you to follow [lit., 'a model, *typos*, for you to imitate, *mimeomai*]" (2 Thess. 3:9).

How could Paul challenge his readers to become like him, to imitate his life? Is this not rather arrogant? Do teachers dare follow Paul in challenging their students to become like them? How can teachers keep this from becoming self-adulation?

It was common in the Greco-Roman world for exemplary figures to be held up as models of conduct.[20] But not one of these writers identi-

---

20. For example, Fowl cites Isocrates *To Demonicus* 4.11; Seneca *Moral Letters* 6.5–6; 7.6–9; 11.9; Quintilian *On the Education of the Orator* 2.28; and Philostratus *Vita Apollonii* 1.19 (Stephen E. Fowl, "Imitation of Paul/of Christ," in *Dictionary of Paul and His Letters*, 430). Michaelis gives other examples ("μιμέομαι κtl.," in *Theological Dictionary of the New Testament*, 4 [1967], 659–66), as does Willis Peter de Boer (*The Imitation of Paul: An Exegetical Study* [Kampen: Kok, 1962], 25–28), and Ernest Best (*Paul and His Converts* [Edinburgh: Clark, 1988], 61–62).

fied *himself* as a model to be followed.[21] Yet Paul did. Why? Two reasons are that Jewish rabbis urged their disciples to imitate them,[22] and Paul urged believers to follow him as a means toward following Christ (1 Cor. 11:1; cf. 1 Thess. 1:6), the ultimate standard ("Be imitators [*mimētai*] of God," Eph. 5:1). Several of Paul's injunctions are based on Christ's example. Believers are to "accept one another . . . just as Christ accepted" them (Rom. 15:7), to "live a life of love just as Christ loved" them (Eph. 5:2), husbands are to love their wives "just as Christ loved the church" (5:25), and the believers' attitude of humility "should be the same as that of Christ Jesus" (Phil. 2:5).

Paul's idea of imitation builds on his personal association with his converts. The exhortations in the five epistles are addressed only to those churches he founded: churches in Galatia, Thessalonica, Philippi, and Corinth. No such command is given in Romans or Colossians, and in Ephesus he exhorted believers to become "imitators [*mimētai*] of God" (Eph. 5:1). Because they had witnessed his life, he could challenge them to remember him and follow him.

In Paul's call to Christians to become imitators of him, he was not directing them to become tentmakers, nor to mimic him in his mannerisms or obey his authority as an apostle.[23] Instead his charge regarding imitation involved his calling them (a) to imitate his endurance in suffering in which he experienced God's strength in spite of his weakness[24] (cf. 1 Cor. 4:10–13); (b) to imitate his godly conduct (his "way of life in Christ" [4:17] probably meaning his pattern of life in which he followed Christ's moral standards[25]); (c) to imitate his giving of himself for the gospel (1 Cor. 11:1 follows his statement in 10:33 that he selflessly was concerned that others be saved[26]); (d) to imitate his

---

21. Adele Reinhartz, "On the Meaning of the Pauline Exhortation: *'mimētai mou ginesthe'*—become imitators of me," *Studies in Religion* 16 (1987): 395.

22. Michaelis, "μιμέομαι κτλ.," 664.

23. Michaelis wrongly proposed this latter idea (Ibid., 668–69, 672).

24. John Howard Schütz, *Paul and the Anatomy of Apostolic Authority* (Cambridge: Cambridge University Press, 1979), 229; and de Boer, *The Imitation of Paul: An Exegetical Study*, 97–99.

25. William David Spencer, "The Power of Paul's Teaching (1 Cor 4:9–20)," *Journal of the Evangelical Theological Society* 32 (March 1989): 57–59. Hans Conzelman, however, says Paul's "ways" refer to his teaching (*1 Corinthians*, Hermeneia, trans. James W. Leitch [Philadelphia: Fortress, 1975], 92).

26. Paul urged the Corinthians to imitate him just as he imitated Christ, the ideal model of one who did not seek his "own good." This imitation demanded that the Corinthians seek the well-being of others rather than their own (Fowl, "Imitation of Paul/of Christ," 429). Cf. Linda L. Belleville, "'Imitate Me, Just as I Imitate Christ': Discipleship in the Corinthian Correspondence," in *Patterns of Discipleship in the New Testament*, ed. Richard N. Longenecker [Grand Rapids: Eerdmans, 1996], 120–42). Paul thus was like a

freedom from the bondage of legalism (Gal. 4:12; cf. 4:8–11); (e) to imitate his example of pressing on toward maturity (Phil. 3:17 follows his words in 3:12–16 about his own life of spiritual discipline and progress[27]); (f) to practice what they had seen in his life and heard from his lips (Phil. 4:9); (g) to imitate his joyful endurance of suffering,[28] something he said the Thessalonians had already done (1 Thess. 1:6) and who therefore were models to others (1:7) including churches in Judea (2:14); and (h) to imitate his industriousness and self-sacrificial living, rather than giving up their work to prepare for the Lord's return (2 Thess. 3:7, 9). Paul's presenting himself as one whose life is to be imitated was a powerful pedagogical tool. Students often learn as much (if not more) by seeing how their teachers live and teach as they do by what their teachers teach. Paul ranked his example alongside his teaching and instruction. In fact, it constituted a part of his teaching and instruction.[29]

Teachers, like Paul, should live in such a way that they, without hesitation, can challenge their students to follow them. This is not bragging or boasting; this is simply urging others to follow Christ by their own model of being consistent and faithful in endurance, godliness, selflessness, humility, spiritual progress, and industriousness.

This matter of imitation is another way of speaking of becoming spiritually mature. As Bryant puts it, "The process of progressing from immaturity to maturity is *mimēsis*."[30] And Grech wrote that imitation of Christ transforms the believer "into the likeness of the Lord."[31]

---

mediator pointing others to Christ (D. M. Stanley, "'Become Imitators of Me': The Pauline Conception of Apostolic Tradition," *Biblica* 40 [1959]: 874; and Elizabeth Anne Castelli, *Imitating Paul: A Discourse of Power* [Louisville: Westminster, 1991], 112).

27. The unusual word *symmimētai* in Philippians 3:17 means either they should be co-imitators with Paul, setting an example for others, or they should collectively as a congregation be examples, thus exhibiting unity. Perhaps the first idea is intended (Jo-Ann A. Bryant, "The Place of *mimēsis* in Paul's Thought," *Studies in Religion* 22 [1993]: 297), though David Stanley advocates the latter ("Imitation in Paul's Letters," in *From Jesus to Paul,* ed. Peter Richardson and John C. Hurd [Waterloo, Ont.: Wilfrid Laurier University Press, 1984], 137–38).

28. Mary Ann Getty, "The Imitation of Paul in the Letters to the Thessalonians," in *The Thessalonian Correspondence,* ed. Raymond F. Collins (Leuven: Leuven University Press, 1991), 277–83.

29. De Boer, *The Imitation of Paul: An Exegetical Study,* 139. Reinhartz suggests another reason why Paul challenged his readers to imitate him: he was thereby pointing out that his opponents lacked those traits that were evident in him ("On the Meaning of the Pauline Exhortation: *'mimētai mou ginesthe'*—become imitators of me," 403).

30. Bryant, "The Place of *mimēsis* in Paul's Thought," 295.

31. Prosper Grech, "Christological Motives in Pauline Ethics," in *Paul de Parse: Apôtre de Notre Temps* (Rome: Abbaye de S. Paul, 1979), 558.

Being an example to our students is as important as knowing the content of our lessons and communicating them well. In fact, if we are not modeling godliness, our teaching sessions will be ineffectual, because people reject what they see as inconsistency between what we are and what we say. Paul's appeals for his followers to imitate him were effective "because he was a teacher who embodied what he taught."[32] Paul stands as a grand example for all of us to imitate—and thereby to be imitators of Christ, and models to our students!

The Goal of Disciple-Making

The verb *mathēteuō* occurs four times in the New Testament, with the meaning "to become a disciple" (Matt. 27:57) or "to make a disciple" (Matt. 13:52;[33] 28:19; Acts 14:21). Interestingly, only once did Luke refer to Paul making disciples, and in that verse (Acts 14:21) it seems to imply becoming a Christian or follower of Christ: "They preached the good news . . . and won a large number of disciples." In Acts, the related noun *mathētēs*, "disciple," used only in the Gospels and Acts, has the same idea of a believer, as in Acts 14:22, 28; 15:10; 16:1; 18:23, 27; 19:9, 30; 20:1, 30; 21:4, 16.[34] In the Gospels, *mathētēs* is used in several ways: (a) those who had been following and listening to Jesus, who were curious but not convinced,[35] (b) Jesus' twelve inner-circle associates, and (c) Jesus' true followers in Christ.[36] However, in Acts *mathētēs* seems limited to the third meaning.

The reference in Acts 9:25 to Paul's disciples (NIV, "his followers") points to individuals who came to Christ as a result of the apostle's ministry, and shows that his early ministry in Damascus was fruitful.

While the Book of Acts and the Pauline Epistles do not speak specifically of Paul training a special group of disciples as Jesus did, Paul obviously was devoted to helping others develop in their Christian walk and develop their spiritual gifts, as already discussed. This is further suggested by his taking men such as Silas, Timothy, Titus, and others with him on his journeys where they could see him in action and be instructed by him. His epistles to Timothy and Titus could be thought of

---

32. Howard Tillman Kuist, *The Pedagogy of Paul* (New York: Doran, 1925), 113.

33. The NIV renders this word in Matthew 13:52, "who has been instructed," whereas the NASB translates it, "who has become a disciple."

34. Dietrich Miller, "Disciple, Follow, Imitate, After," in *New International Dictionary of New Testament Theology*, 1:489; and Karl H. Rengstorf, "μαθητής," in *Theological Dictionary of the New Testament*, 4 (1967), 457–58.

35. J. Dwight Pentecost, *Design for Discipleship* (Grand Rapids: Zondervan, 1971), 14–17.

36. Zuck, *Teaching as Jesus Taught*, 111.

as letters designed to foster their development as disciples and to enhance their leadership abilities. While they and other associates of Paul
are not called his disciples, they were disciples in the sense that a
mathētēs "implies that the person not only accepts the views of his
teacher, but that he is also in practice an adherent."[37] Involved in Paul's
development of his learners was his passing on[38] to them the teachings
he had received from the Lord (1 Cor. 11:2, 23; 15:3; 2 Thess. 2:15; 3:6)
and urging them to pass them on to others (1 Tim. 3:9; 2 Tim. 2:2; Titus
1:9). Thus he was encouraging them, as pupils, to become teachers,
doing for others what he had done for them. Here, too, in his disciple-
making, Paul stands as a great example for teachers not only to win others to Christ and encourage their spiritual growth, but also to train
them in discipleship and leadership.

What Were Paul's Motives?

Why did the apostle Paul strive so vigorously to attain these several
goals? A number of forces and factors forged Paul forward, urging him
on against overwhelming odds.

First, Paul knew God appointed him to this task. God had told Ana-
nias of Damascus, "This man is my chosen instrument" (Acts 9:15).
And Paul told the Jerusalem mob that Ananias had said to him, "The
God of our fathers has chosen you" (22:14). To King Agrippa, Paul re-
ported that God said to him, "I have appeared to you to appoint you
[and] I am sending you" (26:16–17). Twice Paul wrote to his protégé
Timothy that he "was appointed a herald" (1 Tim. 2:7; 2 Tim. 1:11).
God set him apart from birth and called him to preach to the Gentiles
(Gal. 1:15–16), and to represent him as his ambassador (2 Cor. 5:20).
Having been chosen, called, and appointed, how could he possibly turn
his back on his mission?

Second, Paul sensed Christ's constraining love for him (2 Cor. 5:14).
Synechō, the word for compel, means "to hold together, to press together," and thus "to press on, urge, or compel." Because Christ loved

---

37. G. H. Trever, "Disciples," in *International Standard Bible Encyclopedia*, 2 (1924),
851.

38. The verb for "pass on" is *paradidēmi*, "often used in the sense of a teacher passing
on material which he has learned" (Rienecker, *A Linguistic Key to the Greek New Testament*, 422). The related noun *paradosis* means what is passed on and thus in the plural
it means traditions or teachings, as in 1 Corinthians 11:2; Galatians 1:14; Colossians 2:8;
2 Thessalonians 2:15; and 3:6.

him enough to die for him, he felt a strong obligation to return that love by living for and serving him (5:15).

Third, another compelling factor in this teacher's life was his awareness of coming eternal judgment for the unsaved. He often stated that those who are without Christ stand under the wrath of God (Rom. 1:18; 2:5, 8; 3:5; 5:9; 9:22; Eph. 2:3; 5:6; Col. 3:6; 1 Thess. 1:10; 2:16; 5:9), stand condemned before God (Rom. 3:8; 5:16, 18; 2 Thess. 2:12), and are dead spiritually and are without God (Rom. 1:32; 5:12, 14, 17, 21; 6:23; 1 Cor. 15:22; 2 Cor. 5:14; Eph. 2:1, 5; Col. 2:13). With this terrifying truth constantly reverberating in his mind and heart, how could he not always be catapulted toward telling the lost the world's most wonderful news? He was willing to give his very life for his people the Israelites (Rom. 9:2–3) so that they might be saved (10:1), and he willingly did anything necessary to "win as many as possible" to the Savior (1 Cor. 9:19–22). He repeatedly sought to persuade people to turn to Christ, knowing he must face the judgment seat of Christ, to whom he was responsible (2 Cor. 5:10–11). No wonder the apostle said he was "compelled[39] to preach" and that if he did not do so, he would experience "woe," that is, a sense of pain, agony, and despair (1 Cor. 9:16).

Fourth, this great teacher was forcibly driven to help others mature spiritually because he was deeply convinced that Christ would return at any moment.[40] This expectation became a strong, compelling motive. The Lord's coming, for which he longed (Phil. 3:20–21; 2 Tim. 4:8; Titus 2:13), motivated him to patience (1 Cor. 4:5), diligence and steadfastness (15:58), purity (Col. 3:4–5), holiness (1 Thess. 3:13; 5:23), comfort (1 Thess. 4:18), endurance in suffering (2 Thess. 1:7), and faithfulness in ministry (2 Tim. 4:1–2).

These factors—divine appointment, Christ's love, the spiritual condition of the lost, and Christ's coming—kept Paul moving ahead with unflagging zeal and unrelenting zest to see his goals fulfilled. Can teachers today do any less?

---

39. Literally, Paul wrote, "Compulsion [or necessity, *ananke*] presses on me" (1 Cor. 9:16).

40. One evidence that he expected Jesus to return in his lifetime is his words in 1 Thessalonians 4:15, 17: "we who are still alive, who are left till the coming of the Lord" and "we who are still alive and are left will be caught up." His word "we" shows that he put himself in that group of those who will be living at the time of the rapture of the church. Of course that did not happen; but he fully anticipated the imminent return of Christ.

Give It Some Thought . . .

Has everyone in your class received Jesus Christ as his or her Savior? Have you presented the plan of salvation clearly, so that those who are not saved have an opportunity to turn to Christ?

What means are you using in your teaching to convey biblical facts your students need to know? Are you communicating on their level, not speaking above them or below them?

In what specific ways are you helping the Christians in your class to grow?

What evidence of spiritual growth do you see in your students? Do you see in their lives some of the sixty-four maturity traits listed in this chapter?

Sergius Paulus "was amazed at the teaching about the Lord."

Acts 13:12

8

How Did Paul Impact His Learners?

Have you ever wondered if your Bible teaching is really making a difference in your students' lives? Have you ever thought, "Am I getting through? Are they living out what I'm teaching? Are they responding to God's truth?"

It is one thing to know what we want to accomplish, and to be motivated toward those ends. But it is another thing to know whether those goals are being met, to know if we are impacting our learners.

Paul's teaching role shows how the Lord used him to impact his learners. Seeing how he did this can give us clues on how we too can be effective in our teaching ministries.

Jesus ministered to diverse groups, to individuals with varied interests, needs, and concerns.[1] And Paul did the same. Also, like Jesus, Paul dealt with individuals, small groups, and crowds. As with Jesus' teaching ministry, some of Paul's listeners were curious, others were receptive, and still others were antagonistic and even viciously hostile. Seeing how Paul related to the diversity of his audiences and students, and how they responded to him, can enlighten us on how to relate better to our own students.

---

1. Roy B. Zuck, *Teaching as Jesus Taught* (Grand Rapids: Baker, 1995), 115–20.

127

Table 9
People to Whom Paul Ministered

People in synagogues	Acts 9:20 (Damascus); 13:5 (Salamis of Cypress); 13:14 (Antoich of Pisidia); 14:1 (Iconium); 17:2 (Thessalonica); 17:10 (Berea); 17:17 (Athens); 18:1, 4 (Corinth); 18:19; 19:8 (Ephesus); cf. 24:12
People in crowds	Acts 13:44–45; 14:11, 13–14, 18–19; 17:8, 13; cf. 19:33, 35
People in marketplaces	Acts 17:17, 22[a]
People in cities	Acts 13:4; 14:21; 15:35
Women at a riverbank	Acts 16:13
Fellow prisoners	Acts 16:25, 28–31
People in families	Acts 16:15, 33–34; 18:8; 1 Corinthians 16:15
People in a lecture hall	Acts 19:9
People in homes	Acts 16:15, 32, 40; 18:7; 20:8, 20; 21:16
Disciples in churches	Acts 14:22, 27–28; 15:41; 16:5; 18:22–23; 19:1, 9; 20:1, 17

a. Acts 17:22 says that Paul "stood up in the meeting of the Areopagus." Areopagus, literally "Hill of Ares," the Greek god of war ("Mars' Hill," KJV), was the Athenian judicial and legislative council, named after its meeting place on the hill west of the Acropolis. When the council later transferred its meeting place to a building (the "Royal Porch," *stoa basileios*) in the Agora or marketplace, it retained the name Council of Areopagus (F. F. Bruce, *Commentary on the Book of Acts* [Grand Rapids: Eerdmans, 1954], 351–52), and this may have been where Paul met with the council (F. F. Bruce, "Areopagus," in *The Illustrated Bible Dictionary* [Wheaton, Ill.: Tyndale, 1980], 1:108). For a photo of the restored *stoa basileios* near the Athenian Agora, see ibid., 1:147. This roofed colonnade stood about three hundred yards north of Mars' Hill. Colin J. Hemer argues that Paul stood in a small area near the northwest corner of the Agora ("Paul at Athens: A Topographic Study," *New Testament Studies* 20 [1973–1974]: 346).

Whom Did Paul Teach and How Did They Respond?

Paul's amazing evangelistic and pedagogical abilities are seen in the varied audiences and individuals he taught. He debated with religious leaders and spoke boldly to political rulers. He talked with an intelligent government administrator, uncultured pagans, well-to-do craftsmen, sophisticated philosophers, prominent women, prisoners, and Roman soldiers. He addressed huge crowds, religiously oriented groups, families, and individuals in private. This diversity can be seen from the list in table 9.

Most of the people in the synagogues were Jews, of course, but some

throughout the region of Galatia and Phrygia, strengthening all the disciples" (18:23).

...ul "took the disciples with him and had discussions daily in the lecture hall of Tyrannus . . . for two years" (19:9–10).

...e traveled through that area [Macedonia], speaking many words of encouragement to the people, and finally arrived in Greece [i.e., in Achaia], where he stayed three months" (20:2–3).

...e "sailed from Philippi. . . [to] Troas, where [he] stayed seven days" (20:6).

...emember that for three years I never stopped warning each of you [in Ephesus] night and day with tears" (20:31).

...e greeted the brothers [in Ptolemais, south of Tyre] and stayed with them for a day" (21:7).

...e stayed at the house of Philip [in Caesarea] . . . a number of days" (21:8, 10).

...ublius, the chief official of the island [of Malta] . . . welcomed us into his home and for three days entertained us hospitably" (28:7).

...fter three months [on Malta] we put out to sea" (28:11).

...Puteoli, Italy, "we found some brothers who invited us to spend a week with them" (28:14).

...or two whole years Paul stayed there in his own rented house [in Rome] and welcomed all who came to see him [and] he preached . . . and taught" (28:30–31).

...e assurance of salvation brings joy, as is expressed twice in Acts: ...disciples [in Pisidian Antioch] were filled with joy" (13:52); and the ...ppian jailer's family members, all of whom accepted Christ as their ...or, were "filled with joy" (16:34). Paul referred to the Philippians' ...in the faith" and "joy in Christ Jesus" (Phil. 1:25–26) and to the ...salonians' "joy given by the Holy Spirit" (1 Thess. 1:6).

...esides evangelism and teaching, Paul also helped organize ...ches by appointing elders in each congregation of believers in ...a, Iconium, and Antioch of Pisidia (Acts 14:21–23), and Ephesus ...7), which presumably he also did in other churches he founded. ...ncouraged Titus to appoint elders in each church on the island of ...e (Titus 1:5). Thus the apostle's task involved witnessing to the un...d, leading many of them to receive Christ as their Savior, teaching ...truths needed for their spiritual nurture, and organizing believers ...al churches with qualified leaders. These were the measure of his ...ss—not how many miles he traveled, or the number of years he ...stered, or places he visited, or the size of his churches. His success ...measured by spiritual, not numerical, yardsticks.

synagogues were also attended by "God-fearing" Gentiles.[2] These Gentiles (sometimes called "Greeks") were in Antioch of Pisidia (Acts 13:16, 26, 43), Thessalonica (17:4), and Athens (17:17). In each city he entered, Paul usually spoke first to Jews in their places of worship (13:46; 18:5; 26:20; cf. Rom. 1:16, "first for the Jew"), and then to Gentiles (Acts 13:46, 48; 14:27; 15:3, 12, 14, 17, 19; 18:6; 21:19; 26:17–18, 20; 28:28), since God had appointed him the apostle to the Gentiles (Rom. 1:5, 13–14; 3:29; 11:13; 15:9–12, 16, 18; Gal. 1:16; 2:2, 7–9; 3:8, 14; Eph. 3:1, 6, 8; Col. 1:27; 1 Tim. 2:7; 2 Tim. 4:17).

However, in Philippi he altered his strategy, going first to the riverside where he met a God-fearing Gentile woman (Acts 16:14). Both Jews and Gentiles ("Greeks," Acts 18:4; 19:10) heard his message (20:21). He took every opportunity to preach and teach to a variety of audiences in a variety of places.

The crowds he addressed were in Pisidian Antioch, Lystra, Thessalonica, Berea, and Ephesus. The homes in which he witnessed and taught were those of Lydia, the Philippian jailer, Titius Justus, a two-story house in Troas, and Mnason. While it is impossible to know how many were in the various groups, each synagogue may have included scores of individuals. "Almost the whole city" (13:44) of Pisidian Antioch would have included several hundred people. Each crowd would probably have included several hundred people, many would have been in the marketplaces, several dozen may have attended the apostle's daily lectures in Tyrannus's hall,[3] and possibly between four and eight individuals were in each family. Therefore it comes as no surprise to read several times of large numbers of people being saved through Paul's ministry (14:1, 21; 17:4, 12, 34; 18:8, 10; 19:26; 28:23–24), including "many thousands of Jews" (21:20). In hyperbole some unbelieving Jews accused Paul of teaching "all men everywhere" (21:28).

In several cities women were among those who came to Christ. One was Lydia, a religious businesswoman engaged in selling purple-dyed

2. They revered God (*phobeomai*, Acts 13:16, 26) and were religious or devout in worship (*sebomai*, 13:43 [NIV's "devout converts to Judaism" should be translated "devout proselytes"]; 17:4, 17). They were called this because they had renounced idolatry and attended synagogue worship, but were not fully admitted to Judaism. To be "God-fearing" or devout did not mean these individuals were Christian believers, because they needed the message of salvation through faith in Christ (10:2; 13:48; 17:4, 17).

3. Tyrannus may "have been a teacher of philosophy or rhetoric, perhaps the most famous to have lectured in this hall, and hence, for the fame brought to it by him, it was known as 'the hall of Tyrannus'" (Gerald F. Hawthorne, "Tyrannus," in *International Standard Bible Encyclopedia*, 4 [1988], 932). A few Greek manuscripts add that Paul's two-year stint of teaching in this hall each day was "from the fifth to the tenth hour," that is, from 11:00 A.M. to 4:00 P.M., the time "usually reserved for a meal and rest" (ibid.).

woolen goods (16:14).[4] She became Paul's first convert in Europe. Others included the Philippian jailer's wife (16:34), a number of "prominent" women in Thessalonica (17:4) and Berea (17:12), Damaris of Athens (17:34), and the wife of Crispus, a synagogue leader (18:8).

On Cyprus, Sergius Paulus believed on the Lord, being "amazed[5] at Paul's teaching" (13:12). Gentiles in Antioch of Pisidia believed in Christ (13:48) as a result of Paul's ministry there; some of the people of Iconium "sided . . . with the apostles" (14:4); some Jews and many Greeks were saved in Thessalonica (17:4); many Jews and Greeks in Berea came to Christ (17:12); a few in Athens accepted Christ, including Dionysius, a member of the Areopagus (17:34);[6] many Corinthians believed (18:8); some Jews in Rome were convinced by Paul's witnessing (28:24); and Onesimus, a slave from Colossae, came to Christ through Paul's witness while he was in prison (Philem. 10). Many, many lives were changed through the apostle's tireless labors!

Entire cities were impacted by the apostle's preaching and teaching, sometimes with divided results. "On the next Sabbath almost the whole city [of Pisidian Antioch] gathered to hear the word of the Lord" (13:44). "The people of the city [of Iconium] were divided" (14:4). "These men are Jews, and are throwing our city [of Philippi] into an uproar" (16:20). "These men . . . have caused trouble all over the world" (17:6). "Soon the whole city was in an uproar" (19:29). "Paul has convinced . . . large numbers of people here in Ephesus" (19:26). "This is the man who teaches all men everywhere" (21:28).

Paul's evangelistic work stands as a model of a ministry of multiplication. His converts, the objects of his evangelism, in turn became evangelists. This is implied in Acts 13:49 ("the word of the Lord spread through the whole region" of Pisidia, in present-day south-central Tur-

---

4. She was from Thyatira, two hundred miles away, a city well known for manufacturing purple dye and for garment-making.

5. "Amazed" translates *ekplēssō*, "to be astonished or overwhelmed," which is used only here in Acts. Elsewhere in the New Testament it occurs only in the Synoptic Gospels, as the most common word for amazement at Jesus' teaching. Twelve times it expresses the response of groups to Jesus' teaching (Matt. 7:28; 13:54; 19:25; 22:33; Mark 1:22; 6:2; 7:37; 10:26; 11:18; Luke 2:48; 4:32; 9:43). It speaks of "sudden and vehement astonishment" (F. W. Farrar, *The Gospel according to St. Luke*, Cambridge Greek Testament for Schools and Colleges [Cambridge: Cambridge University Press, 1884], 155). *Ekplēssō*, from *plēssō*, "to strike or blow" and *ek*, "out," suggests being struck out of one's senses with astonishment.

6. "The Areopagus was the high court of twelve judges in Athens. A modern equivalent of the believing of Dionysius would be the conversion of a justice of the United States Supreme Court. If such a conversion were to take place because of the message of some contemporary preacher, would that address be considered a failure?" (J. Oswald Sanders, *Paul the Leader* [Colorado Springs: NavPress, 1984], 101).

key) and 19:10 ("all the Jews and Greeks who live Asia [present-day western Turkey] heard the wo 19:26), and in 1 Thessalonians 1:8 ("The Lord's me you not only in Macedonia and Achaia—your faith known everywhere"). Also, on Paul's second mi Turkey, churches "grew daily in number" (Acts 16 then, he told Festus that his ministry "was no (26:26).

Of great significance is the fact that Paul's evang ing, and teaching ministries were urban focused. reach and teach people in large cities in key locat gospel spread to outlying areas. "All the cities, o planted churches were centres of Roman adminis ilization, of Jewish influence, or of some commer

Paul's ministry in his many places of travel be presenting the claims of Christ winsomely and pe not end there. That was only the beginning. Th spent in various locations gave him significant o and nurture believers. How exciting and spiritu have been for new Christians to hear the great ap God's ways. References to the length of time he s no doubt reflect his intense teaching ministry, a key verses:

"Paul and Barnabas spent considerable time (Acts 14:3).

Paul and Barnabas "stayed there [in Antioch disciples" (Acts 14:28).

"Paul and Barnabas remained in Antioch, whe ers taught and preached the word of the Lo

"So Paul stayed for a year and a half [in Corin word of God" (18:11).

"After spending some time in Antioch [on his ney], Paul set out from there and travele

---

7. This Greek word *exēcheomai* refers to the blowing spreads or echoes from one place to another. The Thessaloni in diffusing the gospel in other places, *as if* the sound of a tru among the hills and along the vales of the classic land of Gre *Notes on the New Testament* [reprint, Grand Rapids: Krege Macedonia, where Thessalonica was located, is today nort today southern Greece, the area below the Gulf of Corinth.

8. Roland Allen, *Missionary Methods: St. Paul or Ours?* 1962), 13; cf. 13–17.

While Paul's impact for the gospel was significant in that many came to Christ and were taught by the apostle, his teachings aroused the antagonism of many Jews. These clashes occurred almost everywhere he went, including Damascus (Acts 9:23), Jerusalem (9:29), Antioch of Pisidia (13:45, 50), Iconium (14:2, 4–5), Lystra (14:19), Thessalonica (17:5), Berea (17:13), Corinth (18:12), Ephesus (19:9), Jerusalem (21:27–30, 32, 36; 22:20; 23:12–13), and Caesarea (24:1, 9). Also, workers in both Philippi (16:16–19) and Ephesus (19:23–28) were upset by Paul's teaching, and some Athenian philosophers sneered at him (17:32). His opponents in these various places tried to kill him, they spoke abusively against him, expelled him, slandered and falsely accused him, stoned him, caused citywide riots, sneered at him, agitated crowds against him, publicly maligned his message, beat him, shouted against him, and conspired to kill him. Because the truth ran counter to what many people wanted to believe, they tried to discredit and eliminate the messenger of truth. Yet he did not let their antagonism deter him; he continued on relentlessly.

Who Were Paul's Coworkers?

One of the clearest indications of the impact of the apostle's teaching is his many coworkers.[9] Though he had no disciples *(mathētai),* several dozen individuals were so attracted by Paul's magnetic personality and his dynamic message that they joined with him in his ministry. "Having found a way into the lives of others, they also entered into his. What a large number of personally intimate friends St. Paul had in his heart's affection!"[10] Besides their being encouraged by his role model for them and his friendship, he no doubt benefited from their companionship. Some of them traveled with him, some suffered with him, and several were even imprisoned with him.

Almost 100 individuals were associated in some way at some time or another in his ministry. Redlich includes 95 such companions,[11] and Hiebert lists over 140 individuals who had some contact with Paul, either as coworkers, friends, converts, hosts, or opponents.[12]

9. "The quality of a man's companions is an index, and their number is in some sense a measure, of his soul" (Reginald E. O. White, *Apostle Extraordinary* [Grand Rapids: Eerdmans, 1962], 100).

10. Howard Tillman Kuist, *The Pedagogy of St. Paul* (New York: Doran, 1925), 136.

11. Edwin Basil Redlich, *S. Paul and His Companions* (London: Macmillan, 1913), 200–286.

12. D. Edmond Hiebert, *Personalities around Paul* (Chicago: Moody, 1973), 222. After discussing twenty-eight "prominent personalities" and "lesser lights" on pages 21–219, he lists over one hundred named and unnamed individuals with a brief statement about each one on pages 223–38.

The number depends on how broadly or narrowly the term "companion" is used.

His major coworkers included Barnabas and Mark, who were associated with him on his first missionary trek (Acts 13:1–3, 5); Silas, Timothy, Luke, and Priscilla and Aquila, who were associated with Paul in his second missionary journey (Acts 15:40; 16:1–3, 10; 18:2; Rom. 16:3, 21, 23; 2 Tim. 1:2; 4:10–11; Titus 1:4); and Apollos, Aristarchus, Erastus, who were associated with Paul on his third missionary journey (Acts 19:1, 22, 29; 20:4; 1 Cor. 16:12; Eph. 6:21; Col. 4:7; 2 Tim. 4:12, 20; Titus 3:13). Others may be thought of as short-term itinerant workers. Some of his fellow workers were prominent individuals socially. Barnabas was a property owner (Acts 4:36–37); Lydia was a businesswoman (16:14); Erastus was Rome's public-works director (Rom. 16:24); and Luke was a physician (Col. 4:14).

In speaking of his companions Paul used several compound words with the prefix *syn* ("with"); one of the most frequent is *synergos*, "fellow worker."[13] For anyone to be so designated by Paul must have been in itself an inspiration and honor.[14] All but one of the occurrences of this word in the New Testament are by Paul (the other usage is in 3 John 8). Table 10 lists those whom Paul designated with words using the *syn* prefix.

Table 10
Paul's "Fellow" Companions

Fellow Workers

Priscilla and Aquila (Rom. 16:3)
Urbanus (Rom. 16:9)
Timothy (Rom. 16:21; 1 Thess. 3:2)
Apollos (1 Cor. 3:9)
Titus (2 Cor. 8:23)
Epaphroditus (Phil. 2:25)
Aristarchus (Col. 4:10–11; Philem. 24)
Mark (Col. 4:10–11; Philem. 24)
Jesus Justus (Col. 4:10–11)
Philemon (Philem. 1)
Demas (Philem. 24)
Luke (Philem. 24)

13. See Victor Paul Furnish, "Fellow Workers in God's Service," *Journal of Biblical Literature* 80 (1961): 364–70.
14. T. R. Glover, *Paul of Tarsus* (London: SCM, 1925), 178–79.

Fellow Prisoners[15]

Andronicus (Rom. 16:7)
Junias (Rom. 16:7)
Aristarchus (Col. 4:10)
Epaphras (Philem. 23)

Fellow Slaves

Epaphras (Col. 4:12)
Tychicus (Col. 4:7)

Fellow Soldiers

Epaphroditus (Phil. 2:25)
Archippus (Philem. 2)

Fellow Travelers

Gaius (Acts 19:29)
Aristarchus (Acts 19:29)

Interestingly, Paul called Aristarchus by three "fellow" titles: fellow worker, fellow prisoner, and fellow soldier; Epaphroditus is called the apostle's fellow worker and fellow soldier; and Epaphras is referred to by two titles: Paul's fellow prisoner and fellow slave.[16]

Paul affectionately called each of ten of his colleagues his "brother": Apollos (1 Cor. 16:12), Epaphroditus (Phil. 2:25), Onesimus (Col. 4:9), Philemon (Philem. 7), Quartus (Rom. 16:23), Sosthenes (1 Cor. 1:1), Silas (Acts 15:22), Timothy (2 Cor. 1:1; Col. 1:1; 1 Thess. 3:2; Philem. 1), Titus (2 Cor. 2:13), Tychicus (Eph. 6:21; Col. 4:7), and an unnamed brother who was sent to Corinth with Titus (2 Cor. 8:18, 22; 12:18). "Servant" *(diakonos)* is a term Paul used of Apollos (1 Cor. 3:5), Epaphras (Col. 1:7), and Tychicus (Eph. 6:21; Col. 4:7), and the participle "those who are serving" is used of Timothy and Erastus (Acts 19:22), NIV has "his helpers"). Paul called at least six of his colaborers "apostles" in the sense of their being recommended by God as associates of Paul the apostle, not in the sense of their being one of those who had seen the resurrected Christ: Andronicus (Rom. 16:7), Barnabas (Acts 14:4, 14), Junias (Rom. 16:7), Silas (1 Thess. 2:7), and Timothy (1 Thess. 2:6). [17]

15. On the role of those who helped Paul when he was in prison, see Brian M. Rapske, "The Importance of Helpers to the Imprisoned Paul in the Book of Acts," *Tyndale Bulletin* 42 (1991): 3–30.

16. For a discussion of these coworkers and their ministries with Paul, see F. F. Bruce, *The Pauline Circle* (Grand Rapids: Eerdmans, 1985), 81–90.

17. For more of these designations, see Redlich, *S. Paul and His Companions*, 187–93.

In Romans 16:7, 11, and 21 Paul mentioned six of his relatives by name: Andronicus, Herodion, Jason, Junias, Lucius, and Sosipater. Andronicus and Junias "were very likely Jerusalem relatives who were missionaries from that church to Rome" and were imprisoned, though not at the same time and place as Paul.[18] Jason in Romans 16:21 is probably the Jason of Thessalonica who was Paul's host (Acts 17:5–9), and Sosipater may be the fuller name of Sopater, who represented the church of Berea on the collection visit to Jerusalem (Acts 20:4). "In mentioning these kinfolk coworkers Paul reveals something of the strategy of his mission. He utilized contacts with his relatives in charting the evangelization of Thessalonica and Berea and, upon their conversion, accepted them as fellow workers in the mission. . . ."[19]

Several colleagues of Paul were involved with him in sending and/or writing letters. Co-senders are mentioned near the beginning of eight of his thirteen epistles, as seen in the following list.

1 Corinthians	Sosthenes
2 Corinthians	Timothy
Galatians	"all the brothers with me"
Philippians	Timothy
Colossians	Timothy
1 Thessalonians	Silas, Timothy
2 Thessalonians	Silas, Timothy
Philemon	Timothy

Exactly how they were involved in writing these letters is not known. A secretary, or *amanuensis,* is mentioned in only one epistle: Tertius in Romans 16:22. However, Paul may have dictated some of his epistles to a secretary without mentioning that person's name. This seems to be implied in 1 Corinthians 16:21; Colossians 4:18; 2 Thessalonians 3:17; and Philemon 19, where he said he wrote his greetings in his own hand.[20]

Greetings at the end of several of his letters were sent from Timothy, Lucius, Jason, Sosipater, Tertius, Gaius, Erastus, and Quartus to the Roman believers (Rom. 16:21–23); from Aquila and Priscilla and "the brothers" with Paul to the Corinthians (1 Cor. 16:19); from Epaphras, Mark, Aristarchus, Demas, and Luke from Rome to Philemon (Philem.

---

18. Earle E. Ellis, "Coworkers, Paul and His," in *Dictionary of Paul and His Letters,* ed. Gerald F. Hawthorne, Ralph F. Martin, and Daniel G. Reid (Downers Grove, Ill.: InterVarsity, 1993), 186; cf. idem, "Paul and His Co-Workers," *New Testament Studies* 17 (1970–1971): 437–52.

19. Ellis, "Coworkers, Paul and His," 186.

20. On the use of secretaries in Paul's letters, see E. R. Richards, *The Secretary in the Letters of Paul* (Tübingen: Mohr, 1991), and Richard N. Longenecker, "Ancient Amanuenses and the Pauline Epistles," in *New Dimensions in New Testament Study,* ed. Richard N. Longenecker and Merrill C. Tenney (Grand Rapids: Zondervan, 1974), 281–97.

23–24); and from Eubulus, Pudens, Linus, Claudia and "all the brothers" in Rome to Timothy (2 Tim. 4:21). Tychicus was the courier of at least Ephesians (Eph. 6:21–22) and Colossians (Col. 4:7);[21] and Titus and an anonymous "brother" were the two letter carriers of 2 Corinthians (2 Cor. 8:17–18).

A number of individuals had the honor of hosting Paul in their homes. These twelve are listed chronologically:

Ananias, in Damascus (Acts 9:10–18; 22:12–13)
Judas, in Damascus (Acts 9:11)
Peter, in Jerusalem (Gal. 1:18)
Unnamed jailer, in Philippi (Acts 16:33–34)
Lydia, in Philippi (Acts 16:40)
Jason, in Thessalonica (Acts 17:7)
Aquila and Priscilla, in Corinth (Acts 18:3)
Titius Justus, in Corinth (Acts 18:7)
Gaius, in Corinth (Rom. 16:23)
Mnason, in Jerusalem (Acts 21:16)
Philemon, a potential host (Philem. 22)

Romans 16:1–16 lists twenty-eight of Paul's associates in Rome, whom Paul asked the Roman believers to greet for him. And in Romans 16:21–24 he mentioned by name eight associates who were sending their greetings to the Romans.[22] When these thirty-six individuals are added to others mentioned in Acts and Paul's other epistles, the total number of his colleagues is eighty-three. This total includes his named converts[23] (e.g., Lydia [Acts 16:13–15] and Dionysius and Damaris [17:34]); his friends (such as Chloe, Eunice, James, Lois, Peter, and Philip); and his twelve hosts and hostesses. These eighty-three individuals are listed alphabetically in table 11.[24]

21. Tychicus may have also had the letter to Philemon with him en route from Rome to Ephesus and Colossae (Col. 4:7–9).

22. "This list [of thirty-six persons] reads almost like a roll call of Paul's former 'students.' Many were fellow workers or even fellow apostles, but we can be certain that they all spent time studying and learning from Paul" (Stanley Kent Stowers, *The Diatribe and Paul's Letter to the Romans* [Chico, Calif.: Scholars, 1981], 183).

23. However, three of Paul's converts also became his coworkers: Timothy ("my true son in the faith," 1 Tim. 1:2; "my son," 1:18; 2 Tim. 2:1; "my dear son," 2 Tim. 1:2), Titus ("my true son in our common faith," Titus 1:4), and Onesimus ("who became my son while I was in chains," Philem. 10). Possibly Timothy, though, had been led to the Lord by his mother and/or grandmother.

24. Discussing these names, J. B. Lightfoot points out that many of these same names have appeared in Latin writings (*Saint Paul's Epistle to the Philippians*, 4th ed. [London: Macmillan, 1879], 171).

Table 11
Paul's Colleagues and Coworkers

Achaicus (1 Cor. 1:16; 16:17–18)
Alexander (1 Tim. 1:19–20)
Ampliatus (Rom. 16:8)
Andronicus (Rom. 16:7)
Apelles (Rom. 16:10)
Apollos (Acts 18:24–19:7; 1 Cor. 1:10; 3:5–6; 16:12; Titus 3:13)
Apphia (Philem. 1–2)
Aquila (Acts 18:2–3, 18–19, 26; Rom. 16:3–5; 1 Cor. 16:19; 2 Tim. 4:19)
Archippus (Col. 4:17; Philem. 2)
Aristarchus (Acts 19:29; 20:4; 27:2; Col. 4:10–11; Philem. 24)
Aristobulus (Rom. 16:10)
Artemas (Titus 3:12)
Asyncritus (Rom. 16:14)
Barnabas (Acts 4:36; 9:27; 11:22–26, 30; 12:25; 13:1–15; 1 Cor. 9:6; Gal. 2:1, 9, 13; Col. 4:10)
Carpus (2 Tim. 4:13)
Claudia (2 Tim. 4:21)
Clement (Phil. 4:2–3)
Crescens (2 Tim. 4:10)
Crispus (Acts 18:8; 1 Cor. 1:14)
Demas (Col. 4:14; 2 Tim. 4:10; Philem. 24)
Epenetus (Rom. 16:5)
Epaphras (Col. 1:7; 4:12–13; Philem. 23)
Epaphroditus (Phil. 2:25–30; 4:18)
Erastus (Acts 19:22; Rom. 16:23; 2 Tim. 4:20)
Eubulus (2 Tim. 4:21)
Euodia (Phil. 4:2–3)
Eutychus (Acts 20:7–12)
Fortunatus (1 Cor. 16:17–18)
Gaius of Corinth (Rom. 16:23; 1 Cor. 1:14)
Gaius of Derbe (Acts 20:4)
Gaius of Macedonia (Acts 19:29)
Hermas (Rom. 16:14)
Hermes (Rom. 16:14)
Hermogenes (2 Tim. 1:15)
Herodion (Rom. 16:11)
Hymenaeus (1 Tim. 1:19–20; 2 Tim. 2:16–18)
Jason (Acts 17:5–9; Rom. 16:21)
Jesus Justus (Col. 4:10–11)
Judas Barsabbas (Acts 15:22, 32–33)
Julia (Rom. 16:15)
Junias (Rom. 16:7)
Linus (2 Tim. 4:21)
Lucius (Rom. 16:21)

Lucius of Cyrene (Acts 13:1)
Luke (Acts 16:10–17; 20:6–8, 13–15; 21:1–18; 27:1–28:16 [the word "we" in these passages in Acts include Luke, the author of Acts]; Col. 4:14; 2 Tim. 4:11; Philem. 24)
Manaen (Acts 13:1)
Mark (Acts 12:12, 25; 13:5, 13; 15:37–39; Col. 4:10–11; 2 Tim. 4:11; Philem. 24; 1 Peter 5:13)
Mary (Rom. 16:6)
Narcissus (Rom. 16:11)
Nereus (Rom. 16:15)
Nympha (Col. 4:15)
Olympas (Rom. 16:15)
Onesimus (Col. 4:9; Philem. 10)
Onesiphorus (2 Tim. 1:16–18; 4:19)
Patrobas (Rom. 16:14)
Persis (Rom. 16:12)
Philemon (Philem.)
Philetus (2 Tim. 2:16–18)
Philologus (Rom. 16:15)
Phlegon (Rom. 16:14)
Phoebe (Rom. 16:1–2)
Phygelus (2 Tim. 1:15)
Priscilla (Acts 18:2–3, 18–19, 26; Rom. 16:3–5; 1 Cor. 16:19; 2 Tim. 4:19)[25]
Pudens (2 Tim. 4:21)
Quartus (Rom. 16:23)
Rufus (Rom. 16:13)
Secundus (Acts 20:4)
Silas or Silvanus (Acts 15:22, 27, 32–33, 40: 15:40–18:5; 2 Cor. 1:19; 1 Thess. 1:1; 2 Thess. 1:1; 1 Peter 5:12)
Sopater or Sosipater (Acts 20:4; Rom. 16:21)
Sosthenes (Acts 18:17; 1 Cor. 1:1–2)
Stachys (Rom. 16:9)
Stephanas (1 Cor. 1:16; 16:15–18)
Simeon called Niger (Acts 13:1)
Syntyche (Phil. 4:2–3)
Tertius (Rom. 16:22)
Timothy (Acts 16:1–3; 17:14–15; 18:5; 19:22; 20:4; Rom. 16:21; 1 Cor. 4:17; 16:10–11; 2 Cor. 1:1, 19; Phil. 1:1; 2:19–20; Col. 1:1; 1 Thess. 1:1; 3:2, 6; 2 Thess. 1:1; 1 and 2 Tim.; Philem. 1; Heb. 13:23)
Titus (2 Cor. 2:13; 7:6–7, 13–14; 8:6, 16–17, 23; 12:18; Gal. 2:1, 3; 2 Tim. 4:10; Titus)
Trophimus (Acts 20:4; 21:29; 2 Tim. 4:20)
Tryphena (Rom. 16:12)
Tryphosa (Rom. 16:12)

25. In Romans 16:3, 1 Corinthians 16:19, and 2 Timothy 4:19, the Greek has Prisca, a variant of Priscilla.

Tychicus (Acts 20:4; Eph. 6:21–22; Col. 4:7–9; 2 Tim. 4:12; Titus 3:12)
Urbanus (Rom. 16:9)
Zenas (Titus 3:13)

Table 12
Chronology of Paul's Major Coworkers[26]

Coworkers Associated with Paul	Dates Associated with Paul[a]	Total Years
Barnabas	summer 35–spring 56	20 years
Mark	fall 47–summer 48, and fall 67	ca. 1 year
Titus	fall 47–winter 66/67	19 1/2 years
Timothy	spring 49[b]–fall 67	18 years
Silas	winter 49/50–summer 51	ca. 1 1/2 years
Luke	April 50–fall 67	17 1/2 years
Aquila and Priscilla	March 51–fall 67	16 1/2 years
Aristarchus	spring 53–fall 67	14 1/2 years
Tychicus	spring 53–fall 67	14 1/2 years

a. These dates give the beginnings and endings of the coworkers' associations with Paul. Not all of these companions, however, were physically with him during the entire spread of the years. For a time line of Paul's life, with similar dates, see *The NIV Study Bible*, ed. Kenneth Barker (Grand Rapids: Zondervan, 1985), 1664–65. Cf. Loveday C. A. Alexander, "Chronology of Paul," in *Dictionary of Paul and His Letters*, 115–23; K. P. Donfried, "Chronology: New Testament," in *Anchor Bible Dictionary*, 1:1011–22; and Harold W. Hoehner, "Chronology," in *Dictionary of Jesus and the Gospels*, 118–22.

b. This assumes Timothy began his association with Paul in Derbe on Paul's first missionary journey, though Timothy did not begin traveling with Paul until the apostle's second missionary journey.

According to Hoehner's chronology of the life of Paul,[27] Barnabas and Titus[28] were associated with Paul about twenty years each, Timothy's association with Paul was for about eighteen years, Luke about eighteen years,[29] Aquila and Priscilla about sixteen years, Aristarchus

26. These are listed in the order in which they first appeared with Paul. The dates are based on the chronology worked out by Hoehner ("Chronology of the Apostolic Age", 367–84).

27. Harold W. Hoehner, "Chronology of the Apostolic Age" (Th.D. diss., Dallas Theological Seminary, 1965).

28. Titus, a Greek, traveled with Paul and Barnabas to Jerusalem even before the apostle's first missionary journey (Gal. 2:1–3) and was with Paul on other journeys also (2 Cor. 7:6–7; 8:17).

29. Timothy was very special to Paul as seen in many of Paul's comments about him: "Timothy, my fellow worker" (Rom. 16:21); "Timothy, my son whom I love" (1 Cor. 4:17);

and Tychicus between fourteen and fifteen years each (see table 12). These and others reveal Paul's commitment to teamwork. However, it is of interest that Paul seldom had more than two of these men with him at any given time.

Clearly, the number of people who heard the gospel from Paul, the thousands who became believers through his ministry, the many groups of Christians who received instruction from him over extended periods of times, and the scores of individuals who worked with him or were associated with him in some other way—these all evidence the remarkably widespread and deep impact of this man whose life was given totally to Christ and his cause.

To Consider . . .

Do you take opportunities the Lord gives you to speak to your unsaved students about their need of Christ?

In what ways can you encourage your students who are believers to share their faith in Christ with others?

Are you staying in your teaching position long enough to help establish and nurture your students spiritually?

Are you continuing on in the Lord's work even if you are facing some opposition from students or others?

In what ways can you enlist some of your students or others to work with you or someone else in ministry?

"Timothy . . . is carrying on the work of the Lord, just as I am" (1 Cor. 16:10); "I have no one else like him, who takes a genuine interest in your welfare" (Phil. 2:20); "Timothy has proved himself, because as a son with his father he has served with me in the work of the gospel" (Phil. 2:22); "Timothy . . . is our brother and God's fellow worker in spreading the gospel of Christ" (1 Thess. 3:2); "I have been reminded of your sincere faith" (2 Tim. 1:5); "From infancy you have known the holy Scriptures" (2 Tim. 3:15). For a helpful study of Timothy's career, see William J. Petersen, *The Discipling of Timothy* (Wheaton, Ill.: Victor, 1980).

Paul strengthened "all the disciples."

Acts 18:23

9

How Did Paul Prompt Students to Learn?

Think of a dull class session you have attended. A class you wished would end so you could leave. A class in which you felt you learned little if anything.

Got the class in mind? Now ask yourself, Why was it a waste of time?

Perhaps you could answer that question in a number of ways. But, most likely, the session, simply stated, was not interesting. And if lessons are not interesting, we usually learn less than we would have otherwise.

This is a basic principle in education. We learn a subject or skill largely to the extent we are interested in it. This precept has long been recognized by secular educators.[1] A child does not learn to play the violin well if he or she has no interest in it. A teenager learns little, if any, geometry if interest lags. An adult does not learn to use a personal computer if he or she sees no need for it.

Therefore, it is vital that teachers capture their students' interest from the start, and sustain that interest through each teaching session.

---

1. For example, Willard Abraham, professor of education at Arizona State University, wrote, "The best teachers make learning enjoyable. They have a thorough knowledge of the subjects they teach and know how to arouse their students' interest in them" ("Teaching," in *World Book Encyclopedia,* 19 [1992]: 67).

Lasso pupils' interest and you are on the way to fostering their learning. Without it you may make little headway.

Paul models masterful teaching because he aroused interest and sustained it. No one yawned while he taught;[2] no one ever walked out because of boredom; no one ever said Paul was a dull teacher. People flocked to this teacher, eager to hear him, anxious to learn from him, hungry to be taught by him. Why? Because he engaged their interest.

How Did Paul Acquire Student Interest?

The apostle created a desire for learning by doing several things.

Paul Captured People's Attention

Getting the attention of your students is the first step toward building interest. The apostle did this in several ways.

First, he asked for their attention. In the synagogue in Antioch of Pisidia, his first sentence to the audience included his request, "Listen to me!" (Acts 13:16). When besieged by a riotous mob of Jews in Jerusalem, he began his address to them by saying, "Listen now to my defense" (22:1). And near the beginning of his defense before King Agrippa, Paul requested, "I beg you to listen to me patiently" (26:3).

Second, he addressed his audiences by name. "Men of Israel," "Brother(s),"[3] "Men," "Men of Athens," "Brothers and fathers," "My brothers," "King Agrippa," and "Most excellent Festus" are examples of how he used direct address in some of his speeches.

Third, he engaged his listeners' attention by making forthright, sometimes blunt statements. For example, he confidently affirmed "through Jesus the forgiveness of sins is proclaimed to you" (13:38), and "This Jesus I am proclaiming to you is the Christ" (17:3). He did not stutter. He knew what he wanted to say, and he said it with no hes-

---

2. One exception is Eutychus, who fell asleep while Paul was interacting with (*dialegomai*, "to discuss"; see table 13, note c), not merely lecturing to, a group of believers in an upstairs room (Acts 20:7–12). Eutychus's reaction was not Paul's fault. Maybe Eutychus was sleepy because of his youthful age. Was he accustomed to being up after midnight? Or maybe the close atmosphere of the group in a crowded room made him drowsy. Or possibly the smoke from the "many lamps" in the room (20:8) made the atmosphere stuffy. At any rate, Paul can hardly be considered an inept teacher. After all, though he "kept on talking until midnight" (20:7) he continued conversing (*homileō*; cf. Luke 24:14–15; Acts 24:26), not lecturing, with them till daybreak (20:11), which meant his audience was interacting with and receptive to his teaching.

3. See chapter 5 for a list of Paul's references to fellow Christians as "brothers."

itation. To the unrepentant he wrote, "You are storing up wrath against yourself" (Rom. 2:5), and he wrote to the Galatians, "I am astonished that you are so quickly deserting the one who called you" (Gal. 1:6).

Fourth, Paul acquired student attention by giving commands (see appendix B), asking provocative questions (see chapter 11), and making requests.

Fifth, the apostle gathered listeners' attention by his posture. He sat down by the riverside (Acts 16:13), and he stood up in the synagogue (13:16), on the Areopagus (17:22), and on the ship en route to Rome (27:21).

Sixth, his gestures gained attention. He "motioned" with his hand (13:16; 21:40; 26:1), and he sometimes gazed on his audience (13:9; 14:9; 23:1).

Paul Used Numerous Figures of Speech

The apostle's many figures of speech (discussed in chapters 12 and 13) held his students' attention by challenging them to think.

Paul Appealed to His Listeners' Curiosity

Sergius Paulus may have been curious about Paul's teaching because he said he wanted to hear the word of God (Acts 13:7). The Jews in Pisidian Antioch, after hearing Paul, invited him to speak again (13:42). In Philippi, Lydia, curious about this man's message, listened to Paul speak (16:14), and prisoners in Philippi listened with curious interest to Paul and Silas praying and singing (16:25). Bereans, curious to know if what Paul said was true, examined the Scriptures eagerly (17:11). Curious about what Paul was teaching in the Agora (marketplace), some Athenians asked him to tell them more of what he was teaching (17:19). Then after he spoke of the resurrection of the dead, some were curious to hear even more (17:32). Even in Ephesus, Jews who heard him in their synagogue "asked him to spend more time with them" (18:20). Even rulers were curiously interested in what he taught, including Felix (24:26) and Agrippa (25:22). And Jews in Rome wanted to hear from Paul directly (28:22–23). Because these various individuals were curious, their interest was greater than it would have been otherwise.

Paul Addressed People's Needs and Problems

When people are aware of their needs, their interest in getting solutions climbs. Without that awareness, interest lags. Paul's letters speak to many needs people have. As Bailey wrote, "The fact that the subject matter of most of the epistles was dictated by the needs of the people assured audience interest."[4] He addressed universal needs such as sin, community-oriented needs such as eating idol-offered meat, and personal issues such as restoration for a runaway slave, Onesimus.[5] Note how the following needs are discussed in Paul's letters.

how to have salvation from sin
how to have assurance of salvation
how to have victory over sin
how to have knowledge of God
how to enjoy God's peace
how to face troubles
how to be led by the Holy Spirit
how to pray
how to rest in God's plans
how to trust the Lord
how to know God's will
how to use one's spiritual gifts
how to get along with others
how to respond to people who are hurtful
how to relate to human government
how to behave properly
how to be at peace with others
how to serve the Lord effectively
how to avoid wrong associations
how to be strong spiritually
how to be wise
how to deal with sinful people
how to maintain sexual purity
how to avoid offending others
how to overcome temptation
how to bring glory to God
how to worship God properly
how to help others grow spiritually
how to benefit from suffering
how to forgive others
how to be competent in ministry
how to become more Christ-like
how to avoid discouragement
how to live by faith, not by sight

4. Raymond Bailey, *Paul the Preacher* (Nashville: Broadman, 1991), 80.
5. Ibid., 80–81.

how to express generosity
how to avoid criticism
how to avoid pride
how to avoid legalism
how to have a happy marriage
how to be an effective father
how to keep from giving in to sin
how to have spiritual power
how to know God's love
how to grow spiritually
how to please the Lord
how to be obedient
how to be humble
how to be blameless
how to rejoice in adverse circumstances
how to be steadfast
how to avoid worry
how to enjoy contentment
how to be grateful
how to avoid sinful desires
how to be forgiving
how to be encouraging
how to qualify for leadership
how to serve others
how to be self-disciplined
how to lead productive lives

Can there be any question that Paul addressed many of mankind's most basic needs? Certainly his epistles ring with relevance.

Learning of various problems, Paul did not hesitate to address them. Typical of the basic problem faced by the unsaved was the jailer's question, "What must I do to be saved?" (Acts 16:30). Paul dealt with the problem of twelve Ephesian believers who had not heard of the Holy Spirit (19:1–7). His first epistle to the Corinthians answers a number of concerns brought to his attention from that congregation, including their divisiveness (1 Cor. 1:10–13), their spiritual immaturity (3:1–4), a case of immorality (5:1–5), legal disputes (6:1–8), questions about marriage (7:1–40), the issue of whether to eat food that had been sacrificed to idols in the pagan temples of Corinth (8:1–13), the challenge of his apostleship (9:1–23), the matter of proper order in worship (11:2–34), and proper use of spiritual gifts (12:1–14:39). He also addressed the problem of his apostolic authority in 2 Corinthians. In Galatians he wrote out of concern for the legalistic tendencies of believers in Galatia

(Gal. 1:6–9; 3:1–4). In Philippians he spoke to the problem of two women, Euodia and Synteche, who were not in harmony with each other (Phil. 4:2). His short personal letter to Philemon was designed to encourage his friend to take back and forgive his runaway slave, Onesimus, who had become a believer (Philem. 12–17). Of course, all his epistles with their grand doctrinal teaching and hortatory admonitions were written to help overcome problems of theological ignorance or misinformation and lack of proper moral-ethical conduct.

Paul Commended His Listener-Learners

Another way to hold the interest of students and to motivate and challenge them to learn is to express appreciation for them. Paul often commended or congratulated others, thus gaining their attention and encouraging them. He "strengthened and encouraged" the disciples in Lystra, Iconium, and Antioch (Acts 14:21–22); he "strengthened" churches in Syria, Cilicia, and central Turkey (15:41; 16:5); he encouraged believers who gathered in Lydia's house (16:40);[6] he "strengthened all the disciples" in Galatia and Phrygia on his third missionary journey, evidence of his continued contact with his convert-students (18:23); and he encouraged believers in Ephesus and Macedonia (20:1–2).

Imagine the delight of reading an epistle from the great apostle and noting his words of encouragement and commendation. He wrote to several congregations that he thanked the Lord for them (Rom. 1:8; 1 Cor. 1:4; Eph. 1:16; Phil. 1:3–4; Col. 1:3–5; 1 Thess. 1:2–3; 2:13; 2 Thess. 1:3; 2:13; cf. Acts 28:15), he told Timothy he was mindful of his "sincere faith" (2 Tim. 1:5), and he thanked Philemon for his faith and love (Philem. 4–5, 7). He even told the believers in Thessalonica that he boasted to other churches about their perseverance and faith (2 Thess. 1:4).

He also commended several congregations by telling them they were his "joy and crown" (Phil. 4:1; 1 Thess. 2:19), he commended the Corinthians for maintaining what he had taught them (1 Cor. 11:2), he commended the Thessalonians for their love (1 Thess. 4:10), and he thanked the Philippians for their concern for him (Phil. 4:10, 14). He often wrote of his desire that believers be encouraged (Rom. 1:12; 2 Cor. 7:13; Phil. 2:1; Col. 2:2; 1 Thess. 2:12; 3:2, 7; 4:18; 5:11, 14; 2 Tim. 4:2; Titus 1:9; 2:6, 15; Philem. 7).[7]

6. Since Paul and Silas had just been stripped, beaten, and imprisoned, one would expect them to be the recipients of encouragement, but instead they were the ones giving it to others!

7. For more on this subject, see Albert C. Sundberg, Jr., "Enabling Language in Paul," *Harvard Theological Review* 79 (1986): 270–77.

Teachers who find ways to commend, rather than criticize, their students, both individually and as a group, will see their students' interest climb.

Paul Prayed with and for His Students

Praying with your students goes a long way toward maintaining their interest in your teaching and thus enhancing their learning. Luke wrote of at least two occasions when Paul prayed with believers: the elders of Ephesus (Acts 20:36) and believers in Tyre (21:3–5), and in several of his letters he assured his readers he was praying for them (Rom. 1:9–10; Eph. 1:18–19; 3:16–19; Col. 1:9–12; 1 Thess. 3:12–13; 2 Thess. 1:11–12). Not only did he pray for them; he wrote them that he was doing so.

Do you want your students to be more interested in your teaching? Paul's example suggests several ways to capture that interest: get their attention, use picturesque language, appeal to their curiosity, address their needs, commend them, pray with them, and pray for them and let them know you are doing so.

How Did Paul Vary His Teaching?

Another way Paul prompted people to learn was by varying his teaching. Much as Jesus did, Paul excelled in the use of teaching variety.[8]

Sameness in teaching makes for disinterest. Lack of instructional variety on the part of the teacher results in lack of interest and learning on the part of the students. Conversely, teachers who creatively find ways to vary their teaching approaches enhance student interest and promote greater learning. Variation is not to be used simply for the sake of variation, but because diversity in each class session helps dispel monotony. Learning God's Word ought to be exciting, not monotonous; it ought to be stimulating and challenging, not boring and dull.

Lectures and Discussions

While it is common in many educational circles to downplay lectures, as if they are ineffective, the Bible shows that lecturing—communicating truth verbally from the teacher to his or her students—is a frequently used and highly effective instructional tool, especially when

---

8. For a discussion of Jesus' various teaching methods, see Roy B. Zuck, *Teaching as Jesus Taught* (Grand Rapids: Baker, 1995), 165–78.

Table 13
Verbs Used of Paul's Lecturing and Discussing

English Translations	Greek Verbs	References in Acts
Spoke boldly	*parrēsiazomai*	9:28; 14:3; 19:8
Demonstrated	*symbibazō*[a]	9:22
Debated	*syzēteō*[b]	9:29
Talked, spoke	*laleō*	13:43; 14:1; 17:19
Reasoned, discussed	*dialegomai*[c]	17:2, 17; 18:4, 19; 19:8–9; 20:7, 9; 24:12, 25
Explained, opened	*dianoigō*[d]	17:3
Proved	*paratithēmi*[e]	17:3
Proclaimed	*katangellō*	17:3
Disputed	*symballō*[f]	17:18
Testified, declared	*diamartyromai*	18:5; 20:21, 24; 23:11; 28:23
Testified	*martyreō*	26:22
Set forth	*ektithēmi*	28:23

a. *Symbibazō* means "to bring together" and thus, figuratively, it suggests proving or demonstrating a point by bringing facts together that lead to a certain conclusion (cf. "concluding" in Acts 16:10). When Paul quoted Isaiah 40:13 in 1 Corinthians 2:16, "For who has known the mind of the Lord that he may instruct him?" he used the word *symbibazō* for "instruct." The idea seems to be that no one can put together certain facts before God so that he teaches the Lord.

b. In Acts this verb is used only in 6:9 and 9:29, and it is used eight times in the Gospels (Mark 1:27; 8:11; 9:10, 14, 16; 12:28; Luke 22:23; 24:15). It means "to dispute, argue, or question together." The related noun *syzētsis*, "debate," is used once (Acts 15:2) and the noun *syzētētēs*, "debater," once (1 Cor. 1:20, NIV, "philosopher").

c. *Dialegomai* suggests interaction by discussion that involves questions and answers and is intellectually stimulating (A. T. Robertson, *Word Pictures of the New Testament* [New York: Harper and Brothers, 1930–1933], 3:267). In Acts 20.7 the NIV renders this verb by the rather weak verb "spoke," and in 20:9 the NIV wrongly translates the same verb as "talked on and on," as if Paul were lecturing endlessly. But *dialegomai* conveys discussing along with lecturing, not lecturing only (see note 2 on Eutychus).

d. *Dianoigō* means "to open," as in the opening of the heavens when Stephen saw the resurrected Lord (Acts 7:56) or, figuratively, the opening of the (spiritual) eyes or minds of disciples (Luke 24:31, 45) or the opening of Lydia's heart to the gospel (Acts 16:14). Hence the opening of the Scriptures by Jesus (Luke 24:32) and Paul (Acts 17:3) means to explain or interpret the Scriptures, that is, to open up their meaning.

e. *Paratithēmi*, literally, "to place alongside or to set before," as in setting food before someone (Acts 16:34) or setting forth an obligation (1 Tim. 1:18; NIV, "give") or truths (2 Tim. 2:2; NIV, "entrust") here communicates the thought of presenting evidence or proof from the Scriptures. Compare *ektithēmi*, "to set forth" (NIV, "explained") in Acts 28:23.

f. This verb, used of Stoic and Epicurean philosophers who interacted with what Paul was teaching, etymologically means "to throw together," thus conveying the thought of discussing or throwing ideas back and forth.

combined with discussion or other methods. Jesus often lectured,[9] and so did Paul. However, their lecturing was far from dull. Their discourses were presented with enthusiasm, clarity, and relevance. No wonder people listened! And no wonder people had to decide either for or against what Jesus and Paul were teaching.

In the Book of Acts, Luke used several verbs, listed in table 13, to depict Paul's powerfully communicated lectures, often combined with lively dialogue.

These verbs suggest active, bold presentations of truth in which the apostle carefully explained his content, set forth rational evidence in defense of his position, and gave opportunity for discussion and debate in which questions and challenges raised by his listeners could be dealt with.

These lecture-discussions suggest several principles for teachers today. First, adapt your content to your class. This requires knowing your students and their backgrounds, recognizing that classes and individuals differ. Paul certainly did this, skillfully adapting the way he spoke to various audiences. How he spoke to Jews in Antioch of Pisidia differed from the way he addressed worshipers of Roman gods in Lystra. The presentation he made before a group of philosophically minded Athenians was not the way he spoke with Jews in Jerusalem or the way he talked to King Agrippa.

Second, encourage student interaction. Paul's teaching was not "one way," from him to his listeners. It was two-way communication, in which he invited the learners to participate with him in discussing what he presented (see table 13 and notes a–f).

Third, make teaching challenging. Paul's messages no doubt challenged Jews and Greeks to think. His reasoning stimulated them intellectually. Yet much teaching today falls short in this area. Nonstimulating teaching results in nonstimulated students. A humdrum teacher means students respond with ho hum. Bible teaching needs to be enlivened, motivating, challenging, and invigorating. Paul's teaching certainly was!

Fourth, correct students' false concepts, but do so lovingly. The verbs describing Paul's disputing, reasoning, explaining, declaring, and discussing may suggest that in interacting with his audiences he sought to correct misunderstandings on their part. This important part of instruction ought not be neglected.

Fifth, move your students toward a response to the truth. Paul was never content merely to give a lecture and/or have a discussion and then leave. He pushed for decisions, not simply dialogue. Beyond mental stimulus he wanted spiritual response. Why did he want people to lis-

9. Ibid., 166–70.

ten, think, and discuss? Because he wanted to convince them of the truth of the gospel so they would respond by faith in Jesus Christ. This is seen in the six-time occurrence of *peithō*, "to persuade or urge," in Acts 13:43; 17:4; 18:4; 19:8, 26; 26:28 and the one-time usage of the stronger word *anapeithō*, "to entice or persuade fully," in 18:13.

We too should do more than disseminate Bible facts or doctrinal information. We should call for action and response; we should encourage our students to put into practice what they have learned, to apply the truth to their own lives during the week.

Letters

Paul's thirteen epistles of eighty-seven chapters stand like lectures, sprinkled with questions and other pedagogical elements that call for reflection and action. These letters are outstanding teaching devices, often following up his on-site teaching.[10] His written communications include at least these thirty-six instructional elements.[11]

Admonitions
Affirmations
Analogies
Appeals
Arguments
Assignments
Attacks
Benedictions
Commands
Commendations
Concerns
Conclusions
Defenses
Desires
Doctrines
Exhortations
Expectations
Explanations
Facts

10. However, two epistles—Romans and Colossians—were written to congregations Paul had not visited at the time he wrote the letters.
11. For a discussion of Paul's letter-writing style and his use of many rhetorical devices in those letters, see chapters 12–15.

Goals
Greetings
Illustrations
Objectives
Plans
Pleas
Predictions
Questions
Reasons
Reassurances
Reminders
Reports
Requests
Salutations
Suggestions
Thanksgivings
Warnings

Want a challenging study? Read Paul's epistles, looking for and writing down examples of these many elements. This will give you an excellent grasp of the scope of content in his letters.

Another challenge is to note the many subjects Paul discussed in his speeches and his letters. The table on page 153 lists topics he touched on in four of his speeches.

For an enlightening exercise, read Paul's three other speeches in Acts and write the topics he mentioned: Acts 20:18–35; 22:2–21; 26:2–23.

Of course, the Pauline Epistles are chock full of doctrinal topics, touching on almost every doctrinal subject, including God, Christ, the Holy Spirit, angels, demons, man, sin, salvation, sanctification, the church, Israel, and the end times. These epistles present the apostle's readers with a gold mine of marvelous doctrines! Some of the Bible's greatest theological treatises are included in Paul's writings. These letters abound with profound truths of lasting significance for the modern world.[12]

12. Helpful sources on Pauline theology include the following: Mark L. Bailey, "A Theology of Paul's Pastoral Epistles," in *A Biblical Theology of the New Testament*, ed. Roy B. Zuck (Chicago: Moody, 1994), 243–97; Darrell L. Bock, "A Theology of Paul's Prison Epistles," in *A Biblical Theology of the New Testament*, 299–331; Earle E. Ellis, "Paul," in *Illustrated Bible Dictionary*, 3:1173–74, 1177–78; Paul Enns, *The Moody Handbook of Theology* (Chicago: Moody, 1989), 105–15; Donald Guthrie, *New Testament Theology* (Downers Grove, Ill.: InterVarsity, 1981), passim; Richard N. Longenecker, "Pauline Theology," in *Zondervan Pictorial Encyclopedia of the Bible*, 4:657–65; David K. Lowery, "A Theology

Table 14
Paul's Topics in Four of His Speeches in Acts

Deity of Christ	9:20
Messiahship of Christ	9:22
God's election of Israel	13:17
Exodus of Israel	13:17
Wilderness wanderings	13:18
Conquest	13:19
Judges	13:20
Monarchy (reigns of Saul and David)	13:21–22
Jesus' Davidic descent	13:23
John the Baptist	13:24–25
Crucifixion and burial of Jesus	13:26–29
Resurrection of Jesus	13:30–31
Scriptural support	13:32–37
Invitation/appeal	13:38–41
Challenge to repent	14:15
Existence of God	14:15
God's creative work	14:15
God's forbearance of sin	14:16
God's providential care in the seasons	14:17
Evidence of idolatry	17:22–23
God's creative work	17:24
God's sovereignty	17:24
God's spiritual nature	17:24
God's self-sufficiency	17:25
God's providence	17:25
God's creation of mankind	17:26
God's challenge to man	17:27
God's omnipresence	17:27
Man's existence	17:28
God's spiritual nature	17:29
God's forbearance of sin	17:30
God's call to repentance	17:30
Future judgment by Christ	17:31
Resurrection of Christ	17:31

Narration and Stories

While Paul did not tell parables as Jesus did,[13] he did occasionally use narration. Much of his sermon in the Pisidian Antioch synagogue narrated Israel's history (Acts 13:17–25), her rejection of Jesus (13:27–29), and Jesus' resurrection and exaltation (13:30–37). This lengthy narration led up to Paul's closing appeal in 13:38–41. In his farewell speech to the Ephesian elders, Paul recounted his own ministry in narrative fashion (20:17–21, 26–27, 33–35) as a means of leading up to his admonitions to them (20:28–31). His defense before a Jewish mob and before King Agrippa related in narrative form his background, conversion, and call (22:3–21; 26:4–23). Occasionally in his epistles he recognized the value of brief narratives, as he pointed his readers to various facts in Jewish history (e.g., Rom. 4:2, 18–22; 9:7–13; 11:2–4; 1 Cor. 10:1–5; Gal. 4:21–30).

Carry It Out . . .

In preparing your next lesson, look at the ways Paul captured student interest. Which of these ideas can you use to gain the interest of your class?

What needs and problems do your students have? How do they compare with the list in this chapter?

In what specific ways can you commend your students individually in the days ahead?

---

of Paul's Missionary Epistles," in *A Biblical Theology of the New Testament,* 243–97; Leon Morris, *New Testament Theology* (Grand Rapids: Zondervan, 1986), 19–90; S. Motyer, "Paul, Theology of," in *Evangelical Dictionary of Theology,* 829–31; Herman N. Ridderbos, *Paul: An Outline of His Theology,* trans. John Richard de Witt (Grand Rapids: Eerdmans, 1975); and Charles C. Ryrie, *Biblical Theology of the New Testament* (Chicago: Moody, 1959), 157–222.

13. On Jesus' parables and his techniques in storytelling see Zuck, *Teaching as Jesus Taught,* 305–27.

Evaluate your lecturing and class discussions. In what ways have they been effective? How can they be improved?

Creatively think of other ways you can encourage interaction and participation on the part of your students.

Plan specific ways you can encourage your students to apply your Bible lessons.

Could you write letters to your students to supplement your class sessions? If so, what would you include in those letters?

"There are many who oppose me."

I Corinthians 16:9

10

How Did Paul Respond to His Opponents?

Recently I read a missionary letter in which the writer reported that a person he had led to the Lord had gone astray into false teaching. Unfortunately this happens all too often. A pastor in China recently wrote, "We do not fear persecution, but we fear believers straying from the truth."

Cult members are active everywhere, diligently seeking to bring the unsaved into their clutches and working to win unwary Christians to their ways. Every Bible teacher fears this may happen to one of his or her students. How disturbing to hear that someone to whom you taught the Scriptures and whose life you have helped shape spiritually has turned away from the truth of the Word of God to follow heretical teachings.

Sometimes a student not only becomes entangled in falsehood, but even opposes what his former teacher has faithfully taught from the Scriptures—and perhaps even assails him or her personally and openly.

Such unhappy turns are not new. Even the apostle Paul, though vigorous, faithful, and thorough in his teaching ministry, faced doctrinal antagonists. And not just once or twice. He faced a number of individual opponents and even entire cadres of adversaries in several cities where he preached and taught.

Let's pretend he is addressing us directly about these problem teachers. Reading his "report," we can learn about the kinds of false teachings to be aware of today and how to deal with their proponents.

ᴡhich Opponents Confronted Paul and ᴡhy?

"I am no stranger to opposition; I know what it is to face adversaries, people who pervert the truth. In many of the cities where I preached the gospel and taught the saved, false teachers tried to overturn my teaching.

"In a way this is not surprising. I even expected it, because our Lord told his followers in the upper room, 'If they persecuted me, they will persecute you.'[1] Hardships, as I told converts in Lystra, Iconium, and Antioch, are 'normal' for Christians.[2]

"In my approximately thirty-three years of serving the Lord[3] I faced conflicts with both individuals and groups. Of course, this was not my doing; they 'started' it. These troublemakers were disturbing because many of them infiltrated churches I had founded and they tried to turn my people away from me and from what I taught.

"The first place I encountered difficulty from proponents of faulty doctrines was Galatia, the area (in what you call central Turkey) where Barnabas and I planted churches on my very first missionary endeavor. Of course, soon after I was saved, Jews in Damascus did not like what I preached, so they tried to kill me.[4] And the same thing happened soon after that in Jerusalem.[5] In Pisidian Antioch, unbelieving Jews talked abusively against my message.[6] And in Derbe I was even stoned and left for dead.[7] But I'm not referring to these attempts on my life. I have in mind the problem of unsound views being foisted on people whom I led to the Lord.

"In Galatia these 'alien false brothers,'[8] as I called them, had sneaked into[9] our churches. They joined ranks without the believers realizing they had an ulterior motive: to make them 'slaves' by teaching them they had to obey the Mosaic law, including being circumcised, in order to be saved.[10] These Jews[11] tried to make a good impression on the Gen-

---

1. John 15:20.

2. Acts 14:22.

3. Paul's ministry extended from his conversion in A.D. 35 to his martyrdom in A.D. 67 or 68 (Harold W. Hoehner, "Chronology of the Apostolic Age" [Th.D. diss., Dallas Theological Seminary, 1965], 381–84).

4. Acts 9:23.

5. Acts 9:29.

6. Acts 13:45.

7. Acts 14:19.

8. "Alien" in Galatians 2:4 translates the adjective *pareisaktos*, "alien, foreign, having sneaked in secretly."

9. "Sneaked in alongside" is the meaning of the verb *pareiserchomai*.

10. Galatians 2:4 (cf. 4:9).

11. Most likely these opponents were Jews, possibly from Judea (Bernard H. Brinsmead, *Galatians—Dialogical Response to Opponents* [Chico, Calif.: Scholars, 1982]; Will-

tile believers by telling them that being circumcised would mean the gospel would be less offensive and would result in less persecution. These zealous legalists hoped to be able to boast about their accomplishments by driving a wedge between me and the believers.[12]

"This teaching was serious because it was so different from what I taught; it was like 'another gospel.' It was as if the Galatians were running a race and another runner cut in front of them[13] and slowed them down so that they were kept from obeying the truth. Therefore I was perplexed,[14] wondering if my work there had all been in vain.[15] I was astonished that the Galatian believers had so quickly[16] deserted the truth.[17] The Christians there were confused,[18] joyless,[19] and even 'bewitched';[20] they were foolish to try to add human effort to God's grace.[21]

"How did I respond to this situation? I did several things. For one thing, I stood steadfast, not giving in to these heretics 'for a moment.'[22] Second, I told the believers in my Galatian letter that these 'agitators'[23] deserved to be denounced because their tenets actually perverted the gospel.[24] If works were necessary for salvation, then Jesus' work on the cross was insufficient and Christ is of no value.[25] Third, I was so dis-

---

iam S. Campbell, "Judaizers," in *Dictionary of Paul and His Letters*, ed. Gerald F. Hawthorne, Ralph P. Martin, and Daniel G. Reid [Downers Grove, Ill.: InterVarsity, 1993], 515; George Lyons, *Pauline Autobiography: Toward a New Understanding* [Atlanta: Scholars, 1985], 76–79; Jerome Murphy-O'Connor, *Paul: A Critical Life* (Oxford: Oxford University Press, 1996), 185–210; and Walt Russell, "Who Were Paul's Opponents in Galatia?" *Bibliotheca Sacra* 147 [July–September 1990]: 329–50). Walter Schmithals, however, wrongly suggests they, as well as the adversaries in Corinth and Philippi, were Jewish-Christian Gnostics (*Paul and the Gnostics*, trans. John E. Steely [Nashville: Abingdon, 1972], 29–64).

12. Galatians 4:17; 5:11; 6:12–13.

13. Galatians 5:7.

14. Galatians 4:20.

15. Galatians 4:11.

16. Paul wrote Galatians from Antioch, probably in A.D. 49, soon after his first missionary trek in 48–49. Therefore, their openness to false teaching had occurred soon after he was in Galatia.

17. Galatians 1:6.

18. Galatians 1:7; 5:10.

19. Galatians 4:15.

20. *Baskainō* in Galatians 3:1 means "to cast a magic spell."

21. Galatians 3:3, 5.

22. Galatians 2:5.

23. Galatians 5:12.

24. Galatians 1:7–9. "The curse [*anathema*] is the strongest possible form of denunciation. It tacitly assumes that God shares the speaker's utter abhorrence for the person cursed . . ." (Francis Watson, *Paul, Judaism and the Gentiles: A Sociological Approach* [Cambridge: Cambridge University Press, 1986], 61). The Greek *anathema*, "accursed," is the equivalent of a Hebrew word that means to be designated for destruction.

25. Galatians 5:2.

turbed that I wished these dissenters were more than circumcised; I wished they were castrated![26] Fourth, I pointed out to my converts that these Jewish opponents were cowardly, wanting to avoid persecution, and were hypocritical because even they could not obey the entire law.[27] So I wrote the Galatian letter to give a passionate defense of the truth that justification comes only by faith in Christ, plus nothing else,[28] and that believers should stand in their freedom in Christ without being enslaved by trying to keep the law.[29]

"I felt this error needed to be combated vehemently because it had the potential of leading many, many people away from God's simple plan of salvation by faith alone. Falsehoods brought in secretly, motives that were impure, lives that were hypocritical[30]—all these had to be addressed strongly.

"I had to write sternly to the Galatian believers, to steer them away from such erroneous ideas. But I had another problem—and a serious one—with opponents in Corinth. The environment in that city made it difficult for anyone to lead a pure life. Its open immorality, its secular way of thinking, its arrogance, its emphasis on social prominence and self-display, its abusive behavior, its emphasis on impressive speech—all these elements in the Corinthian culture influenced its residents,[31] including some of those I had led to the Lord when I was in Corinth for a year and a half. Therefore, false teachers had a ready acceptance in Corinth when they pointed out to the church there that I was reticent to boast, that I had an unimpressive physical appearance, that my manner of speaking was inferior to what they were used to, and that I refused to take support from them for my ministry.[32]

"These Jewish migrant preachers had arrived in Corinth from Palestine[33] and were successful in winning over a number of the believers.

---

26. Galatians 5:12.

27. Galatians 6:12–13.

28. Galatians 2:16; 3:21–22, 26.

29. Galatians 4:9; 5:1.

30. When Paul called them "false brothers" *(pseudadelphoi)*, he probably meant they claimed to be Christians, but in reality were not. They were "sham Christians" (NEB).

31. Timothy B. Savage, *Power through Weakness: Paul's Understanding of the Christian Ministry in 2 Corinthians* (Cambridge: Cambridge University Press, 1996), 35–53.

32. Ibid., 54.

33. Though some writers question that they were Jews (e.g., Watson, *Paul, Judaism and the Gentiles: A Sociological Approach,* 85–87), this is clearly supported by the apostle's questions in 2 Corinthians 11:22, "Are they Hebrews? So am I. Are they Israelites? So am I. Are they Abraham's descendants? So am I." Cf. Christopher Forbes, "Paul's Opponents in Corinth," *Buried History* 19 (June 1983): 19–23. Rudolf Bultmann wrongly suggested these errorists in Corinth were Gnostic pneumatics (*The Second Letter to the Corin-*

So again I had to be blunt. The Christians were putting up with 'a different gospel' from the one I preached; in fact, the false teachers were preaching a different Jesus.[34]

"They wanted to put themselves on an equal basis with me, but, as I told the Corinthian church, they were 'false apostles, deceitful workmen, masquerading as apostles of Christ' and as 'servants of righteousness,' just as Satan masquerades as an angel of light.[35] They even thought of themselves as 'super-apostles.'[36] Though they came with letters of recommendation, and commended themselves,[37] they were not what they claimed to be. By deceiving Christians into thinking they had full apostolic authority, they hoped to do two things: cause the believers in Corinth to try to keep the Mosaic law,[38] which is a distortion of the Word of God,[39] and to reject me as an apostle.

"But think of what they were actually doing. They were peddling[40] the Word of God for profit, that is, their real motive in preaching was

---

thians, trans. Roy A. Harrisville [Minneapolis: Augsburg, 1985], 146–47), as did Walter Schmithals (*Gnosticism in Corinth*, trans. John E. Steely [Nashville: Abingdon, 1971], 293–95). The traditional view that the adversaries in Corinth were Judaizers is held, among others, by C. K. Barrett (*Commentary on the Second Epistle to the Corinthians* [New York: Harper and Row, 1973], 30); F. F. Bruce (*1 and 2 Corinthians* [Grand Rapids: Eerdmans, 1971], 172–74); Randall C. Gleason ("Paul's Covenental Contrasts in 2 Corinthians 3:1–11," *Bibliotheca Sacra* 154 [January–March 1997]: 63–66); Murray J. Harris, "2 Corinthians," in *The Expositor's Bible Commentary* [Grand Rapids: Zondervan, 1976–1992], 10 [1976], 312–13); and Alfred Plummer (*A Critical and Exegetical Commentary on the Second Epistle of St Paul to the Corinthians* [Edinburgh: Clark, 1915], xxxvi–xli).

34. 2 Corinthians 11:4.

35. 2 Corinthians 11:13–14; cf. 4:2.

36. Some writers say the "super-apostles" (2 Cor. 11:5; 12:11) and the "false apostles" (11:13) were different groups (e.g., F. C. Baur, *Paul, The Apostle of Jesus Christ*, trans. Eduard Zeller, 2d ed. [London: Williams & Norgate, 1876], 1:277; and Ralph P. Martin, "The Opponents of Paul in 2 Corinthians," in *Tradition and Interpretation in the New Testament*, ed. Gerald F. Hawthorne and Otto Betz [Grand Rapids: Eerdmans, 1987]: 279–87). More likely, however, they were the same (C. K. Barrett, *Essays on Paul* [London: SPCK, 1982], 78–83, 87–107; idem, *Paul: An Introduction to His Thought* [Louisville: Westminster/Knox, 1994], 35–37; P. W. Barnett, "Opposition in Corinth," *Journal for the Study of the New Testament* 22 [1984]: 3–17; Philip Edgcumbe Hughes, *Paul's Second Epistle to the Corinthians* [Grand Rapids: Eerdmans, 1962], 357–58; Doyle Kee, "Who Were the 'Super Apostles' of 2 Corinthians 10–13?" *Restoration Quarterly* 23 [1980]: 65–76; Gerd Luedemann, *Opposition to Paul in Jewish Christianity*, trans. M. Eugene Boring [Minneapolis: Fortress, 1989], 88; and Peter Marshall, *Enmity in Corinth: Social Conventions in Paul's Relations with the Corinthians* [Tübingen: Mohr, 1987], 372).

37. 2 Corinthians 3:1; 10:12.

38. 2 Corinthians 3:9, 11, 14–15; cf. P. W. Barnett, "Opponents of Paul," in *Dictionary of Paul and His Letters*, 646.

39. 2 Corinthians 4:2.

40. "Peddle" translates *kapēleuō* (used in the New Testament only in 2 Cor. 2:17), which pictures a huckster selling goods for more than they are worth. The false teachers were teaching less-than-sound doctrine and, in typical Corinthian fashion, were charging for it!

to make money. Their greed shows they were self-focused, not genuinely concerned for the Corinthian Christians. They were pushing themselves forward.[41]

"And think of the results: The believers in Corinth were being enslaved and exploited, that is, these foes were eating them out of house and home.[42] And the Christians even put up with this![43]

"In dealing with this problem I wrote with irony that since they liked boasting I would boast. But I would boast only in these facts: (a) that I had authority from the Lord to be his apostle, (b) that I confined myself to the field of service the Lord gave (unlike the Judaizers who traveled abroad to spread heresies), (c) that I had visions and revelations from the Lord, and (d) that my weaknesses were actually a means of strength.[44] In fact, I wrote that the things they deplored in speakers as negatives, I affirmed as 'positives.' I delighted in my weaknesses and hardships because Christ's power could then rest on me. In this way I was turning their logic on its head by pointing out that my weakness ensured that my labor was accompanied by divine strength.[45] My ministry was glorious, not shameful. Sarcastically I wrote that one true weakness I had was that I was too weak to mistreat the Corinthian believers.[46] Also, my troubles and hardships demonstrated the authenticity of my apostleship.

"They said I did not have the knowledge they had, but I stated outright that I was not inferior to those so-called super-apostles and that I had more knowledge than they did![47]

"These enemies of the cross held me in low esteem because I worked at a secular job of tentmaking to support myself and did not depend on the Corinthians for finances. So I reaffirmed my position that it was no sin to lower myself that way. I explained that I did that in order not to be a burden to them.[48]

"So I responded to the Christians in sinful Corinth by pointing out that their thinking was secular. They were being exploited by erroneous

41. 2 Corinthians 11:20. Cf. Kee, "Who Were the 'Super-Apostles' of 2 Corinthians 10–13?" 76.

42. "Exploits" translates *katesthiō*, "to eat up." C. K. Barrett suggests the paraphrase, "if anyone eats you out of house and home" (*The Second Epistle to the Corinthians,* Black's New Testament Commentaries [London: Adam and Black, 1973], 288, 291).

43. 2 Corinthians 11:4, 19.

44. 2 Corinthians 10:8; 11:10, 16–18, 21, 30; 12:1, 5, 9; 13:10.

45. 2 Corinthians 12:7–10. Cf. Savage, *Power through Weakness,* 187–88.

46. 2 Corinthians 11:21. Cf. James W. Evans, "Interpretation of 2 Corinthians," *Southwestern Journal of Theology* 32 (Fall 1989): 29.

47. 2 Corinthians 10:10; 11:5–6; 12:11.

48. 2 Corinthians 11:6, 9; 12:14, 16.

teachings, and they were challenging my position as an apostle. I showed them the error of their thinking and defended my position as an apostle and their spiritual father by using irony, with a touch of humor, to get them thinking and set them back on their heels."

"Perverters of the gospel were also present in Philippi, the city where I was first imprisoned. Then years later when I was in prison in Rome I learned that Judaizers had penetrated Philippi as well. In my days, dogs were despised animals because they ran loose, eating garbage and attacking people. So to depict their dislike of Gentiles, my fellow countrymen called them dogs. However, I used the term 'dogs'[49] to describe unsaved Jews who were altering the gospel message by insisting that circumcision is essential for salvation. They were like dogs because they were prowling from one Christian group to another, trying to win Gentile Christians to their way of thinking. These foes pretended to be Christians, but actually, as I called them, they were 'evil workers' (just as I had called the prevaricators in Corinth 'deceitful workers'). To stress how dangerous they were, I used a play on words in my letter to the Philippians. The anti-Paulists were concerned about circumcision *(peritomē)*, but I pointed out that they went further than that; they were mutilators *(katatomē)*! Then I used the word 'circumcision' differently from their normal use. I said Christians—those 'who worship by the Spirit of God [and] who glory in Christ Jesus'[50]—are the true circumcision. As I had written earlier to the Romans, true circumcision is of the heart;[51] that is, salvation is not a matter of outward ceremony, but a cutting off of one's sinful way of life. People who want to alter the flesh are doing more than that; they are actually altering the gospel.

"To alert believers in Philippi to the danger, I told them these mutilators were 'enemies of the cross of Christ.'[52] It brought me to tears to realize there were many who were enemies. Their error was indeed serious, because, not really knowing the Lord, they were lost forever.[53] Meanwhile they took pride in their gluttonous ways.[54] What they gloried in was really shameful, for their minds focused on things of this world, that is, obedience to the Mosaic law.

49. Philippians 3:2.
50. Philippians 3:3.
51. Romans 2:29.
52. Philippians 3:2, 18.
53. Philippians 3:19.
54. The clause, "their god is their stomach," may refer to gluttony or to Jewish regulations about food (Barrett, *Paul: An Introduction to His Thought*, 41; John J. Gunther, *St. Paul's Opponents and Their Background* [Leiden: Brill, 1973], 98; and Barnett, "Opponents of Paul," 652).

"How did I react to these circumcisers? I warned the Philippian Christians to 'watch out for those dogs,' just as you would post a sign on a fence, 'Beware of bad dog!' By this I meant they should be alert to this false doctrine and avoid it."[55]

"I also wrote the Romans, whom I had not yet met, to beware of teachings that contradicted what they had received.[56] Their false views were divisive[57] and hindered the Lord's work like stumbling blocks on a path. While claiming, like the Judaizers in Corinth, to be Christians, they actually were serving their own appetites (like the Philippian Judaizers), not the Lord.[58] They deceived some unsuspecting Roman Christians by 'smooth talk and flattery.' So in response to this alarming situation, I urged the believers there to 'watch out'[59] for such disruptive influences. In fact, I instructed the Romans not to have anything to do with these falsifiers. I urged the Christians to keep away from them."

"Let me share my concern over another church, one established by Epaphras, not me. False teachers may have infiltrated the church at Colossae, but being made aware of that possibility, I urged the Colossian believers not to be taken in[60] by the attractiveness of 'fine-sounding arguments,'[61] and kidnapped[62] by 'philosophy and empty deceit,' that is, deceitful teaching that has no reality. Such philosophies or pseudo-

55. The errorists addressed in Philippians 3:2, 18–19 probably are not the same as those Paul wrote about in Philippians 1:15, 17–18, because there he said that though they preach out of wrong motives, still they were preaching Christ.

56. Romans 16:17. Possibly people in Rome came to Christ through the witness of "visitors from Rome" (Acts 2:10) who were in Jerusalem on the day of Pentecost, got saved, and shared their faith in Christ when they returned home.

57. *Dichostasia*, a strong word used only twice in the New Testament (Rom. 16:17; Gal. 5:20), means dissensions or sharp disagreements resulting in separation.

58. Romans 16:18.

59. "Watch out" in Romans 16:17 translates *skopeō*, "to observe, notice, or scrutinize" (cf. 2 Cor. 4:18; Gal. 6:1; Phil. 3:17), whereas a more frequently occurring synonym, *blepō*, used in Philippians 3:2, means "to see, be on the look out for, beware of."

60. In Colossians 2:4 Paul wrote the word *paralogizomai* (NIV, "deceive"), meaning "to deceive by false reasoning or to cause someone to draw an erroneous conclusion from the reasoning submitted" (James Hope Moulton and George Milligan, *The Vocabulary of the Greek Testament* [1930; reprint, Grand Rapids: Eerdmans, 1974], 487).

61. The word *pithanologia*, found in the New Testament only in Colossians 2:4, was used in the Greek papyri in reference to a court case in which the robber used persuasive speech to try to defend his innocence (ibid., 512). The word suggests arguments that seem acceptable but are actually wrong (James D. G. Dunn, *The Epistles to the Colossians and to Philemon: A Commentary on the Greek Text* [Grand Rapids: Eerdmans, 1996], 133).

62. *Sylagogeō*, "to carry off as a captive," occurs in the New Testament only in Colossians 2:8. This pictures "a marketplace preacher gathering together those impressed by his discourse and taking them off for a fuller exposition and instruction" (ibid., 147).

religious teachings follow traditions of human, not divine origin,[63] and the 'basic principles of the world.'[64]

"I tried to urge the Colossians to beware of not only the deceptive argument of man-made philosophers but also to avoid those who insisted that believers must follow strict ascetic regulations about food and ceremonial observances.[65]

"I wrote that the believers should be on the lookout for such emphases and not become entangled with them."[66]

---

63. Jesus used the same phrase "the tradition of men" in denouncing the Pharisees (Mark 7:8; cf. Matt. 15:3, 6).

64. *Stoicheia*, "elements," means either physical elements of the universe, elementary principles of thought, the zodiac stars ("elementary" stars), or elemental spirits, that is, angels or demons. If it means the last of these in Colossians 2:8, then Paul was saying that human philosophies being taught in and around Colossae were demonic, not godly (cf. ibid., 148–51). See Clinton E. Arnold, *The Colossian Syncretism: The Interface between Christianity and Folk Belief at Colossae* (Grand Rapids: Baker, 1996), 158–94; Günther Bornkamm, "The Heresy of Colossians," in *Conflict at Colossae*, ed. Fred O. Francis and Wayne A. Meeks, rev. ed. [Missoula, Mont.: Scholars, 1975],124; and Ralph P. Martin, *Colossians and Philemon*, New Century Bible Commentary (Grand Rapids: Eerdmans, 1973), 10–14, 79.

65. Many scholars see the falsehood in Colossae as a beginning form of Gnosticism (Barnett, "Opponents of Paul," 651–52; Günther Bornkamm, "The Heresy of Colossians," 123–45; Eduard Lohse, *Colossians and Philemon*, Hermeneia [Philadelphia: Fortress, 1971]; and R. McL. Wilson, "Gnosis, Gnosticism, and the New Testament," in *The Origins of Gnosticism* [Leiden: Brill, 1967], 511–27; and idem, *Gnosis and the New Testament* [Oxford: Blackwell, 1968]).

Others, however, view this error as Jewish mysticism (A. J. Bandstra, "Did the Colossian Errorists Need a Mediator?" in *New Dimensions in New Testament Study*, ed. Richard N. Longenecker and Merrill C. Tenney [Grand Rapids: Zondervan, 1974], 329–43; F. F. Bruce, "The Colossian Heresy," *Bibliotheca Sacra* 141 [July–September 1984]: 195–208; Dunn, *The Epistles to the Colossians and to Philemon*, 24–35; idem, "The Colossian Philosophy: A Confident Jewish Apologia," *Biblica* 76 [1995]: 153–81; Craig A. Evans, "The Colossian Mystics," *Biblica* 63 [1982]: 188–205; Fred O. Francis, "Visionary Discipline and Scriptural Tradition at Colossae," *Lexington Theological Quarterly* 2 [1967]: 71–81; Peter T. O'Brien, "Colossians, Letter to the," in *Dictionary of Paul and His Letters*, 148–50; C. Rowland, "Apocalyptic Visions and the Exaltation of Christ in the Letter to the Colossians," in *Journal for the Study of the New Testament* 19 [1983]: 73–74; Gary S. Shogren, "Presently Entering the Kingdom of Christ: The Background and Purpose of Col 1:12–14," *Journal of the Evangelical Theological Society* 31 [June 1988]: 178; and Edwin M. Yamauchi, "Gnosis, Gnosticism," in *Dictionary of Paul and His Letters*, 353).

As a third view, others see the heresy as a syncretism of Jewish and Greek elements (G. B. Caird, *Paul's Letters from Prison*, New Clarendon Bible [Oxford: Oxford University Press, 1976], 162–64; H. Wayne House, "Heresies in the Colossian Church," *Bibliotheca Sacra* 149 [January–March 1992]: 45–59; Martin, *Colossians and Philemon*, 4–5, 9–19; and Eduard Schweizer, *The Letter to the Colossians* [Minneapolis: Augsburg, 1982], 245–59). Arnold suggests a fourth view, namely, that the error in Colossae was a mixture of Judaistic views and the "folk cult" of the Phrygian mystery cults (*The Colossian Syncretism*, 5, 150–57, 226–27, 310–12).

66. Colossians 2:8. "See to it" renders *blepō*, "to see, be on the lookout for, beware of." See note 59.

"What does it take, then, to avoid pseudo-teachings and false teachers? In summary, you can see that in my church letters, as well as in my epistles to Timothy and Titus, I mentioned several things believers must do to avoid doctrinal entrapment."

Observe and scrutinize false teachings (Rom. 16:17).
Keep away from false teachers (Rom. 16:17).
Beware of and be on the lookout for false teachers (Phil. 3:2; Col. 2:8).
Don't give in to falsehood (Gal. 2:5).
Don't be frightened by it (Phil. 1:28).
Don't let anyone judge you (Col. 2:16).
Avoid false teachers (2 Tim. 2:17).[67]
Gently instruct those who oppose the truth (2 Tim. 2:25).
Be on guard against false teachers (2 Tim. 4:15).[68]
Refute them (Titus 1:9).
Silence[69] them (Titus 1:10–11).
Rebuke them (2 Tim. 4:2; Titus 1:13; 2:15).
Warn them (Titus 3:9–10).

"Besides these groups and individuals who infiltrated the churches in Galatia, Corinth, Philippi, Rome, and Colossae, I was personally opposed by a number of adversaries. On my very first missionary journey I was opposed by a sorcerer named Elymas, a man who used deceit and perverted the Lord's way, and on my second journey I was interrupted by a fortune-teller.[70] Then in Antioch I disputed with Judaizers who taught that circumcision is needed for salvation.[71] In Thessalonica some Jews rounded up some bad fellows from the marketplace and started a riot in order to oppose my teaching.[72] In Athens I was challenged by Epicurean and Stoic philosophers,[73] who called me a bab-

---

67. Since the erroneous teachings of Hymenaeus and Philetus could spread insidiously like gangrene, these men were to be avoided.

68. "Be on guard" renders *phylassō*, "to guard oneself." This directive to Timothy in 2 Timothy 4:15 pertained to Alexander, a metalworker, who harmed Paul by strongly opposing Paul's message (4:15–16). This may or may not be the same Alexander in 1 Timothy 1:20.

69. Deceptive talkers (cf. Col. 2:4, 8), especially Judaizers, were to be muzzled *(epistomizō)* so they could not win entire families by their falsehoods, which were taught out of a motive of greed (cf. 2 Cor. 2:17).

70. Acts 13:8; 16:16–18.

71. Acts 15:1–2.

72. Acts 17:5. Some classical writers spoke of crowds in the marketplace with disdain, for they were easily agitated (John Clayton Lentz, *Luke's Portrait of Paul* [Cambridge: Cambridge University Press, 1993], 99).

73. Epicureanism, founded by Epicurus (341–270 B.C.), taught that the universe was the result of change and materialistically is merely a combination of atoms. Happiness

bler.[74] Demetrius, a silversmith who worshiped Artemis, the Greek goddess of the moon who supposedly protected women, created havoc for me in Ephesus.[75] Alexander, a metalworker, did me a lot of harm by vigorously opposing my words.[76] And, as you know, numerous times Jews who opposed my message stirred up people against me, several times causing riots.[77]

---

comes from limiting desires, withdrawing from public life, and avoiding fear and pain. The gods have no power over humans, and at death a person's body atoms are scattered through space. With these teachings in mind, read Acts 17:24–31, noting which of Paul's statements would counter these views.

Stoicism, founded by Zeno (ca. 335–263 B.C.), was so named because he taught in Athens at the *Stoa Poikile* ("Painted Portico"). Stoics taught that mankind should calmly accept whatever came to them, whether poverty or wealth, disease or health, slavery or freedom. Their aim in life was not, like the Epicureans, to seek happiness in detachment, but rather to live in harmony with the inherent Reason *(logos)* of the universe. Though materialistic, they had high morals. Other well-known Stoic teachers were Cleanthes (ca. 331–232 B.C.), Chrysippus (ca. 280–205 B.C.), Seneca (4 B.C. [?]–A.D. 65, whose brother, by the way, was Gallio, proconsul of Achaia, mentioned in Acts 18:12–17, and who refused to get involved in judging Paul), Epictetus (ca. A.D. 55–135), and the Roman emperor Marcus Aurelius (ca. A.D. 215–275). Read Acts 17:24–31 again and note how Paul's words would appeal to or be disapproved by the Stoics.

For more on these philosophies, see Edwyn Robert Bevan, *Stoics and Skeptics* (Chicago: Ares, 1913); Marcia L. Colish, "Pauline Theology and Stoic Philosophy: An Historical Study," *Journal of the American Academy of Religion* 47 (March 1979): 1–21; M. H. Cressy, "Epicureans," in *Illustrated Bible Dictionary* (Downers Grove, Ill.: InterVarsity, 1980), 1:465; idem, "Stoics," in *Illustrated Bible Dictionary*, 3:1487–88; David A. Desilva, "Paul and the Stoa: A Comparison," *Journal of the Evangelical Theology Society* 38 (December 1995): 549–64; John W. Drane, *Paul* (New York: Harper and Row, 1976), 21–22; Eduard Lohse, *The New Testament Environment*, trans. John E. Steely (Nashville: Abingdon, 1976), 243–50; Terence P. Paige, "Philosophy," in *Dictionary of Paul and His Letters*, 717; Giuseppe Ricciotti, *Paul the Apostle* (Milwaukee: Bruce, 1952), 49–52; John M. Rist, ed., *The Stoics* (Berkeley, Calif.: University of California Press, 1978); Charles C. Ryrie, *Biblical Theology of the New Testament* (Chicago: Moody, 1959), 158–60; Thomas Schmeller, "Stoics, Stoicism," in *Anchor Bible Dictionary*, 6:210–14; and Norman Wentworth de Witt, *Epicurus and His Philosophy* (Minneapolis: University of Minnesota Press, 1954).

74. Acts 17:8. The word rendered "babbler" is *spermologos*, used originally of birds picking up seeds, then of poor people picking up bits of leftover food and goods in the marketplace, and then of those who picked up scraps of information here and there. Thus the word connotes two things: the poor destitutes of society, and people who like birds were noisy and disruptive, picking up scraps of information without really understanding them. *Spermologos* therefore expressed the Athenian philosophers' contempt for a foreign, no-good street preacher who assumed he could instruct others in the Agora of Athens (Albert Barnes, *Barnes' Notes on the New Testament* [reprint, Grand Rapids: Kregel, 1962], 483). Dio Chrysostom (A.D. 40–ca. 120) wrote of these street preachers who in his day attracted the attention of people in the marketplace and told rough jokes and engaged in much babbling (*spermologian; Discourse* 32.9, cited by Abraham J. Malherbe, "'Not in a Corner': Early Christian Apologetic in Acts 26:26," *Second Century* 5 [1985/86]: 198.

75. Acts 19:23–41.

76. 2 Timothy 4:14–15. The Greek word *lian* (NIV, "strongly") suggests something done to the extreme.

77. See chapter 6.

"How did I respond to these opponents? I spoke directly to Elymas, telling him he was a child of the devil and that he would be blind for a time. In the case of the demon-possessed fortune-teller I spoke to the demon, commanding it to leave her.[78] I dealt with the Judaizers in Antioch and at the Jerusalem Council by direct disputation. When the Athenian philosophers accused me of being a babbler, I did not respond to that accusation. I simply used the opportunity to present the gospel. At the riot in Ephesus I wanted to speak to the people, but friends urged me not to. I never took personal revenge on any of my foes; as in the case of Alexander I let the Lord deal with him.[79]

"Obviously, then, the gospel divides people. Some respond in faith to the Good News, others vigorously oppose it, and some are neutral. In spite of the many experiences I had in which groups or individuals tried to forestall my work, I kept on and the Lord blessed his Word and work.

"These experiences of mine prompt me to pass on to you seven important admonitions. First, avoid adding anything to salvation by faith. When any human effort or condition is tacked on to God's way of salvation through simple belief in Christ, it is wrong. Second, realize the importance of true doctrine. We need to know and comprehend what the Bible teaches theologically. Third, be alert to heretical views in cults, other pseudo-religious groups, and human philosophies. Fourth, be grounded in the Word of God, feasting on it with eagerness and regularity. Fifth, help your students and others for whom you are responsible spiritually to be on guard against and avoid false teaching. Sixth, when necessary, warn, rebuke, refute, and silence false teachers if they try to infiltrate your church, class, or other group. Seventh, pray earnestly that God will keep you, your students, and your family true to the Lord and his Word."

What Can We Learn from Paul's Experiences with Opponents?

Several observations can be made about Paul's attitude and response to his assailants. First, he took doctrinal error seriously. This was a big-

78. Several times Jesus exorcised demons by addressing them directly, but this is the only time the New Testament records an apostle or other follower of the Lord doing so. Presumably the pattern today is not to speak directly to demons (since no one has apostolic authority as did Paul), but to turn to the Lord in prayer, asking him to release the person from the demon's struggle.

79. 2 Timothy 4:14.

league issue, not a "it-doesn't-really-matter" issue. Theology, what people believe about God and themselves, is of vital importance. Second, he gave guidance to churches and individual leaders on these important theological matters. He did not sit back and hope the problems would go away. Third, he held firmly to correct beliefs even though it cost him his life. Fourth, he did not hesitate to confront heretics and to urge other leaders to do the same, but he did so with a loving concern for those unbelievers, longing for their salvation. Fifth, he wrote letters to several churches and to two of his protégés to ground them in correct doctrine and guide them in correct practice.

These five practices by Paul suggest what teachers need to do today in dealing with students who may be susceptible to false beliefs or those who may be spreading falsehood. Take doctrine seriously; guide your students to see the importance of doctrine; set a good example of holding steadfastly to correct doctrine regardless of the cost; firmly confront opponents who may be infiltrating your class, church, family, or other group; and use opportunities, including letter writing, to guide others in sound biblical beliefs.

Now What?

Consider the suggestions in the two preceding paragraphs, and ask yourself how you can put these into practice.

Is someone in your class susceptible to being misled by a cult or other false teaching? If so, consider what steps you can take to help him or her avoid that influence.

Are you thoughtfully emphasizing doctrine to your class, and helping them detect the differences between true and false doctrines? (For information on theological concepts to teach children at various age levels, see V. Gilbert Beers, "Teaching Theological Concepts to Children," in *Childhood Education in the Church*, ed. Roy B. Zuck, Robert E. Clark, and Joanne Brubaker, rev. ed. [Chicago: Moody, 1986], 363–80).

Are you making the gospel clear, without adding anything to God's way of salvation by faith in Christ? And are you presenting the plan of salvation, giving opportunity to your students who are not saved to receive Christ as their Savior?

"What shall we conclude then?"

Romans 3:9

11

How Did Paul Use Questions in His Teaching?

Do your students seem uninterested in a subject? Then ask questions.

Do your students seem unclear on a subject? Then ask questions.

Are your students not thinking through the implications of a subject? Then ask questions.

Are you unsure of your students' thinking on a subject? Then ask questions.

Do you wonder what opinions your students have on a subject? Then ask questions.

Do you want to guide your students into learning new facts or ideas? Then ask questions.

Are your students reticent to participate in class? Then ask questions.

Do your students seem to be confused or have misconceptions about a subject? Then ask questions.

Do you sense your students are not adequately challenged? Then ask questions.

Do your students seem to lack excitement about a subject? Then ask questions.

Asking questions in class can be of immense value in helping students learn.[1] But they need to be the right kind of questions, questions

---

1. Stephen G. Fortosis, "Can Questions Make Religious Educators More Effective in the Classroom?" *Christian Education Journal* 12 (1992): 86–103.

that ask for opinions, ideas, clarification, support, and reasoning—not questions that merely ask for recall of facts memorized. Questions constitute such an important role in teaching that Ashner has said the effective teacher is a "question maker."[2]

Paul, the apostle-evangelist-teacher, was certainly a great question maker. He masterfully used questions in his ministry and his writings to stimulate his hearers' and readers' interest and to deepen their learning. His questions aroused interest, stimulated thought, envisioned implications, and encouraged decisions.

How Many Questions Did Paul Ask?

Paul asked a total of 250 questions,[3] a clear indicator that he viewed the asking of thought-provocative questions as a key of an effective teacher. The number of questions recorded in Acts and in each epistle is listed in table 15.

Table 15
Number of Paul's Questions in Acts and Each of His Epistles

Acts	10	Colossians	1
Romans	85	1 Thessalonians	2
1 Corinthians	102	2 Thessalonians	1
2 Corinthians	25	1 Timothy	1
Galatians	20	2 Timothy	0
Ephesians	1	Titus	0
Philippians	2	Philemon	0
			250

As discussed in chapter 9, many of his lectures included discussions. This no doubt meant that he asked questions for his listeners to answer,

2. M. J. Ashner, "Asking Questions to Trigger Thinking," *NEA* [National Education Association] *Journal* 50 (1961): 44.

3. This is slightly more (11 percent) than Jesus' 225 questions (Roy B. Zuck, *Teaching as Jesus Taught* [Grand Rapids: Baker, 1995], 237–39, 258–76). But Paul's writing ministry extended over eighteen years—from Galatians probably written in A.D. 49 to 2 Timothy, probably written in A.D. 67—whereas Jesus' teaching ministry was for only three and a half years. Jesus' 225 questions were asked in his public teaching ministry, and all but ten of Paul's recorded questions were addressed in his letter writing.

and he answered questions they asked. Naturally his written questions prompted his learners to answer in their minds.

As table 15 shows, most of Paul's questions are in Romans, 1 and 2 Corinthians, and Galatians. The questions in these four letters alone constitute ninety-three percent of his questions. Why is this? Possibly because in these epistles he was addressing more local-church problems, both doctrinal and practical, than in the other letters. His letters to Timothy, Titus, and Philemon include only one question because, presumably, those letters called for more forthright directives from the apostle to these friends because of their leadership responsibilities.

Of Paul's ten questions recorded in Acts, five were addressed to individuals (to the Lord, Elymas, a commander, a centurion, and Agrippa; Acts 9:5; 13:10; 21:37; 22:25; 26:27), and five were addressed to groups (officers, Ephesian disciples, and King Agrippa and his associates; Acts 16:37; 19:2–3; 26:8).

Also of note are the nine questions addressed to Paul, as recorded in Acts. Six were asked by individuals (the Philippian jailer, a commander, Festus, and Agrippa; Acts 16:30; 21:37–38; 22:27; 25:9; 26:28) and three by groups (Epicurean and Stoic philosophers, Jerusalem believers, and the Sanhedrin; Acts 17:19; 21:22; 23:4).

What Kinds of Questions Did Paul Ask?

Some truths and implications can best be handled by direct discourse, but others can more effectively be communicated by the use of penetrating questions. Knowing this, Paul, a master questioner, probed his readers' brain cells and spiritual hearts with several kinds of interrogations. These questions addressed issues of profound importance doctrinally and spiritually.

His queries served a variety of purposes, in fact, eleven.

1. To petition for information or to recall facts
2. To pull persons up short
3. To procure assent or agreement
4. To promote thinking or reflection
5. To prod for an opinion
6. To prick the conscience
7. To press for application of the truth
8. To point out something contrary to fact
9. To push for a conclusion
10. To pour out an emotion
11. To probe for motives

All of these except the ninth one are identical to purposes Jesus had in asking his questions.[4]

To Petition for Information or to Recall Facts

Paul often involved his readers in what he was writing by asking them to recall certain truths or facts. For example, he asked, "What does the Scripture say?" (Rom. 4:3; Gal. 4:30), and "Don't you know what the Scripture says in the passage about Elijah?" (Rom. 11:2). His several "Do you not know . . . ?" questions in 1 Corinthians were asked to urge the believers to recall certain truths (1 Cor. 5:6; 6:2, 3, 9, 15, 16, 19). In discussing the law with the Galatians, he asked, "What, then, was the purpose of the law?" (Gal. 3:19) and "Are you not aware of what the law says?" (4:21).

To Pull Persons Up Short

Numerous questions were asked by Paul to get his readers to realize the inconsistency of their positions. A penetrating question like this often proved more effective than a statement. As an example, instead of saying in Romans 2:3, "You will not escape judgment," he asked, "Do you think you will escape God's judgment?" This forced them to think of the matter raised and to respond inwardly. Or instead of remarking in Romans 2:21, "It is wrong for you to preach against stealing and then steal," he probed with the question, "You who preach against stealing, do you steal?" In 1 Corinthians 11:22, when Paul discussed gluttony at fellowship feasts, his readers were more goaded by the question, "Don't you have homes to eat and drink in?" than they would have been if he had merely stated, "You have homes to eat and drink in." And in Galatians 3:3 the question, "Are you so foolish?" penetrated more deeply than the statement, "You are foolish."

To Procure Assent or Agreement

An appropriately worded rhetorical question often acquires mental assent more readily than a declarative sentence. When Paul asked, "Is he not the God of Gentiles too?" (Rom. 3:29), his Roman readers would naturally have nodded in agreement. Most of the questions in this category are in 1 and 2 Corinthians, letters in which he was dealing with errors of doctrine, practice, and opinion. One question in Acts (21:37), one in Romans (3:29), twenty-seven in 1 and 2 Corinthians, and one in

---

4. Jesus had fifteen purposes in His questions (ibid., 241–49).

1 Thessalonians (2:19) were asked in such a way that the readers would be led to respond in the affirmative. This technique effectively won the readers over to Paul's views.

To Promote Thinking or Reflection

Understandably, most of the 250 queries fall in this category. Questions serve as great brain agitators. They are excellent mental stimulants. Browse through the questions in table 16 (starting on page 185), noting the many that have the numeral 4 in the third column. You will see that these questions are introduced by a variety of words, including "what," "who," "how," and "why." The question, "Who has ever given to God, that God should repay him?" (Rom. 11:35) clearly incites the reader to think and to respond mentally with the answer, "No one." "Why do you judge your brother?" (Rom. 14:10) challenges those questioned to try to come up with an answer and to conclude that they have no logical reason for criticizing a fellow believer. To ask, "How can they hear without someone preaching to them?" (Rom. 10:14), leads the readers to think "They can't," and thus to realize that they must share the gospel with those who have not heard of Christ. This question, like the others, compels readers to respond with more reflection than they would have done if Paul's point was a statement.

To Prod for an Opinion

Seven of the apostle's questions seem to urge readers to offer an opinion in their minds: "Do you want to be free from fear of the one in authority?" (Rom. 13:3). "What do you prefer?" (1 Cor. 4:21a). "Shall I come to you with a whip, or in love and with a gentle spirit?" (4:21b). "What then is my reward?" (1 Cor. 9:18). "So what shall I do?" (14:15). "Am I now trying to win the approval of men, or of God?" (Gal. 1:10). "Did you receive the Spirit by observing the law, or by believing what you heard?" (Gal. 3:2).

To Prick the Conscience

To ask, "Where, then, is boasting?" (Rom. 3:27) challenges one to reflect on the fact that boasting of his or her salvation is inappropriate. But it also serves to penetrate the reader's conscience by helping him sense that if he had been boasting of accomplishing his salvation by his works, it is wrong and should be stopped. See the other examples in Romans 2:3–4; 1 Corinthians 6:15–16 and 11:22.

To Press for Application of the Truth

Rightly worded, questions can also be a means of encouraging the ones questioned to put into practice what is being taught. The five questions in Romans 2:21–23 illustrate this point. When Paul challenged Peter, "How is it, then, that you force Gentiles to follow Jewish customs?" (Gal. 2:14), Paul was wanting Peter to do more than think about the wrongness of his actions; he also wanted him to apply or put into action the point made by the question, namely, that since what Peter was doing was wrong he should discontinue it.

To Point Out Something Contrary to Fact

Fifty-eight of Paul's questions raise issues that call for an answer of "no," "nothing," "none," or "no one." These help reverse a person's wrong thinking. By asking, "Shall we go on sinning so that grace may increase?" (Rom. 6:1), Paul helped his Roman readers see that it would be wrong to answer this interrogative "yes." "No one" is the anticipated answer to the question, "Who has known the mind of the Lord?" (Rom. 11:34). When he asked the Corinthians, "Who serves as a soldier at his own expense?" (1 Cor. 9:7), he expected the answer, "No one." The query, "Are all apostles?" (1 Cor. 12:29), called the readers to respond in the negative. When he asked, "What harmony is there between Christ and Belial?" (2 Cor. 6:15), the implied answer is "None."

Paul himself answered fifteen of these fifty-five questions in the negative. By this tactic he prompted the Romans, Corinthians, or Galatians to see the utter illogic of the views suggested in the questions and to reject those views. He answered by several Greek words or phrases, including *ou pantōs*, "not at all!" (Rom. 3:9), *ouchi*, "no" (3:27), and *mē genoito*,[5] which is used fourteen times and is rendered several ways in the New International Version: "Not at all!" (3:3–4, 9, 31; 9:14; 11:11), "Certainly not!" (3:5–6; 7:7), "By no means!" (6:1–2, 15; 7:13; 11:1), "Never!" (1 Cor. 6:15), and "Absolutely not!" (Gal. 2:17; 3:21).

It is interesting to see the false assumptions Paul was denouncing by his *mē genoito* phrases. Stating his questions positively shows what he was defending:

---

5. *Mē genoito*, literally, "let it not be," is a strong negative used in the New Testament only by Paul after rhetorical questions (Walter Bauer, William F. Arndt, and F. Wilbur Gingrich, *A Greek-English Lexicon of the New Testament and Other Early Christian Literature*, 2d ed., rev. F. Wilbur Gingrich and Frederick W. Danker [Chicago: University of Chicago Press, 1979], 158). Also see chapter 18, "Questions," in Stanley E. Porter, *Idioms of the Greek New Testament*, 2d ed. (Sheffield: Sheffield Academic, 1995), 276–80.

Lack of faith does not mean God is unfaithful (Rom. 3:3).

God is not unjust in bringing wrath on unbelievers (3:5).

Jews are no better than Gentiles, for all are under sin (3:9).

Faith does not nullify the law (3:31).

Grace does not mean believers should sin (6:1).

Being out from under the law does not mean believers should sin (6:15).

The law is not sin (7:7).

What was good did not become death (7:13).

God is not unjust (9:14).

God has not rejected his people Israel (11:1).

Israel's rejection does not mean they are beyond recovery (11:11).

A believer should not be involved with a prostitute (1 Cor. 6:15).

Christ does not promote sin (Gal. 2:17).

The law is not opposed to the promises of God (3:21).

Paul followed *mē genoito* with reasons for rejecting the errors presented in the questions.[6] An example is Romans 3:6 in which, after writing *mē genoito,* Paul responded with another question, "If that were so, how could God judge the world?" After he asked, "Do we, then, nullify the law by this faith?" he answered with *mē genoito* and a statement: "Not at all! Rather, we uphold the law" (3:31).

To see these variations, look up these following verses and put a check mark in the appropriate column to indicate whether Paul followed these occurrences of *mē genoito* with a statement or a question. Notice how the apostle used this procedure to establish his viewpoints firmly in his readers' minds.

Reference	Statement	Question
Romans 3:4		
Romans 3:9		
Romans 6:2		
Romans 6:15–16		
Romans 7:7		
Romans 7:13		
Romans 9:14		
Romans 11:1		

6. Abraham J. Malherbe, *"Mē Genoito* in the Diatribe and Paul," *Harvard Theological Review* 73 (1980): 235–37.

Romans 11:11
1 Corinthians 6:15
Galatians 2:17
Galatians 3:21

This practice of first presenting a question as if it were asked by someone objecting to Paul's argumentation, followed by the *mē genoito* rejection and then either a statement or a quotation, is called the diatribe. This rhetorical style was common in the writings of Greek philosophers, including especially Epictetus (ca. A.D. 55–ca. 155), a Stoic philosopher and a contemporary of Paul.[7] In philosophical schools the diatribe served as a useful teaching tool, helpful in giving instruction and exhortation.[8]

To Push for a Conclusion

Questions can help move listeners or readers to think of what conclusion should be drawn from what has been said. At least nine times Paul prompted his readers in this way: "What shall we say?" (Rom. 3:5); "What shall we say, then?" (6:1); "What then?" (6:15); "What shall we say, then?" (7:7); "What, then, shall we say in response to this?" (8:31); "What then shall we say?" (9:14); "What then shall we say?" (9:30); "What then?" (11:7); "What then shall we say, brothers?" (1 Cor. 14:26). In the first six of these occurrences, the question is followed by another question, a query designed to encourage thinking. Here, then, is another excellent technique in teaching: to ask rhetorical questions that keep the students alert to the direction you are moving in your discourse.

To Pour Out an Emotion

Several of Paul's emotions were expressed in questions. These included frustration ("Who will rescue me from this body of death?"[Rom. 7:24]); surprise ("Is it possible that there is nobody among you wise enough to judge a dispute between believers?" [1 Cor. 6:5]); victory ("Where, O death, is your victory? Where, O death, is your sting?" [1 Cor. 15:55]); and disappointment ("Lord, who has believed

---

7. Ibid., 231–32. For more on the diatribe and Paul's use of *mē genoito*, see chapter 14.
8. Duane F. Watson, "Diatribe," in *Dictionary of Paul and His Letters*, ed. Gerald F. Hawthorne, Ralph P. Martin, and Daniel G. Reid (Downers Grove, Ill.: InterVarsity, 1993), 213–14; and Stanley K. Stowers, "The Diatribe," in *Greco-Roman Literature and the New Testament*, ed. David E. Aune (Atlanta: Scholars, 1988), 71–83.

our message?" [Rom. 10:16]; "How is it that you are turning back to those weak and miserable principles?" [Gal. 4:9]; and "What has happened to all your joy?" [4:15]).

Twice the emotions expressed in interrogative form were placed by Paul in the mouths of objectors to express frustration and confusion: "Why am I still condemned as a sinner?" (Rom. 3:7), and "Then why does God still blame us?" (9:19).

To Probe for Motives

Paul also used a few questions to challenge his addressees to evaluate their motives. When he asked the Romans, "You, then, why do you judge your brother? Or why do you look down[9] on your brother?" (Rom. 14:10), he was urging them to see that they had no legitimate reason for criticizing or despising their fellow believers. Doing so meant their motives were faulty and needed to be changed. When he saw Peter's inconsistent actions in living like a Gentile and yet trying to force Gentiles to follow Jewish customs (Gal. 2:14), he asked Peter what possible motive he could have for such hypocrisy.

What Other Features Marked Paul's Questions?

As with Jesus' questions, Paul also often voiced his questions in clusters to add impact to his words.[10] Sometimes the additional question(s) said the same thing as the first question in a different or parallel way; other times one or more additional thoughts were added. The following listing includes only those clusters where no other words are inserted between the questions.

Two-Question Clusters

Romans	2:3–4
	3:1
	3:3
	3:5
	3:7–8
	3:9

9. This verb *exoutheneō* means "to despise, disdain, consider as nothing, treat with contempt." It is stronger than *krinō*, "to judge, criticize."

10. Zuck, *Teaching as Jesus Taught*, 249–52.

	3:27
	3:29
	4:10
	6:1
	6:2–3
	6:15
	7:7
	8:31
	8:32–33
	8:35
	9:14
	14.10
1 Corinthians	4:21
	5:12
	6:7
	7:16
	9:11–12
	10:16
	10:18–19
	10:22
	10:29–30
	11:13–15
	12:17
	14:36
	15:35
	15:55
2 Corinthians	1:17
	3:1
	11:29
Galatians	1:10
	4:9
1 Thessalonians	2:19

Three-question clusters

Romans	10:6–8

	11:34–35
1 Corinthians	1:13
	4:7
	15:29–30
2 Corinthians	12:18–19

Four-question clusters

Romans	10:11–15
1 Corinthians	1:20
	6:1–3
	9:1
	9:4–6
	11:22
	14:6–9

Five-question clusters

Romans	2:21–23
1 Corinthians	3:3–5
2 Corinthians	6:14–16
Galatians	3:2–5

Six-question cluster

| Romans | 9:19–24 |

Seven-question cluster

| 1 Corinthians | 12:29–30 |

Ten-question cluster

| 1 Corinthians | 9:4–10 |

Paul's clusters of multiple (five, six, seven, and ten) questions obviously were used to bring the readers to a fitting climax of argumentation, which his readers could not readily overlook.

As already indicated, Paul began his questions in a variety of ways, all designed to stimulate the readers to respond in thought and/or action.

Paul addressed numerous subjects in his questions, again showing the extent of issues confronting believers. At least sixty-five topics were discussed.

Adultery
Angels

Ascension
Baptism, Spirit
Baptism, water
Calling
Christ
Circumcision
Commandments
Conscience
Death
Disciples
Election
Faith
Family
Finiteness
Folly
Gentiles
God, attributes of (faithfulness, justice, glory, kindness, mercy, omniscience, patience, power, truth, wrath)
Gospel
Grace
Head coverings
Heaven
Hell
Holy Spirit
Husbands
Hypocrisy
Idolatry
Immaturity
Incarnation
Jews
Judging
Judgment
Justification
Kingdom
Lord's Supper
Love
Marriage
Ministry
Missions
Mosaic law
Offense
Prayer
Preaching

Priests
Promises
Prostitutes
Reconciliation
Repentance
Resurrection
Return of Christ
Righteousness
Sin
Soldiers
Spiritual gifts
Temple
Troubles
Truth
Victory
Vinedresser
Will, God's
Wisdom
Wives
Word, God's
World

What Can We Learn from Paul about the Art of Asking Questions?

Noting how Paul asked questions can enhance one's own ability in question asking. There is a skill in asking questions that arouse curiosity, stimulate interest, challenge thinking, guide student learning, and correct false assumptions. And seeing how Paul did it can help teachers today develop that skill effectively. The following suggestions spring from Paul's questions.

Avoid asking questions that are unclear. Paul's questions were always concise and discernible. No one need ever wonder what he meant. For that reason his interrogative arrows quickly hit their target.

Avoid general, sweeping questions. If questions are not sufficiently specific, learners will have difficulty responding.

Avoid questions that belittle the students. While Paul did sometimes reprove or correct his readers with questions, the queries were always written in a spirit of love and pastoral concern.

Avoid sameness in questions. Paul's 250 interrogatives reveal a wide variety of approaches and an extensive variation in the kinds of questions. As can be seen in table 16, he introduced his questions in numerous ways, including, "what," "who," "why," "how." Other words with which he began his questions were "which," "do you," "do we," "did," "can you," "are we," "are you," "do not," "does not," "will," "shall," "is," "was it," "where," "has not," "should," "am I," As in all aspects of teaching, student interest lags when learners can predict what their teachers will do. Variety, on the other hand, spurs interest, which in turn results in greater learning.

Avoid questions that cause students to guess the answers. Perusing Paul's 250 questions in table 16 shows that his readers never had to guess. They usually knew the answers, often to their chagrin and embarrassment. Of course, sometimes he followed his questions with answers. But the questions, being rhetorical, served to get the readers to stay with him and to be interested in hearing the answers.

Following these five suggestions can assist teachers, as question makers, in becoming more effective.

What Do You Think?

Tape record a class session you teach. Then, as you play it back, analyze the questions you asked and determine whether they were effective. Compare your questions with Paul's eleven kinds of queries.

Attend another person's class, observing how he or she uses questions. Write them down and then analyze why they were good or bad questions. If few questions were used, ask yourself where questions could have been used to make the class hour more interesting.

Read Paul's epistles and underline, or mark with a highlighter, all of his questions. As you prepare your next lesson, write out questions you can ask that follow several of Paul's eleven kinds of questions.

184

Table 16
Questions Paul Asked[*]

Questions	References	Kinds of Questions
1. "Who are you, Lord?"	Acts 9:5; 22:8; 26:15	1
2. "What shall I do, Lord?"	Acts 22:10	1
3. "Will you never stop perverting the right ways of the Lord?"	Acts 13:10	2
4. "And now do they want to get rid of us quietly?"	Acts 16:37	2
5. "Did you receive the Holy Spirit when you believed?"	Acts 19:2	1
6. "Then what baptism did you receive?"	Acts 19:3	1
7. "May I say something to you?"	Acts 21:37	3
8. "Is it legal for you to flog a Roman citizen who hasn't even been found guilty?"	Acts 22:25	2
9. "Why should any of you consider it incredible that God raises the dead?"	Acts 26:8	4
10. "King Agrippa, do you believe the prophets?"	Acts 26:27	3
11. "Do you think you will escape God's judgment?"	Romans 2:3	2, 5, 6
12. "Or do you show contempt for the riches of his kindness, tolerance, and patience, not realizing that God's kindness leads you toward repentance?"	Romans 2:4	2, 5, 6
13. "You, then, who teach others, do you not teach yourself?"	Romans 2:21	2, 7
14. "You who preach against stealing, do you steal?"	Romans 2:21	2, 7
15. "You who say that people should not commit adultery, do you commit adultery?"	Romans 2:22	2, 7
16. "You who abhor idols, do you rob temples?"	Romans 2:22	2, 7
17. "You who brag about the law, do you dishonor God by breaking the law?"	Romans 2:23	2, 7

* The numerals in the "Kinds of Questions" column correspond to the eleven numbered questions listed earlier in this chapter on page 172.

18. "If those who are not circumcised keep the law's requirements, will they not be regarded as though they were circumcised?"	Romans 2:26	4, 5
19. "What advantage, then, is there in being a Jew?"	Romans 3:1	4, 5
20. "Or what value is there in circumcision?"	Romans 3:1	4, 5
21. "What if some did not have faith?"	Romans 3:3	4
22. "Will their lack of faith nullify God's faithfulness?"	Romans 3:3	4, 8
23. "But if our unrighteousness brings out God's righteousness more clearly, what shall we say?"	Romans 3:5	4
24. "That God is unjust in bringing his wrath on us?"	Romans 3:5	4, 8
25. "If that were so, how could God judge the world?"	Romans 3:6	4
26. "Someone might argue, 'If my falsehood enhances God's truthfulness and so increases his glory, why am I still condemned as a sinner?'"	Romans 3:7	4, 10
27. "Why not say . . . 'Let us do evil that good may result?'"	Romans 3:8	8
28. "What shall we conclude then?"	Romans 3:9	9
29. "Are we any better?"	Romans 3:9	4, 8
30. "Where, then, is boasting?"	Romans 3:27	4, 6, 7
31. "On what principle?"	Romans 3:27	4
32. "On that of observing the law?"	Romans 3:27	4, 8
33. "Is God the God of Jews only?"	Romans 3:29	4, 8
34. "Is he not the God of Gentiles too?"	Romans 3:29	3, 4
35. "Do we, then, nullify the law by this faith?"	Romans 3:31	4, 8
36. "What then shall we say that Abraham, our forefather, discovered in this matter?"	Romans 4:1	4
37. "What does the Scripture say?"	Romans 4:3	1, 4
38. "Is this blessedness only for the circumcised, or also for the uncircumcised?"	Romans 4:9	4

39. "Under what circumstances was it [his faith] credited?"	Romans 4:10	1, 4
40. "Was it after he was circumcised, or before?"	Romans 4:10	1, 4
41. "What shall we say, then?"	Romans 6:1	9
42. "Shall we go on sinning so that grace may increase?"	Romans 6:1	4, 8
43. "How can we live in it [sin] any longer?"	Romans 6:2	4
44. "Or don't you know that all of us who were baptized into Christ Jesus were baptized into his death?"	Romans 6:3	1
45. "What then?"	Romans 6:15	9
46. "Shall we sin because we are not under law but under grace?"	Romans 6:15	4, 8
47. "Don't you know that when you offer yourselves to someone to obey him as slaves, you are slaves to the one whom you obey—whether you are slaves to sin, which leads to death, or to obedience, which leads to righteousness?"	Romans 6:16	1, 2, 4
48. "What benefit did you reap at that time from the things you are now ashamed of?"	Romans 6:21	1, 4
49. "Do you not know, brothers . . . that the law has authority over a man only as long as he lives?"	Romans 7:1	1
50. "What shall we say, then?"	Romans 7:7	9
51. "Is the law sin?"	Romans 7:7	4, 8
52. "Did that which is good, then, become death to me?"	Romans 7:13	4, 8
53. "Who will rescue me from this body of death?"	Romans 7:24	10
54. "What, then, shall we say in response to this?"	Romans 8:31	9
55. "If God is for us, who can be against us?"	Romans 8:31	4
56. "Will he not also, along with him, graciously give us all things?"	Romans 8:32	3, 4
57. "Who will bring any charge against those whom God has chosen?"	Romans 8:33	4

58. "Who is he that condemns?"	Romans 8:34	4
59. "Who shall separate us from the love of Christ?"	Romans 8:35	4
60. "Shall trouble or hardship or persecution or famine or nakedness or danger or sword?"	Romans 8:35	4
61. "What then shall we say?"	Romans 9:14	9
62. "Is God unjust?"	Romans 9:14	4, 8
63. "One of you will say to me, 'Then why does God still blame us?'"	Romans 9:19	10
64. "'For who resists his will?'"	Romans 9:19	4
65. "But who are you, O man, to talk back to God?"	Romans 9:20	2, 4
66. "Shall what is formed say to him who formed it, 'Why did you make me like this?'"	Romans 9:20	2, 4, 8
67. "Does not the potter have the right to make out of the same lump of clay some pottery for noble purposes and some for common use?"	Romans 9:21	2, 4
68. "What if God, choosing to show his wrath and make his power known, bore with great patience the objects of his wrath—prepared for destruction?"	Romans 9:22	4
69. "What if he did this to make the riches of his glory known to the objects of his mercy, whom he prepared in advance for glory—even us, whom he also called, not only from the Jews but also from the Gentiles?"	Romans 9:23–24	4
70. "What then shall we say?"	Romans 9:30	9
71. "Why not?"	Romans 9:32	4
72. "Do not say in your heart, 'Who will ascend into heaven?'"	Romans 10:6	1, 4
73. "Or 'Who will descend into the deep?'"	Romans 10:7	1, 4
74. "But what does it [the law] say?"	Romans 10:8	1, 4
75. "How, then, can they call on the one they have not believed in?"	Romans 10:14	4
76. "And how can they believe in the one of whom they have not heard?"	Romans 10:14	4

77. "And how can they hear without someone preaching to them?"	Romans 10:14	4
78. "And how can they preach unless they are sent?"	Romans 10:15	4
79. "For Isaiah says, 'Lord, who has believed our message?'"	Romans 10:16	11
80. "Did they not hear?"	Romans 10:18	1, 4
81. "Did Israel not understand?"	Romans 10:19	1, 4
82. "Did God reject his people?"	Romans 11:1	4, 8
83. "Don't you know what the Scripture says in the passage about Elijah?"	Romans 11:2	1
84. "And what was God's answer to him?"	Romans 11:4	1
85. "What then?"	Romans 11:7	9
86. "Did they stumble so as to fall beyond recovery?"	Romans 11:11	4, 8
87. "For if their rejection is the reconciliation of the world, what will their acceptance be but life from the dead?"	Romans 11:15	4
88. "After all, if you were cut out of an olive tree that is wild by nature, and contrary to nature were grafted into a cultivated olive tree, how much more readily will these, the natural branches, be grafted into their own olive tree?"	Romans 11:24	4
89. "Who has known the mind of the Lord?"	Romans 11:34	4, 8
90. "Or who has been his counselor?"	Romans 11:34	4, 8
91. "Who has ever given to God, that God should repay him?"	Romans 11:35	4, 8
92. "Do you want to be free from fear of the one in authority?"	Romans 13:3	5
93. "Who are you to judge someone else's servant?"	Romans 14:4	2
94. "You, then, why do you judge your brother?"	Romans 14:10	2, 4, 11
95. "Or why do you look down on your brother?"	Romans 14:10	2, 4, 11
96. "Is Christ divided?"	1 Corinthians 1:13	4, 8
97. "Was Paul crucified for you?"	1 Corinthians 1:13	4, 8

98. "Were you baptized into the name of Paul?"	1 Corinthians 1:13	4, 8
99. "Where is the wise man?"	1 Corinthians 1:20	4
100. "Where is the scholar?"	1 Corinthians 1:20	4
101. "Where is the philosopher of this age?"	1 Corinthians 1:20	4
102. "Has not God made foolish the wisdom of this world?"	1 Corinthians 1:20	3, 4
103. "For who among men knows the thoughts of a man except the man's spirit within him?"	1 Corinthians 2:11	4
104. "For since there is jealousy and quarreling among you, are you not worldly?"	1 Corinthians 3:3	3, 4
105. "Are you not acting like mere men?"	1 Corinthians 3:3	3, 4
106. "For when one says, 'I follow Paul,' and another, 'I follow Apollos,' are you not mere men?"	1 Corinthians 3:4	3, 4
107. "What, after all, is Apollos?"	1 Corinthians 3:5	4
108. "And what is Paul?"	1 Corinthians 3:5	4
109. "Don't you know that you yourselves are God's temple and that God's Spirit lives in you?"	1 Corinthians 3:16	1, 3, 4
110. "For who makes you different from anyone else?"	1 Corinthians 4:7	4
111. "What do you have that you did not receive?"	1 Corinthians 4:7	4
112. "And if you did receive it, why do you boast as though you did not?"	1 Corinthians 4:7	2, 4
113. "What do you prefer?"	1 Corinthians 4:21	2, 4, 5
114. "Shall I come to you with a whip, or in love and with a gentle spirit?"	1 Corinthians 4:21	2, 4, 5
115. "Shouldn't you rather have been filled with grief and have put out of your fellowship the man who did this?"	1 Corinthians 5:2	2, 3, 4
116. "Don't you know that a little yeast works through the whole batch of dough?"	1 Corinthians 5:6	1, 4
117. "What business is it of mine to judge those outside the church?"	1 Corinthians 5:12	4
118. "Are you not to judge those inside?"	1 Corinthians 5:12	3, 4

119. "If any of you has a dispute with another, dare he take it before the ungodly for judgment instead of before the saints?"	1 Corinthians 6:1	2, 4
120. "Do you not know that the saints will judge the world?"	1 Corinthians 6:2	1, 4
121. "And if you are to judge the world, are you not competent to judge trivial cases?"	1 Corinthians 6:2	2, 4
122. "Do you not know that we will judge angels?"	1 Corinthians 6:3	1, 4
123. "Is it possible that there is nobody among you wise enough to judge a dispute between believers?"	1 Corinthians 6:5	2, 4, 10
124. "Why not rather be wronged?"	1 Corinthians 6:7	2, 4
125. "Why not rather be cheated?"	1 Corinthians 6:7	2, 4
126. "Do you not know that the wicked will not inherit the kingdom of God?"	1 Corinthians 6:9	1, 4
127. "Do you not know that your bodies are members of Christ himself?"	1 Corinthians 6:15	1, 4
128. "Shall I then take the members of Christ and unite them with a prostitute?"	1 Corinthians 6:15	4, 6, 8
129. "Do you not know that he who unites himself with a prostitute is one with her in body?"	1 Corinthians 6:16	1, 4, 6
130. "Do you not know that your body is a temple of the Holy Spirit, who is in you, whom you have received from God?"	1 Corinthians 6:19	1, 4
131. "How do you know, wife, whether you will save your husband?"	1 Corinthians 7:16	4
132. "Or, how do you know, husband, whether you will save your wife?"	1 Corinthians 7:16	4
133. "Was a man already circumcised when he was called?"	1 Corinthians 7:18	1
134. "Was a man uncircumcised when he was called?"	1 Corinthians 7:18	1
135. "Were you a slave when you were called?"	1 Corinthians 7:21	1
136. "Are you married?"	1 Corinthians 7:27	1
137. "Are you unmarried?"	1 Corinthians 7:27	1

138. "For if anyone with a weak con-science sees you who have this knowl-edge eating in an idol's temple, won't he be emboldened to eat what has been sac-rificed to idols?" — 1 Corinthians 8:10 — 3, 4, 5

139. "Am I not free?" — 1 Corinthians 9:1 — 1, 3, 4

140. "Am I not an apostle?" — 1 Corinthians 9:1 — 1, 3, 4

141. "Have I not seen Jesus our Lord?" — 1 Corinthians 9:1 — 1, 3, 4

142. "Are you not the result of my work in the Lord?" — 1 Corinthians 9:1 — 1, 3, 4

143. "Don't we have the right to food and drink?" — 1 Corinthians 9:4 — 3, 4

144. "Don't we have the right to take a be-lieving wife along with us, as do the other apostles and the Lord's brothers and Cephas?" — 1 Corinthians 9:5 — 3, 4

145. "Or is it only I and Barnabas who must work for a living?" — 1 Corinthians 9:6 — 4, 8

146. "Who serves as a soldier at his own expense?" — 1 Corinthians 9:7 — 4, 8

147. "Who plants a vineyard and does not eat of its grapes?" — 1 Corinthians 9:7 — 4, 8

148. "Who tends a flock and does not drink of the milk?" — 1 Corinthians 9:7 — 4, 8

149. "Do I say this merely from a human point of view?" — 1 Corinthians 9:8 — 4, 8

150. "Doesn't the Law say the same thing?" — 1 Corinthians 9:8 — 1, 3, 4

151. "Is it about oxen that God is con-cerned?" — 1 Corinthians 9:9 — 4, 8

152. "Surely he says this for us, doesn't he?" — 1 Corinthians 9:10 — 3, 4

153. "If we have sown spiritual seed among you, is it too much to reap a ma-terial harvest from you?" — 1 Corinthians 9:11 — 4, 8

154. "If others have this right of support from you, shouldn't we have it all the more?" — 1 Corinthians 9:12 — 3, 4

155. "Don't you know that those who work in the temple get their food from the temple, and those who serve at the altar share in what is offered on the altar?"	1 Corinthians 9:13	1, 4
156. "What then is my reward?"	1 Corinthians 9:18	4, 5
157. "Is not the cup of thanksgiving for which we give thanks a participation in the blood of Christ?"	1 Corinthians 10:16	3, 4
158. "And is not the bread that we break a participation in the body of Christ?"	1 Corinthians 10:16	3, 4
159. "Do not those who eat the sacrifices participate in the altar?"	1 Corinthians 10:18	3, 4
160. "Do I mean that a sacrifice offered to an idol is anything, or that an idol is anything?"	1 Corinthians 10:19	4, 8
161. "Are we trying to arouse the Lord's jealousy?"	1 Corinthians 10:22	4, 8
162. "Are we stronger than he?"	1 Corinthians 10:22	4, 8
163. "For why should my freedom be judged by another's conscience?"	1 Corinthians 10:29	4, 5
164. "If I take part in the meal with thankfulness, why am I denounced because of something I thank God for?"	1 Corinthians 10:30	4, 5
165. "Is it proper for a woman to pray to God with her head uncovered?"	1 Corinthians 11:13	4, 5, 8
166. "Does not the very nature of things teach you that if a man has long hair, it is a disgrace to him, but if a woman has long hair, it is her glory?"	1 Corinthians 11:14	4, 5
167. "Don't you have homes to eat and drink in?"	1 Corinthians 11:22	2, 4
168. "Or do you despise the church of God and humiliate those who have nothing?"	1 Corinthians 11:22	2, 4
169. "What shall I say to you?"	1 Corinthians 11:22	4, 5
170. "Shall I praise you for this?"	1 Corinthians 11:22	4, 5, 8
171. "If the whole body were an eye, where would the sense of hearing be?"	1 Corinthians 12:17	4
172. "If the whole body were an ear, where would the sense of smell be?"	1 Corinthians 12:17	4

173. "Are all apostles?"	1 Corinthians 12:29	4, 8
174. "Are all prophets?"	1 Corinthians 12:29	4, 8
175. "Are all teachers?"	1 Corinthians 12:29	4, 8
176. "Do all work miracles?"	1 Corinthians 12:29	4, 8
177. "Do all have gifts of healing?"	1 Corinthians 12:30	4, 8
178. "Do all speak in tongues?"	1 Corinthians 12:30	4, 8
179. "Do all interpret?"	1 Corinthians 12:30	4, 8
180. "Now, brothers, if I come to you and speak in tongues, what good will I be to you, unless I bring you some revelation or knowledge or prophecy or word of instruction?"	1 Corinthians 14:6	4
181. "Even in the case of lifeless things that make sounds, such as the flute or harp, how will anyone know what tune is being played unless there is a distinction in the notes?"	1 Corinthians 14:7	4
182. "Again, if the trumpet does not sound a clear call, who will get ready for battle?"	1 Corinthians 14:8	4
183. "Unless you speak intelligible words with your tongue, how will anyone know what you are saying?"	1 Corinthians 14:9	4
184. "So what shall I do?"	1 Corinthians 14:15	4, 5
185. "If you are praising God with your spirit, how can one who finds himself among those who do not understand say 'Amen' to your thanksgiving, since he does not know what you are saying?"	1 Corinthians 14:16	4
186. "So if the whole church comes together and everyone speaks in tongues, and some who do not understand or some unbelievers come in will they not say that you are out of your mind?"	1 Corinthians 14:23	3, 4
187. "What then shall we say, brothers?"	1 Corinthians 14:26	4, 9
188. "Did the word of God originate with you?"	1 Corinthians 14:36	4, 8
189. "Or are you the only people it has reached?"	1 Corinthians 14:36	4, 8

190. "But if it is preached that Christ has been raised from the dead, how can some of you say that there is no resurrection of the dead?" — 1 Corinthians 15:12 — 4

191. "Now if there is no resurrection, what will those do who are baptized for the dead?" — 1 Corinthians 15:29 — 4

192. "If the dead are not raised at all, why are people baptized for them?" — 1 Corinthians 15:29 — 4

193. "And as for us, why do we endanger ourselves every hour?" — 1 Corinthians 15:30 — 4

194. "But someone may ask, 'How are the dead raised?'" — 1 Corinthians 15:35 — 1, 4

195. "'With what kind of body will they come?'" — 1 Corinthians 15:35 — 1, 4

196. "Where, O death, is your victory?" — 1 Corinthians 15:55 — 10

197. "Where, O death, is your sting?" — 1 Corinthians 15:55 — 10

198. "When I planned this, did I do it lightly?" — 2 Corinthians 1:17 — 4, 8

199. "Or do I make my plans in a worldly manner so that in the same breath I say, 'Yes, yes,' and 'No, no.'" — 2 Corinthians 1:17 — 4, 8

200. "For if I grieve you, who is left to make me glad but you whom I have grieved?" — 2 Corinthians 2:2 — 4

201. "And who is equal to such a task?" — 2 Corinthians 2:16 — 4

202. "Are we beginning to commend ourselves again?" — 2 Corinthians 3:1 — 4, 8

203. "Or do we need, like some people, letters of recommendation to you or from you?" — 2 Corinthians 3:1 — 4, 8

204. "Now if the ministry [of Moses] . . . brought death . . . will not the ministry of the Spirit be even more glorious?" — 2 Corinthians 3:7–8 — 3, 4

205. "For what do righteousness and wickedness have in common?" — 2 Corinthians 6:14 — 4, 8

206. "Or what fellowship can light have with darkness?" — 2 Corinthians 6:14 — 4, 8

207. "What harmony is there between Christ and Belial?" — 2 Corinthians 6:15 — 4, 8

208. "What does a believer have in common with an unbeliever?"	2 Corinthians 6:15	4, 8
209. "What agreement is there between the temple of God and idols?"	2 Corinthians 6:16	4,8
210. "Was it a sin for me to lower myself in order to elevate you by preaching the gospel of God to you free of charge?"	2 Corinthians 11:7	4, 8
211. "Are they Hebrews?"	2 Corinthians 11:22	3
212. "Are they Israelites?"	2 Corinthians 11:22	3
213. "Are they Abraham's descendants?"	2 Corinthians 11:22	3
214. "Are they servants of Christ?"	2 Corinthians 11:23	3, 8
215. "Who is weak, and I do not feel weak?"	2 Corinthians 11:29	4
216. "Who is led into sin, and I do not inwardly burn?"	2 Corinthians 11:29	4
217. "How were you inferior to the other churches, except that I was never a burden to you?"	2 Corinthians 12:13	4
218. "If I love you more, will you love me less?"	2 Corinthians 12:15	4, 5
219. "Did I exploit you through any of the men I sent you?"	2 Corinthians 12:17	8
220. "Titus did not exploit you, did he?"	2 Corinthians 12:18	8
221. "Did we not act in the same spirit and follow the same course?"	2 Corinthians 12:18	4
222. "Have you been thinking all along that we have been defending ourselves to you?"	2 Corinthians 12:19	4, 8
223. "Am I now trying to win the approval of men, or of God?"	Galatians 1:10	4, 5
224. "Or am I trying to please men?"	Galatians 1:10	4, 8
225. "How is it, then, that you force Gentiles to follow Jewish customs?"	Galatians 2:14	4, 7, 11
226. "If, while we seek to be justified in Christ, it becomes evident that we ourselves are sinners, does that mean that Christ promotes sin?"	Galatians 2:17	4, 8
227. "Who has bewitched you?"	Galatians 3:1	1, 4
228. "Did you receive the Spirit by observing the law, or by believing what you heard?"	Galatians 3:2	5

229. "Are you so foolish?"	Galatians 3:3	2
230. "After beginning with the Spirit, are you now trying to attain your goal by human effort?"	Galatians 3:3	2, 5
231. "Have you suffered so much for nothing—if it really was for nothing?"	Galatians 3:4	4
232. "Does God give you his Spirit and work miracles among you because you observe the law, or because you believe what you heard?"	Galatians 3:5	5
233. "What, then, was the purpose of the law?"	Galatians 3:19	1, 4
234. "Is the law, therefore, opposed to the promises of God?"	Galatians 3:21	4, 8
235. "How is it that you are turning back to those weak and miserable principles?"	Galatians 4:9	4, 10
236. "Do you wish to be enslaved by them all over again?"	Galatians 4:9	4, 5
237. "What has happened to all your joy?"	Galatians 4:15	4, 10
238. "Have I now become your enemy by telling you the truth?"	Galatians 4:16	4, 8
239. "Are you not aware of what the law says?"	Galatians 4:21	1, 2
240. "But what does the Scripture say?"	Galatians 4:30	1
241. "Who cut in on you and kept you from obeying the truth?"	Galatians 5:7	1, 2
242. "Brothers, if I am still preaching circumcision, why am I still being persecuted?"	Galatians 5:11	4
243. "What does 'he ascended' mean except that he also descended to the lower, earthly regions?"	Ephesians 4:9	4
244. "But what does it matter?"	Philippians 1:18	4, 5
245. "Yet what shall I choose?"	Philippians 1:22	5
246. "Since you died with Christ to the basic principles of this world, why, as though you still belonged to it, do you submit to its rules: 'Do not handle! Do not taste! Do not touch!'?"	Colossians 2:20–21	2, 4

247. "For what is our hope, our joy, or the crown in which we will glory in the presence of our Lord Jesus when he comes?" — 1 Thessalonians 2:19 — 1, 4

248. "Is it not you?" — 1 Thessalonians 2:19 — 3

249. "Don't you remember that when I was with you I used to tell you these things?" — 2 Thessalonians 2:5 — 1

250. "If anyone does not know how to manage his own family, how can he take care of God's church?" — 1 Timothy 3:5 — 4, 5

*"Our dear brother Paul also wrote you
with the wisdom that God gave him."*

2 Peter 3:15

12

How Did Paul Use Picturesque Expressions in His Teaching?

Can you imagine a world without color? Think of how drab life would be if all the world were, say, a dull gray. No green grass, no blue sky, no red, yellow, purple, orange, pink, or white flowers. No white snow, no fall leaves on trees with their brilliant yellows, reds, and browns. Dresses, shirts, shoes all neutral. Cars, houses, animals, buildings—everything the same drabness.

That would make a rather uninteresting world, wouldn't it? Uninviting, boring, a monotonous sameness.

Now think of language. No figures of speech. No picturesque expressions, no colorful comparisons, no meaningful metaphors, no clever puns. Think of every book, every conversation, every lesson or sermon dull, flat, and lusterless.

Thankfully, God's creative works and man's inventions all have color. And so does language. Picturesque expressions in our teaching, speaking, and writing add sparkle and interest, and help our learners retain what is communicated. For example, it is much easier to remember Paul's references to "savage wolves" (Acts 20:29) than to remember a more flat reference to "false teachers who will viciously oppose you." The imagery of wolves would not readily be forgotten! When the apostle referred to everything in his preconversion days as "rubbish" (Phil. 3:8), that was more memorable than simply calling everything "useless." And challenging believers to be like soldiers wearing "the full armor of God" (Eph. 6:11, 13) is a powerful way of picturing their need to be on the defensive against satanic influences.

Paul's preaching and teaching incorporated many figures of speech, figures that made his communications more interesting, more penetrating, and more easily retained.

As I wrote elsewhere,

> People live and think metaphorically. They commonly compare one object to another to arrest attention. Or they make an overstatement for emphasis. Or they speak with puns to make their point more palatable. They assert contrasts, or they voice riddles, or they personify an inanimate object all for the purpose of communication.[1]

A figure of speech "is simply a word or a sentence thrown into a peculiar form, different from its original or simplest meaning or use."[2] One reason Paul was such a masterful teacher is that he used numerous figures of speech—picturesque expressions that immediately registered with his hearer-readers, aiding them in comprehending the points made, in sensing their force and beauty,[3] and in retaining them mentally. His purpose was not to be clever, but to be communicative.

The apostles' extensive use of figurative language, illustrated in this and the next chapters, reveals that he stands as "a master of metaphor."[4] By moving from the familiar to the unfamiliar in his colorful, graphic word pictures, Paul did what all dedicated teachers want to do—capture attention, clarify issues, stimulate student thinking, delight the reader-listeners,[5] and impact student living.

1. Roy B. Zuck, *Teaching as Jesus Taught* (Grand Rapids: Baker, 1995), 184–85.
2. E. W. Bullinger, *Figures of Speech Used in the Bible: Explained and Illustrated* (London: Eyre and Spottiswoode, 1898; reprint, Grand Rapids: Baker, 1968), xv. Quintilian, the famous first-century Roman rhetorician, wrote that "a figure is a conformation of speech differing from the common and the ordinary . . . a form of speech given a new turn by art" (*On the Education of an Orator* 9.1.4, 14).
3. James Neil, *Figurative Language of the Bible* (London: Woodford Fawcett, 1888), 5.
4. Robert R. Resker, *St. Paul's Illustrations* (Edinburgh: Clark, n.d.), 8.
5. Quintilian wrote that when a speaker uses figurative language "the listener takes pleasure in detecting the speaker's concealed meaning, applauds his own penetration and regards another man's eloquence as a compliment to himself" (*On the Education of an Orator* 9.2.78).

Simile

In a simile one thing is compared to another explicitly by the word "like" or "as."[6] Paul wrote to the Romans about his struggle with sin, referring to his times of spiritual defeat as being "sold as a slave to sin" (Rom. 7:14). Believers undergoing persecution are viewed "as sheep to be slaughtered" (8:36). Israelites are "like the sand by the sea," that is, numerous beyond counting (9:27). Paul addressed the Corinthian Christians as if they were children spiritually (1 Cor. 3:1; 2 Cor. 6:13), and he referred to himself "as an expert builder" in his ministry (1 Cor. 3:10). He told them he and his coworkers were like servants of God (4:1; 2 Cor. 6:4), whereas Satan's servants hypocritically and deceitfully masquerade as servants of righteousness (2 Cor. 11:15). Paul's enemies, he said, treated him like a person condemned to die before beasts in an arena (1 Cor. 4:9), but the Galatians considered him "as if [he] were an angel of God" (Gal. 4:14). He wrote that his ministry was not aimless or useless, like a runner without a goal or a boxer missing his opponent (1 Cor. 9:26).[7]

Like children imitating their parents, so believers, Paul admonished, are to imitate God "as dearly loved children" (Eph. 5:1); they are to live "as children of light" (5:8), shining in their witness for Christ "like stars in the universe" (Phil. 2:15).

In his care for the believers of Thessalonica, Paul was "like a mother caring for [lit., 'nursing'] her little children" (1 Thess. 2:7),[8] and he dealt with them "as a father" (2:11). The day of the Lord, Paul wrote, "will come like a thief" (5:2, 4),[9] and destruction will come "suddenly, as labor pains on a pregnant woman" (5:3).

---

6. Sometimes the NIV adds the words "like" or "as" to make a smoother reading in English in verses that do not have those words (e.g., Rom. 8:22; 2 Cor. 1:22; 5:5; Phil. 2:17).

7. When Paul wrote that he was not like a boxer "beating the air," he probably referred to a boxer missing his opponent rather than a boxer practicing by himself in "shadow boxing." "The allusion is not to . . . a rehearsal of a fight with an *imaginary* adversary . . . but to a fight with a *real* adversary (viz. here, *the body*), in which the boxer vainly hits into the air, instead of striking his antagonist" (Henry Alford, *The Greek Testament* [reprint (4 vols. in 2), Chicago: Moody, 1958], 3:551[italics his]).

8. On this simile, see Abraham J. Malherbe, "'Gentle as a Nurse,': The Cynic Background to 1 Thess ii," *Novum Testamentum* 12 (1970): 203–17.

9. As Gale points out, the point of the comparison is not to suggest that the Lord will steal or will bring material loss or physical harm, but rather that the day of the Lord will come with suddenness (Herbert M. Gale, *The Use of Analogy in the Letters of Paul* [Philadelphia: Westminster, 1964] 29).

Paul used four similes in one chapter of each of his two epistles to Timothy (1 Tim. 5 and 2 Tim. 2). He urged Timothy to exhort an older man "as if he were your father" (1 Tim. 5:1), to "treat younger men as brothers" (5:1), "older women as mothers" (5:2), and "younger women as sisters" (5:2). Timothy was to be serving "like a good soldier" (2 Tim. 2:3) and "as an athlete" (2:5). While in prison Paul wrote that though he was innocent, he was "being chained like a criminal" (2:9), and he warned Timothy that false teaching can "spread like gangrene" (2:17).

In analyzing similes, it is important to note three things: the image, the nonimage or referent (i.e., what is being referred to by the image), and the point of comparison.[10] In table 17, write what you think is the comparison Paul intended in each of his twenty-seven similes discussed in the preceding paragraphs. The first few are filled in to help you get started.

Table 17
Paul's Similes

References	Images	Nonimages (Referents)	Points of Comparisons
Rom. 7:14	Slave	Paul	Spiritually defeated and captured
Rom. 8:36	Sheep	Believers	Persecuted
Rom. 9:27	Sand	Israelites	Innumerable
1 Cor. 3:1; 2 Cor. 6:13	Children	Corinthians	Spiritually immature
1 Cor. 3:10	Builder (of a foundation)	Paul	Winning people to Christ
1 Cor. 4:1; 2 Cor. 6:4	Servants	Paul and coworkers	Devoted to God
1 Cor. 4:9	Person	Paul	Condemned
1 Cor. 9:26	Runner with no goal	Paul	
1 Cor. 9:26	Man beating the air	Paul	
2 Cor. 11:15	Servants	False teachers	
Gal. 4:14	Angel	Paul	
Eph. 5:1	Children	Ephesian believers	
Eph. 5:8	Children of light	Ephesian believers	

10. See Roy B. Zuck, *Basic Bible Interpretation* (Wheaton, Ill.: Victor, 1991), 162–64.

Phil. 2:15	Stars	Philippian believers
1 Thess. 2:7	Mother	Paul
1 Thess. 2:11	Father	Paul
1 Thess. 5:2, 4	Thief	Day of the Lord
1 Thess. 5:3	Labor pains	Destruction
1 Tim. 5:1	Father	Older man
1 Tim. 5:1	Brothers	Younger men
1 Tim. 5:2	Mothers	Older women
1 Tim. 5:2	Sisters	Younger women
2 Tim. 2:3	Soldier	Timothy
2 Tim. 2:5	Athlete	Timothy
2 Tim. 2:9	Criminal	Paul
2 Tim. 2:17	Gangrene	False teaching

Metaphor

A metaphor is a comparison of two normally unlike things, made by using a form of "to be" (is, are, was, were) or "to become." A simile is an explicit comparison, using "like" or "as," but a metaphor is more implicit. By saying "This is that," a metaphor brings together two things that are ordinarily dissimilar, thus creating a shock or surprise. "In the metaphor we have an image with a certain shock to the imagination."[11]

Paul used numerous metaphors in his teaching. Many of them have become commonplace to Bible students, but his initial readers would no doubt have been surprised at some of the associations he made. The surprise element would have jolted their thinking. "Undoubtedly, when two remote referents are juxtaposed in such a fashion that likeness is perceived in the midst of unlikeness, delight and surprise occur."[12]

A few of Paul's metaphors describe unbelievers, who are said to be slaves of sin (Rom. 6:16–17, 20; Gal. 4:3, 7–8), prisoners of sin (Gal. 3:22) and of the law (3:23), foreigners and aliens (Eph. 2:19), and darkness (5:8), whose throats are open graves (Rom. 3:13). A few metaphors relate to Christ, who is the firstborn (Rom. 8:29; Col. 1:15, 18), the church's foundation (1 Cor. 3:11) and cornerstone (Eph. 2:20), the rock

---

11. Amos N. Wilder, *The Language of the Gospel* (New York: Harper and Row, 1964), 80.

12. David M. Park, "The Interpretive Value of Paul's Metaphors," *South East Asia Journal of Theology* 18 (1977): 39.

(1 Cor. 10:4), the firstfruits of the resurrection (15:20, 23), and the head of the church (Col. 1:18). Paul said he was the father of the Corinthians (1 Cor. 4:15); scum and refuse (4:13); and an aroma, smell, and fragrance (2 Cor. 2:15–16). Three objects are referred to metaphorically: the bread is Christ's body (1 Cor. 10:16; 11:24), the cup is his blood (10:16; 11:27), and gifts are a fragrant offering and sacrifice (Phil. 4:18).

Most of Paul's metaphors, however, relate to believers. They are a guide and a light (Rom. 2:19); slaves to righteousness (6:18), to God (6:22), and to God's law (7:25), and in the sinful nature slaves to the law of sin (7:25); God's children (8:16); heirs of God (8:17; Titus 3:7) and co-heirs with Christ (Rom. 8:17); conquerors (8:37); God's field and building (1 Cor. 3:9); God's temple (1 Cor. 3:16–17; 2 Cor. 6:16); a temple of the Holy Spirit (1 Cor. 6:19); the body of Christ (12:27; Col. 1:22); infants regarding evil and adults in thinking (1 Cor. 14:20); a man and an heir (Gal. 4:7); fellow citizens (Eph. 2:19); a dwelling in which God lives (Eph. 2:22); heirs together with Israel (3:6); no longer infants (4:14); members of Christ's body (5:30); circumcision (Phil. 3:3); sons of light and sons of day (1 Thess. 5:5); God's household (*oikos*, lit., "house"; 1 Tim. 3:15); and an instrument (lit., vessel) for noble purposes (2 Tim. 2:21).

In other metaphors Paul said the Corinthians were his letters of recommendation (2 Cor. 3:1–3), the Thessalonians were his crown (1 Thess. 2:19), gifts to him from the Philippians were a fragrant offering (Phil. 4:18), and Onesimus was Paul's "very heart" (Philem. 12).

Regarding the Mosaic law Paul wrote metaphorically that it was a tutor (Gal. 3:24 NASB). "Tutor" translates *paidagōgos* (lit., "child leader"), which is loosely rendered in the New International Version by the words "was put in charge." (The King James Version's translation "schoolmaster" is misleading.) In wealthy homes in the Greco-Roman society a *paidagōgos* was a slave who took a child or youth to school, sat in on his classes, and escorted him back home.[13] The guardian protected the child from harm, taught him manners and morals, and disciplined him when necessary. This responsibility began when the child entered school at age six or seven and continued until the pupil was a late adolescent.[14] The *paidagōgos* thus had a threefold role; he was a guardian, a disciplinarian, and a personal tutor. Some *paidagōgoi* became rather harsh in their disciplining. Paul's point in comparing the law to a *paidagōgos* was to state that it had a restrictive custody, shield-

---

13. Plato *Lysis* 208C; idem *Laws* 808C; Plutarch *On Morals* 439–40; Plutarch *On the Education of Children* 7.

14. For sources that discuss the role of the *paidagōgos*, see Roy B. Zuck, *Precious in His Sight: Childhood and Children in the Bible* (Grand Rapids: Baker, 1996), 145, n. 54.

ing Israel "from the evil heathen rites surrounding them,"[15] and that it was temporary.[16] When Christ came, Paul wrote, the law was no longer needed. Therefore "the attempt of the Judaizers to extend the tenure of the *paidagōgos* beyond the time of Christ's was to lose sight of the law's provisional status and preparatory function [and] to nullify the grace of God."[17]

In 1 Corinthians 4:15 Paul used *paidagōgos* in a different way: "Even though you have ten thousand guardians in Christ, you do not have many fathers, for in Christ Jesus I became your father through the gospel." As Bennett explains, "The Corinthians had had many who had assisted them and watched over them in their Christian life like guardians . . . some as eminent as Peter and Apollos. But there remained a special relationship with the one who had brought them to [spiritual] birth."[18]

In studying these many metaphors, think of the similarity being made between the image and the nonimage. For example, how is Christ similar to the foundation of a building? Or how does a temple picture believers? In what way were Thessalonian Christians like a crown to Paul? Thinking through each of these several dozen metaphors demonstrates the graphic way in which Paul imparted doctrinal truths concretely.

Hypocatastasis

A hypocatastasis is a figure in which a comparison is made between two dissimilar things by direct naming. Whereas a simile uses "like" or "as," and a metaphor uses a form of the verb "to be" or "to become," a hypocatastasis uses neither and instead calls a person, object, or truth something else. When Paul spoke to the elders of Ephesus about finishing his race (Acts 20:24), he was not referring to a literal footrace. Instead he was naming his ministry a race, thus calling attention to a point of similarity between the two. Like a race, serving God involves energy, endurance, and effort toward reaching a goal. These several concepts are all succinctly conveyed by the one word "race."

In this same address he referred, by the use of three hypocatastases, to the elders as shepherds, the believers as a flock of sheep, and false

15. Donald K. Campbell, "Galatians," in *The Bible Knowledge Commentary, New Testament*, ed. John F. Walvoord and Roy B. Zuck (Wheaton, Ill.: Victor, 1983), 600.

16. Frank Thielman, "Law," in *Dictionary of Paul and His Letters*, ed. Gerald F. Hawthorne, Ralph P. Martin, and Daniel G. Reid (Downers Grove, Ill.: InterVarsity, 1993), 539.

17. J. W. MacGorman, "The Law as Paidagōgos: A Study in Pauline Analogy," in *New Testament Studies*, ed. Huber L. Drumwright and Curtis Vaughn (Waco, Tex.: Markham, 1975), 111.

18. David W. Bennett, *Metaphors of Ministry* (Grand Rapids: Baker, 1993), 128.

teachers as savage wolves (20:28–29)—all appropriate verbal pictures. He called heretics in Ephesus "wild beasts" (1 Cor. 15:32).[19]

Similarly, in Philippians 3:2 Paul called false teachers "dogs." When on trial before the Sanhedrin, the Jewish court, Paul addressed Ananias as a "whitewashed wall" (Acts 23:3), not knowing he was the high priest (23:5). Why did he call Ananias a "whitewashed wall"? Because though he looked all right on the outside, inwardly he was unclean, weak, and deteriorating. Sitting as a judge, responsible to follow the law, he violated it by ordering Paul to be struck on the mouth (23:2).

Writing to the Christians at Rome, Paul used a number of hypocatastases. Four times he referred to ministry opportunities as a "way" or a "door" to be opened (Rom. 1:10; 1 Cor. 16:9; 2 Cor. 2:12; Col. 4:3). He called the blessings of the Christian life "the firstfruits of the Spirit" (Rom. 8:23) and fruit (15:28), and he referred to the believers' presence with the Lord in heaven as "our adoption as sons" and the transformation in their bodies at that time as their "redemption."

Unbelieving Israelites "stumbled over the stumbling stone" (9:32) and the "rock that makes them fall" (9:33), a reference to Christ. But elsewhere "stumbling block" refers to any conduct of a believer that causes another Christian to sin (14:13; 2 Cor. 6:3).

Paul considered the advantages of his background as useless as rubbish (Phil. 3:8). And the unsaved condition of the Israelites was like their having a veil over their faces (2 Cor. 3:15–16). Sharing the gospel, however, Paul said, was like laying the foundation of a building (Rom. 15:20; 1 Cor. 3:10) or planting seed (1 Cor. 3:6). To Paul, the gospel was a "treasure in jars of clay" (2 Cor. 4:7).[20] Converts were his "crown" (Phil. 4:1),[21] and Timothy, Titus, and Onesimus were his "sons," that is, ones he had led to the Lord, like a father giving birth to a son (1 Tim. 1:2, 18; 2 Tim. 1:2; 2:1; Titus 1:4; Philem. 10). The difference between being spiritually unregenerate and being saved is the difference between darkness and light (2 Cor. 4:6).

19. On this figure of speech, see Abraham J. Malherbe, "The Beasts of Ephesus," *Journal of Biblical Literature* 87 (1968): 71–80. Malherbe points out that the early church father Ignatius also described heretics as beasts (*Letter to the Ephesians* 7.1; ibid., 80, n. 75).

20. Some writers say the jars of clay, a reference to Paul's body or humanness, suggest weakness, and others say they refer to Paul's own "cheapness" in contrast to the inestimable worth of the treasure, the gospel. Possibly, as Timothy B. Savage suggests, both ideas were intended, for earthern vessels are both weak and inferior (*Power through Weakness: Paul's Understanding of the Christian Ministry in 2 Corinthians* [Cambridge: University Press, 1996], 164–66). Savage adds, "The dual character of clay pots would not be lost on Corinthian readers" (ibid., 166, n. 13). See G. R. Davidson, *Corinth: The Minor Objects*, vol. 12 (Princeton, N.J.: American School of Classical Studies in Athens, 1952).

21. In 1 Thessalonians 2:19 Paul's reference to the believers in Thessalonica as his crown is a metaphor, whereas here in Philippians 4:1 the reference is a hypocatastasis.

Paul called Christ "the Root of Jesse" (Rom. 15:12, a quotation from Isa. 11:10), that is, a "shoot" coming "up from the stump of Jesse" (Isa. 11:1), David's father. In four other hypocatastases Paul referred to Christ as "our Passover lamb" (1 Cor. 5:7), the believers' "husband" (2 Cor. 11:2), the head of the church (Col. 2:19), the head of all things (Eph. 1:22; Col. 2:10), the head of every man (1 Cor. 11:3), and clothing with which believers have been honored (Gal. 3:27).[22]

The Holy Spirit is a seal (2 Cor. 1:22; Eph. 1:13; cf. 4:30), confirming and identifying the believer with Christ, and a deposit (2 Cor. 1:22; 5:5; Eph. 1:14), that is, a down payment *(arrabōna)* guaranteeing more will be paid, in the sense that the indwelling Holy Spirit is a foretaste of future blessings.

Paul called the church several things: a body (1 Cor. 12:13; Eph. 1:23; 4:12, 16; Col. 1:18; 2:19),[23] a building (Eph. 2:21), a pillar and foundation of the truth (1 Tim. 3:15), and a solid foundation (2 Tim. 2:19).

He said sin in a church is yeast and absence of sin is bread without yeast (1 Cor. 5:7–8). Valueless human effort is wood, hay, and straw, and meaningful ministry carried out with Christ's enabling is gold, silver, and costly stones (1 Cor. 3:12–13).[24] Fire is the Lord's testing of the believers' service at the judgment seat of Christ (3:13–15).

Not living a dedicated life is called sleeping (Rom. 13:11), performing deeds of darkness (13:12), and leading deadly "unproductive [lit., 'fruitless'] lives" (Titus 3:14). By contrast, effective Christian living is pictured as bearing fruit (Rom. 7:4; Gal. 5:22–23; Eph. 5:9; Phil. 1:11; Col. 1:6, 10); being clothed with Christ (Rom. 13:14); and completing a race (Acts 20:24; Gal. 2:2; 5:7; 2 Tim. 4:7; cf. Phil. 2:16) toward a goal (Phil. 3:14) after which a prize or crown is given (1 Cor. 9:24–27; Phil. 3:14). Paul also used the figure of fruit to refer to results from his ministry (Rom. 1:13 [NIV, "harvest"]; Phil. 1:22) and to material gifts (Rom. 15:28; Phil. 4:17 [NIV, "gift"]). Spiritual conflict with Satan is likened to a warfare with spiritual weapons (Rom. 13:12; 2 Cor. 6:7; 10:4; Eph. 6:11, 13–17; 1 Thess 5:8), and a fight (1 Tim. 1:18; 6:12; 2 Tim. 4:7).

---

22. "In the Roman society when a youth came of age he was given a special toga which admitted him to the full rights of the family and state and indicated he was a grown-up son. So the Galatian believers had laid aside the old garments of the Law and had put on Christ's robe of righteousness which grants full acceptance before God" (Campbell, "Galatians," 600).

23. "The use of the human body as a metaphor for society was a commonplace in ancient rhetoric, a favorite of the late Stoics" (Wayne A. Meeks, *The First Urban Christians: The Social World of the Apostle Paul* [New Haven, Conn.: Yale University Press, 1983], 89).

24. For other possible interpretations, see David K. Lowery, "1 Corinthians," in *The Bible Knowledge Commentary, New Testament,* 511–12.

In a few other unrelated examples Paul said Christians who might go back under the law would be slaves (Gal. 2:4; 5:1); Gentiles who are saved are a wild olive shoot (Rom. 11:17) grafted into the natural olive branches (11:21); the physical body is a tent (2 Cor. 5:4) and a vessel (1 Thess. 4:4);[25] believers' speech is to be seasoned with salt, that is, gracious (Col. 4:6): and Paul's perils were so fearsome they were like being in a lion's mouth (2 Tim. 4:17). In addition, Paul quoted Proverbs 25:21–22 about heaping burning coals on a person's head (Rom. 12:20). This figurative expression may have as its background the literal act of giving coals in a pan to a person whose fire has gone out, who would then carry the pan home on his head. Thus this act would make an enemy a friend.[26]

As with Jesus, many of Paul's hypocatastases were from nature (shepherds, flock, wolves, beasts, dogs, fruit, seed, darkness, light, root, lamb, bread, body, yeast, gold, silver, precious stones, wood, hay, straw, fire, olive branches, lion, and coals). However, almost as many were drawn from man-made objects (wall, door, rubbish, veil, stumbling block, foundation, jars of clay, clothing, building, pillar, prize, crown, and weapons) or functions or relationships (race, adoption, redemption, sons, seal, deposit, and slavery).

Metonomy

In metonomy a word or phrase is substituted for another word or phrase associated with it. When Paul wrote that the throats of unbelievers are open graves he not only used a metaphor, he also used a metonomy in the word "throats" (Rom. 3:13), for he meant the words that come from one's throat. The same is true of their mouths, which are full of cursing and bitterness (3:14)—not that their mouths are literally filled, but that the words spoken through their mouths were all curses and expressions of bitterness against others. In quoting Psalm 69:22 Paul mentioned the table of the unbelieving Israelites becoming a snare and a trap (Rom. 11:9), by which he meant that the feasts associated with their tables would trap them in their sins, rather than being a means of spiritual blessing. "Macedonia and Achaia were pleased," Paul wrote (15:26), but obviously geographical areas cannot have feelings. So he meant the people living in those two regions.

25. The NIV renders *skeuos*, "vessel," by the word, "body," which is the referent of the image "vessel."

26. Another possible background of this expression is the ancient Egyptian practice of a person carrying a pan of coals on his head as a sign of his repentance. Thus by helping rather than cursing an enemy, he may be encouraged to be repentant and to show it by carrying coals on his head.

Sometimes a metonomy refers to the appearance of something or an opinion of something that differs from the thing itself. Preaching was not foolish; it only seems that way to some (1 Cor. 1:21). Nor is God foolish; unbelievers only think he is (1:25).[27]

No one drinks a cup (1 Cor. 10:21; 11:28; cf. 10:16); we drink the contents associated with the cup. The container represents the contents. The world mentioned in 2 Corinthians 5:19 means the people in the world. Being saved by the blood of Christ means we are saved because of his substitutionary death which involved the shedding of his blood (Rom. 3:25; 5:9; Eph. 1:7; 2:13; Col. 1:20).

When Paul asked the Colossians to remember his chains (Col. 4:18), he wanted them to think not so much of the pieces of metal around his wrists and ankles but of the fact of his imprisonment. Onesiphorus, Paul wrote to Timothy, "was not ashamed of my chains" (2 Tim. 1:16), that is, he was not ashamed to be associated with Paul, a prisoner. When Jesus returns to earth at the end of the tribulation period to establish his millennial reign, he will overthrow the Antichrist ("the lawless one") by "the breath of his mouth" (2 Thess. 2:8); by merely speaking, he will defeat the Antichrist. "House" *(oikos)* in 1 Timothy 3:4 is not the structure, but the family members in it. Here the New International Version renders it "family."

Synecdoche

A synecdoche substitutes a part for the whole, or the whole for a part. In Romans 1:16 and 3:9 the word "Greek" (NASB) stands for the entire non-Jewish population, a part representing the whole. The New International Version translates this word "Gentile," which is the intention of this synecdoche. When Paul wrote that unbelievers' "feet are swift to shed blood" (3:15), he used the part (feet) for the whole (bodies). The silencing of every mouth (3:19) is a synecdoche in which mouth (the part) stands for the individual (the whole). Romans 8:7 includes a synecdoche in which the "sinful mind" which is "hostile to God" represents the whole (the sinner's entire attitude and outlook on life). Other examples are these: "eyes darkened" (11:10) stands for the unbelieving Israelites' entire spiritual life; "bodies" offered to God (12:1) is used for entire persons; when Priscilla and Aquila "risked their necks" for Paul (16:4, NASB), they actually risked their entire lives; persecuting the church (the whole) as Paul did (1 Cor. 15:9; Gal. 1:13) meant persecuting the individuals in it (the part); "flesh and blood" (1 Cor. 15:50) are

27. Bullinger, *Figures of Speech Used in the Bible,* 597.

two parts of the earthly human body that cannot inherit the kingdom. When Paul stated that every knee will bow before the Lord (Phil. 2:10), "knee" (the part) suggests the entire body (the whole); and when he said "every tongue" will confess Jesus as Lord (2:11), he used "tongue" (the part) in place of the individual (the whole). "Every creature under heaven" (Col. 1:23) is a whole that is used instead of the parts (every human). "Bread" (2 Thess. 3:12) probably represents all kinds of food. Sometimes "flesh" stands for the entire person so that the New International Version often renders it "one" (e.g., Rom. 3:20; 1 Cor. 1:29).

Personification

Ascribing a human characteristic or action to inanimate objects, ideas, or animals is called personification. One's conscience is personified like a person in court, as one bearing witness, and one's thoughts, like attorneys, are said to accuse or defend (Rom. 2:15). Sarah's womb, being barren, was personified as if it were "dead" (4:19). In Romans, Paul often personified sin as a king who reigns (5:21; 6:12), as a master (6:14), as a person seizing an opportunity (7:8, 11) or coming to life (7:9). Also, grace reigns as a king (5:21). Four times in Romans 8:19–22 "creation" is mentioned as if it were a person with feelings. He spoke of death, life, the present, the future, height, and depth as if they are persons (8:38–39). "The thing formed" (9:20) is personified as speaking, as is righteousness (10:6), Scripture (10:11; Gal. 3:22), and the foot, ear, eye, and head (1 Cor. 12:15–16, 21). Love is presented as a person with emotions (13:4–8). Death, like an enemy, will be defeated (1 Cor. 15:55), and both death and life are likened to workers (2 Cor. 4:12). Scripture "foresaw" (Gal. 3:8) and faith "came" (3:23, 25). Paul personified "ears" as having desires ("wanting to hear," 2 Tim. 4:3), tongues as confessing (Phil. 2:11),[28] and Christ's peace as ruling like a king (Col. 3:15).

Personifying the inanimate presents truth in a vivid, sometimes startling way.

Anthropomorphism and Anthropopathism

In anthropomorphisms, human characteristics are ascribed to God, as in God's hands (Acts 13:11; Rom. 8:34; 10:21; Eph. 1:20; Col. 3:1), heart (Acts 13:22), and eyes (2 Cor. 8:21).

---

28. In Philippians 2:11 Paul's reference to the tongue is both a synecdoche (see the previous section) and a personification.

Anthropopathisms ascribe human emotions to God. God smells the "aroma" of Paul's ministry (2 Cor. 2:15) and he smells Jesus' sacrifice as a fragrance before God (Eph. 5:2), that is, he finds them pleasing and acceptable. The same is said of the material gifts sent from Philippi to Paul (Phil. 4:18). Also, God walks with his people (2 Cor. 6:16), that is, he fellowships with them, and sin grieves the Holy Spirit (Eph. 4:30).

Apostrophe

An apostrophe is a figure in which an object is addressed directly as if it were a person. "It differs from personification in that in an apostrophe an individual speaks directly *to* an object as if it were a person, whereas in personification someone speaks *about* an object as if it were a person."[29] When Paul was writing to the Corinthian believers, he addressed a wife and a husband as if they were present (1 Cor. 7:16), and in quoting Hosea 13:14 he spoke directly to death as if it were present (1 Cor. 15:55). This latter verse is also an example of personification, as already noted.

Euphemism

A euphemism is a mild expression for a more offensive one. On two occasions Paul referred to being dead as being asleep (Acts 13:36; 1 Thess. 4:13–15). This does not suggest that after death the soul has no conscious existence. Instead, it is simply a euphemism, used because a corpse looks as if the person is asleep.

"Asleep" is used in 1 Thessalonians 5:6 to refer to those who are not spiritually alert. "Asleep" in 1 Thessalonians 5:10 may mean either those who are spiritually lethargic or those who are dead.

Hyperbole

Hyperboles are deliberate exaggerations, in which the writer says more than is literally meant. Thus they effectively add emphasis and surprise to what is said. Several times Paul referred to a large geographical area to convey much of that area, not necessarily its totality. Examples are "in every city" (Acts 20:23), "all over the world" (Rom. 1:8), "all the earth" and "the ends of the world" (10:18), and "everywhere" (2 Cor.

---

29. Zuck, *Teaching as Jesus Taught,* 197 (italics mine).

2:14; 1 Thess. 1:8). Also, he wrote hyperbolically of "everyone" hearing about the Roman believers' obedience (Rom. 16:19), and of "every creature under heaven" hearing the gospel (Col. 1:23). The reference to "ten thousand guardians" (1 Cor. 4:15) is obviously a hyperbole designed to stress his point, since no child would have more than one *paidagōgos*. He also spoke of the Galatians' willingness to tear out their eyes and give them to him (Gal. 4:15), obviously an exaggerated way of referring to their intense desire to help him. To say that a false teacher "understands nothing" (1 Tim. 6:4) is not to suggest that he is totally ignorant of everything in life, but expresses a hyperbole that he is ignorant of spiritual truth. When he referred to his being endangered "every hour" and dying "every day" (1 Cor. 15:30–31), Paul used hyperbole to convey the constant, seemingly unending perils he faced. His reference to the Jews being hostile to all men (1 Thess. 2:15) is also probably an intended exaggeration to emphasize their strong opposition to the gospel.[30]

Litotes

A litotes, the opposite of a hyperbole, is an understatement or a mild negative statement designed to highlight a fact in a unique way. When Paul said to the Jewish mob in Jerusalem, "I am a . . . citizen of no insignificant city" (Acts 21:39 NASB), he meant that Tarsus was in fact a rather significant city.

Sometimes a litotes is an intentional belittling. Paul's words, "I am the least of the apostles" (1 Cor. 15:9), express genuine humility in order, by contrast, to emphasize God's grace in his life (15:10). Not being "in the least inferior" to those who promoted themselves as "super-apostles" (2 Cor. 11:5; 12:11) was Paul's unique backhanded way of saying he was equal to and even superior to them.

To say "we are not unaware of [Satan's] schemes" (2 Cor. 2:11) is a litotes expressing the fact that believers are very much aware of his devices. And to say that the unsaved "will not inherit the kingdom of God" (Gal. 5:21) is a mild way of saying they will suffer eternal punishment.

Irony

Irony is an expression in which the literal meaning is the opposite of what is intended. What sounds like a compliment, for example, may be a ridicule, or what sounds like a ridicule may be a compliment. In

---

30. Carol J. Schlueter, *Filling Up the Measure: Polemical Hyperbole in 1 Thessalonians 2.14–16* (Sheffield: Sheffield Academic, 1994), 93–97.

1 Corinthians 4:8 Paul seemingly complimented the Corinthians with the words, "You have become kings." In the next sentence he added, "I wish that you really had become kings," showing that the first sentence was irony. In his question, "Is it possible that there is nobody among you wise enough to judge a dispute between believers?" (6:5), he may have ironically expressed the affirmation, "Surely, there is at least one wise person who can judge a dispute between believers."

Second Corinthians includes numerous instances of Pauline irony, mostly related to Paul's defense of his apostleship.[31] What sounds like a compliment in 2 Corinthians 11:4, "you put up with [a different gospel] easily enough," is actually ridicule (cf. 11:20). When he urged them to receive him just as they would a fool (11:16), he of course did not really intend to be treated as a fool.[32] He also used irony when he declared, "I too will boast" (11:18; cf. 11:21). And what he boasted about, ironically, was not his strength but his weakness ("If I must boast, I will boast of the things that show my weakness," 11:30). Then he boasted about being lowered in a basket from over a wall in Damascus (11:32–33). The fact that he gloried in this humiliating experience showed he was "parodying the world's idea of boasting. His boasting is rife with irony."[33]

When the apostle said he was "ashamed" to admit he was "too weak" to exploit the Corinthians (11:20–21), he did not mean he was literally ashamed. He meant he was actually glad to have been weak in the sense of being their servant and not being overbearing like his opponents. Writing that he was never a burden to them, he then ironically asked them to forgive him (12:13). Of course he need not be forgiven; it was not wrong for him to preach the gospel to them without charge. But in irony he chided them for thinking he was in error in this regard.[34]

31. See E. M. Blaiklock, "The Irony of Paul," in *New Testament Studies*, ed. Huber L. Drumwright and Curtis Vaughn (Waco, Tex.: Markham, 1995), 85–98; and J. A. Loubser, "A New Look at Paradox and Irony in 2 Corinthians 10–13," *Neotestamentica* 26 (1992): 507–21.

32. Folly had become second nature to Paul's critics in Corinth, but "he deliberately plays the fool for a few minutes, because their folly can be met in no other way" (Alfred Plummer, *A Critical and Exegetical Commentary on the Second Epistle of St Paul to the Corinthians*, International Critical Commentary [Edinburgh: Clark, 1915]: 29).

33. Savage, *Power through Weakness*, 63. Cf. E. A. Judge, "Paul's Boasting in Relation to Contemporary Professional Practice," *Australian Biblical Review* 16 (October 1968): 37–50; Christopher Forbes, "'Unaccustomed as I Am': St. Paul the Public Speaker in Corinth," *Buried History* 19 (March 1983): 11–16; and idem, "Contemporary Self-Praise and Irony: Paul's Boasting and the Conventions of Hellenistic Rhetoric," *New Testament Studies* 32 (1986):1–30.

34. J. B. Phillips brings out the power of this ironic statement by his paraphrase: "What makes you so inferior to the other churches? Is it because I have not allowed you to support me financially? My humblest apologies for this great wrong" (*The New Testament in Modern English* [New York: Macmillan, 1960]).

When Paul added, "I caught you by trickery" like a crafty person (12:16), he did not mean he was actually crafty. In irony he ridiculed them for thinking of him in that way.

His question to the Galatians, "Have I now become your enemy by telling you the truth?" (Gal. 4:16), implies that truth telling should not result in enmity.

Sarcasm

Sarcasm is a form of irony, but it is more caustic or reproachful. This is seen in Paul's exclamations, "You are so wise in Christ!" (1 Cor. 4:10),[35] and "You are so wise" (2 Cor. 11:19). These are clearly "put-downs" in which the opposite of what is stated is intended. He was mockingly saying they were foolish, not wise. Corinth was a city noted for its pride, but Paul sarcastically chided the Christians there for being proud of a case of incest, rather than being grieved (1 Cor. 5:2).

The question, "Don't you have homes to eat and drink in?" (11:22), sarcastically implies that they did have homes to eat in, and that therefore to eat at church without waiting for others (11:21) was wrong. The questions, "Did the word of God originate with you? Or are you the only people it has reached?" (14:36), implying negative answers, are sarcastically affirming the opposite: God's word did not originate with them or reach only them. In sarcasm he accused the Corinthians of easily putting up with those who preach a different message (2 Cor. 11:4).[36] The apostle's injunction, "Examine yourselves to see whether you are in the faith; test yourselves" (2 Cor. 13:5), is often seen as a command to Christians to give themselves a spiritual self-examination to determine whether they are genuinely saved. However, Brown argues cogently that these words of Paul were written sarcastically. The grammar of the verse, he says, is "structured in such a way that Paul fully expected the Corinthians to answer yes" to the question in 13:5b, "Do you not realize, that Christ Jesus is in you?" And the following clause in verse 5, "unless, of course, you fail the test," points sarcastically to the impossibility of

35. On the sarcasm in 1 Corinthians 4:9–13, see Karl A. Plank, *Paul and the Irony of Affliction* (Atlanta: Scholars, 1987), 46, 48–54, 77–86.

36. "Similarly, Demosthenes [in *De Corona* 138] takes the Athenians to task for permitting themselves to be deluded by people who serve their own instead of the national interest" (Frederick W. Danker, "Paul's Debt to the *De Corona* of Demosthenes: A Study of Rhetorical Techniques in Second Corinthians," in *Persuasive Artistry*, ed. Duane F. Watson [Sheffield: Sheffield Academic, 1991], 274).

their failing the test. "He used this remark sarcastically, which fits the emotional tone of much of 2 Corinthians."[37]

Paul spoke with biting sarcasm against the Judaizers who wanted Gentile Christians to be circumcised; he said he wished they would emasculate themselves (Gal. 5:12). He probably intended this as a strong caustic way of rebuking their false teaching.

Paradox

A paradox is a statement that seems to contradict common sense, a statement presenting two apparently (but not actually) contradictory points, both of which may be true. Paradoxes are often startling. For example, one cannot help but be struck with Paul's words that "God's invisible qualities" are "clearly seen" (Rom. 1:20). These facts that seem in conflict are both true. God is invisible and yet something of his character can be seen in what he has made.

To die with Christ (by faith in his substitutionary death) is to be, paradoxically, freed from sin and alive (6:4, 7). Though set free from the slavery of sin, believers are slaves to righteousness (6:18).

How can God's so-called "foolishness" be wise or his "weakness" be strong? (1 Cor. 1:25). This paradox clearly conveys the idea of divine superiority over common wisdom and strength. Paul's inner conflict recorded in Romans 7:15 also seems paradoxical.

The Corinthians prided themselves on their wisdom, but it was an egotistical wisdom, not from God. "Of all the cities in the Graeco-Roman world, none engendered an atmosphere of self-centredness [*sic*] more striking than Corinth."[38] Therefore, they would have been startled to read Paul's exhortation that if any one of them thought himself wise "by the standards of this age, he should become a 'fool' so that he may become wise" (1 Cor. 3:18). To think of becoming truly wise before God by becoming foolish before others would have jolted the Corinthians. Continuing this paradox, Paul added, "For the wisdom of this world is foolishness in God's sight" (3:19). It is also paradoxical to think of something not coming to life unless it dies (15:36).

Second Corinthians is filled not only with irony and sarcasm but also with a number of paradoxes. It is paradoxical for a valuable treasure (the gospel) to be stored in valueless clay jars (humans; 2 Cor. 4:7). Paul's suffering for the sake of the gospel is also stated in a paradox:

37. Perry C. Brown, "What Is the Meaning of 'Examine Yourselves' in 2 Corinthians 13:5?" *Bibliotheca Sacra* 153 (April–June 1997): 188.
38. Savage, *Power through Weakness,* 18.

"We always carry around in our body the death of Jesus, so that the life of Jesus may also be revealed in our body" (4:10). Though alive, he added, he was "given over to death for Jesus' sake so that his [Jesus'] life may be revealed" in Paul's "mortal body" (4:11). His physical suffering ("death is at work in us") resulted in spiritual life in the Corinthians (4:12). In a similar vein, he wrote in 6:9–10 that though dying, he was living on; that he experienced both sorrow and rejoicing; and that his poverty resulted in others becoming spiritually rich. Though he had nothing of this world's goods, in contrast to the wealth of Corinth,[39] he was "possessing everything" spiritually. Though poor in one sense, he paradoxically was rich in another sense.[40] And unsaved Corinthians, though rich in one sense, were poor in another.

The Macedonians, Paul wrote the Corinthians, were poor but they gave generously to the Lord's work (8:2). And Jesus' poverty has resulted in many becoming spiritually rich (8:9).

It sounds paradoxical for Paul to write that because God's power was revealed in the apostle's weakness, he would boast of his weaknesses and hardships (12:8–10; 13:4). These statements would have been especially shocking and disturbing to the Corinthians who prided themselves in power, applause, esteem, and social prominence, and disdained weakness.[41]

In another paradox Paul wrote that "the widow who lives for pleasure is dead even while she lives" (1 Tim. 5:6). Though alive physically, the unsaved person who seeks only his or her own pleasure is actually dead spiritually.

Oxymoron

An oxymoron puts together two terms that are opposite or contradictory.[42] A paradox unites seemingly contradictory concepts or statements, whereas an oxymoron links two words that are incongruous. "Cruel kindness" and "sweet sorrow" are examples. Paul used oxymo-

---

39. Ibid., 36, 41–43, 52.

40. Mealand and Fitzgerald point out that Paul drew here on the Stoic idea that "all things belong to the wise," and that, paradoxically, the sage is rich, however needy he may be (David L. Mealand, " 'As Having Nothing, and Yet Possessing Everything' 2 Kor 6 10c," *Zeitschrift für neutestamentliche Wissenschaft* 67 [1967]: 277–79; and John T. Fitzgerald, *Cracks in an Earthen Vessel* [Atlanta: Scholars, 1988], 200). Cf. Plutarch *On Morals* 1058c and Seneca *Moral Letters* 66.22.

41. Fitzgerald, *Cracks in an Earthen Vessel*, 22–23, 52, 187.

42. The word *oxymoron* comes from two Greek words—*oxys* ("sharp") and *moros* ("stupid").

rons when he wrote of offering "living sacrifices" (Rom. 12:1); of Christ, who had no sin, being made "sin for us" (2 Cor. 5:21); of the "glory" of unbelievers being their "shame" (Phil. 3:19), that is, they prided themselves in things they should have been ashamed of.

Paul urged the Thessalonians (1 Thess. 4:11) to strive eagerly *(philotimeomai)* to live quietly *(euēsychazō)*. And some Thessalonian believers were idle; though they were not "busy" *(ergazomai)*, they were "busybodies" *(periergazomai;* 2 Thess. 3:11).

Humor

What makes a statement funny? Why do people laugh at certain comments? The reason is surprise—an unexpected association of ideas, an unanticipated putting together of the incongruous, the paradoxical, the absurd. That is why hyperboles, litotes, irony, paradoxes, oxymorons, and word puns are often amusing; they surprise the hearer or reader with something unexpected.

A teacher's humorous remark can help make a point more palatable. When a teacher and students laugh together, a bond builds between them.

Though it may seem surprising to think of Paul using humor, he did in fact say and write some things that surely made his listeners and readers smile. Reviewing the previous sections in this chapter on hyperboles, litotes, irony, paradoxes, and oxymorons reveals that many of these examples were no doubt amusingly humorous. In addition, the following are also instances of humor, statements that led to smiles, which in turn meant his hearers and readers did not fail to comprehend his points.

Murphy suggests that when Paul was brought before the Sanhedrin (Acts 23:1–10), he "saw something of the humor of the situation, in the alliance against him of the otherwise hostile Pharisees and Sadducees."[43] Perhaps with a mischievous twinkle in his eye, he shouted out that he was a Pharisee and he believed in the resurrection (23:6). This was clever because the Pharisees, believing in a future resurrection, would have sided with Paul, but the Sadducees, denying a future resurrection, would have disagreed with Paul and the Pharisees. As these two groups argued vigorously, Paul may have chuckled under his

43. DuBase Murphy, "The Lighter Side of Paul's Personality," *Anglican Theological Review* 11 (1928–29): 248.

breath,[44] because this split between his opponents weakened their case against him.

No doubt the Corinthians smiled as they read Paul's ludicrous comments about a human foot or ear thinking it does not belong to the body, or the whole body being nothing but an eye or an ear (1 Cor. 12:15–17, 21). Since all the parts of a body are needed, so all members of the church, the body of Christ, are needed. Jealousy and competition[45] or a sense of superiority or inferiority on the part of the Corinthians made for absurd contradictions. Surely Paul's humor made its mark.

In 1 Corinthians 15:8 Paul joked about himself being "abnormally born" *(tō ektrōmati)*, that is, one with an untimely birth. This may refer to the fact that "he lacked the 'gestation' period of having been with Christ during His earthly ministry. . . ."[46] This was a humorous way of saying that though the Lord appeared to him a year or two after Christ was resurrected, Paul still possessed genuine apostleship.[47]

Paul humorously referred to his receiving gifts from other churches as "robbing" them so he could help the Corinthians (2 Cor. 11:8). And since he did not burden the Corinthians by receiving offerings from them, he said he hoped they would forgive him! (12:13). He continued his playful humor with them by calling himself "crafty," saying he caught them "by trickery" (12:16).

His sarcastic remark that he wished the Judaizers, who promoted circumcision, would emasculate themselves (Gal. 5:12) surely caused the Galatians to smile.

Pun

A pun is a subtle form of humor, a use of close-together words with different meanings but similar sounds. Only transliterations can bring out the significance of these puns in Greek.

> "Since they did not approve [*edokimasan*] having God in their knowledge, God gave them over to a disapproved or unqualified [*adokimon*] mind" (Rom. 1:28, author's trans.).
> "At whatever point you judge [*krineis*] the other, you are condemning [*katakrineis*] yourself" (Rom. 2:1).

44. Ibid.
45. Jakob Jónsson, *Humour and Irony in the New Testament* (Leiden: Brill, 1985), 233.
46. Lowery, "1 Corinthians," 542.
47. Paul W. Barnett, "Apostle," in *Dictionary of Paul and His Letters*, 48.

"The disobedience [*parakoēs*] of the one man [and] the obedience [*hypakoēs*] of the one man" (Rom. 5:19; cf. *parakoēn* and *hypokoē* in 2 Cor. 10:6).

"Do not think of yourself more highly [*hyperphronein*] than you ought [to think, *phronein*], but rather think [*phronein*] of yourself with sober judgment [*sōphronein*]" (Rom. 12:3).

"If you owe taxes, pay taxes [*phoron*] . . . if respect, then respect [*phobon*]" (Rom. 13:7).

"Those who use [*chrōmenoi*] the things of the world as if not engrossed [*katachrōmenoi*] in them" (1 Cor. 7:31).

"But if we judged [*diekrinomen*] ourselves, we would not come under judgment [*ekrinometha*]. When we are judged [*krinomenoi*] by the Lord, we are being disciplined so that we will not be condemned [*katakrithōmen*] with the world" (1 Cor. 11:31–32).

"You yourselves are our letter, written on our hearts, known [*ginōskomenē*] and read [*anaginoskomenē*] by everybody" (2 Cor. 3:2).

"Perplexed [*aporoumenoi*] but not in despair [*exaporoumenoi*]" (2 Cor. 4:8).

"Having [*echontes*] nothing; and yet possessing [*kataechontes*] everything" (2 Cor. 6:10).

"So I will very gladly spend [*dapenēsō*] for you everything I have and expend myself [*ekdapanēthēsomai*] as well" (2 Cor. 12:15).

"In my presence [*parousia*] . . . in my absence [*apousia*]" (Phil. 2:12).

"Watch out for . . . those mutilators [*katatomē*] . . . for it is we who are the circumcision [*peritomē*]" (Phil. 3:2–3).

"They are not busy [*ergazomenous*]; they are busybodies [*periergazomenous*]" (2 Thess. 3:11).

"Formerly he was useless [*achrēston*] to you, but now he has become useful [*euchrēston*] both to you and to me" (Philem. 11).

Also the word "benefit" [*onaimēn*] in Philemon 20 is related to "Onesimus" [*Onēsimon*] in Philemon 10.

Alliteration

In alliteration two or more words close together begin with the same letter, as seen in the following examples. They would have been pleasing to the ear as congregations heard Paul's letters read to them. Some occurrences of alliteration are based on different words, whereas others are based on different forms of the same word.

"Envy [*phthonon*], murder [*phonon*]" (Rom. 1:29).

"They disobey [*apeitheis*] their parents; they are senseless [*asynet-ous*], faithless [*asynthetous*], heartless [*astorgous*], ruthless [*aneleēmonas*]" (Rom. 1:30–31). In Greek, these five words follow one after the other with no intervening words. Paul got carried away in his alliteration!

"How unsearchable [*anexereunēta*] his judgments, and his paths beyond tracing out [*anexichniastoi*]" (Rom. 11:33).

"To the weak [*asthenesin*] I became weak [*asthenēs*], to win the weak [*astheneis*]. I have become all things [*panta*] to all men [*pasin*] so that by all possible means [*pantōs*] I might save some" (1 Cor. 9:22).

"Then the Son himself will be made subject [*hypotagēsetai*] to him who put everything [*hypotaxanti*] under him" (1 Cor. 15:28).

"Our brother who has often [*pollakis*] proved to us in many ways [*pollois*] . . ." (2 Cor. 8:22).

"God is able to make all [*pasan*] grace abound to you, so that in all things [*panti*] at all times [*pantote*], having all [*pasan*] that you need, you will abound in every [*pan*] good work" (2 Cor. 9:8). In the Greek, three of these five words all occur together with no intervening words: *panti, pantote, pasan*.

"Finally, be strong [*endynamousthe*] in the Lord. . . . Put on [*endysasthe*] the full armor of God" (Eph. 6:10–11).

"We always [*pantote*] thank God for [*peri*] all [*pantōn*] of you" (1 Thess 1.2). Again, these three alliterated words occur one after the other in Greek.

"May God himself . . . sanctify you through and through [*holoteleis*, 'thoroughly']. May your whole [*holoklēron*] spirit, soul and body be kept blameless at the coming of our Lord Jesus Christ" (1 Thess. 5:23).

"People will be lovers of themselves [*philautoi*], lovers of money [*philargyroi*]" (2 Tim. 3.2).

People will be "ungrateful [*acharistoi*], unholy [*anosioi*], without love [*astorgoi*], unforgiving [*aspondoi*], slanderous, without self-control [*akrateis*], brutal [*anēmeroi*], not lovers of the good [*aphilagathoi*]" (2 Tim. 3:2–3).

People will be "treacherous [*prodotai*], rash [*propeteis*], conceited, lovers of pleasure [*philēdonoi*] rather than lovers of God [*philotheoi*]" (2 Tim. 3:4).

Besides these alliterations being pleasant to the ear and eye, they would also have helped the hearers and readers remember those statements.

Assonance

In alliteration, words close together begin with the same letter. In assonance, words close together have similar sounds within or at the ends of the words. This does not occur often in Paul's writings, but the few instances are striking. Second Corinthians 12:21 includes reference to "sexual sin [*porneia*] and debauchery [*aselgeia*]." In 1 Thessalonians 2:9 Paul wrote of "toil [*kopon*] and hardship [*mochthon*]," and in 2:10 he wrote that his conduct was "holy [*hosiōs*], righteous [*dikaiōs*] and blameless [*amemptōs*]." Another example is the last three words of 1 Thessalonians 4:18: "Therefore encourage each other with these words [*tois logois toutois*]."

Your Turn . . .

Think of one or more figures of speech you could use in your next lesson. Can you make a statement more picturesque by using a simile, metaphor, or hypocatastasis?

How might you use a hyperbole, irony, paradoxical statement, or word pun to communicate a point in your lesson?

Is there some way you could appropriately use humor in your next lesson?

After using one of these figures of speech, ask yourself how you felt the students responded.

"Fis letters are weighty and powerful."

2 Corinthians IO:IO, NKJV

13

How Did Paul Use Other Rhetorical Devices in His Teaching?

Besides the twenty figures of simile, metaphor, hypocatastasis, metonomy, synecdoche, personification, anthropomorphism, anthropopathism, apostrophe, euphemism, hyperbole, litotes, irony, sarcasm, paradox, oxymoron, humor, pun, alliteration, and assonance, discussed in chapter 12, Paul used a number of other figures of speech and rhetorical devices. These include maxims, repetitions, synonyms, antitheses, enumerations, idioms, and various structural patterns. These too demonstrate Paul's unusual versatility as an outstanding communicator-teacher.

Maxims

A maxim is a brief statement given in a concise, witty manner. The Gospels abound with dozens of Jesus' maxims or aphorisms.[1] Paul, how-

---

1. Roy B. Zuck, *Teaching as Jesus Taught* (Grand Rapids: Baker, 1995), 207–14.

ever, used only a few, but the ones he wrote were effective and have become memorable.

A proverb is similar to a maxim in that both compress a thought in a brief, memorable fashion. But they differ in that proverbs relay "collective wisdom" and "are popular" in origin,[2] whereas maxims "are the product of an individual voice."[3] Not every pithy, pointed statement becomes a proverb.

The succinctness of Paul's obvious aphorisms helped convey important principles. When he wrote, "A little yeast works through the whole batch of dough" (1 Cor. 5:6), he was illustrating the danger of not dealing with a sinner in the congregation. If the sinner were not confronted with his sin, others might be inclined to duplicate his heinous evil. He quoted the same maxim to the Galatians (5:9) to point out that false teaching may begin in a small way, affecting only a few believers, but, like the yeast, it can spread and influence many others.

Warning the Corinthians not to follow the evil deeds of the Israelites, Paul admonished, "So, if you think you are standing firm, be careful that you don't fall!" (1 Cor. 10:12). Encouraging the Corinthians to be generous in their giving, the apostle spoke a maxim based on an analogy from agriculture: "Whoever sows sparingly will also reap sparingly, and whoever sows generously will also reap generously" (2 Cor. 9:6). Just as the quantity of a crop depends on the farmer's quantity of sown seed, so the amount of spiritual blessing obtained from giving is in direct proportion to the amount given.

For Thessalonians who felt they need not work because Christ would soon return, Paul reminded them of the truism, "If a man will not work, he shall not eat" (2 Thess. 3:10). When Paul wrote, "To the pure, all things are pure" (Titus 1:15), he was saying that a person who is inwardly pure cannot be corrupted by something externally impure.[4]

---

2. Leo G. Perdue, "The Wisdom Sayings of Jesus," *Foundations and Facets Forum* 2 (September 1986): 6.

3. Marcus J. Borg, "The Teaching of Jesus Christ," in *Anchor Bible Dictionary*, 3 (1992), 807.

4. The words "Everything is permissible for me," stated twice in 1 Corinthians 6:12, and "Food for the stomach and the stomach for food" (6:13) may have been Corinthian slogans by which they sought to justify their immoral actions. Paul quoted these slogans to refute and correct them. He also quoted their slogan, "We all possess knowledge" (8:1), in order to qualify it. And he affirmed their slogans, "An idol is nothing at all" and "There is no God but one" (8:4), to show that eating food sacrificed to idols is of no consequence since idols have no reality (Archibald Robertson and Alfred Plummer, *A Critical and Exegetical Commentary on the First Epistle of St Paul to the Corinthians*, International Critical Commentary, 2d ed. [Edinburgh: Clark, 1914], 121–22, 163–64; and David K. Lowery, "1 Corinthians," in *The Bible Knowledge Commentary, New Testament*, ed. John F. Walvoord and Roy B. Zuck [Wheaton, Ill.: Victor, 1983], 517, 521).

Other memorable Pauline statements, well known throughout the centuries, are these: "And now these three remain: faith, hope, and love. But the greatest of these is love" (1 Cor. 13:13); "God is not a God of disorder but of peace" (14:33); "For to me to live is Christ and to die is gain" (Phil. 1:21); "Do not be anxious about anything" (4:6); "Give thanks in all circumstances" (1 Thess. 5:18); "The love of money is a root of all kinds of evil" (1 Tim. 6:10); "I have fought the good fight" (2 Tim. 4:7).

Repetition

Paul often repeated words or phrases in order to reinforce those concepts in his readers' minds, and to enable them to recall important points.[5] The following examples of his use of repetition no doubt riveted the truth home with sledgehammer effect.

Table 18
Paul's Use of Repetition

References	Words or Phrases	Number of Times Repeated
Romans 2:21–23	"You who"	5
Romans 2:25–29	"Circumcision"	6
Romans 4:9–11	"Uncircumcision"	4
Romans 4:13, 16, 18	"Offspring"	3
Romans 6:13, 16, 18–20	"Righteousness"	5
Romans 8:28, 32, 37	"All things"	3
Romans 8:32–35	"Who"	4
Romans 8:38–39	"Neither . . . nor"	4
1 Corinthians 3:9	"God's"	3
1 Corinthians 6:12	"Everything is permissible for me"	2
1 Corinthians 6:15–16	"Do you not know?"	2
1 Corinthians 9:22	"Weak"	3
1 Corinthians 11:3–7	"Head"	9
1 Corinthians 12:4–6	"Different kinds"	3
1 Corinthians 12:4–6	"The same"	3

5. Repetition brings "vigour and force" to Paul's words (P. C. Sands, *Literary Genius of the New Testament* [Oxford: Clarendon, 1932], 144).

1 Corinthians 12:8–11	"To another"	8
1 Corinthians 12:8–9, 11	"Same Spirit"	3
1 Corinthians 12:12–20, 22, 24–25, 27	"Body"	17
1 Corinthians 13:1–3	"If"	3
1 Corinthians 13:1–3	"Have not love"	3
1 Corinthians 13:7	"Always"	4
1 Corinthians 13:8	"Where there are/is"	3
1 Corinthians 13:11	"Child"	4
1 Corinthians 15:42–44	"Is sown"	4
1 Corinthians 15:42–44	"It is raised"	4
2 Corinthians 3:7–11	"Glory"	6[a]
2 Corinthians 4:10–11	"Our body"	3
2 Corinthians 9:6	"Sows" and "reap"	2 each
2 Corinthians 9:6	"Sparingly" and "generously"	2 each
2 Corinthians 11:26	"Danger"	8
Ephesians 1:6, 12, 14	"To the praise of his glory"	3
Ephesians 4:4–6	"One"	7
Ephesians 4:6	"All"	4
Ephesians 5:21–22, 24	"Submit"	4
Ephesians 6:12	"Against"	5
Ephesians 6:18	"All"	3
Philippians 4:4	"Rejoice"	2
Philippians 4:8–9	"Whatever"	7
Colossians 1:16–17	"All things"	4

a. Though the New International Version has "glory" three times and "glorious" three time in these verses, the Greek has the noun *doxa*, "glory," all six times.

In addition, in 2 Corinthians 10–12, Paul used the verb "boast" and the noun "boasting" nineteen times (in the Greek)!

Synonyms

Synonyms are like many-sided diamonds. One part of a diamond's surface looks magnificent, but it does not convey all the beauty of the diamond. Looking at other facets of a diamond helps us capture more of its full attractiveness.

So it is with words and the concepts they transmit. Sometimes one word portrays only part of the picture; similar words—synonyms—are needed to fill out the import of what is being communicated. Note how Paul took advantage of synonyms to round out his subject matter.[6]

Romans 2:4	God's "kindness, tolerance and patience"
Romans 2:8–9	"Trouble and distress"
Romans 2:10	"Glory, honor and peace"
Romans 2:19–20	"A guide," "a light," "an instructor," "a teacher"
Romans 9:33	"A stone," "a rock"
2 Corinthians 7:11	"Earnestness," "eagerness," "longing," "concern"
Galatians 1:12	"Receive," "taught"
Ephesians 1:4; 5:27; Titus 2:12	"Holy and blameless"
Ephesians 1:20–21	"Rule and authority, power and dominion"
Ephesians 3:17	"Rooted and established"
Ephesians 5:19; Colossians 3:16	"Psalms, hymns and spiritual songs"
Philippians 1:10; 2:15	"Blameless and pure"
Colossians 1:9	"Spiritual wisdom and understanding"
Colossians 1:11	"Endurance and patience"
Colossians 1:16	"Thrones or powers or rulers or authorities"
Colossians 2:7	"Rooted and built up"
Colossians 2:10, 15	"Power and authority/ies"
1 Timothy 3:15	"God's household," "the church of the living God, the pillar and foundation of the truth"

For a fascinating study, search the Book of Philippians for the numerous synonymous word pairs Paul employed there.

Antitheses

Besides repeated words and phrases and synonyms, Paul often cited a number of concepts or words that stand in contrast. Just as a synonym adds luster to its companion word, so an antonym or a contrasting word or phrase can round out a concept being conveyed. Weiss has suggested that "antithesis is perhaps the most distinctive characteristic of

6. E. W. Bullinger lists many of these and others (*Figures of Speech Used in the Bible* [London: Eyre and Spottiswoode, 1898; reprint, Grand Rapids: Baker, 1968], 332–38).

[Paul's] style. We may say, perhaps with some exaggeration, that all his speaking and thinking has an antithetical rhythm to it. . . ."[7]

In Romans 5:15–18 Paul presented several contrasts between Adam's sin and Jesus' grace. The trespass of one person (Adam) resulted in death for many, in condemnation, and in the reign of death. By contrast, the gift of God through one person (Christ) resulted in grace for many, in justification, and in the reign of life. For believers to be united with Christ in his death means they will also be united with him in his resurrection (Rom. 6:5, 8). Though they are dead to sin, by contrast they are alive to God (6:11). Set free from sin, they are slaves to righteousness and to God (6:18, 22). In contrast to death, which results from sin, believers have eternal life (6:23).

Romans 8:5–6, 13 presents a contrast in two ways of living: according to the sinful nature or according to the Holy Spirit. One results in death and the other in life and peace.

Paul challenged Christians to live out the anthitheses of hating what is evil while at the same time clinging to what is good (12:9), and not being vengeful but doing what is right (12:17).

The apostle's contrast between five intelligible words and ten thousand words spoken in a foreign language for which there is no interpretation (1 Cor. 14:19) highlights the total lack of value in tongues-speaking, since it does not edify (14:5, 12, 17).

The believer's resurrection body will differ significantly from the present physical body in several ways. The contrasts in 1 Corinthians 15:42–44 may be graphed in this way:

Sown perishable	Raised imperishable
Sown in dishonor	Raised in glory
Sown in weakness	Raised in power
Sown a natural body	Raised a spiritual body.[8]

By means of these four contrasting pairs, Paul set forth various aspects of the spiritual, resurrected body and how it will differ from the earthly body.

Evidences of Paul's hardships are seen in his four descriptions of himself in 2 Corinthians 4:8–9: hard pressed, perplexed, persecuted,

---

7. Johannes Weiss, *Earliest Christianity,* trans. Frederick C. Grant (New York: Harper and Brothers, 1937), 2:411.

8. Ibid., 298.

and struck down.[9] Yet these did not defeat him, for he added a contrasting fact about himself after each one: not crushed, not in despair,[10] not abandoned, and not destroyed.[11] While his difficulties meant he was constantly facing physical death, they resulted, by contrast, in the Corinthians' spiritual life (4:10, 12). Outwardly, that is, physically, Paul was wasting away (*diaphtheirō* means "to be decaying"), but inwardly, that is, within his soul, he was refreshed daily (4:16). The believer's glory in heaven will exceed by far any troubles in this life, for they, by contrast, are light and temporary (4:10). What can be seen in this life will not last, but what cannot be seen is eternal (4:18).

To suffer so intensely might lead the Corinthians, Paul said, to think he was insane ("out of our mind"), but his suffering was because of his devotion to God. But if, by contrast, they considered him sane, he was committed selflessly to them ("it is for you"; 2 Cor. 5:13).

In discussing his troubles in 2 Corinthians 6:8–10 Paul cited nine contrasts between his positive and negative experiences. The first pair lists the positive element first ("through glory and dishonor"), the second pair cites the negative first ("bad report and good report"), and the next two pairs list the positives first ("genuine, yet regarded as imposters; known, yet regarded as unknown"). Then the last five pairs introduce the negative element first: "dying, and yet we live on; beaten, and yet not killed; sorrowful, yet always rejoicing; poor, yet making many rich; having nothing, and yet possessing everything."

The truth of justification is stated in Galatians 2:16a both negatively ("a man is not justified by observing the law") and positively ("but by faith in Jesus Christ"). Then later in the verse (2:16b) these two are stated again, but in reverse order: "justified by faith in Christ and not by observing the law." The Mosaic law was given to Israel not as a way

---

9. "Hard pressed" translates *thlibō*, "to be pressed, or afflicted, or troubled" (the related noun *thlipsis* means pressure or trouble); "perplexed" renders *aporeō*, "to be at a loss as to how to act" (Timothy B. Savage, *Power through Weakness: Paul's Understanding of the Christian Ministry in 2 Corinthians* [Cambridge: University Press, 1996], 169, n. 33); "persecuted" *(diōkō)* suggests the idea of being hunted down like an animal; and "struck down" translates *kataballō*, "to knock down, to throw down" as in wrestling (Fritz Rienecker, *A Linguistic Key to the Greek New Testament*, ed. Cleon L. Rogers, Jr. [Grand Rapids: Zondervan, 1980], 464).

10. "Not in despair" is NIV's translation of *exaporeō*, "to be completely despondent or at a total loss." This verb, used only once in the New Testament, presents an interesting play (as noted in chapter 12) on the word "perplexed" *(aporeō*, "to be at a loss").

11. These lists of suffering were common in Cynic-Stoic writings, particularly Plutarch and Epictetus (Savage, *Power through Weakness*, 169–70). Of note in this list of antitheses is Paul's use of the negative *ouk*, which indicates that he was by no means defeated by his problems (ibid., 171).

of salvation ("by observing the law no one will be justified," 2:16c), but as a way of life and worship for Old Testament believers.

Christians who succumb to the pull of their sin nature may become involved in sins that are sexual, religious, or societal (Gal. 5:19–21). By contrast, those who live by the power of the Holy Spirit manifest nine graces, listed in 5:22–23 as "the fruit of the Spirit," that is, the result or evidence of living by the Spirit (5:16, 25). These verses point up the two kinds of lives believers may live: following the influences of sin or following the guidance of God. Rather than "unwholesome [*sapros*, 'putrid, rotten'] talk," Jesus' followers should speak words that edify and benefit others (Eph. 4:29).

Paul contrasted the self-based, outward righteousness of the law with genuine righteousness that comes through faith in Jesus Christ (Phil. 3:9). In still another contrast the apostle urged his readers not to be anxious *(merimnaō)*, "to fret, worry") about anything, but "in everything" to make known *(gnōrizō)* their requests to God (4:6).

These examples of contrasts show how presenting both negative and positive elements can help amplify an issue or a truth. (For other examples, in which the contrast between two elements is pointed up by the word "but," see Rom. 2:7–8; 1 Cor. 1:18; 2:4, 6; 8:1b–3; 2 Cor. 2:17; Eph. 5:8, 15, 17–18; Phil. 2:3–4; Col. 1:21–22; 1 Thess. 4:7; 5:9, 15; 2 Thess 3:15; 1 Tim. 2:9; 2 Tim. 2:9).

Enumerations or Lists

Paul frequently cited lists of virtues to cultivate or vices to avoid. While synonyms, antitheses, and the repetition of identical words add variation to concepts, numerical sequences provide a coordinated series of related terms. Such lists were common in Stoic literature and in other Hellenistic writings. Onosander, a contemporary of Paul, gave a list of qualifications for a general that compares with Paul's list of requirements for elders in 1 Timothy 3:2–7. "The general should be chosen as sober minded, self-controlled, temperate, frugal, hardy, intelligent, no lover of money, not too young or old, if he be the father of children, about to speak well, of good repute."[12] This similarity need not suggest that Paul copied a secular list; it may simply mean this was a conventional way of first-century writing. Clearly, Paul adapted his lists to the needs of the congregations he addressed. Even in 1 Timothy 3:2–7 he included statements pertaining to the church: "How can he take care of

12. Burton Scott Easton, "New Testament Ethical Lists," *Journal of Biblical Literature* 51 (1932): 10–11.

God's church?" (v. 5), "he must not be a recent convert" (v. 6), and he must not fall "into the devil's trap" (v. 7).[13]

Kruse's suggestion that Paul's lists fall into five categories is a helpful way of reviewing these enumerations.[14] These are illustrated in table 19.

Table 19
Paul's Lists of Virtues and Vices

Purposes	References	Items
To depict the depravity of unbelievers	Romans 1:29–31	Wickedness, evil, greed, depravity, envy, murder, strife, deceit, malice, gossiping, slander, hating God, insolent, arrogant, boastful, inventing evil, disobedient to parents, senseless, faithless, heartless, ruthless
	1 Corinthians 5:10–11	immoral, greedy, swindlers, idolaters, sexually immoral, greedy, idolater, slanderer, drunkard, swindler
To encourage believers to avoid the vices and practice the virtues	Romans 13:13	*Vices:* Orgies, drunkenness, sexual immorality, debauchery, dissension, jealousy
	1 Corinthians 6:9–10	Sexually immoral, idolaters, adulterers, male prostitutes, homosexual offenders, thieves, greedy, drunkards, slanderers, swindlers
	2 Corinthians 12:20	Quarreling, jealousy, outbursts of anger, factions, slander, gossip, arrogance, disorder
	Galatians 5:19–21	Sexual immorality, impurity, debauchery, idolatry, witchcraft, hatred, discord, jealousy, fits of anger, selfish ambition, dissensions, factions, envy, drunkenness, orgies
	Ephesians 4:31	Bitterness, rage, anger, brawling, slander, malice
	Ephesians 5:3–4	Sexual immorality, impurity, greed, obscenity, foolish talk, coarse joking

13. James L. Bailey and Lyle D. Vander Broek, *Literary Forms in the New Testament* (Louisville: Westminster/Knox, 1992), 67.

14. Colin G. Kruse, "Virtues and Vices," in *Dictionary of Paul and His Letters*, ed. Gerald F. Hawthorne, Ralph P. Martin, and Daniel G. Reid (Downers Grove, Ill.: InterVarsity, 1963), 962.

	Colossians 3:5, 8–9	Sexual immorality, impurity, lust, evil desires, greed, idolatry, anger, rage, malice, slander, filthy language, lying
	Titus 3:3	Foolish, disobedient, deceived, enslaved by all kinds of passions and pleasures, malice, envy, being hated, hating one another
	Galatians 5:22–23	*Virtues:* Love, joy, peace, patience, kindness, goodness, faithfulness, gentleness, self-control
	Philippians 4:8	True, noble, right, pure, lovely, admirable, excellent, praiseworthy
	Colossians 3:12	Compassion, kindness, humility, gentleness, patience
	Titus 2:2	Temperate, worthy of respect, self-controlled, sound in faith, love, endurance
	Titus 2:5	Self-controlled, pure, busy at home, kind, subject to their husbands
	Titus 2:7–8	Integrity, seriousness, soundness of speech
	Titus 3:1–2	Subject to rulers and authorities, obedient, ready to do whatever is good, slanders no one, peaceable, considerate, true humility
To expose and/or denounce the failure of the false teachers	1 Timothy 1:9–10	Lawbreakers, rebels, ungodly, sinful, unholy, irreligious, murderers, adulterers, perverts, slave traders, liars, perjurers
	1 Timothy 6:4–5	Conceited, understands nothing, interest in controversies and arguments resulting in envy, quarreling, malicious talk, evil suspicions, friction
To describe what is required of church leaders	1 Timothy 3:2–7	*Elders:* Above reproach, the husband of one wife, temperate, self-controlled, respectable, hospitable, able to teach, not given to much wine, not violent but gentle, not quarrelsome, not a lover of money, managing his family well, his children obeying him, not a recent convert, a good reputation with outsiders

	Titus 1:6–9	Blameless, the husband of one wife, his children believe and are not wild and disobedient, not overbearing, not quick-tempered, not given to much wine, not violent, not pursuing dishonest gain, hospitable, loving what is good, self-controlled, upright, holy, disciplined, holding firmly to the message
	1 Timothy 3:8–10, 12	*Deacons:* Worthy of respect, sincere, not indulging in much wine, not pursuing dishonest gain, holding the deep truths of the faith, a clear conscience, the husband of one wife, managing his children and his household well
	1 Timothy 6:11	*Timothy:* Righteousness, godliness, faith, love, endurance, gentleness
	2 Timothy 2:22–25	Righteousness, faith, love, peace, avoiding foolish and stupid arguments, not quarrelsome, kind, able to teach, not resentful, gently instructing opponents
To advise a young pastor	2 Timothy 3:2–5	*Unbelievers in the last days:* Lovers of themselves, lovers of money, boastful, proud, abusive, disobedient to their parents, ungrateful, unholy, without love, unforgiving, slanderous, without self-control, brutal, not lovers of the good, treacherous, rash, conceited, lovers of pleasure rather than lovers of God, having a form of godliness but denying its power
	2 Timothy 3:10	*Paul's virtues:* Teaching, way of life, purpose, faith, patience, love, endurance

These enumerations of virtues and vices occur in ten of Paul's epistles (all except 1 and 2 Thessalonians and Philemon). Some of the lists are surprisingly lengthy, particularly Romans 1:29–31 and 2 Timothy 3:2–5. Thirteen lists enumerate virtues and thirteen, vices. A number of the lists of virtues include the same characteristics, and a number of the vice lists include the same items. For an interesting study, analyze the virtue lists, noting the items that are listed more than once, and analyze the vice lists to determine the same.[15]

Other lists in 2 Corinthians describe the apostle's many hardships: four items are noted in 4:8–9, ten are in 6:4–5, nine in 6:8–10, twenty-five in 11:23–28, and five in 12:10![16] In listing his hardships in 2 Corinthians 6, Paul also included nine positive qualities of his life in verses 6–7.

In Romans, Paul included several enumerations, some of which are rather lengthy.[17] After the injunction "Let love be without hypocrisy" (12:9a NASB), he elaborated on that command with twenty-eight specific admonitions in 12:9–21. Ten forms of opposition to believers are listed in Romans 8:38–39, ten claims of Jewish superiority are cited in 2:17–20, and eight attributes of Israel are given in 9:4–5. Seven Old Testament passages are quoted in 3:10b–18,[18] and seven rhetorical questions are raised in 8:31–35. In verse 35 the seventh of these questions includes seven forms of opposition, and seven spiritual gifts are recounted in 12:6–8: prophesying, serving, teaching, encouraging, contributing to others' needs, leading, and showing mercy.[19]

15. Paul's vice lists, with their repetition of several key sins, are similar to Hellenistic Jewish writings (Bailey and Vander Broek, *Literary Forms in the New Testament*, 67). For discussions on whether the forms of Paul's virtue and vice lists were taken from Hellenistic philosophy or from Old Testament concepts, see Hans Dieter Betz, *Galatians*, Hermenia (Philadelphia: Fortress, 1979), 281–83; Burton Scott Easton, "New Testament Ethical Lists," *Journal of Biblical Literature* 51 (1932): 1–12; Neil J. McEleney, "The Vice Lists of the Pastoral Epistles," *Catholic Biblical Quarterly* 36 (1974): 203–19; David Schroeder, "Lists, Ethical," in *Interpreter's Dictionary of the Bible Supplementary Volume*, 546–47; and Ralph P. Martin, "Virtue," in *New International Dictionary of New Testament Theology*, 3:928–32.

Martin also discusses whether the style of the so-called house tables (lists of imperatives to wives, husbands, children, parents, slaves, and masters) stemmed from Stoicism ("Virtue," 3:931).

16. The enumerations in 2 Corinthians 6 and 11 are also known as "pleonasms" (George A. Kennedy, *New Testament Interpretation through Rhetorical Criticism* [Chapel Hill, N.C.: University of North Carolina Press, 1984], 91). This term was used in Greek rhetoric to refer to lists that seemingly had more items than were necessary.

17. Robert Jewett, "The Rhetorical Function of Numerical Sequences in Romans," in *Persuasive Artistry*, ed. Duane F. Watson (Sheffield: Sheffield Academic, 1991), 227–45.

18. This catena of quotations condemning the unsaved is as follows:

Romans 3:10b	(Ecclesiastes 7:20)
Romans 3:11–12	(Psalms 14:1–3)
Romans 3:13a	(Psalms 5:9)
Romans 3:13b	(Psalm 140:3)
Romans 3:14	(Psalm 10:7)
Romans 3:15–17	(Isaiah 59:7–8)
Romans 3:18	(Psalm 36:1)

19. "The seven types of congregational service and leadership do not appear to be exhaustive, because several other types are listed elsewhere. The choice of the sacred, rounded number of seven conveys the sense that these examples stand for the wide range of gifts, in which every member of the congregation was thought to participate" (ibid., 238).

Series of sixes include the six questions in Romans 3:27–31 and the six Old Testament quotations in 10:15–21.

A series of four questions, each beginning with "How?" addresses the need for messengers to bear the Good News to the lost (10:14–15). Romans 13:7 presents a series of four forms of civil obligation, in which each Greek phrase begins with *tō* ("to whom"): "taxes to whom taxes [are due], revenue to whom revenue [is due], respect to whom respect [is due], and honor to whom honor [is due]."[20]

Paul utilized a number of triads throughout Romans.[21]

2:4	God's "kindness, tolerance and patience"
2:7	The good seek "glory, honor and immortality"
7:12	The law is "holy, righteous and good"
12:1	Sacrifices that are "living, holy and pleasing to God"
12:2	God's "good, pleasing and perfect" will
14:17	The kingdom of God is "righteousness, peace and joy"

Jewett observes that these many numerical series in Romans may rhetorically reinforce the argument of the epistle. "The large number of series associated with completeness convey the comprehensive argument concerning the triumph of divine righteousness through the gospel."[22]

Paul seemed to enjoy using a good number of triads in 1 Thessalonians. These verses or groups of verses each include this recurring pattern, which would have had aesthetic value to those hearing the epistle read to them: 1:3, 5, 9–10; 2:3, 5, 11–12, 15, 19; 3:2–3, 11–13; 4:3–4, 11, 16; 5:12, 23.[23]

Besides the lists of virtues and vices and the many enumerations in Romans, 2 Corinthians, and 1 Thessalonians, Paul incorporated other listings as well. Note the following passages, count the number of items in each list, and write that number beside the reference.

These many lists in Paul's letters serve to amplify and refine points he was making and to add emphasis to them. No one could miss the compounding, accumulating effect of such lists.

---

20. Alliteration and wordplays are also present in these four phrases, as noted in chapter 12.

21. Ibid., 240.

22. Ibid., 244–45.

23. Cf. Stanley B. Marrow, *Paul: His Letters and His Theology* (New York: Paulist, 1986); and Carol J. Schleuter, *Filling Up the Measure: Polemical Hyperbole in 1 Thessalonians 2:14–16* (Sheffield: Sheffield Academic, 1994), 116–20.

References	Number of Items
1 Corinthians 9:1	
1 Corinthians 9:7–9	
1 Corinthians 12:4–6	
1 Corinthians 12:8–10	
1 Corinthians 12:28	
1 Corinthians 12:29–30	
1 Corinthians 13:4–8a	
1 Corinthians 13:13	
1 Corinthians 14:26	
1 Corinthians 15:39	
2 Corinthians 7:11	
2 Corinthians 8:7	
Ephesians 4:4–6	
Ephesians 4:11	
Ephesians 6:14	
Philippians 3:5–6	
1 Thessalonians 5:14	
1 Thessalonians 5:16–22	
1 Timothy 1:2	
1 Timothy 1:5	
1 Timothy 1:17	
1 Timothy 2:1	
2 Timothy 1:2	
2 Timothy 2:11–13	
2 Timothy 3:16	
Titus 3:1–2	

Idioms

An idiom is a figure of speech which is an expression peculiar to a given language or to people in a certain geographical location. The combination of words differs from the normal literal meaning of each individual word. We use the phrase "down in the dumps" to say a person is discouraged or depressed. To "hit the sack" means to go to bed, not to beat against a bag. If we are "snowed under," we mean we have a lot to do, not that we are literally under a pile of snow. A person who "flies off the handle" expresses sudden, great anger.

In Hebrew and Greek the idiom "the son of" followed by a characteristic indicates that the person possesses that quality or destiny. "The sons of disobedience" (Eph. 2:2; 5:6 Greek) is an idiom meaning disobedient individuals. "Sons of wrath" (2:3 Greek) refers to those who are subject to God's wrath. "The son of destruction" (2 Thess. 2:3 Greek; "man of lawlessness" NIV) means the one who is destined to be destroyed.

Many times idioms are expressed in verbs. "To hear" *(akouō)* often means more than merely listening with one's ears. It means "reported" (1 Cor. 5:1), "understand" (14:2), and "be aware of" (Gal. 4:21). Sometimes "to see" suggests more than looking with one's eyes. In 1 Corinthians 10:12 and Colossians 4:17 it means "to give attention to." "To open one's mouth" is an idiomatic expression for speaking freely (2 Cor. 6:11).[24] In 2 Timothy 2:19 "to know" indicates more than having knowledge; it implies "to care for." And in 1 Thessalonians 5:12 it even conveys the sense of "showing respect for."

The verb "to walk" idiomatically suggests not mobility by means of one's legs and feet, but one's manner of life or conduct, as in "we walk [live] by faith" (2 Cor. 5:7), and "walk [live] by the Spirit" (Gal. 5:16, 25). "To run" is to carry out a project (Phil. 2:16); "to cause someone to stumble" is to cause him or her to make a mistake in his Christian life (Rom. 14:20).

Being "yoked" with unbelievers was Paul's idiom for joining with them in a cooperative endeavor (2 Cor. 6:14).[25] To be "dead" in sins is to be unsaved, with no spiritual fellowship with God (Eph. 2:1; Col. 2:13). When Epaphras "wrestled" in prayer for the Colossians, he was praying with great intensity and earnestness (Col. 4:12). The Thessalonians "trumpeted" *(exēchomai)* the word of the Lord (1 Thess. 1:8) in the sense that when they told others the message of salvation, those who heard and received it passed it on to others, like a trumpet sound going from one spot to many other areas. To be "shipwrecked" as some were, including Hymenaeus and Alexander (1 Tim. 1:19–20), is a graphic idiom for the personal disaster that comes to those who reject what they have heard.

Other Pauline idioms include (a) the members of Paul's body (i.e., his sin nature) "waging war" against his mind (his new nature; Rom. 7:23);

24. Bullinger, *Figures of Speech Used in the Bible,* 842.
25. For discussion on whom Paul had in mind by these unbelievers, see William J. Webb, "Who Are the Unbelievers (ἄπιστοι) in 2 Corinthians 6:14?" *Bibliotheca Sacra* 149 (January–March 1992): 27–44; and idem, "What Is the Unequal Yoke (ἑτεροζυγου'ντε") in 2 Corinthians 6:14?" *Bibliotheca Sacra* 149 (April–June 1992): 162–79.

(b) sinners being "redeemed" in the sense of being set free from sin like a slave being purchased in the marketplace and released (Rom. 3:24; 1 Cor. 6:20; 7:23; Gal. 3:13–14; 4:5; Eph. 1:7, 14; Col. 1:14; Titus 2:14); (c) being "at home in the body" (2 Cor. 5:6, 9) meaning to be alive; and (d) to reap what one sows (Gal. 6:7) speaks as an idiom in an agricultural society of a person experiencing the consequences that stem inexorably from his sins. Paul wrote an idiom in 2 Corinthians 4:17 that is difficult to render literally. He spoke of believers' eternal glory that "far outweighs" *(hyperbolēn eis hyperbolōn)* all their troubles. Since the adjective *hyperbolē* means "extraordinary or beyond all measure," the idiom "the extraordinary unto the extraordinary" masterfully conveys the fact that our future glory will be so great it will be immeasurable.

Another idiomatic form of which Paul was fond was the use of the superlative *hyper* ("abundant, surpassing, utterly, superior, more earnestly") as a prefix to a number of nouns, verbs, adverbs, and adjectives. Examples taken from the New American Standard Bible include "abounded all the more" *(hyperperisseuō,* Rom. 5:20); burdened "excessively" *(hyperbolē,* 2 Cor. 1:8); "surpassing greatness [*hyperbolē*] of the power" (4:7); "surpassing greatness [*hyperbolē*] of the revelations" (12:7); "overflowing [*hyperperisseuō*] with joy" (7:4); the "surpassing [*hyperballō*] grace of God" (9:14), "the love of Christ which surpasses [*hyperballō*] knowledge" (Eph. 3:19); "praying most earnestly [*hyperekperissou*]" (1 Thess. 3:10); "esteem them very highly [*hyperekperissōs*] in love" (5:13); "your faith is greatly enlarged [*hyperauxanō*]" (2 Thess. 1:3). Perhaps one of Paul's best known superlatives using the prefix *hyper* is in Romans 8:37: "we overwhelmingly conquer [*hypernikaō*]."

Another form of Greek idiom is what Bullinger calls antimereia,[26] in which one part of speech is used in place of another, such as a noun in place of its corresponding adjective. When Paul wrote, he "will justify the circumcised by faith" (Rom. 3:30), he used the Greek noun for "circumcision." By this he meant those who are circumcised, and most English translations bear this out (cf. 15:8). "The body of this death" (7:23) is an idiomatic way of saying "this mortal body." The Greek phrase "the body of our humiliation" (Phil. 3:21) is an idiom for "our lowly body." "The Son of his love" (Col. 1:13) means "the Son he loves." "His powerful angels" translates the Greek phrase, "the angels of his power" (2 Thess. 1:7). In writing of Jesus as "our hope" (1 Tim. 1:1), Paul was saying that Jesus is the object of our hope.[27]

---

26. Bullinger, *Figures of Speech Used in the Bible,* 491–506.
27. For other idioms in Greek, see C. F. D. Moule, *An Idiom Book of New Testament Greek,* 2d ed. (Cambridge: University Press, 1971).

Structural Patterns

Several structural patterns used by Paul add rhetorical luster to his epistles and provide means of emphasis. The artistry of these forms intrigue readers, boosting their ability to remember the passages.

Parallelism

Paul's prose occasionally bursts into poetic brilliance. In quoting Isaiah 54:1 in Galatians 4:27 he cited some lines that stand in comparative parallel: "O barren woman" in the first line is coupled with the synonymous phrase "who bears no children," and the admonition "Be glad" is paralleled by "break forth and cry aloud."

Following the exclamation, "How unsearchable [are] his judgments," is the synonymous remark, "his paths [are] beyond tracing out!" (Rom. 11:33). The next verse makes the same point by parallel questions: "Who has known the mind of the Lord? Or who has been his counselor?"

The command "Wake up" in the quotation in Ephesians 5:14 is paralleled by the corresponding injunction "rise from the dead." In contrastive parallelism the second line presents a contrast to the first line. The two parts of Romans 6:23 contrast "wages" and "gift," "sin" and "God," and "death" and "eternal life."

Diversity in spiritual gifts is contrasted by the fact that the same Holy Spirit enabled believers to exercise those gifts (1 Cor. 12:4). The same antithesis between diversity and unity is seen in verses 5 and 6. At the same time these three sentences, each with a contrast, parallel each other in form, thus making a memorable rhythm. First Corinthians 13:1–3 evidences a rhythm of three contrastive sentences, each with a similar structure, including an "if" clause, the phrase, "but have not love," and a clause that states the effect of the gift apart from love.[28] Many of the verses with antitheses (see the earlier section on "Antitheses") include other antithetical parallels.

Alternations

Occasionally Paul alternated his points between negative and positive assertions, and/or between warnings and exhortations. After the negative warning, "But do not use your freedom to indulge the sinful nature," Paul added positively, "Serve one another in love" (Gal. 5:13).

28. Bailey and Vander Broek, *Literary Forms in the New Testament*, 77.

Then continuing the alternating pattern, verse 14 of the same chapter positively urges believers to love each other, and verse 15 signals the danger of its opposite, the negative of "devouring each other." Paul followed the subject of sowing to please one's sinful nature with its alternative about sowing to the Spirit (6:8).

Romans 5:18–19 includes an alternation in the same A, B, A', B' fashion, speaking first of (A) one trespass and (B) one act of righteousness, and then of (A') the disobedience of one man and (B') the obedience of one man. The statements by Paul in 1 Corinthians 15:42–44 about the earthly body and the heavenly body are given in an alternating pattern (as well as in contrast, as discussed earlier under "Antitheses").

Inclusios

An inclusio is a group of verses in which what is said near the beginning of the segment is repeated near the end. These repeated words or phrases are like string tying the intervening verses together. The purpose is to separate that position of Scripture from what precedes and follows, thus setting it off as a unit and adding emphasis to the unifying "string."

The following are among the inclusios in Paul's writings. After the general injunction, "Love must be sincere," Paul began a series of admonitions with the words, "Hate what is evil; cling to what is good" (Rom. 12:9). Then in verse 21 he concluded the pericope by another challenge having to do with evil and good: "Do not be overcome by evil, but overcome evil with good."

Having stated, "I make myself a slave to everyone" (1 Cor. 9:19), Paul wrote in verse 22, "I have become all things to all men." In the statements between these verses he cited specific ways in which he had done that. The inclusio statements are general and the intervening verses are specific.

Paul's lengthy discussion on spiritual gifts in 1 Corinthians 12–14 begins with the desire, "I do not want you to be ignorant [*agnein*]" (12:1), and concludes with a recurrence of the words "ignorant": "But if anyone is ignorant [*agnoei*], let him be ignorant [*agnoeitai*]" (14:38 NKJV).[29]

A smaller unit of nine verses in 1 Corinthians 12 refers to the fact that though the human body has many parts it forms one body (12:12), and the unit concludes by affirming the same fact: "There are many parts, but one body" (12:20).

---

29. Other translations render 1 Corinthians 14:38 differently: "If he ignores this, he himself will be ignored" (NIV); "But if anyone does not recognize this, he is not recognized" (NASB); "If he does not acknowledge this, God does not acknowledge him" (NEB).

Christ "is the head over every power and authority" (Col. 2:10), for he has disarmed those same "powers and authorities" (2:15).

Chiasms

A chiasm is a verbal pattern in which the first and fourth portions of a verse or passage are parallel, and points two and three are similar. Or if the segment has an uneven number of parts, the first and last are parallel, the second and next-to-last are parallel, and the middle part is the focal point. This pattern may be noted as A, B, B' A', or A B, C, B' A'. If a chiastic passage has, say, seven corresponding elements the pattern is A B C D, C', B' A. "Where only two pairs of elements are present in the chiastic structure (i.e., in the form A B B' A'), emphasis is not so likely intended by the two central elements; the main focus in such a structure is the correspondence of each pair of elements."[30] Besides serving as an interpretive focal point, a chiasm may mark an important transition in the passage.[31]

By placing corresponding elements in reverse order, the chiastic art form takes on a special beauty, aids the reader's memory, focuses on and elucidates points emphasized, highlights contrasts and repetitions, and divides one section from another.[32] Chiasms occur "to one degree or another in most languages and literature, though with varying frequencies and effects."[33] In ancient literature they occur in abundance,[34] as evidenced in Welch's collection of essays on chiasms in a variety of ancient literatures, including Sumero-Akkadian, Ugaritic, Old Testament Hebrew, Aramaic, New Testament Greek, and ancient Greek and Latin.[35]

Some chiasms are brief, as in the following examples.

Food
   for the *stomach*
   and the *stomach*
for *food* (1 Cor. 6:13a).

---

30. Ronald E. Man, "The Value of Chiasm for New Testament Interpretation," *Bibliotheca Sacra* 141 (April–June 1984): 148–49.

31. Bailey and Vander Broek illustrate this from Romans 11:33–35 (*Literary Forms in the New Testament*, 52–53).

32. Man, "The Value of Chiasm for New Testament Interpretation," 146–57; Nils Wilhelm Lund, *Chiasmus in the New Testament* (1942; reprint, Peabody, Mass.: Hendrickson, 1992), 30–31; H. van Dyke Parunak, "Oral Typesetting: Some Uses of Biblical Structure," *Biblica* 62 (1981): 153–68; Ian H. Thomas, *Chiasmus in the Pauline Letters* (Sheffield: Sheffield Academic, 1995), 34–43; and David Noel Freedman, "Preface," in *Chiasmus in Antiquity,* ed. John W. Welch (Hildesheim: Gerstenberg, 1981), 12.

33. Freedman, "Preface," 7.

34. Ibid.

35. Welch, ed., *Chiasmus in Antiquity.*

The *body* is . . .
> for the *Lord*
> and the *Lord*
for the *body* (1 Cor. 6:13b).

For *man*
> did not come from *woman*,
> but *woman*
from *man* (1 Cor. 11:8).

Neither was *man* created
> for *woman*,
> but *woman*
for *man* (1 Cor. 11:9).

For as *woman*
> came from *man*,
> so also *man* is born
of *woman* (1 Cor. 11:12).

Greek or
> *Jew*,
> *circumcised* or
uncircumcised (Col. 3:11a).

Romans 2:7–10 is chiastic in structure, with verses 7 and 10 being parallel and verses 8 and 9 parallel.

Some chiastic structures are not so evident in some English translations. Romans 10:19 with its quotation from Deuteronomy 32:21 is a chiasm, though it appears as a parallelism in the New International Version and the New King James Version. The New American Standard Bible brings out the chiastic pattern with its reverse order.

I will *make you jealous*
> by that which is *not a nation*,
> by a *nation without understanding*
will I *anger you.*

Philemon 5, chiastic in Greek, needs to be altered in translation to make sense in English.

I hear of your *love*
> and of the *faith*
> which you have *toward the Lord Jesus*
and *toward all the saints.*[36]

---

36. The NIV reads, "I hear about your faith in the Lord Jesus and your love for all the saints."

Other examples of chiasms follow.

Christ [is] the *power* of God
  and the *wisdom* of God.
  For the foolishness of God is *wiser* than man's wisdom,
And the weakness of God is *stronger* than man's strength (1 Cor. 1:24–25).[37]

I [am] preaching to the *Gentiles*
  just as Peter [is preaching] to the *Jews*.
  Peter [is] *an apostle to the Jews*
. . . my ministry [is] as an *apostle to the Gentiles* (Gal. 2:7–8).

For the *sinful nature* desires
  what is contrary *to the Spirit*
  and *the Spirit* what is contrary
to the *sinful nature* (Gal. 5:17).

A longer chiastic pattern is evident in Ephesians 2:12–19. The following summarizes the points in each element.

"Excluded . . . and *foreigners* (v. 12)
  Now . . . brought *near* (v. 13)
    Made the two *one* [and] destroyed . . . *hostility* (v. 14)
      His purpose was to create in himself *one* new man (v. 15)
    One body [and] put to death their *hostility* (v. 16)
  Near [and] access (vv. 17–18)
No longer *foreigners* and aliens" (v. 19).[38]

Interpreters must avoid the temptation to find chiasms where there are none, foisting chiasms on passages that were not so intended. Shorter passages more readily reveal chiastic structures; the longer the passage, the more difficult it is to certify that a chiasm was in fact intended by the Holy Spirit.[39]

37. Bullinger, *Figures of Speech Used in the Bible*, 362.

38. Other chiasms in Romans, 1 Corinthians, Ephesians, Philippians, Colossians, and Philemon are listed by Lund (*Chiasmus in the New Testament*, 145–225; and Welch cites numerous chiasms in the New Testament, including some in each of Paul's letters (John W. Welch, "Chiasmus in the New Testament," in *Chiasmus in Antiquity*, 211–49). Also see examples in Nels Wilhelm Lund, "The Presence of Chiasmus in the New Testament," *Journal of Religion* 10 (1930): 75–93; idem, "The Literary Structure of Paul's Hymn to Love," *Journal of Biblical Literature* 50 (1931): 266–76; idem, "The Significance of Chiasmus for Interpretation," 105–23; and E. Randolph Richards, *The Secretary in the Letters of Paul* (Tübingin: Mohr, 1991), 207–8.

39. Thomson's excellent discussion presents some chiasms of longer passages, in which his proposed parallel elements do not all seem to match, such as those in Romans 5:15–21 and Colossians 2:6–19 (Thomson, *Chiasmus in the Pauline Letters*, 236–37).

Crescendos

Another rhetorical device Paul used may be called the crescendo or the climax. These add particular focus to the last element in the list. In some cases a word or phrase at the end of a clause is repeated at the beginning of the next clause. Augustine recognized this pattern and called it *klimax,* which Latins called *gradioto.*[40] Since this "chain" device was popular in Hellenistic literature,[41] it is not surprising that Paul used it several times, and with great impact.[42]

Romans 8:17 moves from "heirs" to "heirs of God" to "co-heirs with Christ." In similar fashion Galatians 4:7 progresses from reference to a slave, to a son, to an heir. Paul's list of ten items, none of which is able to separate believers from Christ's love, concludes with the climactic, all-embracive phrase, "nor anything else in all creation" (Rom. 8:38–39).

In the chain-link structure of Romans 8:30, "predestined," "called," and "justified" are each mentioned twice, leading to the climax of believers being glorified. Romans 5:2–5 presents a chain link or stairstep pattern in which key words are repeated in succeeding phrases as seen in the following:[43]

    Rejoice
    Rejoice
       Sufferings
       Suffering
          Perseverance
          Perseverance
             Character
             Character
                Hope
                Hope

The stairstep pattern, leading to a crescendo, is also used in Romans 10:13–15:

40. Augustine *On Christian Doctrine* 4, cited in Frank Witt Hughes, *Early Christian Rhetoric and 2 Thessalonians* (Sheffield: Sheffield Academic, 1989), 19–20.

41. Raymond Bailey, *Paul the Preacher* (Nashville: Broadman, 1991), 91.

42. Quintilian, first-century Roman rhetorician, said one way to amplify or enhance the power of one's words is to build words on words, proceeding step by step "to the highest degree or even beyond it" (*On the Education of an Orator* 8.4.3).

43. Kummel notes that this rhetorical form is called a sorites (Werner G. Kummel, *Exegetical Method*, ed. Otto Kaiser and Werner G. Kummel, trans. E. V. N. Goetchius and M. J. O'Connell, rev. ed. [New York: Seabury, 1981], 61).

Calls
Call
  Believed
  Believe
    Heard
    Hear
      Preaching
      Preach
        Sent

First Corinthians 15:12–14 has a similar stairstep climax:

If . . . Christ has not been raised from the dead
  how can some . . . say that there is no resurrection of the dead?
  If there is no resurrection of the dead,
    then not even Christ has been raised,
  And if Christ has not been raised.
    our preaching is useless
    and so is your faith.

Verses 16–17 of the same chapter have a similar pattern of argumentation:

If the dead are not raised,
  then Christ has not been raised either.
  And if Christ has not been raised,
    your faith is futile;
    you are still in your sins.

While not in a stairstep pattern, 1 Timothy 3:16 includes six progressive statements about Christ, culminating in his being "taken up in glory."

Paul's artful use of these patterns—parallelisms, alternations, inclusios, chiasms, and crescendos—would have added to the impact of his words on those who heard and read his epistles. They can do the same for present-day readers as well.

Ask Yourself . . .

Could you think of some maxims to use in your teaching? Could your students create some maxims that would summarize Bible truths they have learned?

How could you make use of synonyms or antitheses?

Tape record a class session you teach, and then play it at home, listening for idioms you used.

In your Bible study, be alert to idioms and various structural patterns in the Scriptures. Note how these add clarity and emphasis.

*"By the meekness and gentleness of Christ,
J appeal to you."*

2 Corinthians IO:I

14

How Did Paul Use Logical Reasoning in His Teaching?

Another factor that made Paul such a dynamic teacher was his use of logic. He employed a number of reasoning techniques and kinds of argumentation to help his reader-students think logically and accurately, and to seek to persuade them to his point of view. His reasoning led them from certain assumptions to related conclusions and from false notions to correct concepts.

A Fortiori Reasoning

In the argumentation known as a fortiori the person reasons from the lesser to the greater,[1] or from the greater to the lesser. If one accepts the

---

1. Rabbi Hillel (30 B.C.–A.D. 9) called this form of argument *qal wahomer*, "light and heavy." For Hillel's seven interpretive rules, see E. Earle Ellis, *Paul's Use of the Old Testament* (Grand Rapids: Eerdmans, 1957), 41; and Richard N. Longenecker, *Biblical Exegesis in the Apostolic Period* (Grand Rapids: Eerdmans 1975), 117–18.

premise as true, then the conclusion drawn from it is also logical and even more so. By granting the validity of the first premise, which is readily accepted, a reader is obliged to accept the second premise as valid too. If one premise is certain, the other is even more so. Paul put to advantage this powerful form of persuasion, especially in Romans, an epistle arranged in an intensely logical form, and in 1 and 2 Corinthians. The well-known "how much more" phrases occur four times in Romans 5. Since believers are justified, they will certainly "be saved from God's wrath" (5:9), and since they are reconciled by his death, they will be "saved through his life" (5:10).[2] Since Adam's sin resulted in spiritual death for the human race, of even greater significance is God's provision of grace through Christ which overflows to many people (5:15). Death reigns because of one man's sin, but of greater impact is the fact that believers "reign in life through the one man, Jesus Christ" (5:17).

To illustrate the truth that believing Gentiles share God's grace with believing Jews, the apostle compared the former to a wild olive tree being grafted into a cultivated olive tree (11:24).[3] Then, using an a fortiori argument, Paul asserted a question to show that believing Israelites ("the natural branches") would enjoy God's blessing ("grafted into their own olive tree").

The Mosaic law served to condemn people in their sin; so since it was glorious, the ministry of the new covenant, which "brings righteousness," is "much more glorious" (2 Cor. 3:9). The glorious Mosaic law faded away; therefore, the glory of the ministry of the Spirit "which lasts" is "much greater" (3:7–8, 11).

In the logic of these a fortiori arguments Paul reasoned from a lesser fact to a greater fact, from an accepted truth to an even more profound fact. Now in the following instances he argued in the opposite direction: If something of great import is valid, then a fact of lesser significance is also unquestionably true. This second approach is seen in several verses. In Romans 8:31 Paul asked the rhetorical question, "If God is for us (the greater fact), who can be against us?" (the lesser fact). Since God defends believers, certainly no one is strong enough to oppose them successfully. And the apostle wrote that if Christ did not please himself (the greater truth), certainly Christians should not please themselves

---

2. The antithesis between Jesus' death and his present life presents an arresting contrast, pointing to the value of his present resurrected-ascended state in which he now lives.

3. This was actually contrary to normal agricultural procedure; usually a cultivated olive branch would be grafted to a wild olive tree. But Paul knew he was reversing the usual procedure, doing so for the purpose of his illustration; he said his point was "contrary to nature" (11:24).

but should be concerned about helping others (the lesser fact, 15:2–3). Since saints will judge the world,[4] they certainly ought to be able to judge trivial cases now (1 Cor. 6:2). Similarly, since believers will judge angels,[5] saints ought to be competent in judging "the things of this life" (*biōtikos*, matters pertaining to daily living on the earth, 6:3).

Since Paul had "sown spiritual seed," that is, won some Corinthians to Christ (the more important), then he had the right to have a "material harvest" from them, that is, to receive monetary support from them (9:11). Also, since others had that right (the more significant because of the numbers), then Paul and Sosthenes (1:1), only two individuals, also had that right (9:12).

Reductio ad absurdum

In this line of reasoning, the logician seeks to reduce a person's view to its absurd logical outcome. If a position logically leads to an absurdity, then the view is untenable.

If someone could be saved and become an heir of eternal life by means of keeping the law, then the absurd conclusion of that premise would be, Paul pointed out, that faith has no value and that the promise to Abraham (that faith is credited to the believer as righteousness) was worthless (Rom. 4:14).

The Corinthians' quarreling, divisive spirit—in which some were followers of Paul, others of Apollos, others of Cephas, and still others saying they were "of Christ"—meant, illogically, Paul argued, that Christ was divided or that he, Paul, was crucified for them and baptized them (1 Cor. 1:13–14).

The logical absurdity stemming from some Corinthian Christians thinking they were superior to others (and that the others with their

4. "To judge" is probably used here in the sense of ruling, and the future tense of the verb ("will judge") points to the millennium when "the saints will share in Christ's reign over the created universe" (Archibald Robertson and Alfred Plummer, *A Critical and Exegetical Commentary on the First Epistle of St Paul to the Corinthians*, 2d ed. [Edinburgh: Clark, 1914], 111); cf. Daniel 7:22; Matthew 19:28; 2 Timothy 2:12; and Revelation 5:10; 20:4, 6; 22:5. Reigning with Christ, however, may include making judicial decisions as Christ's representatives.

5. This judgment of angels points to the highest class of created beings over which saints will have authority as they reign with Christ (ibid., 112). Or it may point to saints participating in Christ's sentencing of judgment on fallen angels at the end of the millennium—judgment of fallen, nonbound angels "on the great Day," as Jude put it (Jude 6), that is, probably at the time Satan, the Antichrist, and Satan's false prophet will be thrown into the lake of fire (Rev. 20:10).

spiritual gifts were not needed) was like supposing the human body had only one part, such as an eye (12:14–19)—clearly an absurd conclusion!

Other uses of reductio ad absurdum logic are evident in 1 Corinthians 15:14, 32; Galatians 3:3; 4:9; and 5:11.

Pointing out these absurd conclusions of various notions revealed the fallacy of those ideas, thus strengthening the thrust of Paul's arguments against them.

Non Sequitur

A person using non sequitur reasoning shows that a conclusion presumably held by an opponent does not logically follow from the premise being presented.

Paul argued this way in Romans 3:3–4 when he said that the fact (Paul's premise) that some Jews do not believe in Christ does not mean God is not faithful. And in 3:5–6 God's exercising of wrath on unbelievers does not mean he is unjust. This would not follow (it would be a non sequitur) because if God could not judge the unsaved then he could not carry out his role as Judge of the world.

In Romans 3:9 the first premise—that sin, which highlights God's truthfulness and glory—does not logically suggest the conclusion that sin is excusable (3:7). Also, it is wrong to assume that Jews are better than Gentiles (3:9) because all are "under sin."

Suppose someone were to argue that since God's grace increases when sin increases (5:20), people ought to sin more (6:1). Paul answered that false idea with a non sequitur: It does not follow that Christians should go on sinning and "live in" sin because they have "died" to it and are to "live a new life" (6:2, 4). And if some argued that since believers are not under law, sin is allowable, that too, Paul wrote, would be a non sequitur. Why? Because sin leads to spiritual slavery whereas Christians "have been set free from sin" (6:15–18). Also see 3:31.

Argumentum ad Hominem

In this kind of reasoning technique a person argues against an opposing view by attacking the antagonist himself rather than his arguments as such. For instance, Paul challenged the Romans in their misjudging others by means of his belittling question, "Who are you . . . ?" (Rom. 14:4). And to the Corinthians he wrote, "Come back to your senses . . . and stop sinning; for there are some who are ignorant of God—I say this to your shame" (1 Cor. 15:34). Paul made use of this only a few times. He called the Galatians "foolish" (Gal. 3:1), and later added, "Are you so foolish?" (3:3).[6] His wish that the Judaizers, who were promoting the need for circumcision as essential for salvation, would emasculate themselves (Gal. 5:12) may be seen as a sarcastic argument ad hominem, an argument against the Judaizers themselves.

Excluded Middle

In this form of reasoning the logician shows that only two opposites exist in a given situation. Since no middle ground exists, one of the two bipolar positions must be accepted. This argumentation often forces a person to face the two options and, hopefully, to make the right choice. Belittling the role of those who plant and water (God's servants) in contrast to God himself (the one who brings about spiritual growth), Paul emphasized the Corinthians' folly of divisively following Paul or Apollos (1 Cor. 3:5–7). Since one was foolish and since only God causes spiritual progress, the choice in attitudes was clear.

Paul also gave them a choice of two attitudes with which he might go to them (4:21). And he excluded any third "middle" option by his statement, "You cannot drink the cup of the Lord and the cup of demons too" (10:21). This implied that worship of demons, through idol worship, was to be avoided. Since having the Holy Spirit does not come from law observance, the Galatians must have received the Spirit by faith (Gal. 3:2, 5). These bipolar options show that the Galatians were inconsistent in trying to advance spiritually by keeping the law. Also "the inheritance" of eternal life depends either on obeying the Mosaic law or on God's promise (3:18); it cannot be based on both. And since eternal life is clearly not attainable by keeping the law, it is based on faith in God's promise.

Other examples of the excluded middle may be seen in the antitheses discussed in chapter 13.

Noncontradiction

Noncontradiction is a kind of reasoning in which the exponent presents an argument, often in the form of a question, to which the listener must

---

6. In both instances the word *anoētoi* is used. It suggests the lack of intelligence or wisdom. In the New Testament this word occurs only in Paul's writings (Rom. 1:14; Gal. 3:1, 3; 1 Tim. 6:9; Titus 3:3).

respond with a yes or a no. The purpose is to challenge the opponent to affirm the proponent's view and to reject the undesirable option.

The question, "Is God the God of Jews only?" (Rom. 3:29), clearly implies a negative answer, thereby affirming Paul's position that God is over both Jews and Gentiles. Paul made a similar point in 4:9. To ask whether Abraham was justified before or after he was circumcised (4:10a) is a meaningful way to stress that circumcision has no bearing on justification.

Sometimes the answer to the question raised in a noncontradiction point of logic is answered by the arguer, as Paul did in Romans 11:1, "I ask then, Did God reject his people? Not at all!" and in 11:11, "Again I ask, Did they stumble so as to fall beyond recovery? Not at all!"

To see how the reasoning apostle used this technique frequently, look up each of the following verses and jot down by each one whether Paul expected an affirmative or a negative answer.

    Romans 6:16
    Romans 7:1
    Romans 9:21
    Romans 10:18
    Romans 10:19
    Romans 11:1
    Romans 11:11
    1 Corinthians 3:3a
    1 Corinthians 3:3b
    1 Corinthians 9:1a
    1 Corinthians 9:1b
    1 Corinthians 9:1c
    1 Corinthians 9:1d
    1 Corinthians 9:4
    1 Corinthians 9:5
    1 Corinthians 9:6
    1 Corinthians 9:9
    1 Corinthians 9:10
    1 Corinthians 9:24
    1 Corinthians 10:16
    1 Corinthians 10:18
    1 Corinthians 10:19
    1 Corinthians 11:13
    1 Corinthians 11:14
    1 Corinthians 11:15
    1 Corinthians 12:29–30 (seven questions)
    2 Corinthians 11:7

2 Corinthians 12:17
2 Corinthians 12:18a
2 Corinthians 12:18b
Galatians 3:4
Galatians 4:16
1 Thessalonians 2:19b
2 Thessalonians 2:5

Analogies

Paul also used analogies to support his views. In an analogy, something unfamiliar is likened to a familiar or already accepted fact, thus encouraging the audience to accept the less familiar as readily as they have accepted its analogous counterpart.[7]

Similarities exist between Adam and Christ as Paul explained in his "just as . . . so also" sentences in Romans 5:19 and 21. His readers, acknowledging the consequences of one man's sin, would be led to accept the truth of righteousness and eternal life being made available through Christ. Just as priests are allowed to eat meat from animals sacrificed at the temple, so "in the same way" those who preach the gospel should receive financial support from those they serve (1 Cor. 9:13–14). In an analogous fashion, the one accepted premise calls for acceptance of the other.

A similarity and a contrast are simultaneously suggested in 1 Corinthians 11:12, "For as woman came from man, so also man is born of a woman." Though the nature and origins of man and woman differ, they are analogous in that male and female have, in a sense, originated from each other: Eve came from Adam, and every person since then has come from his or her mother's womb. In affirming his integrity, Paul stated that just as God is fruitful, so his own message was faithful and trustworthy (2 Cor. 1:18).

What comparative analogies did Paul make between Christ and believers in Romans 6:4; 2 Corinthians 1:5; and Colossians 3:13? What is the analogy between a man-made covenant and God's promises? (Gal. 3:15). How are sons in a home similar to spiritual children? (Gal. 4:2–3). In what ways are Hagar and Sarah analogous? (Gal. 4:22–31). What is the point of the analogy between wives and the church? (Eph. 5:24). What is the point of the analogy between husbands and Christ? (Eph.

---

7. An analogy uses an "as . . . so" pattern, whereas a simile uses the word "like" or "as" (e.g., "as servants of God," 2 Cor. 6:4), and a metaphor uses a form of the verb "to be" or "to become" (as in "you are God's field," 1 Cor. 3:9).

4:29). How were Jannes and Jambres in Moses' day like false teachers in Paul's day? (2 Tim. 3:8).

Inductions

In inductive reasoning a person argues from several observations or examples to a general conclusion. Based on certain premises, conclusions can be drawn. Paul introduced such premise-based conclusions with words such as "therefore," "consequently," "so then." He used this strategy numerous times in his writings, often as appeals for action based on truths previously presented.

The common Greek word for "therefore" or "then" is *oun*, used almost one hundred times by Paul. Not surprisingly, almost half that number are in Romans, a book in which the apostle used numerous means of logic to persuade his readers. Well-known examples are Romans 5:1 ("Therefore, since we have been justified through faith, we have peace with God through our Lord Jesus Christ"); and 12:1 ("Therefore, I urge you, brothers, in view of God's mercy, to offer your bodies as living sacrifices, holy and pleasing to God—this is your spiritual act of worship"). Whereas the New International Version often (twenty-two times) renders *oun* as "therefore," it more often (about thirty-five times) translates *oun* as "then" (e.g., 2:21; 3:1), occasionally (eleven times) as "so" (e.g., 11:5; 2 Tim. 1:8), twice as "so then" (1 Cor. 8:4; Col. 2:6), and once as "now" (1 Tim. 3:2). *Oun* is not translated at all in the New International Version in twenty-five of its occurrences.[8]

A stronger inferential word in Greek is *ara*, which occurs twenty-seven times in the Pauline Epistles. It too is variously translated: "so" (Rom. 7:21; 2 Cor. 7:12), "therefore" (Rom. 8:1), "consequently" (10:17), "otherwise" (1 Cor. 7:14), "then" (1 Cor. 15:15, 18; Gal. 3:7, 29), and "in that case" (Gal. 5:11).[9] *Ara* introduces the logical result or consequence or what was previously asserted.[10]

Twelve times an even stronger inference is indicated by combining *ara* and *oun*. The New International Version renders this combination in three ways: "so then" (Rom. 7:3, 25; 14:12; 1 Thess. 5:6; 2 Thess. 2:15),

8. These are Romans 2:26; 4:9, 10; 5:9, 10; 6:21; 11:11, 13; 14:16; 1 Corinthians 3:5; 6:7; 7:26; 9:25; 11:20; 16:18; 2 Corinthians 1:17; 7:1; Galatians 3:5; 4:15; Philippians 2:1, 29; 3:15; 1 Thessalonians 4:1; 1 Timothy 2:8; and 2 Timothy 2:21.

9. Several times it too is not translated in the NIV (1 Cor. 5:10; 15:14; 2 Cor. 1:17; 5:15; Gal. 2:21).

10. Walter Bauer, William F. Arndt, and F. Wilbur Gingrich, *A Greek-English Lexicon of the New Testament and Other Early Christian Literature*, 2d ed., rev. F. Wilbur Gingrich and Frederick W. Danker (Chicago: University of Chicago Press, 1979), 103–4.

"consequently" (Rom. 5:18; Eph. 2:19), and "therefore" (Rom. 8:12; 9:16, 18; 14:19; Gal. 6:10).

Another variation of *oun* is the Greek *toigaroun,* used only twice in the New Testament (1 Thess. 4:8 and Heb. 12:1). It marks an emphatic conclusion based on what was previously discussed and may be rendered "for that very reason."[11] In view of the fact that it is God who has called believers to lead a holy life, it is emphatically clear, Paul wrote, that to reject his instructions about purity is to reject not man, but God.

Another word introducing consequential sentences is *dio,* "wherefore, therefore, for this reason," which Paul used twenty-six times (e.g., Rom. 1:24; 3:1; 1 Cor. 14:3; 2 Cor. 5:9; Eph. 2:11; 1 Thess. 5:11).[12] A variation of *dio* is *dioper,* "therefore," used only twice in the New Testament, both times by Paul (1 Cor. 8:13; 10:14). Two other related words that suggest a logical induction are *dia touto,* "on account of this, therefore, for this reason";[13] *hōste,* "so, therefore;"[14] *houtōs,* "so, hence" ("that is why," Rom. 1:15; "in the same way," 6:11), and *toinyn,* "hence, therefore," which Paul used once (1 Cor. 9:26).

These many instances of conclusions inferred from previously stated premises firmly demonstrate Paul's ability to argue with deductive reasoning. Unquestionably, his epistles "bristle with complex, passionate arguments."[15]

Explanations

Paul backed up many of his scores of injunctions and exhortations with reasons. These explanations helped motivate his readers to follow his imperatives. Other times he gave logical reasons or explanations for truths presented. These explanatory statements are often introduced by the words "because" or "for."[16]

---

11. Ibid., 821; cf. Fritz Rienecker, *A Linguistic Key to the Greek New Testament,* ed. Cleon L. Rogers, Jr. (Grand Rapids: Zondervan, 1980), 713.

12. *Dio* usually designates a self-evident inference (Bauer, Arndt, and Gingrich, *A Greek-English Lexicon of the New Testament and Other Early Christian Literature,* 198).

13. *Dia touto,* occurring twenty-one times, is rendered by the NIV as "therefore" (Rom. 4:16; 5:12; 15:9; 2 Cor. 4:1; Eph. 5:17; 6:13; 1 Thess. 3:7; 2 Tim. 3:10), "for this reason" (1 Cor. 4:17; 11:10; Eph. 1:15; Col. 1:9; 1 Thess. 3:5; 2 Thess. 2:11), and a few similar terms.

14. *Hōste,* in an inferential sense, was used by Paul twenty-four times, most often in 1 and 2 Corinthians. One of the better known occurrences of *hōste* is in 1 Corinthians 15:58; "Therefore [*hōste*], my dear brothers, stand firm. Let nothing move you. Always give yourselves fully to the work of the Lord. . . . " These admonitions flow from the truth of the resurrection of the body which Paul discussed in 15:12–57.

15. Neil Asher Silberman, "The World of Paul," *Archaeology* 49 (November/December 1996): 30.

References	The Facts	The Explanations
Romans 8:1–2	There is no condemnation for believers in Christ.	Why? Because the Holy Spirit has set them free from sin and death.
Romans 8:6–7	The mind of sinful man is death.	Why? Because the sinful mind is hostile to God.
Romans 8:12–13a	We are not to live according to the sinful nature.	
Romans 8:13b–14		
Romans 8:19–20		
Romans 8:23–24		
Romans 14:10		
Romans 14:16–17		
Romans 15:2–3		
Romans 16:17b–18		
Ephesians 5:6		
Ephesians 5:8a–9		
Ephesians 6:1		

For a challenging study, read through Paul's epistles, noting every explanation or reason he stated and the truth or command it supports. Beginning with a shorter epistle, such as 1 Thessalonians or 1 Timothy, may be a helpful way to carry out this project.[17]

16. The Greek *gar* occurs over three hundred times in Paul's epistles, with more than a third of them in Romans. Occasionally Paul omitted "because" and "for," and simply declared the reason. For example, after urging the Philippians to put into practice what he had taught them, he wrote, "And the God of peace will be with you" (Phil. 4:9).

17. As discussed earlier (see n. 13), the phrase *dia touto* occurs twenty-one times in Paul's writings to point to an inference. It is also used several times to introduce an explanation. In these instances the NIV translates it "this is why" (Rom. 13:6; 2 Cor. 13:10), "that is why" (1 Cor. 11:30), "by all this" (2 Cor. 7:13), and "because of such" (Eph. 5:6).

Diatribes

Perhaps in your teaching you have presented a viewpoint, expounded a doctrinal truth, or suggested an idea, only to have one or more students say they disagree. Or perhaps you have discovered in class discussion that some students have drawn the wrong conclusions from what you have been teaching. So you needed to take time to correct the objections and to clarify the false assumptions.

Another way, however, to deal with this kind of student response in class is to anticipate their objections or faulty responses and to voice them yourself in your presentation. Presenting an imaginary dialogue in which you pose questions students may ask, and then you answer them is called diatribe.[18]

Including in your lectures a hypothetical exchange between two persons with opposing viewpoints—yourself and an imaginary student— helps lead students to draw correct conclusions and to be persuaded of your view,[19] while at the same time enhancing student interest.

Paul used the diatribe a number of times in some of his epistles, notably Romans. This is not surprising, since this was a common form of teaching for several centuries before Paul as well as during his day. Several philosophers, for example, often used this pedagogical technique, including Bion, Teles, Cicero (106–43 B.C.), Seneca (4 B.C.–A.D. 65), the Jewish philosopher Philo (ca. 13 B.C.–A.D. 45), Plutarch (A.D. 46–?110), the Stoic Musonius Rufus and his student Epictetus (ca. A.D. 55–ca. 135), Dio Chrysostom, and Hermogenes, orator of the second century A.D.[20] Any traveler in the Greco-Roman world would know of the dia-

18. E. W. Bullinger calls it dialogue (*Figures of Speech Used in the Bible* [London: Eyre and Spottiswoode, 1898; reprint, Grand Rapids: Baker, 1968], 898–99).

19. Eduard Lohse, *The New Testament Environment*, trans. John E. Steely (Nashville: Abingdon, 1976), 247.

20. Stanley K. Stowers, "The Diatribe," in *Greco-Roman Literature and the New Testament*, ed. David E. Aune (Atlanta: Scholars, 1988), 48–78; Abraham J. Malherbe, "*Mē Genoito* in the Diatribe and Paul," *Harvard Theological Review* 73 (1980): 231; and George C. Kustas, *Diatribe in Ancient Rhetorical Theory* (Berkeley, Calif.: Center for Hermeneutical Studies in Hellenistic and Modern Culture, 1976), 5, 7, 9. Diatribe was also used by Menander (343–291 B.C.), the Greek playwright (ibid., 10, 12), whom Paul quoted in 1 Corinthians 15:33 from Menander's *Thais* 218. Menander's writings were highly regarded in Paul's day (Abraham J. Malherbe, " 'The Beasts at Ephesus,'" *Journal of Biblical Literature* 87 [1968]: 73).

The anonymous *Rhetorica ad Herennium* (ca. 80 B.C.) also refers to the "hypothetical dialogue" in rhetoric (4.52.65). For examples of the Stoic use of the diatribe see excerpts from Epictetus's discourse on anxiety (*Discourses* 2.13) in Stowers, "The Diatribe," 76–80. For other examples, see idem, *The Diatribe and Paul's Letter to the Romans*, 86–118.

tribe, for "schools often operated in public view, a teacher gathering a circle of students in a market, gymnasium, or stoa."[21]

However, Paul's use of the diatribe in his epistles did not follow the style of wandering Cynic-like street preachers, with their polemical harangues. Instead, his diatribes followed the pedagogical style philosophers used in their schools.[22] His exchanges exhibit "not two enemies arguing, but a teacher leading his students to the truth."[23]

Rather than slavishly following the diatribe of Greco-Roman teachers and writers, Paul adapted it to his congregations. He posed questions to an imaginary interlocutor and/or he put hypothetical questions in the mouth of an alleged questioner; he responded to the fictitious discussion partner with terse answers (often with *mē genoito*, "by no means!") and often with reasons for his responses; and sometimes he addressed the questioner with a derogatory epithet. Epictetus, known for his use of diatribes in his *Discourses*, and Paul are similar in their employment of the diatribe, but Paul raised and answered false conclusions more often than did Epictetus.[24] These false conclusions, placed in the mouth of an imaginary student, often arose when his argumentation reached a significant point from which some readers might draw wrong inferences. Then he rejected those inferences and told why. In this way he sought to offset possible misunderstandings and objections and to clarify the truth. His diatribes, typical of most diatribal writings, include rhetorical questions,[25] quotations from other writings to support his responses, irony, and personification.

Another feature of the diatribe the apostle used in Romans is the figure of speech known as apostrophe, in which an individual(s) is addressed as "you" as if he were present. In using the apostrophe Paul seemed to stop addressing the recipients of the letter as a whole and wrote as if he were addressing an individual. He spoke directly to an imaginary person who criticized others for what he himself did (Rom.

21. Stowers, "The Diatribe," 81.

22. Ibid., 73; and idem, *The Diatribe and Paul's Letters to the Romans* (Chicago, Calif.: Scholars, 1981), 175.

23. *The Diatribe and Paul's Letter to the Romans,* 165, 174–75, 177. "The body of Romans is written in the style he would use in teaching a group of Christians" (ibid., 182). "The dialogical style of Romans is evidence for what might best be described as Paul's 'school'" (ibid., 183). In the Book of Romans he was teaching Roman believers, not engaging in argumentation against Judaism (Duane F. Watson, "Diatribe," in *Dictionary of Paul and His Letters,* ed. Gerald F. Hawthorne, Ralph P. Martin, and Daniel G. Reid [Downers Grove, Ill.: InterVarsity, 1993], 214).

24. Stowers, *The Diatribe and Paul's Letter to the Romans,* 148.

25. See chapter 11 on Paul's use of questions.

2:1–5), to a Jewish believer boasting of his superiority over Gentiles (2:17–29), a person who questioned God's sovereignty (9:19–21), a Gentile believer, pictured as a wild olive tree branch, who boasted of his superiority over the Jews (11:17–24), and a believer who criticizes another Christian (14:4, 10).[26] Paul answered the Jewish boaster of 2:17–29 in 3:1–9 and 3:27–4:2.[27] By using the apostrophe, Paul's indictments were made more personal and thus more stinging in their impact.

Table 20 demonstrates Paul's several uses of the diatribe in fifteen passages, twelve of which are in Romans.

Table 20
Paul's Diatribes

References	Preceding Premises	False Conclusions	Initial Brief Responses	Reason for Rejections
Romans 2:1–5	All humanity is depraved and condemned (1:24–31).	"Do you[a] think you will escape God's judgment?" (2:3). Don't you realize the point of God's kindness? (2:4).	Wrath will come on you (v. 5).	God will reward people in accord with their deeds (v. 6).[b]
Romans 3:1–9	A person is not a Jew simply because he is circumcised (2:28–29).	Is there no advantage to being a Jew, or to being circumcised? (3:1).	"Much in every way!" (v. 2).	The Jews have the words of God (v. 2).
		Will lack of faith annul God's faithfulness? (v. 3).	"Not at all! [*mē genoito*]" [c] (v. 4).	God is the one who is true (v. 4).[b]
		Does our unrighteousness mean God is unjust? (v. 5).	"Certainly not! [*mē genoito*]" (v. 6).	Then God could not judge the world (v. 6).[b]

26. Stowers, *The Diatribe and Paul's Letter to the Romans*, 79–81.

27. Stowers, "The Diatribe," 81; and Watson, "Diatribe," 214.

		Does falsehood mean God is unfair in condemning us? (v. 7). Why not sin so that good may result? (v. 8).	"Their condemnation is deserved" (v. 8).	
		Are Jews better? (v. 9).	"Not at all! [*oupantōs*]" (v. 9).	All are "under sin" (v. 9).[b]
Romans 3:31	God justifies both Jews and Gentiles who believe, apart from the law (3:28–30).	Does faith nullify the law?	"Not at all! [*mē genoito*]."	Instead, the law is upheld.
Romans 6:1–3	Where sin increased, grace abounded even more (5:20–21).	Shall we sin so grace may increase? (6:1).	"By no means! [*mē genoito*]" (v. 2a).	How can we live in sin, to which we have died? Don't you know we were all baptized into Christ? (vv. 2b–3).
Romans 6:15–16	You are under grace, not law (6:14).	Shall we sin? (v. 15).	"By no means! [*mē genoito*]" (v. 15).	Don't you know that you are slaves to whom you offer yourselves? (v 16).
Romans 7:7	The law aroused sinful passions (7:5–6).	"Is the law sin?"	"Certainly not! [*mē genoito*]."	The law brings the knowledge of sin.
Romans 7:13	The law is holy (7:12).	Did something good lead to death?	"By no means! [*mē genoito*]."	The law made sin "utterly sinful."
Romans 9:14–15	God loved Jacob and hated Esau (9:13).	"Is God unjust?" (v. 14).	"Not at all! [*mē genoito*]" (v. 14).	God can bestow mercy on whom he wishes (v. 15).[b]

Romans 9:19–21	God has mercy on whom he wishes (9:18).	Why does God blame us? (v. 19).	"Who are you, O man [*ō anthrōpe*], to talk back to God?" (v. 20).	An object has no right to complain to its maker (vv. 20–21).[b]
Romans 11:1–5	Israel is disobedient and obstinate (10:21).	"Did God reject his people?" (11:1).	"By no means! [*mē genoito*]" (v. 1).	Paul's own experience (v. 1), God's foreknowledge of his people (v. 2), Elijah's experience (vv. 2b–4),[b] and the fact of a present remnant (v. 5) show that God has not rejected Israel.
Romans 11:11–12	Israel was hardened against God (11:7–10).	Did Israel fall beyond recovery? (11:11).	"Not at all! [*mē genoito*]" (v. 11a).	Salvation has come to Gentiles and Israel will be enriched (vv. 11b–12).
Romans 11:19–21	You, a branch, are supported by the roots (11:18).	But the broken branches (Israel) enabled Gentiles to be grafted in (saved, v. 19).	"Granted" (v. 20). Israel's rejection of Christ is admitted (v. 20a).	Since the reason for Israel's fall is unbelief, Gentile Christians should not be arrogant (vv. 20b–21).
1 Corinthians 6:15b–16	Believers' bodies are members of Christ (6:15a).	Shall we unite the members of Christ with a prostitute? (v. 15b).	"Never!" [*mē genoito*]. (v. 15c)	To unite with a prostitute is to become one with her in body (v. 16).
1 Corinthians 15:35–44	The dead will be resurrected (15:12–34).	How are the dead raised? (v. 35).	"How foolish!" (v. 36a).	What is sown differs from what comes to life from the seed (vv. 36b–44).

Galatians 2:17–21	Justification is by faith, not by law keeping (2:15–16).	Does Christ promote sin? (v. 17).	"Absolutely not! [*mē genoito*]" (v. 17).	We are to live for God, not the law (vv. 18–21).
Galatians 3:21–22	Salvation depends on God's promise, not the law (3:15–20).	Does the law oppose God's promises? (v. 21).	"Absolutely not! [*mē genoito*]" (v. 21a).	The law and God's promises have different purposes (vv. 21b–22).

a. Changing abruptly to the second person singular, Paul used "you," "yourself," and "your" fourteen times in five verses! Also Romans 2:1, 3 each have the derogatory epithet *ō anthrōpe* (lit., "O man"), though the NIV does not translate it in verse 1, and renders it "mere man" in verse 3. *Ō anthrōpe* also occurs in Romans 9:20. Other writers who used this same form of address in their diatribes include Plutarch, Dio Chrysostom, and especially Epictetus (Stowers, *The Diatribe and Paul's Letters to the Romans*, 93).

b. This symbol "b" is added in this table each time Paul cited Scripture in support of his rejection of the false conclusion.

c. Of the diatribal authors, only Epictetus used *mē genoito* (ibid., 130). He used it twenty-five times in his *Dissertations* (Malherbe, "Mē Genoito in the Diatribe and Paul," 232, n. 8). Other rejection phrases used by Greek diatribal writers include *oudamōs* ("by no means"), *ou pantōs* ("not at all"), *ou ma dia* ("indeed not"), or *minime* ("by no means") (ibid., 231).

As seen in the table, the false conclusions that are put in the mouth of imaginary respondents follow after the development of major theological treatises. The questions addressed in apostrophe to imaginary individuals raise potential misconceptions about the apostle's teaching. Then Paul responded to the objections or erroneous conclusions, first by brief exclamations that deny the deviant thinking, and then by additional argumentation in support of his initial response. Sometimes Paul buttressed the added support by one or more quotations from the Old Testament. This teaching tactic was a clever way of developing the doctrines he addressed. The diatribe, a pedagogical tool familiar to his readers from classical writers, would have had a dramatic impact on Paul's initial readers. "A sudden turning to an imaginary interlocutor, indictments, rhetorical questions, exclamations, strong statements of rejection—these are powerful literary and rhetorical tools!"[28]

28. James L. Bailey and Lyle D. Vander Broek, *Literary Forms in the New Testament* (Louisville: Westminster/Knox, 1992), 40.

Quotations

Quotations from Secular Greek Writers

As already noted, Paul often quoted the Old Testament to document and augment his own teaching. In addition he cited four quotations from Greek writers. "In him we live and move and have our being" (Acts 17:28a) is from Epimenides, the sixth-century poet of Crete, in his *Cretica*. By this quotation Paul added logical support to the point in his previous sentence (17:27) that though God is the transcendent Creator (17:24–26) he is also imminent and therefore "not far from each of us." "We are his offspring" (Acts 17:28b) comes from the poet Aratus (ca. 315–240 B.C.) in his *Phaenomena*, as well as from Cleanthes (331–233 B.C.) in his *Hymn to Zeus*. Paul cited this sentence in order to set forth the logical conclusion in the next sentence (17:29) that God is not a man-made image. Man is made by God, not God by man! By citing these writings known and appreciated by the Athenians, and with which they would be in agreement, Paul cleverly led his hearers on Mars' Hill to accept his own affirmations more easily. Of course, he was not endorsing everything these Greek poets wrote; he simply selected these sentences from their writings because those statements, well known to his audience, were useful in his sermon.

"Bad company corrupts good character" (1 Cor. 15:33) quotes the Greek dramatist Menander in his comedy *Thais*. Recognizing and agreeing with this proverbial statement, the Corinthians were influenced by Paul to acknowledge that those who denied the resurrection were "bad company" who would corrupt the "good character" of those who believed the doctrine of the resurrection. Writing to Titus on the island of Crete, Paul again quoted Epimenides, who had written "Cretans are always liars, evil brutes, lazy gluttons" (Titus 1:12). Thus Paul verified his denunciation of false teachers in Crete by a quote from a Cretan writer!

Quotations from the Old Testament

To support an assertion, to lead to a conclusion, to illustrate a point—these are also some of the reasons Paul quoted from the Old Testament. Paul's extensive quoting from the Old Testament is seen in the fact that he wrote about one-third of the almost three hundred Old Testament quotations in the New Testament. The exact number is difficult to determine because ancient writings did not have quotation marks to mark the beginnings and endings of citations, some quotations alter the wording, and some are strung together, thus making it difficult to know how many to count as quotations.

Nicole suggests a total of 295 separate quotations of the Old Testament in the New,[29] and the New International Version has 296 footnote references to Old Testament citations.[30] Bratcher observes that these occur in twenty-three of the twenty-seven New Testament books—all except Philemon and 1, 2, and 3 John.[31]

Writers differ in their listing of the number of Old Testament quotations in the Pauline letters.[32] Some citations viewed by some writers as quotations are seen by others as allusions or indirect references. For example, some authors include Romans 9:20 as a quotation of Isaiah 29:16 and 45:9, whereas others say it is an allusion.[33] If Silva's list of ninety-seven Pauline quotations of the Old Testament is accepted (excluding ten others he lists as "debated"[34]) then ten Pauline books cite passages from seventeen Old Testament books. More than half of Paul's quotations are in Romans (fifty-five out of ninety-seven), and the books he most frequently quoted are Isaiah (twenty-four times) and Psalms (twenty times). Next in order are Genesis (cited fifteen times) and Deuteronomy (thirteen times). As Silva notes in his chart of Paul's quotations, the apostle frequently (fifty-nine times) quoted from the Septuagint, the Greek translation of the Old Testament, which was in common use in New Testament times. The wording of seven of Paul's quotations accords with the Hebrew wording rather

29. Roger Nicole, "The Old Testament in the New Testament," in *The Expositor's Bible Commentary* (Grand Rapids: Zondervan, 1979), 1:617.

30. Ronald J. Youngblood, "Old Testament Quotations in the New Testament," in *The NIV: The Making of a Contemporary Translation*, ed. Kenneth L. Barker (Grand Rapids: Zondervan, 1986), 113. Samuel Davidson, however, gave the total as 255 (*Sacred Hermeneutics* [Edinburgh: Clark, 1843], 446).

31. Robert G. Bratcher, ed., *Old Testament Quotations in the New Testament*, 3d ed. (New York: United Bible Societies, 1987), v.

32. Longenecker lists 83, Ellis 93, Bonsirven 95, Silva 97, Turpie 101, Archer and Chirichigno 106, Toy 127, and Bratcher 132 (Longenecker, *Biblical Exegesis in the Apostolic Period*, 107–11; Ellis, *Paul's Use of the Old Testament*, 11, 150–52; Joseph Bonsirven, *Exégèse Rabbinique et Exégèse Paulinienne* [Paris: Beauchesne, 1934], 277–80; Moisés Silva, "Old Testament in Paul," in *Dictionary of Paul and His Letters*, 631; David McCalman Turpie, *The New Testament View of the Old* [London: Hodder and Stoughton, 1872], 4–5, 15–19; Gleason L. Archer and Gregory Chirichigno, *Old Testament Quotations in the New Testament* [Chicago: Moody, 1983], xx–xxi; Crawford Howell Toy, *Quotations in the New Testament* [New York: Scribner's Sons, 1884], 289–92; and Bratcher, *Old Testament Quotations in the New Testament*, 35–36).

33. Examples of the many allusions are Romans 5:12–14 on Adam's sin, 1 Corinthians 10:1–15 with references to Israel's disobedience, and Galatians 4:21–31 on Hagar and Sarah and their sons (Longenecker, *Biblical Exegesis in the Apostolic Period*, 111).

34. Silva, "Old Testament in Paul," 631.

than the Septuagint, and in thirty-one other cases his wording differs from both.[35]

A feature in many of Paul's quotations is his clustering of citations from various parts of the Old Testament. This "pearl stringing," as Longenecker calls it, also characterized rabbinic teaching.[36] Clusters of three or more quotes occur in Romans 3:10–18; 9:12–13, 25–29; 10:18–21; 11:8–10; 15:9–12; 2 Corinthians 6:16–18; and Galatians 3:10–13. In six other places Paul combined two quotations, one after the other: Romans 4:17–18; 9:33; 11:26–27; 12:19–20; 1 Corinthians 3:19–20; 15:54–55.

Paul introduced these many quotations in a variety of ways: "as it is written," "it is written," "the Scripture says."[37] Four times he added "says the Lord" (Rom. 12:19; 1 Cor. 14:21; 2 Cor. 6:17–18). Paul pointed to human authors of Old Testament books by "David says" (Rom. 4:6; 11:9), "Moses describes" (10:5), "Moses says" (10:19), "Isaiah cries out" (9:27), "Isaiah said" (9:29), "Isaiah says" (10:16, 20; 15:12). And Paul acknowledged the divine nature of the Old Testament by writing "he [God] says" (9:15, 25; 2 Cor. 6:2) and "as God said" (6:16). Many times he simply quoted an Old Testament passage without any introductory formula (e.g., Rom. 10:13; 11:34; 1 Cor. 2:16). Clearly Paul viewed the Old Testament as originating from God and thus divinely authoritative. The most frequent reason he cited Old Testament Scriptures was to validate truths he was presenting. These citations showed that what he was writing was verified by and in full accord with the Old Testament and therefore, like the Old Testament, his writings should be accepted as from God.

---

35. For a summary of the kinds of grammatical variations in New Testament quotations of the Old, see Roy B. Zuck, *Basic Bible Interpretation* (Wheaton, Ill.: Victor, 1991), 254–57; and Bullinger, *Figures of Speech Used in the Bible*, 792–97. Yet in spite of those variations, Paul certainly was not careless in quoting the Scriptures (Silva, "Old Testament in Paul," 640–41, Christopher D. Stanley, *Paul and the Language of Scripture* [Cambridge: University Press, 1992], 359–60). Roger Nicole suggests several principles to keep in mind regarding the New Testament writers' quotations from the Old Testament: they had to translate their quotations; they did not have the same rules for quotations as are nowadays enforced in works of a scientific character; they sometimes paraphrased their quotations; they often simply alluded to Old Testament passages without intending to quote them; they sometimes recorded quotations made by others ("New Testament Use of the Old," in *Revelation and the Bible*, ed. Carl F. H. Henry [Grand Rapids: Baker, 1958], 142–47).

36. Longenecker, *Biblical Exegesis in the Apostolic Period*, 115.

37. "As it is written" occurs twenty times (Rom. 1:17; 2:24; 3:4, 10; 4:17; 8:36; 9:13, 33; 10:15; 11:8, 26; 15:3, 9, 21; 1 Cor. 1:31; 2:9; 3:19; 10:7; 2 Cor. 8:15; 9:9). Paul used the clause "it is written" eleven times (Rom. 12:19; 14:11; 1 Cor. 1:19; 9:9; 14:21; 15:45; 2 Cor. 4:13; Gal. 3:10, 13; 4:22, 27), and "the Scripture says" seven times (Rom. 4:3; 10:11; 11:2; Gal. 3:16, 22; 4:30; 1 Tim. 5:18).

A few examples of Paul's many cases of substantiating his arguments from the Old Testament are these:

Romans 1:17	Habakkuk 2:4
Romans 2:24	Isaiah 52:5
Romans 3:4	Psalm 51:4
Romans 4:3	Genesis 15:6
Romans 9:15	Exodus 33:19
Romans 9:33	Isaiah 8:14; 28:16
Romans 10:11	Isaiah 28:16
Romans 10:16	Isaiah 53:1
Romans 14:11	Isaiah 45:23
Romans 15:9–12	Deuteronomy 32:43; Psalms 18:49; 117:1; Isaiah 11:10
1 Corinthians 1:19	Isaiah 29:14
1 Corinthians 3:19	Job 5:13
Galatians 3:6	Genesis 15:6
Galatians 3:8	Genesis 12:3; 18:18; 22:18
Galatians 3:10	Deuteronomy 27:26
Galatians 3:11	Habakkuk 2:4
Galatians 3:12	Leviticus 18:5
Galatians 3:13	Deuteronomy 21:23
2 Timothy 2:19a	Numbers 16:5

In a number of verses in which Paul's citations support his principles, he modified the quotation from its original setting to relate it to a new situation. Psalm 69:9 refers to David, but in citing it in Romans 15:3, Paul related it to Christ. What was true of David, the apostle argued, was also true of Christ. Psalm 44:22, written about Israel, was applied in Romans 8:36 to church-age believers. Isaiah 10:22–23 discusses Israel's future believing remnant and God's judgment, and Paul quoted these verses in Romans 9:27–28 to support his argument that God has a believing remnant "not only from the Jews but also from the Gentiles" (9:24). What Moses said to Israel in Deuteronomy 30:12–14 about God's word being available to them so that they need only ask for someone to go to heaven or across the sea to bring it to them was applied to the gospel in Romans 10:6–8. The "voice" of natural creation testifying of God's glory (Ps. 19:4) was accommodated by Paul to refer to special revelation (Rom. 10:18). In 2 Corinthians 4:13 Paul applied to himself what an anonymous psalmist said about believing and therefore speaking (Ps. 116:10). Other examples of Paul's modifying an Old Testament verse(s) to a different situation, but following the same general principle, are these: Romans 10:20–21; 15:3, 21; 1 Corinthians 5:13; 6:16; 10:26; 14:21; 2 Corinthians 6:16–18; 8:15; 9:9; 13:1.

Another reason Paul cited Scripture was to explain what the passages did or did not mean. This is evident in 1 Corinthians 9:9, which quotes Moses' injunction against muzzling an ox (Deut. 25:4), and 1 Corinthians 15:27, in which Paul explained Psalm 8:6 (he "has put everything under his feet"). Similar to this purpose are Paul's citations to point out contrasts, as in 1 Corinthians 2:9 (no one knows what God has prepared for those who love him [Isa. 64:4], but, by contrast, the Holy Spirit has revealed it [1 Cor. 2:10]), and Galatians 3:12 (the basis of the law is not faith, but actions, Lev. 18:5).

Another reason Paul cited Old Testament verses was simply to "borrow" the language. In 1 Corinthians 15:32b Paul could have written, "If there is no future resurrection, then people may as well live for selfish pleasure." Instead he cited Isaiah 22:13, "Let us eat and drink for tomorrow we die." These familiar words no doubt added to the impact of Paul's argument.

Still another purpose in Pauline quotations was to state a principle from the Old Testament (e.g., God "will give to each person according to what he has done," Rom. 2:6 citing Ps. 62:12) in order to then designate some specifics that spell out the principle (as in Rom. 2:7–10).

Another of Paul's purposes was to cite an Old Testament historical incident to support the truth he presented. For example, God's answer to Elijah about a believing remnant illustrates the apostle's point that God has not rejected his people (Rom. 11:1–5).[38]

References to and Possible Echoes of Jesus' Sayings

The fact that Paul seldom quoted Jesus' words seems strange in light of the fact that the apostle's teachings and attitudes align so closely with those of Jesus.[39] Yet on a number of occasions Paul's words do seem to

---

38. Bailey and Vander Broek point out that in Galatians 3:6–9 Paul developed a theme by referring to several Scripture passages and commenting on them in an alternating pattern. Galatians 3:6 refers to Genesis 15:6, and Galatians 3:7 relates it to those who have faith. Galatians 3:8 cites Genesis 12:3, and Galatians 3:9 comments on it. The same alternation between citation and explanation is given on two different themes in Galatians 3:10–14 and 3:15–18 (*Literary Forms in the New Testament*, 43).

39. Seyoon Kim, "Jesus, Sayings of," in *Dictionary of Paul and His Letters*, 474.

reflect Jesus' words, even though they are not direct quotations. Six times Paul referred to the words of the Lord: 1 Corinthians 7:10 ("I give this command [not I, but the Lord]"); 9:14 ("the Lord has commanded"); 11:24–25 ("he said . . . he took the cup, saying"); 14:37 ("what I am writing to you is the Lord's command"); 2 Corinthians 12:9 ("he said to me"); 1 Thessalonians 4:15 ("according to the Lord's own word"). Probably Paul's only explicit quotation of Jesus is recorded in Acts 20:35, where Paul told the Ephesian elders to remember Jesus' words, "It is more blessed to give than to receive."

Additional allusions, not quotations, to Jesus' sayings, in which Paul's words seem dependent on Jesus' words, are evident in the passages listed in table 21.

Table 21
Paul's Allusions to Jesus' Sayings

Paul's Words	Reference in the Gospels
"Bless those who persecute you; bless and do not curse" (Rom. 12:14).	Matthew 5:44
"Do not repay anyone evil for evil" (Rom. 12:17).	Matthew 5:39–42
"If it is possible, as far as it depends on you, live at peace with everyone" (Rom. 12:18).	Matthew 5:9
"Do not be overcome by evil, but overcome evil with good" (Rom. 12:21).	Matthew 5:43–44
"Give everyone what you owe him: If you owe taxes, pay taxes; if revenue, then revenue; if respect, then respect; if honor, then honor" (Rom. 13:7).	Matthew 22:15–21
"Let no debt remain outstanding, except the continuing debt to love one another, for he who loves his fellow man has fulfilled the law" (Rom. 13:8).	Matthew 22:37–40
"You then, why do you judge your brother? Or why do you look down on your brother? For we will all stand before God's judgment seat" (Rom. 14:10).	Matthew 7:1
"No food is unclean in itself" (Rom. 14:14).	Matthew 15:11
"When we are cursed, we bless; when we are persecuted, we endure it; when we are slandered, we answer kindly" (1 Cor. 4:12b–13a).	Matthew 5:11–12
"Put to death, therefore, whatever belongs to your earthly nature: sexual immorality, impurity, lust, evil desires and greed, which is idolatry" (Col. 3:5).	Matthew 5:29–30; 18:8–9

"Bear with each other and forgive whatever grievances you may have against one another. Forgive as the Lord forgave you" (Col. 3:13).	Matthew 6:12
"Devote yourselves to prayer, being watchful and thankful" (Col. 4:2).	Matthew 26:41
"Let your conversation be always full of grace, seasoned with salt, so that you may know how to answer everyone" (Col. 4:6).	Matthew 5:13
"Therefore, he who rejects this instruction does not reject man but God, who gives you his Holy Spirit" (1 Thess. 4:8).	Luke 10:16
"For you know very well that the day of the Lord will come like a thief in the night" (1 Thess. 5:2).	Matthew 24:32
"While people are saying, 'Peace and safety,' destruction will come on them suddenly, as labor pains on a pregnant woman, and they will not escape" (1 Thess. 5:3).	Luke 21:34
"So then, let us not be like others, who are asleep, but let us be alert and self-controlled" (1 Thess. 5:6).	Matthew 24:42
"Live in peace with each other" (1 Thess. 5:13).	Mark 9:50b
"Make sure that nobody pays back wrong for wrong, but always try to be kind to each other and to everyone else" (1 Thess. 5:15).	Matthew 5:39–44

In addition to these allusions, possibly made consciously by Paul, he may have also echoed Jesus' words, several times unconsciously. Kim lists thirty-one such echoes in nine of Paul's epistles.[40] However, they do not show direct dependence on Jesus' sayings, and they are more disputed than the allusions listed in table 21. Scholars differ on both the number of allusions and echoes.[41] Yet it is clear that Paul was "steeped in the mind and words of his Lord."[42]

40. Ibid., 481.

41. For discussions on this subject, see W. D. Davies, *Paul and Rabbinic Judaism: Some Rabbinic Elements in Pauline Theology* (New York: Harper and Row, 1948), 137–42; Victor Paul Furnish, *Theology and Ethics of Paul* (Nashville: Abingdon, 1968), 51–65; David L. Dungan, *The Sayings of Jesus in the Churches of Paul* (Philadelphia: Fortress, 1971); F. F. Bruce, *Paul: Apostle of the Heart Set Free* (Grand Rapids: Eerdmans, 1977), 95–112; idem, *Paul and His Converts* (Downers Grove, Ill.: InterVarsity, 1985), 34–37; Dale C. Allison, Jr., "The Pauline Epistles and the Synoptic Gospels: The Pattern of the Parallels," *New Testament Studies* 28 (1982): 1–32; David Wenham, *The Rediscovery of Jesus' Eschatological Discourse*, Gospel Perspectives 4 (Sheffield: JSOT, 1984); idem, *Paul: Follower of Jesus or Founder of Christianity?* (Grand Rapids: Eerdmans, 1995), 380–408; Frans Neirynck, "Paul and the Sayings of Jesus," in *L' Apôtre Paul*, ed. A. Vanhoye (Leuven: University Press, 1986), 265–321; A. J. M. Wedderburn, "Paul and Jesus: The Problem of Continuity," in *Paul and Jesus*, ed. A. J. M. Wedderburn and C. Wolff (Sheffield: JSOT, 1989), 99–115; idem, "Paul and Jesus: Similarity and Continuity," in *Paul and Jesus*, 117–43; and Kim, "Jesus, Sayings of," 474–92.

42. Davies, *Paul and Rabbinic Judaism*, 140.

What does this all suggest for Bible teachers today? First, like Paul, we should be saturated with the Scriptures. We ought to know it so well that its wording comes to mind readily. Second, like Paul, we should use the Scriptures in our teaching to substantiate and verify our content, to explain what Scripture passages do or do not mean, or to cite a biblical principle in order then to elaborate on it with specific applications. Of course, teachers can draw on all sixty-six books of the Bible for these purposes, which are much more than what Paul had as his "Bible."

Think It Through . . .

As you hear sermons or class sessions, listen for the forms of logical reasoning discussed in this chapter. Then ask yourself, What impact did the use of these forms of reasoning make on you? How do you think they may have affected the listeners?

Analyze your own teaching in the light of these aspects of logic. Which of them have you used or could you use? As you use them in your teaching, note how they affect your students' understanding of the material.

How often do you support your teaching by citing other Scripture passages? Can you make more use of references to historical incidents in the Bible to buttress the points you are making?

"Since, then, we know what it is to fear the Lord, we try to persuade men."

2 Corinthians 5:11

15

How Did Paul Use Rhetorical Persuasion in His Teaching?

With which of the following statements would you agree?

"I think teachers are explainers. They are responsible for introducing new concepts, clarifying problems and issues, and explaining ideas."

"No, I think teachers are to be persuaders. Their task is to motivate students to take or avoid certain attitudes and actions, to convince learners of the propriety or impropriety of certain causes or issues."

Actually, both are correct. Effective teachers inform, explain, clarify, expound, and interpret. Then, based on ideas the students understand, effective teachers seek to move students to act on what they do, to change their course of action if necessary.

Paul's epistles abound with both explanation and exhortation. His theological ideas were impressive, and his persuasive influence was compelling. His profound ability, prompted by the Holy Spirit, influenced others through his writings, which followed certain patterns of rhetorical persuasion common in the Greco-Roman world. The art of

269

speaking or writing effectively, in order to persuade, is known as rhetoric. Bible teachers today can become more effective persuaders as they examine Paul's writings in light of classical rhetoric.

In classical Greek and Latin, several works became "handbooks" for instruction in rhetorical speech and writing. These include Aristotle's *The Art of Rhetoric* (mid-fourth century B.C.), the anonymous *Rhetorica ad Alexandrum* (early third century B.C.), Cicero's *On Inventions*, the anonymous *Rhetorica ad Herennium* (first century B.C.), and Quintilian's *On the Education of the Orator* (A.D. 92). Handbooks on writing style were fewer in number. One important work in existence before Paul's day was *On Style* (ca. first century B.C.). Instruction in the rhetoric of speech preparation included five aspects: invention (choosing the right subject and proofs), arrangement (outlining the material in the best sequence), style (utilizing figures of speech, appropriate grammar, and the right words), memory (memorizing the speech), and delivery (using one's voice, gestures, and pauses).[1] Of course, the first three aspects applied to writing material as well.

Today rhetoric often denotes style of delivery; but in Greece and Rome, rhetoric was broader, including all aspects of communication and especially the art of persuasion. As Aristotle wrote, rhetoric is "the faculty of discovering the possible means of persuasion."[2] As a tool for persuasion, rhetoric emphasized three factors: ethos, the speaker's moral character; pathos, emotions aroused in the hearers by the speech; and logos, logical arguments.[3]

Knowledge and use of rhetoric was not limited to sophisticated philosophers; it became commonplace among the Greco-Roman populace, as speeches were given in the marketplace, the gymnasium, and the theater. "To be engulfed in the culture of Hellenism meant to have ears trained for the rhetoric of speech."[4]

1. Burton L. Mack, *Rhetoric and the New Testament* (Minneapolis: Fortress, 1990), 31–34; and Philip E. Satterthwaite, "Acts against the Background of Classical Rhetoric," in *The Book of Acts in Its Ancient Literary Setting*, ed. Bruce W. Winter and Andrew W. Clarke (Grand Rapids: Eerdmans, 1993), 343–79.

2. Aristotle *The Art of Rhetoric* 1.2.1.

3. G. Walter Hansen, "Rhetorical Criticism," in *Dictionary of Paul and His Letters*, ed. Gerald F. Hawthorne, Ralph P. Martin, and Daniel G. Reid (Downers Grove, Ill.: InterVarsity, 1993), 822.

4. Mack, *Rhetoric and the New Testament*, 31. Also see these four works by George A. Kennedy: *The Act of Persuasion in Greece* (Princeton, N.J.: Princeton University Press, 1963); *The Art of Rhetoric in the Roman World, 300 B.C.–A.D. 300* (Princeton, N.J.: Princeton University Press, 1972); *Classical Rhetoric and Its Christian and Secular Tradition from Ancient to Modern Times* (Chapel Hill, N.C.: University of North Carolina Press, 1980); and *New Testament Interpretation through Rhetorical Criticism* (Chapel Hill, N.C.: University of North Carolina Press, 1984).

Was Paul Trained in Classical Rhetoric?

Since rhetoric was a public affair, and since the skill of rhetoric for speaking and writing[5] was taught in Greek and Roman schools, it is not surprising to find patterns of rhetorical composition evident in the New Testament, and especially in Paul's letters.

Not everyone, however, has believed that Paul was trained in or even knew of rhetorical techniques. Rudolf Bultmann, for example, wrote in 1910 that Paul did not consciously follow rhetorical principles in his epistles,[6] and a hundred years ago Orello Cone wrote that Paul "does not write like a man who has formed his style upon Greek models, and he certainly does not reason after the manner of a student of the Grecian philosophers."[7] Hans Conzelman maintained a similar view about Paul and Greek education.[8]

Current scholars, however, argue that Paul did in fact consciously use a number of rhetorical devices;[9] some writers even suggest he may have been schooled in rhetoric. Since Tarsus, Paul's birthplace, had "all kinds of schools of rhetoric,"[10] as the Greek geographer Strabo (64 B.C.– A.D. 23) wrote, Paul may have had some formal educational training in rhetorical patterns.

5. Malherbe has shown that instruction in letter writing was part of the curriculum of grammar schools in the early Greek Empire (Abraham J. Malherbe, "Ancient Epistolary Theorists," *Ohio Journal of Religious Studies* 5 [October 1977]: 12–15).

6. Cited by William Wuellner, "Greek Rhetoric and Pauline Argumentation," in *Early Christian Literature and the Classical Intellectual Tradition*, ed. William R. Schoedel and Robert L. Wilkin (Paris: Beauchesne, 1979), 178, n.8.

7. Orello Cone, *Paul, the Man, the Missionary, and the Teacher* (New York: Macmillan, 1898), 5.

8. Hans Conzelmann, *An Outline of the Theology of the New Testament*, trans. J. Bowden (London: SCM, 1909), 246.

9. For example, Christopher Forbes, "Comparison, Self Praise and Irony: Paul's Boasting and the Conventions of Hellenistic Rhetoric," *New Testament Studies* 32 (1986): 23; Peter Marshall, *Enmity in Corinth: Social Conventions in Paul's Relations with the Corinthians* (Tübingen: Mohr, 1987), 393; J. Paul Sampley, "Paul, His Opponents in 2 Corinthians 10–13, and the Rhetorical Handbooks," in *The Social World of Formative Christianity and Judaism*, ed. Jacob Neusner, Peder Borgen, Ernest S. Frerichs, and Richard Horsley (Philadelphia: Fortress, 1988), 162; and Edwin Yamauchi, *Harper's World of the New Testament* (San Francisco: Harper and Row, 1981), 101. Since Greek rhetorical figures in Paul "are far more abundant in his epistles than in other parts of the New Testament, and some are found in him alone, may we not conclude that as a boy in Tarsus he had attended some elementary class in Greek rhetoric, perhaps as a part of his education in the grammatical knowledge of the language?" (F. W. Farrar, *The Life and Work of St. Paul* [1902; reprint, Minneapolis: Klock & Klock, 1981], 1:630.

10. Strabo *Geography* 14.5.13–14.

Yet even if Paul was not formally trained in a Tarsian school of rhetoric, he could not have been ignorant of rhetoric. "The persuasive models of the classical, rhetorical handbooks were well known during Paul's day, and one did not have to be formally trained in rhetoric to use them."[11] While it is unlikely that Paul, a Jew, was a trained Greek rhetorician like his Gentile contemporaries, he may well have been influenced by the use of rhetoric and oratory in the Greek culture all around him.[12]

Besides hearing speeches by itinerant street preachers, civil leaders, and dramatists, all of whom used rhetorical devices, Paul may have been introduced to basic aspects of rhetoric in his Jewish schooling. This may well have been the case since Greek culture, including Greek rhetoric, had been so assimilated by the Jews.[13] In the Diaspora and even in Palestine, Jewish education was strongly Hellenized.[14] Even the seven hermeneutical principles of Hillel, the well-known first-century Jewish rabbi, were derived from Hellenistic rhetorical theory.[15] Also, the fact that Paul spent more than ten years in Hellenized Tarsus, Cilicia, and Antioch (Acts 9:30; 11:25–26; 12:25–13:1; Gal. 1:21) after his conversion, before launching his missionary program,[16] means he

11. Peter O'Brien, "Letters, Letter Forms," in *Dictionary of Paul and His Letters*, 553. Cf. Jürgen Becker, *Paul: Apostle to the Gentiles* (Louisville: Westminster/Knox, 1993), 52; Martin Hengel, *The Pre-Christian Paul* (Philadelphia: Trinity, 1991), 2–3; C. Joachim Classen, "St Paul's Epistles and Ancient Graeco-Roman Rhetoric," in *Rhetoric and the New Testament*, ed. Stanley E. Porter and Thomas H. Olbricht (Sheffield: Sheffield Academic, 1993), 269; and E. A. Judge, "Paul's Boasting in Relation to Contemporary Professional Practice," *Australian Biblical Review* 16 (October 1968): 40–41.

12. E. A. Judge, "St Paul and Classical Society," *Jahrbuch für Antike und Christentum* 15 (1972): 19–36; Duane Litfin, *St. Paul's Theology of Proclamation: 1 Corinthians 1–4 and Greco-Roman Rhetoric* (Cambridge: University Press, 1994), 139; and Carol J. Schlueter, *Filling up the Measure: Polemical Hyperbole in 1 Thessalonians 2.14–16* (Sheffield: Sheffield Academic, 1994).

13. Litfin, *St. Paul's Theology of Proclamation*, 139. "The Jews had their own traditional methods of writing letters, but it is not unreasonable to assume that they were given some instruction in Greco-Roman letters" (E. Randolph Richards, *The Secretary in the Letters of Paul* [Tübingen: Mohr, 1991], 151; cf. 153). "Hellenistic influences also affected, consciously or unconsciously, education in orthodox, Rabbinic circles" (John T. Townsend, "Ancient Education in the Time of the Early Roman Empire," in *The Catacombs and the Colosseum: The Roman Empire as the Setting of Primitive Christianity*, ed. Stephen Benko and John J. O'Rourke [Valley Forge, Penn.: Judson, 1971], 154. Also see Nathan Morris, *The Jewish School* (New York: Bloch, 1937), 27–30, 37–41, 72–73.

14. Richards, *The Secretary in the Letters of Paul*, 150.

15. David Daube, "Rabbinic Methods of Interpretation and Hellenistic Rhetoric," *Hebrew Union College Annual* 22 (1949): 240.

16. If Paul was converted in A.D. 35, his time in Tarsus, Cilicia, and Antioch may have extended from A.D. 37 to A.D. 48, before he went on his first missionary journey from the spring of 48 to the fall of 49 (Harold W. Hoehner, "Chronology of the Apostolic Age" [Th.D. diss., Dallas Theological Seminary, 1965], 381–82).

would have had further contact with Greco-Roman culture, particu-larly oratory and letter writing.[17]

The possibility of Paul having read some Greek works in his upbring-ing seems evident from his epistles, which bear a number of similarities to ancient writing style. Köster, in 1854, and Danker, in 1991, pointed out numerous ways in which the Pauline Epistles correspond to the lan-guage and style of Demosthenes (384–322 b.c.), the Athenian orator whose writings would have been familiar to almost everyone in the Greco-Roman world.[18] And Sampley discusses how Paul's arguments in 2 Corinthians 10–13 were indebted to the rhetorical conventions of Cicero (106–43 b.c.), Roman orator, in his *On Inventions,* especially on ways to cultivate good will with one's audience.[19]

What Forms of Persuasion Were Used in Classical Rhetoric?

Aristotle discussed three kinds of rhetorical speech: forensic, delibera-tive, and epideictic.[20] Forensic (or judicial) rhetoric was used in the courtroom to accuse or defend; deliberative speeches were used in civil assemblies to persuade or dissuade; and epideictic rhetoric offered praise or blame. The first addresses the question, Is the court just or un-just? The second asks, Is the issue helpful or harmful? The third asks, Is the matter honorable or disgraceful?[21] Fact and legality are the focus of the forensic speech, expediency is the issue in the deliberative speech, and honor is the concern in epideictic rhetoric.[22]

Paul's speech before Felix, in which he defended himself against Jew-ish opponents recorded in Acts 24:1–21, is a grand example of the apos-tle's use of judicial rhetoric, structured according to the parts of a clas-sical discourse: exordium (introduction), narratio (statement of facts),

17. Richards, *The Secretary in the Letters of Paul,* 152.

18. Friedrich Köster, "Did Paul Model His Language after That of Demosthenes?" *Bibliotheca Sacra* 11 (July 1854): 514–27; and Frederick W. Danker, "Paul's Debt to the *De Corona* of Demosthenes: A Study of Rhetorical Techniques in Second Corinthians," in *Persuasive Artistry,* ed. Duane F. Watson (Sheffield: Sheffield Academic, 1991), 262–79.

19. Sampley, "Paul, His Opponents in 2 Corinthians 10–13 and the Rhetorical Hand-books," 162–77.

20. *The Art of Rhetoric* 1.3.1–3.

21. Ibid., 1.3.5; cf. Frank Witt Hughes, "The Rhetoric of 1 Thessalonians," in *The Thessalonian Correspondence,* ed. Raymond F. Collins (Leuven: University Press, 1990), 97.

22. Mack, *Rhetoric and the New Testament,* 34.

confirmatio (establishment of facts), refutatio or confutatio (refutation of opposing arguments), and peroratio (conclusion).[23]

Many of his epistles give evidence of being patterned according to these three main forms of rhetorical strategy.[24] Numerous articles and book chapters, published in the last two decades, reveal the growing awareness of Paul's use of rhetorical persuasion in his epistles.[25]

23. These are the five parts of speech according to Quintilian (*On the Education of the Orator* 3.9.1–5; 4.3.15). Aristotle said a speech basically has two parts: a statement of the case, and proof of it (*The Art of Rhetoric* 3.13). The *Rhetorica ad Herennium* said an effective speech has six parts, adding *partitio* (outline of main points to be made) after *narratio*. In one place Cicero suggested four parts (*On Oratory* 1.4; 8.27) and in another place six parts (*On Inventions* 1.14.19; cf. *On Oratory* 1.31.143; 219.80; 2.76.307). See Insawn Saw, "Paul's Rhetoric in 1 Corinthians 15" (Lewistown, N.Y.: Mellen Biblical, 1995), 84–85; Donald Lemen Clark, *Rhetoric in Greco-Roman Education* (New York: Columbia University Press, 1957), 70; and Hughes, *Early Christian Rhetoric and 2 Thessalonians*, 32–43.

24. Writers disagree, however, on how to designate the epistles rhetorically. For example, Betz classifies Galatians as forensic rhetoric, whereas Aune and Smit see it as deliberative (David E. Aune, *The New Testament in Its Literary Environment* [Phildelphia: Westminster, 1987], 206–8; Joop Smit, "The Letters of Paul to the Galatians: A Deliberative Speech," *New Testament Studies* 35 [1989]: 1–26), and Hansen views it as a mixture of both. Watson considers Philippians deliberative, but others see it as epideictic or both (cf. Hansen, "Rhetorical Criticism," 823).

25. The following are among the growing number of essays on this subject, arranged by Bible book.

Romans: Donald A. Campbell, "The Rhetoric of Righteousness in Romans 3:21–26" (Sheffield: Sheffield Academic, 1992); Michael R. Cosby, "Paul's Persuasive Language in Romans 5," in *Persuasive Artistry*, 209–20; David Hillholm, "Amplificiatio in the Macro-Structure of Romans," in *Rhetoric and the New Testament*, 123–51; Robin Scroggs, "Paul as Rhetorician: Two Homilies in Romans 1–11," in *Jews, Greeks and Christians: Religious Cultures in Late Antiquity*, ed. Robert Hamerton-Kelly and Robin Scroggs (Leiden: Brill, 1976), 271–98; Johannes N. Vorster, "Strategies of Persuasion in Romans 1.16–17," in *Rhetoric and the New Testament*, 152–70; and Wilhelm Wuellner, "Paul's Rhetoric of Argumentation in Romans," *Catholic Biblical Quarterly* 38 (1976): 330–51.

1 Corinthians: Benjamin Fiore, "'Covert Allusion' in 1 Corinthians 1–4," *Catholic Biblical Quarterly* 47 (1985): 85–102; idem, "Passion in Paul and Plutarch: 1 Corinthians 5–6 and the Polemic against Epicureans," in *Greeks, Romans, and Christians*, ed. David L. Balch, Everett Ferguson, and Wayne A. Meeks (Minneapolis: Fortress, 1990), 135–43; E. Schüssler Fiorenza, "Rhetorical Situation and Historical Reconstruction in 1 Corinthians," *New Testament Studies* 33 (1987): 386–403; Judge, "Paul's Boasting in Relation to Contemporary Professional Practice," 37–50; Mack, *Rhetoric and the New Testament*, 56–66; M. M. Mitchell, *Paul and the Rhetoric of Reconciliation* (Tübingen: Mohr, 1991); Saw, *Paul's Rhetoric in 1 Corinthians 15;* Joop Smit, "The Genre of 1 Corinthians 13 in the Light of Classical Rhetoric," *Novum Testamentum* 33 (1991): 193–216; idem, "Argument and Genre in 1 Corinthians 12–14," in *Rhetoric and the New Testament*, 211–30; Duane F. Watson, "1 Corinthians 10:23–11:1 in the Light of Greco-Roman Rhetoric: The Role of Rhetorical Questions," *Journal of Biblical Literature* 108 (1989): 301–18; idem, "Paul's Rhetorical Strategy in 1 Corinthians 15," in *Rhetoric and the New Testament*, 231–49; Wuellner, "Greek Rhetoric and Pauline Argumentation," 177–88; and idem, "Paul as

Pastor: The Function of Rhetorical Questions in First Corinthians," in *L'Apôtre Paul: personnalité, style et conception du ministère,* ed. A. Vanhoye (Leuven: University Press, 1986), 49–77.

2 Corinthians: Danker, "Paul's Debt to the *De Corona* of Demosthenes: A Study of Rhetorical Techniques in Second Corinthians," 262–80; Glenn Hollard, "Speaking Like a Fool: Irony in 2 Corinthians 10–13," in *Rhetoric and the New Testament,* 250–64; Frank Witt Hughes, "The Rhetoric of Reconciliation: 2 Corinthians 1.1–2.13 and 7.5–8.24," in *Persuasive Artistry,* 246–61; Kennedy, *New Testament Interpretation through Rhetorical Criticism,* 86–96; Mack, *Rhetoric and the New Testament,* 59–60; Marshall, *Enmity in Corinth;* Sampley, "Paul and His Opponents in 2 Corinthians 10–13 and the Rhetorical Handbooks," 162–77.

Galatians: H. D. Betz, "The Literary Composition and Function of Paul's Letter to the Galatians," *New Testament Studies* 21 (1975): 353–79; B. H. Brinsmead, *Galatians—Dialogical Response to Opponents* (Chico, Calif.: Scholars, 1982); Robert G. Hall, "The Rhetorical Outline for Galatians: A Reconsideration," *Journal of Biblical Literature* 106 (1987): 271–87; idem, "Historical Inference and Rhetorical Effect: Another Look at Galatians 1 and 2," in *Persuasive Artistry,* 308–20; G. Walter Hansen, *Abraham in Galatians—Epistolary and Rhetorical Contexts* (Sheffield; Sheffield Academic, 1989); James D. Hester, "The Rhetorical Structure of Galatians 1:11–2:14," *Journal of Biblical Literature* 103 (1984): 223–33; idem, "Placing the Blame: The Presence of Epideictic in Galatians 1 and 2," in *Persuasive Artistry,* 281–307; P. E. Koptak, "Rhetorical Identification in Paul's Autobiographical Narrative: Galatians 1:13–2:14," *Journal for the Study of the New Testament* 40 (1990): 97–115; Mack, *Rhetoric and the New Testament,* 66–73; Smit, "The Letter of Paul to the Galatians: A Deliberative Speech," 1–26.

Philippians: Loveday Alexander, "Hellenistic Letter-Forms and the Structure of Philippians," *Journal for the Study of the New Testament* 37 (1989): 87–101; Claudio Basevi and Juan Chapa, "Phil. 2:6–11: The Rhetorical Function of a Pauline 'Hymn,'" in *Rhetoric and the New Testament,* 338–56; J. G. Bloomquist, *The Function of Suffering in Philippians* (Sheffield: Sheffield Academic, 1993); John W. Marshall, "Paul's Ethical Appeal in Philippians," in *Rhetoric and the New Testament,* 357–74; Charles Robbins, "Rhetorical Structure of Philippians 2:6–11," *Catholic Biblical Quarterly* 42 (1980): 73–82; A. H. Snyman, "Persuasion in Philippians 4:1–20," in *Rhetoric and the New Testament,* 325–37; Duane F. Watson, "A Rhetorical Analysis of Philippians and Its Implications for the Unity Question," *Novum Testamentum* 30 (1988): 57–88.

1 and 2 Thessalonians: Frank Witt Hughes, *Early Christian Rhetoric and 2 Thessalonians* (Sheffield: Sheffield Academic, 1989); idem, "The Rhetoric of 1 Thessalonians," in *The Thessalonian Correspondence,* ed. Raymond F. Collins (Leuven: University Press, 1990); Robert Jewett, *The Thessalonian Correspondence* (Philadelphia: Fortress, 1986); Abraham J. Malherbe, "Exhortation in First Thessalonians," *Novum Testamentum* 25 (1983): 238–56; idem, *Paul and the Thessalonians* (Philadelphia: Fortress, 1987); Thomas H. Olbricht, "An Aristotelian Rhetorical Analysis of 1 Thessalonians," in *Greeks, Romans and Christians,* 216–36; Steve Walton, "What Has Aristotle to Do with Paul? Rhetorical Criticism and 1 Thessalonians," *Tyndale Bulletin* 46 (1995): 229–50; Wilhelm Wuellner, "The Argumentative Structure of 1 Thessalonians as Paradoxical Encomium," in *The Thessalonian Correspondence,* 117–36.

1 Timothy: Barth Campbell, "Rhetorical Design in 1 Timothy 4," *Bibliotheca Sacra* 154 (April–June 1991): 189–204.

Philemon: F. Forrester Church, "Rhetorical Structure and Design in Paul's Letter to Philemon," *Harvard Theological Review* 71 (1978): 17–33; Clarence J. Martin, "The Rhetorical Function of Commercial Language in Paul's Letter to Philemon (verse 18)," in *Persuasive Artistry,* 321–37.

Many of Paul's letters were designed after deliberative rhetoric, written to persuade. This is true of 1 Corinthians,[26] Galatians 4:12–6:18,[27] 1 Thessalonians,[28] and Philemon.[29]

Other portions of the Pauline literature are epideictic, composed to praise or blame.[30] For example, in Galatians 1:6–4:11 Paul blamed his adversaries for altering the gospel message. Romans and 2 Corinthians 1–7 may be forensic.[31]

Was the Form of Paul's Epistles Similar to Greco-Roman Letters?

Most ancient Greco-Roman letters consisted of three parts: opening, body, and closing.[32] Paul followed this pattern but modified it by adding two sections, thus having a five-part format[33] consisting of (a) the opening (sender, addressee[s], greetings);[34] (b) thanksgiving to God for the addressees' faithfulness (not included in Galatians); (c) the body; (d) exhortations; and (e) the closing (wish for peace, greetings, benediction).[35] In his salutations Paul used "grace" *(charis)* rather than the

26. Mitchell, *Paul and the Rhetoric of Reconciliation.*

27. Hansen, "Rhetorical Criticism," 823.

28. Kennedy, *New Testament Interpretation through Rhetorical Criticism,* 142–44. However, Hughes sees 1 Thessalonians as epideictic ("The Rhetoric of 1 Thessalonians").

29. Church, "Rhetorical Structure and Design in Paul's letter to Philemon."

30. On epideictic writing, see Theodore C. Burgess, "Epideictic Literature," *University of Chicago Studies in Classical Philology* 3 (1900): 89–261.

31. Kennedy, *New Testament Interpretation through Rhetorical Criticism,* 86–96, 152–56.

32. See John L. White, "Ancient Greek Letters," in *Greco-Roman Literature and the New Testament,* ed. David E. Aune (Atlanta: Scholars, 1988), 85–105; and idem, *Light from Ancient Letters* (Philadelphia: Fortress, 1988), 189–220.

33. Sidney Greidanus, "Preaching from Paul Today," in *Dictionary of Paul and His Letters,* 738–39; and John L. White, *The Form and Function of the Body of the Greek Letters* (Missoula, Mont.: Scholars, 1972), 45.

34. Several studies have been made of Paul's epistolary introductions. See Aune, *The New Testament in Its Literary Environment,* 184–86; Judith M. Lieu, "Grace to You and Peace: The Apostolic Greeting," *Bulletin of the John Rylands University Library* 68 (1986): 161–78; Terence Y. Mullin, "Formulas in New Testament Epistles," *Journal of Biblical Literature* 91 (1972): 380–90; Peter T. O'Brien, *Introductory Thanksgiving in the Letters of Paul* (Leiden: Brill, 1977); idem, "Thanksgiving within the Structure of Pauline Theology," in *Pauline Studies,* ed. Donald A. Hagner and Murray J. Harris (Grand Rapids: Eerdmans, 1980), 50–66; Jeffrey T. Reed, "Are Paul's Thanksgivings 'Epistolary'?" *Journal for the Study of the New Testament* 61 (1996): 87–99; and Paul Schubert, *Form and Function of the Pauline Thanksgiving* (Berlin: Töpelmann, 1939).

35. Sands compares elements in Paul's epistles to these elements common in Greco-Roman personal or private letters (P. C. Sands, *The Literary Genius of the New Testament* [Oxford: Clarendon, 1932], 128–32), as listed on the following page.

Greco-Roman "greetings" *(chairein)*. The opening thanksgiving is an epistolary form found occasionally in papyrus letters.[36]

Corresponding to Greek letters, Paul utilized six kinds of opening formulas in his epistles: disclosure formula (his desire that the addressee[s] know something), the request formula (common in papyrus letters[37]), the joy expression, the expression of astonishment, the statement of compliance, and the use of a verb of hearing or learning.[38]

Besides these transitional formulas, the bodies of the Pauline Epistles also include elements similar to other ancient letters: themes or motifs called *topoi* (such as concern for the health of the sender or the recipient, business matters, wish for reunion with the addressees, government matters), autobiographical statements, travel plans, and concluding points of advice or exhortation *(paraenesis)*.[39]

The conclusions of Paul's letters all have a benediction of grace. Other optional items in several of his epistles are a wish for peace (2 Cor. 13:11; Gal. 6:16; Phil. 4:9), a request for prayer for himself and/ or others, closing greetings from himself and/or others (typical of many papyrus letters), an exhortation to greet each other with a holy kiss (Rom. 16:16; 1 Cor. 16:20; 2 Cor. 13:12; 1 Thess. 5:26), and an autographed greeting.[40] Sometimes an exhortation is also included in the closing.[41] Schmithals charts five elements in Paul's epistolary closings:

Dear . . . Salutation
I am glad to hear you are well . . . The health and interests of the person
I congratulate you on . . . written to
I have not been too well myself . . . The health or interests of the writer
I have been very well since I saw you . . . Ditto
I want to explain . . . Information or
They tell me you have . . . criticism
My advice is . . . Advice
I shall be seeing you soon . . . The next meeting
Keep well . . . Do your best to . . . Closing injunctions
Remember me to . . . Greetings sent
Yours affectionately . . . Signature

36. Stowers, *Letter Writing in Greco-Roman Antiquity*, 21.

37. Ibid., 24.

38. John L. White, "Introductory Formulae in the Body of the Pauline Letters," *Journal of Biblical Literature* 90 (1971): 91–97; cf. idem, "Ancient Greek Letters," (99; idem, *The Form and Function of the Body of the Greek Letter*, 95–96; and Terence Y. Mullins, "Formulas in New Testament Epistles," 380–90.

39. Aune, *The New Testament in Its Literary Environment*, 188–91.

40. Ibid., 186–87. Many papyrus letters and "even literary letters reflect this practice (Cicero *To Atticus* 12:32; 13:28; 14:21)" (ibid., 187).

41. Jeffrey A. D. Weima, *Neglected Endings: The Significance of the Pauline Letter Closings* (Sheffield: Sheffield Academic, 1994), 145–48.

personal notes, intercession and/or doxology, paraenesis, salutations, and benediction.[42]

In Romans 16:22 Paul referred to Tertius, his secretary or amaneunsis, who recorded the epistle. In four other epistles Paul wrote that he added his own autographed greeting (1 Cor. 16:21; Gal. 6:11; Col. 4:18; 2 Thess. 3:17), thereby suggesting the use of an amanuensis in the writing of those letters also. Whether he used a secretary in his other nine epistles is not known, but using a secretary to record or edit letters was common in the ancient world.[43]

Besides grouping ancient letters according to the three major forms of rhetoric (forensic, deliberative, epideictic), some Greco-Roman writers categorized them into further types according to their function. In *Epistolary Types* Pseudo-Demetrius described twenty-one types, and in *Epistolary Styles* Pseudo-Libanius discussed forty-one types, most of which were epideictic (commending or blaming). Stowers has suggested these be grouped into six categories: (a) letters of friendship, (b) family letters, (c) letters of praise and blame, (d) hortatory letters, (e) letters of recommendation or mediation, and (f) accusing, apologetic, and accounting letters.[44] Paul's letters are in categories c, d, and e.

Of course, while Paul's epistles followed, and to some degree modified, the style of letters in the Greco-Roman world, we should remember that he wrote under the inspiration of the Holy Spirit (2 Tim. 3:16). His letters were accepted by the early church as authoritative along with Old Testament books (2 Peter 3:15–16). Thus the Pauline Epistles, while rhetorical in form and persuasive in nature, like letters of his contemporaries, stand far above them as part of God's written revelation.

Why Did Paul Say He Was Not a Trained Speaker?

If Paul had some formal training in rhetoric or was at least exposed to it in some of his school classes or in public life, why did he write, "I may not be a trained speaker, but I have knowledge" (2 Cor. 11:6)? And since

42. Walter Schmithals, *Paul and the Gnostics* (Nashville: Abingdon, 1972), 130.
43. On the use of secretaries in Paul's writings, see Richard N. Longenecker, "Ancient Amanuenses and the Pauline Epistles," in *New Dimensions in New Testament Study*, ed. Richard N. Longenecker and Merrill C. Tenney (Grand Rapids: Zondervan, 1974), 281–97; Michael Prior, *Paul the Letter-Writer and the Second Letter to Timothy* (Sheffield: Sheffield Academic, 1989); and Richards, *The Secretary to the Letters of Paul*.
44. *Letter Writing in Greco-Roman Antiquity*, 58–173. Aune adds two other categories: private or documentary letters, and literary letters (*The New Testament in Its Literary Environment*, 162–69). Also see Luther Stirewalt, Jr., *Studies in Ancient Greek Epistolography* (Atlanta: Scholars, 1993), 1–26.

his epistles, as we have seen, reveal the use of numerous rhetorical devices and patterns, how could he say he was untrained in oratory?

The word for "untrained" is *idiōtēs*, which means "one who confines himself to his own affairs, τὰ ἴδια, and takes no part in public life."[45] The word then came to mean "one who had no technical or professional training with regard to some particular art or science; unskilled, a layman or amateur, as distinct from an expert or professional."[46] Using this word, Paul was disclaiming expert, professionally trained ability in the art of speaking.[47]

While the Greeks lauded the display of flowery oratory, Paul repudiated the use of humanly designed tricks of language and sophisticated arguments of philosophy to sway people's minds.[48] He made this clear in 1 Corinthians 1:17–2:4, where he wrote that his preaching was "not with words of human wisdom" (1:17), or "eloquence or superior wisdom" (2:1),[49] or "with wise and persuasive words" (2:4). Paul even acknowledged that some Corinthians said "his speaking amounts to nothing" (2 Cor. 10:10).[50] His preaching avoided arrogant, humanly contrived efforts of delivery so that faith on the part of his hearers would be the work of the Holy Spirit, not Paul's.[51] The apostle con-

---

45. Alfred Plummer, *A Critical and Exegetical Commentary on the Second Epistle of St Paul to the Corinthians*, International Critical Commentary (Edinburgh: Clark, 1915), 299. For example, the *Sybilline Oracles* 847.16 refer to five *idiōtai* as private citizens (James Hope Moulton and George Milligan, *The Vocabulary of the Greek Testament* [1930; reprint, Grand Rapids: Eerdmans, 1974], 299). And the Athenian philosopher Isocrates (436–338 B.C.) used the verb *idiōteuō* "to live in private" (*Antidosis* 204).

46. Plummer, *A Critical and Exegetical Commentary on the Second Epistle of St Paul to the Corinthians*, 299.

47. C. K. Barrett, *A Commentary on the Second Epistle to the Corinthians* (New York: Harper and Row, 1973), 279. Betz suggests, however, that Paul used this term of himself tongue-in-cheek. "This concession is to be taken ironically and as such belongs in the tradition of the controversy between philosophers and sophists, going all the way back to Socrates. In his debates with the sophists . . . Socrates . . . always emphasizes that he is 'unskilled in rhetoric' while the sophists are said not only to know everything but also to know how to persuade everybody. In Socrates' strategy this concession is, of course, only one of the moves to defeat the sophists" (Hans Dieter Betz, "Paul's Apology [in] II Cor. 10–13 and the Socratic Tradition," in *Protocol of the Second Colloquy* [Berkeley, Calif.: Center for Hermeneutical Studies in Hellenistic and Modern Culture, 1970], 11).

48. Philip Edgcumbe Hughes, *Paul's Second Epistle to the Corinthians* (Grand Rapids: Eerdmans, 1962), 381.

49. *Hyperochē* means "superiority" so that the phrase may be rendered, "I have not come in superiority of speech or wisdom." Thus Paul was rejecting speech characterized by pride or arrogance (Savage, *Power through Weakness*, 72).

50. "Amounts to nothing" translates *exouthenēmenos*, a perfect passive participle of *exoutheneō*, "to despise, consider as nothing" (cf. 1 Cor. 1:28; 6:4).

51. Litfin, *St. Paul's Theology of Proclamation*, 247. Rhetorical delivery "was fundamentally a human approach which produced human results" (ibid., 249).

trasted his preaching ministry with public orators whose goal was to amuse their audiences by "startling effects, sensational topics, and powerful deliveries," sometimes sacrificing truth—all in order to overwhelm gullible hearers and win their applause and praise,[52] and receive money from them. Paul wanted his listeners to be persuaded by the genuine work of the Holy Spirit, not by clever oratorical manipulations.

Why then did Paul say he refused to follow human sophistication in his delivery, while obviously utilizing many rhetorical conventions in his epistles? The answer lies in recognizing the difference between his preaching and his writing.[53] Litfin emphasizes this distinction between Paul's oral and writing style, pointing out that the epistles written to believers were didactic and therefore possess rhetorical design, whereas his preaching, being oral in nature, and addressed to unbelievers, involved the proclamation of the gospel—a proclamation that Paul determined would be by the "Spirit's power" (1 Cor. 2:4).[54] Even Paul's critics recognized this difference between these forms of communication (2 Cor. 10:10), acknowledging that while his preaching *(logos)* was contemptible, his letters were "weighty" *(bareiai)* and "forceful" *(ischyrai)*. *Bareiai* possibly means impressive or even severe.[55]

Though refusing to preach with artificial rhetorical polish to trick audiences (for which "deficiency" the Corinthians criticized Paul), he did employ genuine rhetoric in his letters, sometimes with devastating effect.[56] In fact, his correspondence was rich by virtue of "the wealth of words at his command, the abundance of illustration, the wealth of apt quotation, the flow of ideas, and rapid suggestion of one topic to another."[57] These and many other elements in his letters demonstrate his

---

52. Savage, *Power through Weakness*, 31, 71. "The rhetoric of Paul's day was almost totally preoccupied with the *ornamental aspects*of public speaking" (Donald R. Runukjian, "The Preacher as Persuader," in *Walvoord: A Tribute*, ed. Donald K. Campbell [Chicago: Moody, 1982], 292 [italics added]).

53. The ancient writings distinguished between "primary" rhetoric, which was public speaking in social and civic life, and "secondary" rhetoric, which was the use of "primary" rhetoric techniques in literature such as in historical accounts, treatises, drama, and poetry (Kennedy, *Classical Rhetoric in Its Christian and Secular Tradition from Ancient to Modern Times*, 4–6; cf. Satterthwaite, "Acts Against the Background of Classical Rhetoric," 338–43). Also, Litfin observes that ancient writers, including Aristotle and Pliny, "distinguished between how letters and speeches were to be judged" (Litfin, *St. Paul's Theology of Proclamation*, 155, n. 16).

54. Litfin, *St. Paul's Theology of Proclamation*, 257. Cf. Duane F. Watson, "Review of Duane Litfin, *St. Paul's Theology of Proclamation*," *Biblica* 77 (1996): 128–31.

55. Plummer, *A Critical and Exegetical Commentary on the Second Epistle of St Paul to the Corinthians*, 282.

56. Winter, "Rhetoric," 821.

57. Sands, *Literary Genius of the New Testament* , 135.

skill as a writing rhetorician, a man whose compositions were Spirit-empowered works of honesty and integrity. Without any deceptive conniving (2 Cor. 4:2), Paul presented doctrinal truths (he had knowledge of God's ways; 11:6) and injunctions to his readers by means of the persuasive dynamic of the Holy Spirit (1 Cor. 2:13). His competence was not his own; it was divine in origin (2 Cor. 3:5).

Think It Over . . .

Think of the spiritual needs of each of your students. Then ask yourself these questions about each one: Are there areas in his or her life where he or she needs to be persuaded to follow a course of action or to acquire a desirable attitude? Are there areas in his or her life where he or she needs to be dissuaded from a wrong course of action or a wrong attitude? What can you do to help in that persuading or dissuading?

As you prepare for your next class, think of ways you can gently persuade and/or dissuade your students regarding the biblical content you will be teaching.

Plan ways to commend and thank your class for their spiritual progress.

Do you avoid using unnecessary flowery language designed simply to impress others? Yet at the same time are you careful to use proper grammar and to teach with colorful imagery?

Consider writing a letter to your students to confirm some of the truths you are teaching and to prompt them to respond to the truth properly.

As you prepare each lesson, pray that the Lord will use you to make a difference in the lives of those you teach. Depend on the Holy Spirit to guide you and use you as you prepare and then teach each lesson.

Appendix A

Paul's Illustrations Arranged Topically

As discussed in chapters 11 and 12, Paul's many figures of speech and illustrations are drawn from numerous sources. As Resker wrote, "There is hardly a chapter in which he does not make clear his meaning to the mind and fix it in the memory by the use of illustrations, gathered for the most part from circumstances or facts with which both he and his readers were familiar."[1] These many illustrations and verbal images reveal "the wide range of his knowledge and observation."[2] The number of illustrations Paul used is truly amazing!

A most profitable study can be enjoyed by looking up each verse in this appendix and noting the points—doctrinal or applicational—the apostle was depicting.[3] Look for the way Paul illustrated these and other truths: the nature of the unsaved, the nature of salvation, Christian disciplines, spiritual growth, Christian living and service, spiritual freedom, relationships (of believers to each other, believers to the unsaved, individual believers to Christ, the church to Christ, the church to Israel, Christ to God the Father), Christian values, Christian ministry, dedication, opportunities, remuneration for ministry, difficulties in the Christian life, spiritual opposition, character of false teachings and false teachers, death and resurrection, and God's judgment of believers.

---

1. Robert R. Resker, *St. Paul's Illustrations* (Edinburgh: Clark, n.d.), 8.
2. Ibid.
3. Only those verses with illustrations are included. Verses that refer to literal items with no metaphorical meaning are excluded. For example, "wall" in 2 Corinthians 11:33, being literal, is not listed under "Architecture," but "wall" in Ephesians 2:14 is included because it is used in a figurative sense.

Agriculture

Branches	Romans 11:16–19, 21, 24
Crops	2 Timothy 2:6
Fields	1 Corinthians 3:9; 2 Corinthians 10:13
Firstfruits	Romans 8:23; 11:16; 16:5 (NIV, "first convert"); 1 Corinthians 15:20, 23; 16:15 (NIV, "first converts")
Fruit	Romans 7:4–5; 15:28; Galatians 5:22–23; Ephesians 5:9; Philippians 1:11, 22; 4:17 (NIV, "gift"); Colossians 1:6, 10
Grain	1 Corinthians 9:9; 1 Timothy 5:18
Grapes	1 Corinthians 9:7
Harvest	Romans 1:13; 1 Corinthians 9:10; 2 Corinthians 9:6, 10; Galatians 6:9
Hay	1 Corinthians 3:12
Olive branch, olive tree	Romans 11:17, 24
Reaping	Romans 6:21–22; Galatians 6:7–8
Roots	Romans 11:16, 18; 15:12; 1 Timothy 6:10
Seeds	1 Corinthians 3:6; 9:11; 15:37–38; 2 Corinthians 9:10; Galatians 3:16, 19, 29
Sowing	1 Corinthians 15:36–37; Galatians 6:7–8
Straw	1 Corinthians 3:12
Thorn	2 Corinthians 12:7
Vineyard	1 Corinthians 9:7
Wheat	1 Corinthians 15:37
Yoke	2 Corinthians 6:14; Galatians 5:1; Philippians 4:3; 1 Timothy 6:1

Animal World

Animals	Romans 1:23; 1 Corinthians 15:39
Birds	Romans 1:23; 1 Corinthians 15:39
Dogs	Philippians 3:2
Fish	1 Corinthians 15:39
Flock	1 Corinthians 9:7
Lion	2 Timothy 4:17
Oxen	1 Corinthians 9:9; 1 Timothy 5:18

Reptiles, serpents, snakes, vipers	Romans 1:23; 3:13; 9:7; 1 Corinthians 10:9; 15:32, 39; 2 Corinthians 11:3
Sheep	Romans 8:36
Wild beasts	1 Corinthians 15:32

Architecture[4]

Architect	1 Corinthians 3:10 (NIV, "expert builder")
Build, building (verb: *oikodomeō*)	Romans 15:20; 1 Corinthians 3:10, 12; 8:10 (NIV, "emboldened"); 10:23 (NIV, "is constructive"), 17 (NIV, "edified"); 2 Corinthians 12:19 (NIV, "strengthening"); 13:10; Galatians 2:18 (NIV, "rebuild"); Ephesians 4:16, 29; 1 Thessalonians 5:11
Building (noun: *oikodomē*)	Romans 14:19 (NIV, "edification"); 15:2 (NIV, "build him up")
	1 Corinthians 3:9; 14:3 (NIV, "strengthening"), 5 (NIV, "edified"), 12 (NIV, "build up"), 26 (NIV, "strengthening"); 2 Corinthians 5:1; 10:8; 12:19 (NIV, "strengthening"); 13:10; Ephesians 2:21; 4:12 (NIV, "built up"), 16 (NIV, "builds itself up"), 29
Door	1 Corinthians 16:9; 2 Corinthians 2:12; Colossians 4:3
Dwelling	2 Corinthians 5:2, 4; Ephesians 2:22
Foundation	Romans 15:20; 1 Corinthians 3:10–12; Ephesians 2:20; 3:17 (NIV, "established"); Colossians 1:23 (NIV, "established"); 1 Timothy 3:15; 6:19; 2 Timothy 2:19
House	2 Corinthians 5:1
Pillar	Galatians 2:9; 1 Timothy 3:15
Tent	2 Corinthians 5:4
Wall	Ephesians 2:14, 16
Wood	1 Corinthians 3:12

Athletics

Athlete	2 Timothy 2:5
Boxing[a]	1 Corinthians 9:26
Compete (*athleō*)	1 Corinthians 9:25; Philippians 1:27 (NIV, "contending"); 2 Timothy 2:5

---

4. "This is one of the Apostle's favourite metaphors" (Resker, *St. Paul's Illustrations,* 26).

Crown	1 Corinthians 9:25; 2 Timothy 2:5; 4:8
Fight (noun: *agōn*, verb: *agōnizomai*)	Colossians 1:29 (NIV, "struggling"); 2:1 (NIV, "struggling"); 4:12 (NIV, "wrestling"); 1 Timothy 4:10 (NIV, "strive"); 6:12; 2 Timothy 4:7
Goal[b]	Philippians 3:14
Judge	2 Timothy 4:8
Physical training	1 Corinthians 9:25; 1 Timothy 4:8
Prize	1 Corinthians 9:24; Philippians 3:14
Race[c]	1 Corinthians 9:24; Galatians 2:2; 5:7; Philippians 2:16; 3:13–14; 2 Timothy 4:7
Rules	2 Timothy 2:5
Wrestling (*palē*)[d]	Ephesians 6:12 (NIV, "struggle")

a. On boxing in the ancient world see E. Norman Gardiner, *Athletics of the Ancient World* (1930; reprint, Chicago: Ares, 1978), 197–211; Mitchell P. Poliakoff, *Combat Sports in the Ancient World* (New Haven. Conn.: Yale University Press, 1987), 68–88; and Waldo E. Sweet, *Sport and Recreation in Ancient Greece* (New York: Oxford University Press, 1987), 68–80.

b. *Skopos* ("goal") "refers to the winning post of the race on which the runner intently fixes his gaze" (Victor C. Pfitzner, *Paul and the Agon Motif* [Leiden: Brill, 1967], 139).

c. The Greek stadium, where foot races and other athletic contests were held, was a long parallelogram, semicircular at one end, and about two hundred yards long and thirty yards wide. See Gardiner, *Athletics of the Ancient World*, 128, 133–36; and William Smith, *A Dictionary of Greek and Roman Antiquities*, 2d ed. (Boston: Little, Brown, 1870), 1055–56. The Isthmian games were played every two years at a stadium near Corinth. Also see Sweet, *Sport and Recreation in Ancient Greece*, 27–30.

d. On wrestling in the ancient world see Gardiner, *Athletics of the Ancient World*, 181–96; and Sweet, *Sport and Recreation in Ancient Greece*, 63–67.

Commerce

Buy	Ephesians 5:16 (NKJV, "redeeming")
Credit	Romans 4:3–6, 9, 11, 22, 24; 2 Corinthians 5:19 (NIV, "counting")
Debt	Romans 1:14 (NIV, "obligated"); 8:12 (NIV, "obligation"); 13:8; 15:27; Galatians 5:3 (NIV, "obligated"); Colossians 2:14 (NIV, "written code"[a]); Philemon 18
Deposit[b]	2 Corinthians 1:22; 5:5; Ephesians 1:14
Loss[c]	Philippians 3:7
Peddling[d]	2 Corinthians 2:17
Wages	Romans 4:4; 6:23

a. The word *cheirographon* in Colossians 2:14 is literally "handwriting," a written acknowledgement of debt.

b. On the Greek word *arrabōn* see Eric C. Malte, "Light from the Papyri on St. Paul's Terminology," *Concordia Theological Monthly* 18 (1947): 503–4.

c. The word *zēmia* ("loss") is used in the papyri of a business loss (James Hope Moulton and George Milligan, *The Vocabulary of the Greek Testament* [1930; reprint, Grand Rapids: Eerdmans, 1974], 273; cf. Wayne A. Meeks, ed., *The Writings of St. Paul* [New York: Norton, 1972], 99, n. 3).

d. *Kapēleuō*, used only here in the New Testament, means "to pawn off a product for gain." Some people, Paul wrote, were selfishly trying to make money off the Word of God by cheapening it and degrading it with false elements, just as a dishonest merchant diluted wine with a lot of water to cheat the buyers (C. K. Barrett, *A Commentary on the Second Epistle to the Corinthians* [New York: Harper and Row, 1973], 103; and Philip Edgcumbe Hughes, *Paul's Second Epistle to the Corinthians*, New International Commentary on the New Testament [Grand Rapids: Eerdmans, 1962], 83).

Creation

Clay	Romans 9:21; 2 Corinthians 4:7; 2 Timothy 2:20
Cloud	1 Corinthians 10:1–2
Coals	Romans 12:20
Darkness	Romans 13:12; 1 Corinthians 4:5; 2 Corinthians 4:6; 6:14; Ephesians 5:8, 11, 13; Colossians 1:13; 1 Thessalonians 5:4–5
Fire	1 Corinthians 3:13; 1 Thessalonians 5:19; 2 Thessalonians 1:7
Gold	1 Corinthians 3:12
Rock, stone	Romans 9:33; 1 Corinthians 3:12; 10:4
Salt	Colossians 4:6
Silver	1 Corinthians 3:12
Wind	Ephesians 4:14

Domestics

Adoption	Romans 8:15, 23; 9:4; Galatians 4:5; Ephesians 1:5
Child, children	Romans 8:16–17, 21; 9:8; 1 Corinthians 4:14; 13:11; 14:20; 2 Corinthians 6:13; 12:14; Galatians 3:7; 4:1, 3, 19, 28, 31; Ephesians 5:1, 8; Philippians 2:15; 1 Thessalonians 2:7, 11
Daughters	2 Corinthians 6:18
Family	Galatians 6:10; Ephesians 3:15
Fathers	1 Corinthians 4:15; 1 Thessalonians 2:11
Firstborn	Romans 8:29; Colossians 1:15, 18

Guardians	Galatians 4:2
Household	Ephesians 2:19; 1 Timothy 3:15
Husband	2 Corinthians 11:2
Infants	Romans 2:20; 1 Corinthians 3:1; 14:20; Ephesians 4:14
Labor pains, childbirth	Romans 8:22; Galatians 4:19; 1 Thessalonians 5:3
Marriage	Romans 7:2–4
Mother	Galatians 4:26; 1 Thessalonians 2:7
Pedagogue	Galatians 3:24 (NASB, "tutor")
Son(s)	Romans 8:14, 19; 9:26; 1 Corinthians 4:17; 2 Corinthians 6:18; Galatians 3:26; 4:6–7; Ephesians 1:5; Philippians 2:22; 1 Thessalonians 5:5; 1 Timothy 1:2, 18; 2 Timothy 1:2; 2:1; Philemon 10

Food

Dough	Romans 11:16
Loaf	1 Corinthians 10:17
Milk	1 Corinthians 3:2
Yeast	1 Corinthians 5:6–8; Galatians 5:9

Human Body

Body	Romans 12:4–5; 1 Corinthians 10:17; 12:12–27; Ephesians 1:10, 23; 3:6; 4:12, 15–16, 25; 5:23, 28, 30; Colossians 1:18, 24; 2:19
Death	Romans 6:2, 7–8, 10; 7:4, 9; Galatians 2:19; Colossians 2:20; 3:3; 2 Timothy 2:11
Ear	1 Corinthians 12:16–17
Eye	1 Corinthians 12:16–17, 21; 15:52
Feet	Romans 3:15; 10:15; 1 Corinthians 12:21; Ephesians 1:22; 6:15
Gangrene	2 Timothy 2:17
Hand(s)	Romans 8:34; 10:21; 1 Corinthians 12:15, 21; 2 Corinthians 6:7; Galatians 2:9; Ephesians 1:20; Colossians 3:1
Head	1 Corinthians 11:3, 5; 12:21; Ephesians 1:10, 22; 4:15; 5:23; Colossians 1:18; 2:10, 19; 2 Timothy 4:5

Heart	Romans 1:9; 2:5, 29; 9:2; 10:6, 8–10; 15:6; 1 Corinthians 14:25; 2 Corinthians 2:4; 4:1, 16; 5:12; 6:13; 7:2; 8:16; 9:7; Ephesians 1:18; 5:19; 6:5–6; Philippians 1:7; Colossians 2:2; 3:22–23; 1 Timothy 1:5; 3:1; 2 Timothy 2:22; Philemon 12, 20
Lips	Romans 3:13
Mouths	Romans 3:14
Stomach	Philippians 3:19
Swallow	1 Corinthians 15:54; 2 Corinthians 5:4
Throats	Romans 3:13
Tongue	Romans 3:13; 14:11
Wake	Romans 13:11; Ephesians 5:14; 1 Thessalonians 5:10
Walk	Romans 4:12; 2 Corinthians 6:16; Colossians 3:7

Legal Matters

Accusation	Romans 8:33
Aliens, foreigners	Ephesians 2:12; Colossians 1:21
Citizenship	Ephesians 2:12, 19; Philippians 3:20
Covenant(s)	Galatians 3:15; 4:24
Free, freedom	Romans 6:18, 20–22; 8:2; 1 Corinthians 7:22; 8:9; 12:13; 2 Corinthians 3:17; Galatians 2:4; 3:28; 4:26; 5:1, 13
Heirs, inheritance	Romans 4:13–14; 8:17; Galatians 3:18, 29; 4:1, 7, 30; Ephesians 1:14, 18; 3:6; 5:5; Colossians 1:12; 3:24; Titus 3:7
Redeem, purchase, set free by paying a ransom	Romans 3:24; 8:23; 1 Corinthians 1:30; 6:20; 7:23; Galatians 3:13; Ephesians 1:7; 4:30; 5:16; Colossians 1:14
Slavery, slaves	Romans 6:6, 16–20, 22; 1 Corinthians 7:22–23; Galatians 2:4; 4:3, 7–8, 24–25; 5:1; Ephesians 6:6
Witness(es)	Romans 1:9; 2:15; 2 Corinthians 1:23; 1 Thessalonians 2:5, 10

ℳilitary[5]

Armor, weapons	Romans 13:12; 2 Corinthians 6:7; 10:4; Ephesians 6:11, 13
Battle, fight	1 Corinthians 14:8; 2 Corinthians 10:3; 1 Timothy 1:18[a]
Breastplate	Ephesians 6:14; 1 Thessalonians 5:8
Commanding officer	2 Timothy 2:4
Enemy	Romans 5:10; 11:28; 1 Corinthians 15:25–26; Philippians 3:18; Colossians 1:21; 1 Timothy 5:14
Guard	1 Corinthians 16:13; Philippians 4:7
Helmet	Ephesians 6:17; 1 Thessalonians 5:8
Prisoners of war, captives	Romans 7:23; 2 Corinthians 10:5; Ephesians 4:8
Shield	Ephesians 6:16
Soldier	1 Corinthians 9:7; Philippians 2:25; 2 Timothy 2:3–4; Philemon 2
Sword	Ephesians 6:17
Trumpet	1 Corinthians 15:52; 1 Thessalonians 4:16
Victory parade[b]	2 Corinthians 2:14–16; Colossians 2:15

a. "Fight" in 1 Timothy 1:18 probably refers to a military conflict rather than an athletic contest because the Greek word is *strareuō*, "to fight as a soldier."

b. The triumph referred to in these verses was the victory procession of a military hero entering Rome. The parade was led by city magistrates, "followed by trumpets, then the spoils taken from the enemy followed by white oxen intended for sacrifice, then the captives headed by the king of the conquered country, then officials of the victorious army and musicians dancing and playing, and at last the general himself in whose honor the whole wonderful pagent [sic] was taking place" (Fritz Rienecker, *A Linguistic Key to the Greek New Testament*, ed. Cleon L. Rogers, Jr. [Grand Rapids: Zondervan, 1980], 457–58; cf. Smith, *A Dictionary of Greek and Roman Antiquities*, 1163–67; and H. A. Trebel and K. M. King, *Everyday Life in Rome* [Oxford: Oxford University Press, 1958], 115–18). Believers are likened to soldiers marching behind Christ, their "general" (W. M. Ramsey, *Like the Physician* [London: Hodder and Stoughton, 1968], 297, n.1).

5. "Wherever [Paul] resided, military uniforms and military quarters were familiar objects; wherever he traveled, he was liable to meet troops on their march from one province to another, or in the pursuit of banditti, or acting as an escort of prisoners" (John S. Howson, *The Metaphors of St. Paul* [London: Strahan, 1870], 6).

Miscellaneous

Fragrance	2 Corinthians 2:15; Ephesians 5:2
Music	1 Corinthians 13:1; 14:7–8
Nautical	Ephesians 4:14; 1 Timothy 1:19
Vessels, pottery	Romans 9:20–21; 2 Corinthians 4:7; 1 Thessalonians 4:4 (NIV, "body"); 2 Timothy 2:20–21

Appendix B

Paul's 390 Commands[1]

Romans

"Let God be true, and every man a liar" (3:4).

"Count yourselves dead to sin but alive to God in Christ Jesus" (6:11).

"Therefore do not let sin reign in your mortal body so that you obey its evil desires" (6:12).

"Do not offer the parts of your body to sin, as instruments of wickedness" (6:13a).

"Offer yourselves to God, as those who have been brought from death to life" (6:13b).

"Now offer them [the parts of your body] in slavery to righteousness leading to holiness" (6:19).

"May their table become a snare and a trap, a stumbling block and a retribution for them" (11:9).

"May their eyes be darkened so they cannot see, and their backs be bent forever" (11:10).

"Do not boast over those branches" (11:18).

"Do not be arrogant" (11:20a).

---

1. This list includes only the commands that are Greek imperatives. Most English versions have many more commands because many Greek participles can be understood as imperatives. An example is Romans 12:3, in which the Greek participle "thinking more highly" is clearly a command. Also, the three commands in Romans 12:12 are participles in Greek. See H. E. Dana and Julius R. Mantley, *A Manual Grammar of the Greek New Testament* (New York: Macmillan, 1927), 229; A T. Robertson, *A Grammar of the Greek New Testament in the Light of Historical Research*, 4th ed. (Nashville: Broadman, 1934), 944–46; and Nigel Turner, *Syntax*, vol. 3 of James Hope Moulton, *A Grammar of New Testament Greek* (Edinburgh: Clark, 1903), 303, 343.

"Be afraid" (11:20b).
"Consider therefore the kindness and sternness of God" (11:22).
"Do not conform any longer to the pattern of this world" (12:2a).
"Be transformed by the renewing of your mind" (12:2b).
"Bless those who persecute you; bless and do not curse" (12:14).
"Do not be conceited" (12:16).
"Leave room for God's wrath" (12:19).
"If your enemy is hungry, feed him" (12:20a).
"If he is thirsty, give him something to drink" (12:20b).
"Do not be overcome by evil" (12:21a).
"Overcome evil with good" (12:21b).
"Everyone must submit himself to the governing authorities" (13:1).
"Do what is right and he [the one in authority] will commend you" (13:3).
"If you do wrong, be afraid" (13:4).
"Give everyone what you owe him" (13:7).
"Owe nothing to anyone except to love one another" (13:8 NASB[2]).
"Clothe yourselves with the Lord Jesus" (13:14a).
"Do not think about how to gratify the desires of the sinful nature" (13:14b).
"Accept him whose faith is weak, without passing judgment on disputable matters" (14:1).
"Let not him who eats regard with contempt him who does not eat, and let not him who does not eat judge him who eats, for God has accepted him" (14:3 NASB).
"Let each man be fully convinced in his own mind" (14:5 NASB).
"Therefore let us stop passing judgment on one another" (14:13).
"Do not by your eating destroy your brother for whom Christ died" (14:15b).
"Do not allow what you consider good to be spoken of as evil" (14:16).
"Do not destroy the work of God for the sake of food" (14:20).
"So whatever you believe about these things keep between yourself and God" (14:22).
"Let each of us please his neighbor for his good, to his edification" (15:2 NASB).
"Accept one another, then, just as Christ accepted you, in order to bring praise to God" (15:7).
"Rejoice, O Gentiles, with his people" (15:10).
"Greet Priscilla and Aquila, my fellow workers in Christ Jesus" (16:3).

2. While most of the commands in this appendix are from the NIV, a few are from the NASB because that version more accurately reflects the Greek imperative mood in those verses by the word "let" rather than the NIV's "should" or "must."

"Greet my dear friend Epenetus, who was the first convert to Christ in the province of Asia" (16:5).

"Greet Mary, who worked very hard for you" (16:6).

"Greet Andronicus and Junias, my relatives who have been in prison with me" (16:7).

"Greet Ampliatus, whom I love in the Lord" (16:8).

"Greet Urbanus, our fellow worker in Christ, and my dear friend Stachys" (16:9).

"Greet Apelles, tested and approved in Christ" (16:10a).

"Greet those who belong to the household of Aristobulus" (16:10b).

"Greet Herodion, my relative" (16:11a).

"Greet those in the household of Narcissus who are in the Lord (16:11b).

"Greet Tryphena and Tryphosa, those women who work hard in the Lord" (16:12a).

"Greet my dear friend Persis, another woman who has worked very hard in the Lord" (16:12b).

"Greet Rufus, chosen in the Lord, and his mother, who has been a mother to me, too" (16:13).

"Greet Asyncritus, Phlegon, Hermes, Patrobas, Hermas and the brothers with them" (16:14).

"Greet Philologus, Julia, Nereus and his sister, and Olympas and all the saints with them" (16:15).

"Greet one another with a holy kiss" (16:16).

"Keep away from them" (16:17).

I Corinthians

"Therefore, as it is written: 'Let him who boasts boast in the Lord'" (1:31).

"Let each man be careful how he builds upon it" (3:10 NASB).

"Let no man deceive himself" (3:18a NASB).

"If any man among you thinks that he is wise in this age, let him become foolish that he may become wise" (3:18b NASB).

"So then, let no one boast in men" (3:21 NASB).

"Let a man regard us in this manner, as servants of Christ, and stewards of the mysteries of God" (4:1 NASB).

"Therefore, judge nothing before the appointed time" (4:5).

"Therefore I urge you to imitate me" (4:16).

"Get rid of the old yeast that you may be a new batch without yeast—as you really are" (5:7).

"Expel the wicked man from among you" (5:13).

"Therefore, if you have disputes about such matters, appoint as judges even men of little account in the church!" (6:4).

"Do not be deceived" (6:9).

"Flee from sexual immorality" (6:18).

"Therefore honor God with your body" (6:20).

"But because of immoralities, let each man have his own wife, and let each woman have her own husband" (7:2 NASB).

"Do not deprive each other except by mutual consent and for a time" (7:5).

"But if they do not have self-control, let them marry" (7:9 NASB).

"But if she does leave, let her remain unmarried or else be reconciled to her husband" (7:11 NASB).

"If any brother has a wife who is an unbeliever, and she consents to live with him, let him not send her away" (7:12 NASB).

"And a woman who has an unbelieving husband, and he consents to live with her, let her not send the husband away" (7:13 NASB).

"But if the unbeliever leaves, let him do so" (7:15).

"As God has called each, in this manner let him walk" (7:17 NASB).

"Was any man called already circumcised? Let him not become uncircumcised" (7:18 NASB).

"Let each man remain in that condition in which he was called" (7:20 NASB).

"Were you a slave when you were called? Don't let it trouble you" (7:21).

"You were bought at a price; do not become slaves of men" (7:23).

"Brethren, let each man remain with God in that condition in which he was called" (7:24 NASB).

"Are you married? Do not seek a divorce" (7:27a).

"Are you unmarried? Do not look for a wife" (7:27b).

"Let him do what he wishes, he does not sin" (7:36 NASB).

"Let her marry" (7:36 NASB).

"Be careful, however, that the exercise of your freedom does not become a stumbling block to the weak" (8:9).

"Run in such a way as to get the prize" (9:24).

"Do not be idolaters" (10:7).

"Do not grumble" (10:10).

"Be careful that you don't fall!" (10:12).

"Flee from idolatry" (10:14).

"Consider the people of Israel" (10:18).

"Let no one seek his own good, but that of his neighbor" (10:24 NASB).

"Eat anything sold in the meat market without raising questions of conscience" (10:25).

"Eat whatever is put before you without raising questions of conscience" (10:27).

"But if anyone says to you, 'This has been offered in sacrifice,' then do not eat it" (10:28).

"So whether you eat or drink or whatever you do, do it all for the glory of God" (10:31).

"Do not cause anyone to stumble, whether Jews, Greeks or the church of God" (10:32).

"Follow my example, as I follow the example of Christ" (11:1).

"For if a woman does not cover her head, let her also have her hair cut off" (11:6a NASB).

"But if it is disgraceful for a woman to have her hair cut off or her head shaved, let her cover her head" (11:6b NASB).

"Judge for yourselves" (11:13).

"Do this in remembrance of me" (11:24).

"Do this, whenever you drink it, in remembrance of me" (11:25).

"Let a man examine himself" (11:28a NASB).

"Let him eat of the bread and drink of the cup" (11:28b NASB).

"So then, my brothers, when you come together to eat, wait for each other" (11:33).

"If anyone is hungry, he should eat at home" (11:34).

"But eagerly desire the greater gifts" (12:31).

"Follow the way of love and eagerly desire spiritual gifts, especially the gift of prophecy" (14:1).

"Try to excel in gifts that build up the church" (14:12).

"Therefore let one who speaks in a tongue pray that he may interpret" (14:13 NASB).

"Brethren, do not be children in your thinking" (14:20a NASB).

"Yet in evil be babes" (14:20b NASB).

"In your thinking be mature" (14:20c NASB).

"Let all things be done for edification" (14:26 NASB).

"Let one interpret" (14:27 NASB).

"But if there is no interpreter, let him keep silent in the church" (14:28a NASB).

"Let him speak to himself and to God" (14:28b NASB).

"And let two or three prophets speak, and let the others pass judgment" (14:29 NASB).

"But if a revelation is made to another who is seated, let the first keep silent" (14:30 NASB).

"Let the women keep silent in the churches" (14:34a NASB).

"Let them subject themselves" (14:34b NASB).

"Let them ask their own husbands at home" (14:35 NASB).

"If anybody thinks he is a prophet or spiritually gifted, let him acknowledge that what I am writing to you is the Lord's command" (14:37).

"Desire earnestly to prophecy" (14:39a NASB).

"Do not forbid to speak in tongues" (14:39b NASB).
"But let all things be done properly and in an orderly manner" (14:40 NASB).
"Do not be misled" (15:33).
"Come back to your senses" (15:34a).
"Stop sinning" (15:34b).
"Stand firm" (15:58).
"Do what I told the Galatian churches to do" (16:1).
"Let each one of you put aside and save" (16:2 NASB).
"If Timothy comes, see to it that he has nothing to fear" (16:10).
"Send him on his way in peace so that he may return to me" (16:11).
"Be on your guard" (16:13a).
"Stand firm in the faith" (16:13b).
"Be men of courage" (16:13c).
"Be strong" (16:13d).
"Do everything in love" (16:14).
"Acknowledge such men" (16:18 NASB).
"Greet one another with a holy kiss" (16:20).
"Let him be accursed" (16:22 NASB).

2 Corinthians

"Be reconciled to God" (5:20).
"Open wide your hearts also" (6:13).
"Do not be yoked together with unbelievers" (6:14).
"Come out from them" (6:17a).
"Be separate" (6:17b).
"Touch no unclean thing" (6:17c).
"Make room for us in your hearts" (7:2).
"Finish the work" (8:11).
"If any one is confident in himself that he is Christ's, let him consider this again within himself" (10:7 NASB).
"Receive me just as you would a fool" (11:16).
"Forgive me this wrong!" (12:13).
"Be that as it may" (12:16).
"Examine yourselves to see whether you are in the faith" (13:5a).
"Test yourselves" (13:5b).
"Rejoice" (13:11a NASB).
"Be made complete" (13:11b NASB).
"Be comforted" (13:11c NASB).
"Be like-minded" (13:11d NASB).
"Live in peace" (13:11e NASB).

Galatians

"Let him be eternally condemned" (1:8).
"Let him be eternally condemned" (1:9).
"Understand, then, that those who believe are children of Abraham"
    (3:7).
"Become like me" (4:12).
"Tell me" (4:21).
"Be glad, O barren woman" (4:27a).
"Break forth" (4:27b).
"Cry aloud" (4:27c).
"Get rid of the slave woman and her son" (4:30).
"Stand firm" (5:1b).
"Do not let yourselves be burdened again by a yoke of slavery" (5:1c).
"Serve one another in love" (5:13).
"Watch out or you will be destroyed by each other" (5:15).
"Live by the Spirit" (5:16).
"Brethren, even if a man is caught in any trespass, you who are spiri-
    tual, restore such a one in a spirit of meekness" (6:1 NASB).
"Carry each other's burdens" (6:2).
"But let each one examine his own work" (6:4 NASB).
"Let the one who is taught the word share all good things with him who
    teaches" (6:6 NASB).
"Do not be deceived" (6.7).
"See what large letters I use as I write to you with my own hand!" (6:11).
"Let no one cause me trouble" (6:17).

Ephesians

"Therefore, remember that formerly you who are Gentiles by birth . . .
    were separate from Christ" (2:11–12).
"Speak truthfully" (4:25).
"Be angry" (4:26a NASB).
"Do not sin" (4:26b NASB).
"Do not let the sun go down on your anger" (4:26b NASB).
"Do not give the devil a foothold" (4:27).
"Let him who steals steal no longer" (4:28a NASB).
"But rather let him labor" (4:28b NASB).
"Do not let any unwholesome talk come out of your mouths" (4:29).
"Do not grieve the Holy Spirit of God" (4:30).
"Get rid of all bitterness, rage, and anger, brawling and slander, along
    with every form of malice" (4:31).

"Be kind and compassionate to one another" (4:32).

"Be imitators of God" (5:1).

"Live a life of love" (5:2).

"Do not let immorality or any impurity or greed even be named among you" (5:3 NASB).

"Be sure: No immoral, impure, or greedy person . . . has any inheritance in the kingdom of Christ and of God" (5:5).

"Let no one deceive you with empty words" (5:6).

"Do not be partners with them" (5:7).

"Live as children of light" (5:8).

"Have nothing to do with the fruitless deeds of darkness" (5:11a).

"But rather expose them" (5:11b).

"Wake up, O sleeper" (5:14a).

"Rise from the dead" (5:14b).

"Be very careful, then, how you live" (5:15).

"Therefore do not be foolish" (5:17a).

"But understand what the Lord's will is" (5:17b).

"Husbands, love your wives" (5:25).

"Let each individual among you also love his own wife even as himself" (5:33 NASB).

"Children, obey your parents in the Lord" (6:1).

"Honor your father and mother" (6:2).

"Fathers, do not exasperate your children" (6:4).

"Slaves, obey your earthly masters" (6:5).

"Masters, treat your slaves in the same way" (6:9).

"Be strong in the Lord" (6:10).

"Put on the full armor of God" (6:11).

"Put on the full armor of God" (6:13).

"Stand firm" (6:14).

"Take the helmet of salvation and the sword of the Spirit, which is the word of God" (6:17).

Philippians

"Conduct yourselves in a manner worthy of the gospel of Christ" (1:27).

"Make my joy complete by being like-minded" (2:2).

"Have this attitude in yourselves which was also in Christ Jesus" (2:5 NASB).

"Continue to work out your salvation with fear and trembling" (2:12).

"Do everything without complaining or arguing" (2:14).

"Be glad" (2:18a).

"Rejoice with me" (2:18b).

"Welcome him [Epaphroditus] in the Lord with great joy" (2:29a).
"Honor men like him" (2:29b).
"Rejoice in the Lord!" (3:1).
"Watch out for those dogs" (3:2a).
"Beware of the evil workers" (3:2b NASB).
"Beware of the false circumcision" (3:2c NASB).
"Join with others in following my example" (3:17a).
"Take note of those who live according to the pattern we gave you" (3:17b).
"Stand firm in the Lord" (4:1).
"Help the women who have contended at my side in the cause of the gospel" (4:3).
"Rejoice in the Lord always" (4:4a).
"I will say it again: Rejoice!" (4:4b).
"Let your gentleness be evident to all" (4:5).
"Do not be anxious about anything" (4:6a).
"But . . . present your requests to God" (4:6b).
"Think about such things" (4:8).
"Whatever you have learned or received or heard from me, or seen in me—put it into practice" (4:9).
"Greet all the saints in Christ Jesus" (4:21).

Colossians

"So then, just as you received Christ Jesus as Lord, continue to live in him" (2:6).
"See to it that no one takes you captive through hollow and deceptive philosophy" (2:8).
"Therefore do not let anyone judge you by what you eat or drink, or with regard to a religious festival, a New Moon celebration or a Sabbath day" (2:16).
"Do not let anyone who delights in false humility and the worship of angels disqualify you for the prize" (2:18).
"Set your heart on things above" (3:1).
"Set your mind on things above" (3:2).
"Put to death, therefore, whatever belongs to your earthly nature" (3:5).
"Put them all aside: anger, wrath, malice, slander, and abusive speech from your mouth" (3:8 NASB).
"Do not lie to each other" (3:9).
"Clothe yourselves with compassion, kindness, humility, gentleness and patience" (3:12).
"Let the peace of Christ rule in your hearts" (3:15a).

"Be thankful" (3:15b).
"Let the word of Christ dwell in you richly" (3:16).
"Wives, submit to your husbands, as is fitting in the Lord" (3:18).
"Husbands, love your wives" (3:19a).
"Do not be harsh with them" (3:19b).
"Children, obey your parents in everything, for this pleases the Lord" (3:20).
"Fathers, do not embitter your children" (3:21).
"Slaves, obey your earthly masters in everything" (3:22).
"Whatever you do, work at it with all your heart" (3:23).
"Masters, provide your slaves with what is right and fair" (4:1).
"Devote yourselves to prayer" (4:2).
"Be wise in the way you act toward outsiders" (4:5).
"If he [Mark] comes to you, welcome him" (4:10).
"Give my greetings to the brothers at Laodicea, and to Nympha and the church in her house" (4:15).
"After this letter has been read to you, see that it is also read in the church of the Laodiceans and that you in turn read the letter from Laodicea" (4:16).
"Tell Archippus, 'See to it that you complete the work you have received in the Lord'" (4:17).
"Remember my chains" (4:18).

I Thessalonians

"Therefore, encourage each other with these words" (4:18).
"Therefore encourage one another" (5:11a).
"Build each other up" (5:11b).
"Live in peace with each other" (5:13).
"Warn those who are idle" (5:14a).
"Encourage the timid" (5:14b).
"Help the weak" (5:14c).
"Be patient with everyone" (5:14d).
"Make sure that nobody pays back wrong for wrong" (5:15a).
"Always try to be kind to each other and to everyone else" (5:15b).
"Be joyful always" (5:16).
"Pray continually" (5:17).
"Give thanks in all circumstances" (5:18).
"Do not put out the Spirit's fire" (5:19).
"Do not treat prophecies with contempt" (5:20).
"Test everything" (5:21a).
"Hold on to the good" (5:21b).

"Avoid every kind of evil" (5:22).
"Brothers, pray for us" (5:25).
"Greet all the brothers with a holy kiss" (5:26).

2 Thessalonians

"Stand firm" (2:15a).
"Hold to the teachings we passed on to you" (2:15b).
"Pray for us" (3:1).
"If anyone will not work, neither let him eat" (3:10 NASB).
"If anyone does not obey our instruction in this letter, take special note of him" (3:14).

I Timothy

"Let a woman quietly receive instruction with entire submissiveness" (2:11 NASB).
"If there is nothing against them, let them serve as deacons" (3:10).
"Let deacons be husbands of only one wife" (3:12 NASB).
"Have nothing to do with godless myths and old wives' tales" (4:7a).
"Train yourself to be godly" (4:7b).
"Command . . . these things" (4:11a).
"Teach these things" (4:11b).
"Don't let anyone look down on you because you are young" (4:12).
"Devote yourself to the public reading of Scripture, to preaching and to teaching" (4:13).
"Do not neglect your gift" (4:14).
"Be diligent in these matters" (4:15a).
"Give yourselves wholly to them" (4:15b).
"Watch your life and doctrine closely" (4:16a).
"Persevere in them" (4:16b).
"Exhort him [an older man] as if he were your father" (5:1).
"Give proper recognition to those widows who are really in need" (5:3).
"If any widow has children or grandchildren, let them first learn to practice piety in regard to their own family" (5:4 NASB).
"Give the people these instructions, too" (5:7).
"Let a widow be put on the list only if she is not less than sixty years old" (5:9 NASB).
"As for younger widows, do not put them on such a list" (5:11).
"If any woman who is a believer has dependent widows, let her assist them" (5:16a NASB).
"Let not the church be burdened" (5:16b NASB).

"Do not entertain an accusation against an elder unless it is brought by two or three witnesses" (5:19).

"Those who continue in sin, rebuke in the presence of all" (5:20a).

"Do not be hasty in the laying on of hands" (5:22a).

"Do not share in the sins of others" (5:22b).

"Keep yourself pure" (5:22c).

"Stop drinking only water" (5:23a).

"Use a little wine because of your stomach and your frequent illnesses" (5:23b).

"Let all who are under the yoke as slaves regard their own masters as worthy of all honor" (6:1 NASB).

"Let those who have believers as their masters not be disrespectful to them" (6:2a NASB).

"Let them serve them all the more" (6:2b NASB).

"Teach . . . these principles" (6:2c NASB).

"Preach . . . these principles" (6:2d NASB).

"Flee from all this" (6:11a).

"Pursue righteousness, godliness, faith, love, endurance and gentleness" (6:11b).

"Fight the good fight of the faith" (6:12a).

"Take hold of the eternal life to which you were called" (6:12b).

"Guard what has been entrusted to your care" (6:20).

2 Timothy

"Join with me in suffering for the gospel" (1:8).

"What you heard from me, keep as the pattern of sound teaching" (1:13).

"Guard the good deposit" (1:14).

"Be strong in the grace that is in Christ Jesus" (2:1).

"And the things you have heard me say in the presence of many witnesses entrust to reliable men who will be qualified to teach others" (2:2).

"Endure hardship with us like a good soldier of Christ Jesus" (2:3).

"Reflect on what I am saying" (2:7).

"Remember Jesus Christ" (2:8).

"Keep reminding them of these things" (2:14).

"Do your best to present yourself to God as one approved, a workman who does not need to be ashamed and who correctly handles the word of truth" (2:15).

"Avoid godless chatter" (2:16).

"Let every one who names the name of the Lord abstain from wickedness" (2:19 NASB).

"Flee the evil desires of youth" (2:22a).

"Pursue righteousness, faith, love and peace" (2:22b).

"Don't have anything to do with foolish and stupid arguments" (2:23).

"But mark this: There will be terrible times in the last days" (3:1).

"Have nothing to do with them" (3:5).

"Continue in what you have learned" (3:14).

"Preach the Word" (4:2a).

"Be prepared in season and out of season" (4:2b).

"Correct" (4:2c).

"Rebuke" (4:2d).

"Encourage" (4:2e).

"Keep your head in all situations" (4:5a).

"Endure hardship" (4:5b).

"Do the work of an evangelist" (4:5c).

"Discharge all the duties of your ministry" (4:5d).

"Do your best to come to me quickly" (4:9).

"Get Mark and bring him with you" (4:11).

"When you come, bring the cloak that I left with Carpus at Troas, and
my scrolls, especially the parchments" (4:13).

"Be on guard against him [Alexander] yourself" (4:15 NASB).

"Greet Priscilla and Aquila and the household of Onesiphorus" (4:19).

"Do your best to get here before winter" (4:21).

Titus

"Rebuke them sharply" (1:13).

"Speak the things which are fitting for sound doctrine" (2:1 NASB).

"Encourage the young men to be self-controlled" (2:6).

"These things speak" (2:15a NASB).

"Exhort" (2:15b NASB).

"Reprove with all authority" (2:15c NASB).

"Remind the people to be subject to rulers and authorities" (3:1).

"Avoid foolish controversies and genealogies and arguments and quar-
rels about the law" (3:9).

"Warn a divisive person once, and . . . a second time" (3:10).

"Do your best to come to me at Nicopolis" (3:12).

"Do everything you can to help Zenas the lawyer and Apollos on their
way" (3:13).

"Greet those who love us in the faith" (3:15).

Philemon

"So if you consider me a partner, welcome him [Onesimus] as you
   would welcome me" (v. 17).
"Refresh my heart in Christ" (v. 20).
"Prepare a guest room for me" (v. 22).

*   *   *

For a challenging project, assign each command in this appendix to
one of these categories:

Commands regarding positive attitudes or actions in the Christian life
Commands regarding attitudes or actions to avoid
Commands regarding personal relationships
Commands regarding Christian service and ministry
Commands regarding false teachings
Commands regarding Paul's own ministry
Commands addressed to Paul's companions

Subject Index

Scripture Index

Roy B. Zuck is senior professor emeritus of Bible exposition at Dallas Theological Seminary and editor of the theological journal *Bibliotheca Sacra*. He is the author or editor of numerous works, including *Teaching as Jesus Taught, Teaching with Spiritual Power, The Bible Knowledge Commentary,* and *Precious in His Sight: Childhood and Children in the Bible.*